MW01201623

Shōbōgenzō

Shōbōgenzō

The Treasure House of the
Eye of the True Teaching

A Trainee's translation of
Great Master Dōgen's
Spiritual Masterpiece

Rev. Hubert Nearman, O.B.C.
Translator

Shasta Abbey Press,
Mount Shasta,
California

First Edition—2007
© 2007 Shasta Abbey

This edition reformatted—2022

ISBN: 978-0-930066-37-6
Imprint: Shasta Abbey Press

Shasta Abbey
3724 Summit Drive
Mt. Shasta, California 96067-9102
(530) 926-4208

Volume III of III

This Volume contains Chapters 71 to 96

Acknowledgments

Considering the scope and length of this work and the demands, both monastic and scholarly, that it puts on any translator, a reader may well wonder what could possibly motivate anyone to take on such an enormous task. Whatever may be the motives for other translators, mine has been quite simple. I had finished translating the various texts that were included in *Buddhist Writings on Meditation and Daily Practice* (Shasta Abbey Press, 1994) and asked Rev. Daizui MacPhillamy, my editorial consultant at the time, whether Rev. Master Jiyu-Kennett had anything else she wanted me to translate for her. He took my question to her, and, he said, he was dumbfounded when, without a moment's pause, she replied "*The Shōbōgenzō,*" for such a monumental undertaking would obviously take me many years to complete, not only because of its length but also because of its reputed obscurity and even incomprehensibility. Simply because she was my Master, I agreed to her request, knowing that I would never have taken on such a task for any other reason. It has been my monastic offering to the Sangha over some fourteen years. During that time I have had the great good fortune to live at Shasta Abbey, a traditional Buddhist monastery where the life that Dōgen extolled is practiced. I wish to express my deep gratitude for all the assistance my fellow monks have given me, and in particular:

—Rev. Master Jiyu-Kennett, Abbess of Shasta Abbey when the initial volume of the first eleven of Dōgen's discourses was published. (This has been reworked in light of the whole of the present book and is not simply a reprint.) She can never be thanked enough for opening the Way of the Buddha, and of Dōgen, to an immeasurable number of people;

—Rev. Daizui MacPhillamy, whose sharp intellect and broad experience in the Dharma provided me with critical editing and consultation, but who sadly died unexpectedly before he could work with me on the last half of the discourses;

—Rev. Ekō Little, successor to Rev. Master Jiyu-Kennett as Abbot of Shasta Abbey, who has given me the unflagging support, encouragement, and assistance needed to complete the work;

—Rev. Oswin Hollenbeck of the Eugene Buddhist Priory for help with the introduction and who, together with Rev. Meikō Jones of Portland Buddhist Priory and Rev. Chōsei Swann of Shasta Abbey, read and commented on a number of the discourses;

—Rev. Fidelia Dolan who not only transformed electronic information into formats that could be made available to all, but also worked tirelessly as my editorial consultant after Rev. Daizui passed on, and helped me find ways to convey Dōgen's medieval Japanese and Chinese into hopefully comprehensible English;

—Rev. Meian Elbert, Rev. Shikō Rom, and Rev. Veronica Snedaker, who brought the book to completion;

—and to all the monastics, known and unknown, who have kept the Buddha's Transmission of the living Dharma vibrant down the centuries.

May the merit of this work benefit all beings.

Acknowledgments for the reformatted edition

The reformatting of this edition into three volumes to enable the use of print-on-demand services was undertaken by Rev. Lambert Tuffrey of Throssel Hole Buddhist Abbey, UK.

Contents

Volume III of III

The *Shōbōgenzō*

A Trainee's Translation
of Great Master Dōgen's Spiritual Masterpiece

Translator's General Introduction

The *Shōbōgenzō* is the recognized spiritual masterpiece by the thirteenth-century Japanese Sōtō Zen Master Eihei Dōgen. It is comprised of discourses that he gave to his disciples, in person or in writing, at various times between 1231 and his death twenty-two years later at age fifty-three.[†] These discourses cover a wide range of topics pertinent to those in monastic life though often also relevant to those training in lay life. He discusses matters of daily behavior and religious ceremonial as well as issues involving the Master-disciple relationship. He also explores the deeper meaning that informs the so-called Zen kōan stories, which often puzzle readers by their seeming illogicality and contrary nature.

I have translated the title as *The Treasure House of the Eye of the True Teaching*, though a fuller, more comprehensive rendering would be *The Treasure House for What the Spiritual Eye of Wise Discernment Perceives from the Vantage Point of the True Teachings of Shakyamuni Buddha and His Heirs*. The term 'Teaching' in the title is synonymous with the Buddhist use of the term 'Dharma', which refers not only to what the historical Buddha taught to His disciples but also to the Truth that flows from the Unborn and which all things give expression to when they are functioning directly from their innate True Self. However, it does not address what may be a scholar's particular interest in producing a translation, though it is obvious that translating anything from medieval Japanese and Chinese requires

---

special academic training: hence the subtitle "A Trainee's Translation of Great Master Dōgen's Spiritual Masterpiece". That is, it is intended primarily for those who practice Zen Buddhism rather than those whose interest is purely academic.

There are various ways in which Dogen's discourses can be presented, each having its particular advantages. The way I have chosen is simply to divide the discourses into those that were completed before his death and those that were still in draft form when he died, ordered where possible chronologically by the date when the discourse was given.

The discourses were originally written out by hand, primarily by his chief disciple and amanuensis, the Second Japanese Sōtō Zen Ancestor, Kōun Ejō. Most of the discourses have a two-part postscript (printed in italics, usually at the end of a discourse). The first half indicates who the recipients of the discourse were, along with when and where it was presented. If this is signed, it will customarily be by Dōgen. The second half supplies a short account of when and where the copy was made. These copies are most often signed by Ejō, though three were signed by Giun, one of Ejō's Dharma-heirs who later became the fifth abbot of Dōgen's Eihei-ji Monastery.

The majority of the discourses focus on exploring the spiritual significance of some topic drawn from Buddhist Scriptures or Chinese Chan (Zen) texts. Dōgen's commentaries on these texts are not lectures as would be understood in academic circles, but are talks that arise from a Zen Master's deepest understanding of the spiritual meaning and relevance of his topic to Buddhist training and practice. They come out of Dōgen's mind of meditation and are being presented to his monastic and lay disciples, who are presumably listening from their mind of meditation.□

The discourses carry a strong flavor of the conversational and the personal, and he enriches them with colorful Chinese and Zen phrases, as well as with medieval Chinese and Japanese colloquialisms. When translated literally, many of these metaphors and figures of speech may well have little meaning for English-speaking readers. However, by the thirteenth century they would have been a common way for a Buddhist Meditation Master to refer to That which is the True Nature of all beings. The function of these metaphors is, to some extent, to 'ground' a Master's disciples by providing them with a colorful and more easily remembered image instead of some more abstract, 'intellectual' definition. They point to the Great Matter for which one trains in Serene Reflection Meditation, which is to awaken to one's True Nature.▫

Dōgen sometimes uses a manner of speaking that closely resembles a dialogue. One specific instance occurs in 'A Discourse on Doing One's Utmost in Practicing the Way of the Buddhas' (*Bendōwa*), his earliest dated text in the *Shōbōgenzō*. The major part of this particular discourse consists of an imaginary dialogue between Dōgen and a potential disciple. While it takes the form of someone asking questions and Dōgen giving answers, it is not a catechism. That is, it is not a series of formal questions and answers. Rather, the questions arise from an attitude of mind which has misgivings about the efficacy and worth of the type of seated meditation that Dōgen advocates. Dōgen's responses, by contrast, arise from a place that lies beyond the intellective, duality-based mind and are aimed at helping the questioner to recognize that duality and to let go of it. Hence, the attitude of mind of both the questioner and the Master is as important as the specific question being asked. For the translator, one challenge in rendering Dōgen's text is to convey to the reader the attitudes implied in the exchanges between the two.

These interchanges between a Master and a potential or real disciple are not speculative in nature, but invariably have the purpose of helping disciples find that spiritual certainty which is the hallmark of a genuine kenshō, 'the seeing of one's Original Face', that is, the direct experiencing of one's innate Buddha Nature. This is not the same as having an intellectual understanding or intuition, since the experience takes one beyond those functions associated with the so-called rational mind, which are the foundation and authority for those who are not dedicated to spiritual pursuits. Furthermore, the certainty arising from a kenshō is not speculative in nature or the product of rational persuasion or a form of blind faith.

Dōgen's teaching in the *Shōbōgenzō* is neither confined to nor limited by conventional mental categories, which is why practitioners of Dōgen's type of meditation are admonished to be willing to be disturbed by the Truth, that is, to have not only their intellectual preconceptions questioned but also to have their reliance on solely what makes conventional, worldly sense called into question. Despite the view of some that Dōgen is therefore 'anti-intellect', once the spiritual certainty arises in those who are doing the training, the previous need to depend solely on the 'boxes' fabricated by their intellect disappears. Or as several Meditation Masters describe it, once we give up 'the walls and fences' that our intellect constructs from the bits and pieces of experience, this dependency disappears, and we metaphorically 'drop off our body and mind' but without rejecting the intellect itself or denying its natural and useful functions.

Conventions

In the present work, when a common word is used having spiritual significance, I have employed initial capitals to signal to the reader that word X is not intended literally but is part of a code which Zen Masters have used to convey spiritual meaning. Indeed, when people spiritually awaken, this is customarily signaled by their expressing their understanding in some unique and personal way. When the use of this code is ignored or overlooked by a translator, a kōan story may well become totally unintelligible and give rise to the erroneous notion that Zen promotes the indescribable. To avoid this, I have added some footnotes intended to point out places where the code may not have been spotted by readers.

An example of this may occur in a dialogue in which a Master and his disciple use the same words but with a totally different meaning. For example, a Master and his disciple are having a discussion, and the Master tests his disciple's understanding of what his True Nature is by asking, "Do you get It?" with the disciple answering, "No, I don't get it." The Master's question is a spiritual one: "Have you got to the heart of your spiritual question?" to which the disciple's reply reveals that he is still attached to conventional, worldly ways of thinking.

Elements of Style

In the present translations, four stylistic elements are used whose purpose may not be immediately apparent:

First is the capitalizing of words that would not usually be proper nouns, such as 'Original Nature', 'the Self', 'the Truth', 'It', 'One's Original Face'. Such words refer either to one's own Buddha Nature or to That which is the spiritual source of one's Buddha Nature. For instance, there is a difference between the term 'good friend' which refers to a Buddhist who has the ability to teach and train others in Buddhism (usually synonymous with a Zen Master), and the term 'Good Friend', which is another name for one's Buddha Nature.

Second, a word that is underlined is to be understood as emphatic within the context of the particular sentence in which it occurs. Were the text to be read aloud, the underlined word would be given emphasis.

Third, Dōgen sometimes abruptly changes his topic within his talks. Whereas many of these shifts are signaled by some introductory word, such as 'further' and 'also', which appears at the beginning of a new paragraph, in some instances this is not the case. Thus it has seemed advisable to aid the reader by inserting a plum blossom asterisk (`) between paragraphs where a sudden shift might otherwise prove disconcerting.

Fourth, single quotation marks are often used in the sense of 'so-called', 'what I (or someone else) would call', or 'the term' or 'the phrase', in addition to their customary use for marking a quote within a quote.

Special Terms

Dōgen often alludes to 'training and practice'. This consistently refers specifically to doing seated meditation, applying 'the mind of meditation' to all one's daily activities, and attempting to live in accord with the Precepts of Mahayana Buddhism, that is, the Precepts as spelled out in Dōgen's *Text for a Precepts Master's Giving the Mahayana Precepts* (*Kyōjukaimon*) and *The Scripture of Brahma's Net* (*Bommō Kyō*). Similarly, references to 'studying' denote training under a Zen Master, and do not signify the undertaking of a scholastic regimen.

To render the Japanese word *tennin* (or *ninden*) I have used the phrase 'ordinary people and those in lofty places'. Some translators render it as 'gods and men'. There is the danger that some readers may therefore assume that it means 'immortals and mortals'. However, in a Buddhist context it refers to those who are in the celestial and human realms among the six Realms of Existence, the four others being those of beasts, those in a hellish state, those who are hungry ghosts, and those who are asuras (heaven stormers). Those in the celestial and human realms are potentially able to hear the name of Buddha and absorb the Dharma, whereas those in the other four are so preoccupied with their suffering that it is exceedingly difficult for them to believe that they can transcend their suffering long enough to hear the Teaching and thereby free themselves from their spiritual obsessions.

Dōgen often uses the terms Mahayana and Hinayana (translated as 'the Greater Course' and 'the Lesser Course'). A widely voiced view is that references in Mahayana writings to those who follow a Lesser Course denote practitioners of the Theravadan Buddhist tradition. The Theravadan tradition, however, was not active in medieval Japan during Dōgen's lifetime. Also, the Pali Canon upon which the Theravadan tradition is grounded was known to Dōgen through Chinese translations and was held in great esteem by him. Allusions in Dōgen's writings to 'those who follow the Lesser Course' are clearly to persons whom trainees may well encounter in their daily life. Thus it is likely that he is referring to shravakas (those who merely seek to gain an intellectual understanding of Buddhism) or to pratyekabuddhas (those who undertake some aspects of Buddhist practice but only for their own personal benefit).

The Issue of Gender and Sex

This issue is sometimes raised in regard to translating medieval Chinese and Japanese texts into English. It involves the attitude of Buddhism in general, and Dōgen in particular, toward women in spiritual life. While it is true that in some cultures during some periods negative social attitudes toward women have unfortunately colored the practice of Buddhism, Dōgen's view is unequivocal: males and females are spiritual and monastic equals, for enlightenment knows no such distinction as sex. The English language, however, has not yet developed a universally accepted way to express what is gender neutral. When Dōgen refers to monks or laity in general or as 'someone who', it should be understood that he is including both males and females, even though the English pronominal reference is, for brevity's sake, 'he', 'him', or 'his': I have used 'she', 'her', and 'hers' only where the sex of the person is known to be female.

Appendices

Two appendices have been added to the book. The first is a listing of the Japanese names of the major figures in the various kōan stories along with their Chinese equivalents. The second is a glossary of words and idiomatic phrases, such as hossu and kōan, which need some explanation because they do not have an easy equivalent in English.

On Kōan Stories

Dōgen makes wide use of stories from Zen kōan collections. Since these stories may strike some readers as strange or incomprehensible, the following observations may prove helpful.

Originally, the term 'kōan' meant 'a public case', and in Chinese Zen referred to a notable, authenticated instance when a disciple came to realize his or her True Nature. By Dōgen's time, the term 'kōan' had become synonymous with the spiritual question which epitomizes that which keeps disciples, as well as anyone else, from directly experiencing what their Original Nature is. It is the spiritual doubt that keeps someone 'looking down'. The kōan stories, then, are usually accounts of how a particular trainee's doubt was resolved.

In these stories, the spiritual problem of a trainee often involves a habitual acting counter to at least one of the ten major Mahayana Buddhist Precepts on either a literal or a figurative level. That is, in some way the disciple will have persisted in taking the life from someone or something, in taking things that are not given, in giving in to covetous feelings, in saying that which is not so, in trafficking in something that intoxicates or deludes, in putting oneself up and others down, in insulting others, in giving in to anger or resentfulness, in being stingy, or in acting in a disrespectful manner toward Buddha, Dharma, or Sangha.

When reading such dialogues, it is prudent to consider what the mental attitude of the questioner is and not just what is being asked. This is important because the question asked arises from a particular frame of mind. Determining who is asking the question (and sometimes where and when) will help clarify what this frame of mind is and, therefore, what is really being asked, since the answer given will not be an absolute one, independent of the questioner, but one that speaks to the questioner's mental attitude and perspective. This is sometimes referred to in Zen writings as 'two arrows meeting in mid-air', one meaning of which is that the questioner thinks he knows what the target, or goal, is and has 'shot his arrow' of discriminatory thought at that target only to have his 'arrow' deflected by the Master's response so that, to mix metaphors, the disciple's 'train of discriminatory thought' is derailed. At the same time, the Master's 'arrow' points to a way for the disciple to go in his Buddhist training.

However, in some cases the roles are reversed: the Master asks the disciple a question or 'invites' him to respond from a perspective beyond the discriminatory mind. If the disciple has truly awakened, he will respond appropriately from the mind of meditation and not from the discriminatory mind of duality. In such an instance, the 'two arrows meeting in mid-air' is an expression for their oneness of mind.

The stories may follow any of several different patterns or their combination. Almost all will involve at least one of the following three patterns:

In the first, a disciple will ask the Master a question which arises from a reliance on dualistic thinking to comprehend his own spiritual doubt. This encounter with the Master will often occur in the context of a formal spiritual examination ceremony, but this will not always be made explicit in the text. The Master will then do or say something which cuts through the disciple's confusion and points him directly toward 'seeing' his Original Nature. What the Master does or says arises from a source that transcends the dualistic, intellective mind: it is not a philosophical, doctrinal, or 'rational' answer to the question. If the disciple is 'ripe'—that is, spiritually ready to shift his perspective away from reliance on what his intellect is doing so that he can realize That which transcends intellect—he has an experience referred to by some such phrase as 'realizing the Truth' or 'awakening to his True Nature'. In some kōan stories, the trigger for this experience may not be directly supplied by the Master but by some other external condition, such as seeing peach blossoms or hearing a piece of tile strike bamboo.

In the second, a Meditation Master initiates an exchange with a disciple who is still in doubt, and tries through his conversation with the disciple to steer him toward facing up to what his spiritual problem is. In such dialogues, the Master's questions may seem upon first reading to be casual ones. In kōan stories, when a Master asks a question, he is not trying to engage the disciple in some social interchange: his question will have a deeper purpose or meaning, which the disciple may or may not pick up on. If the disciple fails to 'get it', the Master will usually persist in his questioning until either the disciple has an awakening or until the Master decides that the disciple is still not yet 'ripe' enough.

In the third pattern, a Master-disciple interchange occurs, but with a disciple who has already awakened to the Truth. In such an instance, since what the disciple is saying or doing no longer arises from the mind of duality, there will be some clear indication of the Master's approval.

In those cases where the disciple is still in doubt, one useful clue as to what his spiritual problem is can be found in how the Master addresses the disciple. For instance, in one story, a monk who is given to striving too hard is addressed as 'Shibi the Austere Monk'. In another, a monk who has become entangled in erudition through his academic pursuit of studying Scriptures is addressed by his Master as 'you who are a learned scholar of considerable intelligence'.

In identifying the disciple's spiritual problem, it is helpful to determine what the disciple's attitude of mind is, and not to treat his questions or responses on a purely informational level. Once the disciple's spiritual problem has been identified, how he responds to his Master will reflect that problem until he has an awakening, at which time he may compose a poem which expresses the change in perspective that has emerged.

Another aspect which may be difficult for the reader to fathom immediately is the relevance of the Master's actions in word or deed to what the disciple's problem is. Since such actions are not 'pre-planned' but reflect the on-the-spot skillful means of the Master, it can only be said that whatever is done will arise from the mind of meditation, will be free of any dualistic tendency, will not break any of the Precepts, and will arise out of his compassion for the suffering of the disciple. In one famous kōan story (Nansen's cat), the roles are reversed: Meditation Master Nansen puts himself in a spiritually unsupportable position by trying to teach his monks to keep to the Precepts by seriously breaking one himself, and it is his chief disciple who points this out to him.

Another topic that arises from the kōan stories deals with who the participants are. The Master is easily identified. On the other hand, the one who asks a question is often referred to simply as a monk. In such cases the person is most likely a junior monk, one who has not yet been Transmitted and who is asking his question at a ceremony called shōsan. This is the formal spiritual examination ceremony which is customarily held twice a month in Zen monasteries during which junior trainees ask a question that reflects their present spiritual state.

When the monk asking a question is specifically identified, this refers to a senior monk, one who is already Transmitted or who will be Transmitted. These are monks who will ultimately function as a Master, and often as the founder of a temple or a lineage. Whether in the kōan story they have already been Transmitted or are still juniors can only be determined by the nature of their question.

Applying the Principles

To see how the preceding principles apply to an actual kōan story, the following one, taken from Dōgen's *Bendōwa*, is given with my exegetical remarks in square brackets. The kōan story itself is given in indented text:

> Long ago, there was a monk in Meditation Master Hōgen's monastic community named Gensoku, who was a subordinate under the Temple's administrative director. Master Hōgen asked him, "Director Gensoku, how long have you been in our community?"

[Although Gensoku is not the director, he is apparently acting as though he thought he was, thus breaking a Precept by 'putting himself up'. Hōgen's question is not a casual but a leading one, arising from his compassionate sensitivity to Gensoku's spiritual suffering from pride.]

> Gensoku replied, "Why, I've been in the community for three years now."

[Gensoku tacitly acknowledges recognition of his importance as self-evident and responds in a casual manner. Had he not been absorbed in his pride, he might have responded, as would be expected not only from a novice but also from any Chinese, by some such statement as "You flatter me by addressing me by too exalted a title, considering that I have been training here for only three years now." Had he already had a kenshō, his response, though not predictable, would not be impolite or disrespectful in tone but, on the other hand, would probably not be a conventional, 'socially correct' one either.]

The Master asked, "As you are still a junior monk, why have you never asked me about the Buddha Dharma?"

[Hōgen gently corrects Gensoku by now pointing out his actual position as a junior monk. He then asks another leading question, which implies that Gensoku thinks that he is above all other novices and does not need instruction.]

Gensoku replied, "I will not lie to Your Reverence. Previously, when I was with Meditation Master Seihō, I fully reached the place of joyful ease in the Buddha Dharma."

[The delusion underlying Gensoku's pride begins to emerge more clearly, for he claims to have attained a spiritual state which he has not yet reached. This is what Hōgen had probably surmised and which had led him to engage Gensoku in this dialogue. Gensoku is now breaking the Precepts by saying that which is not so and by having sold himself the wine of delusion.]

The Master said, "And what was said that gained you entry to that place?"

[Hōgen now probes directly into the heart of Gensoku's problem.]

Gensoku said, "I once asked Seihō what the True Self of a novice is, and Seihō replied, 'Here comes the Hearth God looking for fire.' "

[The nature of the question and the response suggest that this interchange had occurred as part of a shōsan ceremony (referred to above) held before the assembled monks, during which novices ask a Meditation Master a question which presumably reflects their current spiritual understanding. Because at this point Gensoku is still operating from the mind of duality, it is likely that the question was asked from the intellect rather than from the heart. The significance of Seihō's response will be discussed later.]

> Hōgen responded, "Nicely put by Seihō. But I'm afraid you may not have understood it."

[Gensoku had heard Master Seihō's words but had not grasped their import. Hōgen makes a complimentary remark about Seihō's comment. Had Hōgen suspected that Gensoku had already had a kenshō, it is unlikely that he would have done this, but instead might have made some remark that on the surface looked as though he were disparaging Seihō, such as "That old rascal! Is he still going around saying such things?" but which Gensoku would see as being the way a Master may acknowledge another Master whilst avoiding judgmentalism.]

> Gensoku said, "A Hearth God is associated with fire, so I understand it to mean that, just as fire is being used to seek for fire, so the True Self is what is used to seek for the True Self."

[Gensoku has worked out an intellectual interpretation of Seihō's remark, and therefore thinks that this type of understanding is what constitutes awakening to one's True Self. Gensoku's error is in thinking that there are two True Selves: the one that seeks and the one that is sought.]

> The Master said, "Just as I suspected! You have not understood. Were the Buddha Dharma like that, it is unlikely that It would have continued on, being Transmitted down to the present day."

[The Master now sets Gensoku straight as to where he is spiritually, in order to shake up his proud complacency and break through his deluded view.]

> Gensoku was so distressed at this that he left the monastery. While on the road, he thought to himself, "In this country the Master is known as a fine and learned monastic teacher and as a great spiritual leader and guide for five hundred monks. Since he has chided me for having gone wrong, he must undoubtedly have a point." So, he returned to his Master,

respectfully bowed in apology, and said, "What is the True Self of

a novice?"

[Leaving the monastery when asked to confront one's spiritual problem 'head on' is not an uncommon occurrence in kōan stories. Similarly, the turning about in one's heart by recognizing that it is oneself who may be wrong is a crucial moment in the life of a trainee. Here it marks Gensoku's letting go of his pride, so that he now returns with the appropriate attitude of mind for asking his spiritual question, which now arises from his heart-felt need to know the truth, and without any preconceptions.]

The Master replied, "Here comes the Hearth God looking

for The Fire." Upon hearing these words, Gensoku awoke fully to

the Buddha Dharma.

[What a Meditation Master says or does at a formal spiritual examination ceremony in response to a spiritual question is often multilayered in meaning and application. Since it is not intellectually contrived but arises from the Master's spiritual depths, it may in some way speak not only to the questioner but also to others who are present.]

[In Master Seihō's original remark to Gensoku several layers of meaning were occurring simultaneously. On one level, he was inviting Gensoku to give up his attitude of self-importance and 'play' with him; hence, the form in which the response was given: it forms a first line for a couplet and would have been spoken in the equivalent of English doggerel, the translated version read to the rhythmic pattern of *dum-dum-di-dum-dum dum-di-dum-di-dum*. If Gensoku were open enough, he would have come up with a second line, such as 'Burning up his false self upon the funeral pyre'.]

[On another level, Master Seihō was pointing Gensoku toward his spiritual problem. A 'Hearth God' is the title given to the temple boy whose task it is to light the monastery lamps. Thus, Seihō was saying in effect, "You are acting like a temple boy, not like a monk, and are seeking for that which you already have—in your case, the spiritual flame of your training."]

[Hōgen uses the same words and intonation as Seihō did, but context brings out a third level of meaning, which Gensoku now hears, "Here comes the one most innocent of heart whose practice lights the way for all of us, truly seeking That which is the True Light (The Fire)." Gensoku, upon hearing this, realized that this is what he has been truly seeking—not social position or erudition—and awoke to the Truth where the distinction of self and other completely drops away.]

[In the original Chinese text, as given by Dōgen, the words used by Seihō and Hōgen are the same, but the context indicates that there has been a shift in meaning from how Gensoku interpreted these words when spoken by Seihō and what they implied to him when reiterated by Hōgen. To convey that difference in meaning in English, the two quotes are translated in a slightly, but significantly, different way. In other kōan stories where the same phrase is used in two different contexts, the translation will also attempt to convey the shift in meaning, rather than leave it to the reader to puzzle out from a mere repetition what that shift may be. While footnotes have occasionally been supplied to help readers over such difficult points in a kōan story, the translator has not attempted to supply full explanations of these stories, trusting that the preceding guidelines, plus the footnotes, will be sufficient.]

71

On Turning the Wheel of the Dharma

(Tembōrin)

Translator's Introduction: The main point of this discourse is that even if a Buddha or an Ancestor quotes a line from a work of questionable authenticity, it may still be valid Teaching if it results from, and with, a turning of the Wheel of the Dharma.

My late Master, the Old Buddha of Tendō, once began a Dharma talk by saying, "The World-honored One once remarked, 'When someone gives rise to Truth by returning to the Source, the whole of space in all ten quarters falls away and vanishes.'" My Master, commenting on this quote, made the following remarks:

> This is what was expounded long ago by the World-
> honored One, but His Teaching has not escaped from people's
> capacity to create thoroughly strange and wondrous interpretations
> of It. I, Tendō, am not like that. When someone gives rise to Truth
> by returning to the Source, that 'begging child' will have broken his
> rice bowl.[1] The Venerable Abbot Goso Hōen once said, "When
> someone gives rise to Truth by returning to the Source, he will keep
> bumping up against the Space in all the ten quarters."[2] The
> Venerable Abbot Busshō Hōtai once said, "When someone gives
> rise to Truth by returning to the Source, for him the whole of space
> in the ten quarters will simply be, for him, the whole of space in the
> ten quarters." Meditation Master Engo Kokugon once said, "When
> someone gives rise to Truth by returning to the Source, he will

---

1. That is, such a one no longer needs to beg for the Truth.

2. That is, having awakened to the Truth, he will keep encountering Buddha Nature, no matter which way he may turn.

965

embellish the whole of Space in the ten quarters with his brocaded flowerings."

I, Dōgen, of Daibutsu-ji Temple would put it this way, "When someone gives rise to Truth by returning to the Source, the whole of space in the ten quarters gives rise to Truth by returning to the Source." What has initially been quoted as, "When someone gives rise to Truth by returning to the Source, the whole of space in all ten quarters falls away and vanishes," is a verse from the *Shurangama Scripture*. This verse has been cited by various Buddhas and Ancestors alike. Up to this very day, this verse is truly the Bones and Marrow of the Buddhas and Ancestors. It is the very Eye of the Buddhas and Ancestors. As to my intention in saying so, there are those who say that the ten-fascicle *Shurangama Scripture* is a spurious scripture, whereas others say that it is a genuine Scripture: both views have persisted from long in the past down to our very day.[3] There are older translations and there are newer translations, but the one considered spurious is the doubtful translation made during the Chinese Shenlung era (705-706). Be that as it may, the Venerable Abbot Goso Hōen, the Venerable Abbot Busshō Hōtai, and my late Master, the Old Buddha of Tendō, have just now recommended this verse. So, this verse has already been set in motion by the Dharma Wheel of the Buddhas and Ancestors; it is the turning of Their Dharma Wheel. As a result, this verse has already set Them in motion; it has already given voice to Them. Because it is set in motion by Them and sets Them in motion, even were the Scripture a spurious one, if They continue to offer its turning, then it is a genuine Scripture of the Buddhas and Ancestors, as well as the Dharma Wheel intimately associated with Them. For instance, even tiles and stones, even yellow leaves, even udumbara

---

3.   A spurious scripture is one that purports to be a genuine translation of a Sanskrit original, but is not considered canonical because it contradicts fundamental Buddhist doctrine. In this discourse, 'a genuine Scripture' refers to one that was originally composed in Chinese, but one that does not contradict basic Buddhist teaching.

   The *Shurangama Scripture* discussed here should not be confused with the three-fascicle and unequivocally genuine *Shurangama Samadhi Scripture*, translated by Kumārajīva from the Sanskrit.

blossoms, even robes of gold brocade, once they have been held aloft by a Buddha or an Ancestor, they become the Dharma Wheel of the Buddha. They are the Buddha's Treasure House of the Eye of the True Teaching.

You need to keep in mind that when sentient beings transcend a genuine awakening,[4] they are an Ancestor of the Buddha, they are the teachers and disciples of the Buddhas and the Ancestors, and they are the Skin and Flesh, Bones and Marrow of the Buddhas and Ancestors. They no longer consider sentient beings who were their brothers to be their brothers, but treat the Buddhas and Ancestors as their brothers. Likewise, even if this verse were from a text considered to be spurious, it is the verse for the present moment, it is the verse of a Buddha and the verse of an Ancestor, and it should not be grouped with other phrases or verses from that particular Scripture. Even if there are other verses in that Scripture that far surpass this verse, you should not consider each and every passage to be absolutely, or even provisionally, a saying of the Buddha or the words of an Ancestor, nor should you treat them as the Eye for exploring the Great Matter.[*]

There are many reasons why you should not compare this particular verse with the other verses. Let's take up just one of them. What is called 'the turning of the Wheel of the Dharma' is a matter for Buddhas and Ancestors. There have not been any Buddhas or Ancestors who have not turned the Wheel of the Dharma. Some will turn the Wheel of the Dharma by using sound and form to free Their disciples from attachment to sound and form, and some will turn the Wheel of the Dharma by Their leaping free of sound and form, and some will turn the Wheel of the Dharma by scraping out Their Eyes, and some will turn the Wheel of the Dharma by holding Their Fist aloft. And there are times when the disciple comprehends what his Nose is or comprehends what the Unbounded is, which are instances of the Wheel of the Dharma naturally turning Itself. To comprehend what this verse is about is to grasp what the morning star is about, what one's Nose is about, what the plum blossom is about, and what the Unbounded is about. It is comprehending what Buddhas and Ancestors are

---

4.   That is, having dropped off body and mind, one then drops off 'dropping off'.

*   See *Glossary.*

about and what the Wheel of the Dharma is about. The underlying principle of these is, clearly, what the turning of the Wheel of the Dharma is about.

'Turning the Wheel of the Dharma' means doing your utmost to explore the Matter through your training with your Master without leaving the temple throughout the rest of your life. I call it sitting with others on the long meditation benches and asking for the Master's benevolence whilst doing your utmost to train in the Way.

Delivered to the assembly on the twenty-seventh day of the second lunar month in the second year of the Kangen era (April 6, 1244), whilst in Echizen Province at Kippō-ji temple.

Copied by me on the first day of the third lunar month in the same year (April 8, 1244), whilst in the quarters of the Abbot's assistant in the same temple.

Ejō

72

On the Meditative State of One's True Nature

(Jishō Zammai)

Translator's Introduction: In the first part of this discourse, Dōgen explores what the proper attitude of mind is for one who is serious about coming to know what one's True Nature is and how It functions.

In the latter part of the discourse, Dōgen devotes considerable time to presenting stories concerning the Rinzai Master Daie, who is credited with introducing the method of kōan study that is particular to the Rinzai tradition. Dōgen's purpose seems to be to describe someone who exemplifies the failure to realize the meditative state of his True Nature. Because what is happening in these stories is not always easily grasped and the significance of the exchanges may not be immediately apparent, it has seemed worthwhile to supply more extensive footnotes for the sake of modern readers.

What has been authentically Transmitted by the Buddhas from the Seven Buddhas* on is that the meditative state of one's training is identical with one's inherent enlightenment. In other words, we sometimes submit ourselves to what a good spiritual friend advises and sometimes we submit ourselves to what Scriptural texts advise, for these are both the Eye of the Buddhas and Ancestors. This is why the following dialogue occurred.

> The Old Buddha Daikan Enō once put the question to a monk, asking, "And is this a substitute for training and enlightenment?"[1]
>
> The monk replied, "It is not that there is no training and enlightenment, but rather, there is nothing to be had that will stain It."

---

* See *Glossary.*

1. The monk in question was Enō's Dharma heir, Nangaku Ejō. Enō's question was in response to Ejō's statement, "Were I to try to put the One Matter into words, they would miss the mark."

969

So, keep in mind that one's training and enlightenment being unstained by attachments is a characteristic of Buddhas and Ancestors. It is the meditative state of the Buddhas and Ancestors being experienced like a flash of lightning, like a gust of wind, like a roll of thunder.

At the very moment when we submit ourselves to what a good spiritual friend advises, sometimes we see half of each other's Countenance, sometimes we see half of each other's Body, sometimes we see the whole of each other's Countenance, and sometimes we see the whole of each other's Heart and Mind. And there are times when we both see half of our own self and times when we both see half of each other's self. There are times when we become aware that a deity's head is enveloped in hair and times when we notice that a demon's countenance has sprouted horns.[2] There are times when we come, attending on others so that we might rescue all manner of beings from their suffering, and there are times when we go, transforming ourselves amongst those with whom we live. In situations like these, we do not know how many thousands of myriad times we have discarded our sense of self for the sake of the Dharma. And we do not know for how many billions of eons we have sought the Dharma for the sake of our own self. This is our basing our life upon submitting ourselves to what a good spiritual friend advises, and it is the state of our exploring through our training what Self is and how we may submit ourselves to that Self. There was the occasion when Makakashō broke out into a smile when he saw the twinkle in Shakyamuni's eye. And Eka bowed to Bodhidharma in deepest respect upon realizing the latter's Marrow, which is connected with Eka's having 'cut off his arm'.[3]

In summary, from the sequence of the Seven Buddhas down though the Sixth Chinese Ancestor and beyond, good spiritual teachers who have encountered the Self have been more than just one or two. And good spiritual teachers who could see It in others are not limited to the past nor are they limited to the present.

2.　That is, there are times when the Master seems to resemble a lay person, just as there are times when the Master seems like a raging bull.

3.　The Second Chinese Ancestor, Taiso Eka, is said to have cut off his arm in order to find the Truth. This 'severing' may refer to giving up one's attachments rather than to a literal, physical act.

When we submit ourselves to Scriptural Writings, we thoroughly explore Their Skin and Flesh, Bones and Marrow. When we let go of our own skin and flesh, bones and marrow, the Peach Blossom is seen jutting out from our Eye, and the sound of the Bamboo is heard thundering in our Ear.

In general, when we are following the path of studying Scriptures, Scriptures truly come forth. What we call Scriptures are the whole world of the ten quarters, the great earth with its mountains and rivers, grasses and trees, self and other. And They are our eating meals, putting on our clothes, and doing our daily activities. When we study the Way by submitting ourselves to each of the Scriptural texts, one by one, the thousands of myriad volumes of Scriptures that we have not yet encountered are emerging right in front of us. Fortunately, They contain verses stating the Matter* with words of affirmation and poems clearly stating It with words of negation.[4] When we have succeeded in encountering Them, we employ our body and mind to explore Them through our training, exhausting long eons and making use of Them over long periods of time. Through this, we ultimately reach our goal of understanding Them thoroughly. When we explore Them by letting go of body and mind, we scrape out all traces of duality and leap beyond the first signs of anything arising, while, at the same time, we inevitably realize the merits of accepting and retaining the Scriptures.

The Sanskrit texts of India that have been translated into Chinese books of Dharma number barely five thousand scrolls. Among these are the three vehicles, the five vehicles, the six divisions, and the twelve divisions. All these are Scriptural texts that you should study and follow. Even if we were to attempt to stay aloof from Them, we could not. Thus, sometimes They are 'the Eye' and sometimes They are what 'my Marrow' is.[5] When horns on the head are right, then a tail will be right.[6] Whether we receive Them from others or impart Them to others, They are just one's Eye springing

---

4. That is, some statements express what the Matter is, whereas other statements express what the Matter is not.

5. 'Eye' refers to spiritual 'seeing' as the Master 'sees', and 'my Marrow' refers to what one 'sees', which is completely in accord with one's Master.

6. To paraphrase, in either case the Scriptures are right from beginning to end.

to life as we drop off self and other. They are simply the conferring of 'my Marrow' as we free ourselves from the delusion of self and other. Because both the Eye and 'my Marrow' are beyond self and beyond other, the Buddhas and Ancestors have continued to accurately Transmit Them and confer Them from the distant past, to this present moment, and to the next present moment. There is the traveling staff* as a Scripture, which gives free expression to the Dharma in every conceivable way, spontaneously breaking up 'emptiness' and breaking up 'existence'. And there is the ceremonial hossu* as a Scripture, as it sweeps away snow and sweeps away frost. And there are the one or two sessions of seated meditation as Scriptures. And there is the kesa* as a Scripture, which has ten scrolls per volume. These are what Buddhas and Ancestors safeguard and keep to. Following such 'Scriptures' as These, we awaken to training and realize the Way. And there are times when we bring forth into existence the face of someone in a lofty position or the face of some ordinary person, and times when we bring forth the countenance of the Sun or the countenance of the Moon, as we do our utmost to realize our pursuit of Scriptures.

At the same time, whether people are following a good spiritual teacher or following the Scriptures, all such persons are following their True Self. The Scriptural texts are, naturally, the Scriptural texts of Self, and good spiritual teachers are, naturally, good spiritual teachers of Self. Thus, you should investigate through your training that thorough training means thoroughly training oneself, that studying the hundreds of things which sprout up like grass means studying oneself, that studying the myriad things that take root and branch out like trees means studying oneself, and that this self is, of necessity, synonymous with making such an effort. By exploring like this through your training, you drop off self and you promise enlightenment to yourself.

Accordingly, in the Great Way of the Buddhas and Ancestors there are tools for awakening to one's True Self and for realizing what that Self truly is. If there were no Buddhas or Ancestors who were genuine Dharma heirs, there would be no genuine Transmission. But there are tools that Dharma heir after Dharma heir has received, for were there not the Bones and Marrow of the Buddhas and Ancestors, there would not be a genuine Transmission.

Because we explore the Matter in this way, when we pass on the Transmission for the sake of others, we confer it by saying such things as "You have gotten what my Marrow is" and "I have the Treasure House of the Eye of the True Teaching which I confer on Makakashō." Expressing It for someone's sake does not necessarily depend on self and others. To express It for the sake of others is to express It for one's own sake. It is one's Self and another's Self harmoniously hearing and expressing the same thing. One ear is hearing and one ear is expressing: one tongue is expressing and one tongue is hearing. The same holds true for the sense organs of eye, ear, nose, tongue, body, and mind, as well as for their forms of consciousness and their sense objects. Further, there is one Body and there is one Mind, and there is enlightenment and there is training. It is the hearing and expressing of one's ears, and it is the hearing and expressing of one's tongue. Even though we may have expressed an exception to the rule yesterday for the sake of others, today we are expressing the established rule for our own sake. In this way, the faces of the sun line up one after another, as do the faces of the moon.

To give expression to the Dharma for the sake of others and to put the Dharma into practice for oneself is to hear the Dharma, to clarify what It is, and to realize It for many lives. Even in this life, if we are sincere in giving expression to It for the sake of others, it will be easy for us to realize the Dharma. If we help others to hear and promote the Dharma, we will establish good causes for our own learning of the Dharma. We will establish good causes both physically and mentally. Should we hinder others from hearing the Dharma, then we ourselves will be hindered in hearing the Dharma. To express the Dharma, as well as to hear It over many lives in many bodies, is to hear the Dharma over many generations. It is to hear It once more in this generation as well as hearing the Dharma that has been genuinely Transmitted to us from the past. We are born in the Dharma and we die in the Dharma, and so, having had the Dharma genuinely Transmitted to us whilst being within the whole universe of the ten quarters, we listen to It in life after life and train with It in body after body. Since we have made life after life manifest in the Dharma and have made body after body into Dharma, we bring together each molecule of dust and the whole realm of thoughts and things, and we help them to realize the Dharma.

Thus, having heard a verse whilst in eastern regions, when we come to some western region, we should give expression to it for someone's sake. This means that we do our utmost, first and foremost, to listen to it and give expression to it in our own way and that we simultaneously practice and experience our eastern self and our western self. In any case, we should delight in having our own body and mind keep close company with the Buddha's Teaching and with the words and ways of the Ancestors, to say nothing of our hoping and intending to do so, and to our putting Them into practice. We should extend our practice from an hour to a whole day until we have extended it from a year to a whole lifetime. We should give free rein to the Buddha Dharma as our very essence. In this way, we will not pass through life after life in vain pursuits.

At the same time, if you have not yet fully clarified the Matter, do not think that you cannot express It for someone's sake. Were you to wait until you had fully clarified It, you would not be equal to the task even for immeasurable eons. Even if you clarify what a human Buddha is, you will need to clarify what a celestial Buddha is. Even if you clarify what the heart of a Mountain is, you will need to clarify what the heart of the Water is. Even if you clarify what the causes and conditions are for the arising of thoughts and things, you will need to clarify what makes the causes and conditions for the arising of thoughts and things an irrelevant issue. Even if you clarify what the environs of the Buddhas and Ancestors are, you will need to clarify what is above and beyond Buddhas and Ancestors. If you are aiming at first completely clarifying these within your lifetime and only then acting for the benefit of others, you are not doing your utmost, nor are you being stout-hearted, nor are you exploring the Matter through your training with your Master.

In short, as someone who is studying the words and ways of the Buddhas and Ancestors, after you have explored through your training a single method or a single model, you then enthusiastically let your intention to help others rise to the very heavens. Accordingly, we let go of 'self and other'. Further, if you thoroughly awaken to your Self, you will have thoroughly awakened to others. And if you can thoroughly awaken to others, you will have thoroughly awakened to your Self. Even though we call the model of a Buddha 'One who has been born wise', if such a person has not received the Teaching through a Master, that person cannot realize It through direct bodily experience. If those born wise have not yet encountered a Master, they do not know what is beyond being born wise and they do not know what the Unborn and Unknowing is. Even though we speak of those who have been born wise, that does not mean that they will know the Great Way of the Buddhas and Ancestors; only by exploring It through their training with their Master will they come to know It. Being thoroughly awakened to one's Self and being thoroughly awakened to the Self of others is the Great Way of the Buddhas and Ancestors. They just need to turn their attention to exploring their own beginner's mind and do the same with exploring the beginner's mind of others. In bringing out from that beginner's mind the harmonization of self and other, they will be able to arrive at harmonization with the Ultimate and they will be able to promote the diligent efforts of others just as they do their own.

At the same time, upon hearing such phrases as 'awakening to one's True Self' and 'realizing what that Self truly is', rude and boorish people think that they do not need to receive Transmission from a Master, but need only to do self-study. This is a great mistake. Those who erroneously consider everything to be based on their personal ruminations and discriminations and have not received the Teaching through a Master are non-Buddhist followers of Indian naturalism.[7] How could that bunch who do not understand this possibly call themselves persons of the Buddha's Way? What is more, upon hearing the phrase 'awakening to one's True Self', they reckon that it refers to the accumulation of the five skandhas,* and so equate it with the self-discipline of the Lesser Course.* There are many folks who do not understand the difference between the Greater Course* and the Lesser Course, and many of them call themselves offspring of the Buddhas and Ancestors. Even so, what bright-eyed person would be deceived by such folks?

During the Shaohsing era (1131-1162) in Great Sung China, there was a certain Sōkō, later known as Meditation Master Daie of Mount Kinzan. He was originally a scholastic student of Scriptural texts and commentaries. During his travels

---

7.   Indian naturalism is the belief that everything arises spontaneously, without a cause.

from teacher to teacher, he became a follower of Meditation Master Shōri in Hsüanchou Province, with whom he studied Ummon's comments on kōan[*] stories, as well as Setchō's verse and prose commentaries on kōan stories, which was the beginning of his formal training under a Master. Failing to grasp Ummon's turn of mind, he eventually went to train under Abbot Tōzan Dōbi, but Dōbi did not permit Sōkō to enter his private quarters. Abbot Dōbi was a Dharma heir of Abbot Fuyō Dōkai; he was head-and-shoulders above those idle ones who seat themselves in the back row. Even though 'Meditation Master' Sōkō did the training for a rather long time, he did not succeed in getting hold of his Master's Skin and Flesh, Bones and Marrow, much less did he even know that there is an Eye amidst the dust motes of defiling passions.[8]

And then there was the time when he had just heard of the practice in the Way of the Buddha's Ancestors of burning incense on one's elbow whilst requesting the Record of Transmission.[9] All eager, he begged Abbot Dōbi for the Record of Transmission. However, Abbot Dōbi refused his request.

> In time, the Abbot said to Sōkō, "If you want to receive the Record of Transmission, do not be in such a hurry. Just by all means do your utmost to be diligent in your training here and now. What you are asking the Buddhas and Ancestors for is never given indiscriminately. It is not that I am unwilling to bestow It. It is simply that you are not yet equipped with the Eye."
>
> Sōkō now responded, "Having been endowed with genuine eyes from the first, I have awakened to my True Self and

---

8. Since Sōkō was the name given to Daie upon being ordained as a novice monk, Dōgen's referring to him as Meditation Master Sōkō is clearly sarcastic, implying Daie's propensity for putting himself above his teachers, a trait that becomes more evident in what follows.

9. This was apparently a symbolic reenactment of Eka's offering up his arm when requesting Transmission from Bodhidharma.

have realized what that Self truly is, so how can you be so arbitrary and not give It to me?"

Abbot Dōbi laughed and left it at that.

Later, Sōkō went to train under Abbot Tandō Bunjun.

One day Tandō asked Sōkō, "And why are you lacking half your nose today?" [10]

Sōkō replied, "I am a disciple in the monastery of the Hōbō Peak." [11]

Tandō responded, "Inaccurate, and far from the mark!"

Once when Sōkō was reading a Scripture, Tandō asked him, "What Scripture are you reading?"

Sōkō replied, "The Diamond-Cutting Scripture." [12]

Tandō then asked him, "It says in that Scripture, 'This Teaching is impartial; there is no higher or lower,' so why is Mount Ungo exalted and Mount Hōbō devalued?" [13]

---

10. Tandō is asking in effect, "Why don't you let go of that arrogant attitude of yours, so that you can realize the fullness of your innate True Nature?"

11. Hōbō Peak is the mountain on which Tandō's monastery lies, and by extension is a reference to Abbot Tandō himself. In effect, Daie is holding the Abbot responsible for his not having fully realized his True Self—an extremely rude remark.

12. This is the Scripture that Daikan Enō heard being recited, which triggered his kenshō.

13. Mount Ungo was a Sōtō monastery, whereas Mount Hōbō was a Rinzai monastery. Tandō is trying to point out to Sōkō his arrogant, judgmental way of thinking.

Sōkō responded, "This Teaching is impartial, without high or low."[14]

Tandō responded, "You have certainly succeeded in making yourself into a full-fledged scholastic," and had him go do seated meditation.[15]

On another occasion, Tandō was watching a government official placing adornments on figures of the Ten Lords who preside over the ten hells. He asked Sōkō, who was still a novice who had not yet been Chief Junior,[16] "What is this official's family name?"

Sōkō responded, "His family name is Ryō."

Tandō, stroking his own head with his hand, said, "My family name was Ryō, so how come I lack a hat like his?"

Sōkō replied, "Even though you lack a hat, your nose closely resembles his."

Tandō remarked, "You are wide of the mark!"[17]

---

14. Sōkō's response is merely a mouthing of Scripture. He does not see the relevance of his Master's remark to his kōan of intellectual arrogance.

15. In Zen contexts, the term translated here as 'a full-fledged scholastic' is a strong rebuke, implying that someone is content to merely pursue intellectual interests, which he is not all that good at in the first place, rather than to do the practice needed to resolve the One Great Matter.

16. The Chief Junior is a novice monk who as been given the responsibility to oversee the behavior of junior monks for a variable period of time, in accordance with the guidance of the senior officers of the temple. A novice who has not yet done his stint in this position is considered to be still quite new to the ways of monastic life.

17. Sōkō's remark is ambiguous, but it sounds as if he were saying, 'The only difference between you and some government official is that you lack a fancy hat."

One day, Tandō said to Sōkō, "Veteran novice Sōkō, you have been able to comprehend at once what my 'meditate here and now' means. Were I to let you explain it, you could put it in your own words. Were I to let you demonstrate how to do it, again, you could demonstrate it. Were I to let you compose comments on it in verse or prose, expound it to trainees, give the monks informal talks on it, or request teaching from a Master, you could also do any of these. But there is just one thing that you do not yet have in place. Do you know what it is?"[18]

Sōkō responded, "What is that thing that I do not yet have in place?"

Tandō answered, "There is just one bit of understanding that you lack: HAH![19] If you are lacking this one bit of understanding, then whenever we are in my private quarters and I give teaching for your sake, you have the mind of meditation, but as soon as you leave my quarters, it is completely gone. Whenever you are clearly pondering the Matter, you have the mind of meditation, but as soon as you do the least bit of drifting off into sleep, it is completely gone. If that is the way you are, how can you possibly be up to handling the matter of life and death?"

Sōkō replied, "That is precisely what Sōkō is suspicious of."

After a few years had passed, Tandō showed signs of illness. Sōkō asked him, "Venerable Abbot, a hundred years from

---

18. This question has a double meaning, the other being "Do you know what It is?"

19. HAH! represents the spontaneous sound made upon realizing what It truly is. It is also what is known as a kwatz, a sudden shout by a Master, used to interrupt the flow of intellectual thought in a disciple.

now who should I rely upon that I may resolve this Great Matter of life and death?"[20]

Tandō responded to his request by saying, "There is a Master by the name of Engo Kokugon. He is from the State of Pa. I do not know him personally. Even so, if you meet him, I am sure you will be able to resolve this Matter. Once you have met him, do not go around visiting other Masters. In generations yet to come, explore the mind of meditation through your training."

When we examine just this one part of the stories, it is clear that Tandō still had not endorsed Sōkō. Even though time and time again Tandō aimed at opening Sōkō up, the latter ultimately kept missing that one experience, and there is no way of compensating for that, for one cannot omit that experience. Obviously, we can trust to Abbot Dōbi's clearly seeing Sōkō's makeup by his denying him the Record of Transmission yet continuing to encourage him, saying that there was still something that needed doing. Sōkō did not thoroughly explore his own statement, "That is precisely what Sōkō is suspicious of," nor did he drop it off, or break it open, or give rise to the Great Doubt, or break through that doubting.[21] In fact, his impertinence in asking for the Record of Transmission was his attempt to rush past his exploring the Matter with his Master. It was the utmost limit of a mind for which there was no such thing as Truth. It was an extreme lack of respect for the ancients. We must say that it was not only lacking in discretion, it was lacking in the markings of the Way. It was the height of negligence in the practice. Greedy for fame, craving personal gain, he attempted to crash his way into the private quarters of the Ancestors of the Buddha. It is so pitiful how he failed to understand what the Ancestors of the Buddha were saying to him in their talks and writings. He did not grasp that to study and train is to awaken to one's True Self. He did not hear that to delve deeply into the writings of myriad

---

20. The phrase 'a hundred years from now' was a polite way of saying 'after you are dead', as it implies that the Master will surely live for another century.

21. The Great Doubt is "I could be wrong."

generations is to come to realize what that Self truly is. Without proper study, there are errors like these and there is self-deception like his. Because this was the way 'Meditation Master' Sōkō was, in his assembly there was not a single disciple, or even half a one, who had a trustworthy nose ring, but there were many who were pretend monks.[22] Failure to intuitively grasp what the Buddha Dharma is and failure to intellectually understand what the Buddha Dharma is are both just like this. Beyond any question, novice trainees here and now should explore the Matter in detail with their Master. Do not be negligent out of pride.

   After Tandō's passing, Sōkō, in accord with Tandō's recommendation, went to train under Meditation Master Engo at Tennei Temple in the capital city. One day, upon Engo's entering the Dharma Hall, Sōkō reported to Engo that, thanks to Engo, he had had a spiritual awakening. Engo said, "Not yet. Even though a disciple's state may be like what you describe, nevertheless, you have still not clarified what the Great Dharma is."

   On another day, whilst giving a Dharma talk, Engo quoted the words of the Venerable Abbot Goso Hōen on asserting existence and non-existence. Upon hearing this, Sōkō grasped a principle that brought him great comfort. Once again, he reported his understanding to Engo. Engo laughed and said, "It is not I who has deluded you!"

This is the story of how 'Meditation Master' Sōkō subsequently trained under Engo.

   While in Engo's assembly, he served in the post of Abbot's Secretary, but there is no visible evidence of his attaining any understanding before or after that. Even when he was giving formal or informal talks, he offered nothing of what he had

---

22. A nose ring is used in training a water buffalo. The term is often used in Zen contexts to refer to the practice of mastering self-control.

grasped. You need to know that his biographer speaks of his having had a spiritual awakening and records that he had grasped a principle that brought him great comfort, but there is nothing to support this.[23] Do not think of him as someone of prominence, for he was simply another person who was training under a Master.

Meditation Master Engo was an Old Buddha, as venerable as anyone within all ten quarters. Not since Ōbaku had there been one so worthy of veneration as Engo, for he was an Old Buddha who would be rare in any other world. Even so, ordinary folks and those in lofty positions who have recognized this are few, for the everyday world is a sad place indeed.

Now when we examine Old Buddha Engo's giving voice to the Dharma and investigate Sōkō's Dharma talks, it is clear that the latter still did not have wise discernment that came up to that of his Master, nor did he have wise discernment that resembled that of his Master, and what is more, he never realized wise discernment that surpassed that of his Master even in his dreams. So, you need to recognize that 'Meditation Master' Sōkō did not have abilities that even equaled half those of his Master. He merely parroted lines from texts like the *Avatamsaka Scripture* and the *Shurangama Scripture*, but he never grasped what 'the Bones and Marrow of the Buddhas and Ancestors' means. From Sōkō's point of view, he considered the Buddha Dharma to be merely the opinions supported by the greater and lesser hermits—those who are led by the spirit that permeates grasses and trees.[24] If this is what he imagined the Buddha Dharma to be, then clearly he did not know what the Great Way of the Buddhas and Ancestors is. After Engo, he did not wander off to other temples or seek

---

23.　That is, his biographer quotes what Sōkō said he had experienced, but he does not record Engo's responses.

24.　'Hermits' in this context refer to those who have removed themselves from worldly ways of thinking. The greater hermits were those who resided among ordinary folks, practicing the Bodhisattva vows. The lesser hermits were those who resided in mountains and forests, practicing to acquire merit which they could then transfer to all sentient beings. 'The spirit that permeates grasses and trees' is an allusion to the Buddha Nature that is innate in all things that 'sprout up and grow tall'.

out good spiritual friends, but as head of a large temple, he functioned haphazardly as the monk who greets incoming novices.[25] The sayings he has left behind do not even approach the outskirts of the Great Dharma. At the same time, folks who do not recognize this are apt to think that it is not shameful to classify 'Meditation Master' Sōkō with the ancients, whereas those who see and know have decisively concluded that he was not enlightened. Ultimately, he had not clarified what the Great Dharma is and just irresponsibly babbled on.

Thus, you need to recognize that, in truth, Abbot Dōbi of Mount Tōzan had clearly made no mistake in what he saw in Sōkō's future. Folks who trained under 'Meditation Master' Sōkō ultimately became jealous and resentful of Abbot Dōbi, and have not stopped being so even to this very day. All Abbot Dōbi did was to refuse to acknowledge Sōkō's claim. Abbot Tandō's refusals to acknowledge Sōkō's claims were far stronger than Dōbi's, for he found fault with Sōkō every time he encountered him. Even so, Abbot Tandō is not resented by Sōkō's followers. Oh, how embarrassed we should feel for those who have been resentful in the past and are still so in the present!

In general, offspring of the Buddhas and Ancestors in Great Sung China have been many, but trainees who have learned what Truth is have been few, so there are few who teach what is true. You should clearly recognize this principle in these stories. It was no different in Sōkō's Shaohsing era. The present is incomparably worse than that era. Today, folks who do not even know what the Great Way of the Buddhas and Ancestors is have become the masters for novices.

You need to realize that the genuine passing on of the Record of Transmission in India and China by Buddha after Buddha and Ancestor after Ancestor is the genuine Transmission that has come down from Seigen's mountain. After it came down from Seigen's mountain, it was naturally Transmitted to Tōzan, which is something unknown to any but ourselves throughout all the ten quarters. Those who know this are all offspring of Tōzan and they bestow their fame upon their trainees. Still, throughout his life, 'Meditation Master' Sōkō did not understand what the

---

25. That is, despite his being nominal head of a large temple, he was unable to spiritually lead novices beyond the level of newcomers.

phrases 'awakening to one's True Self' and 'realizing what that Self truly is' meant. How much less could he have penetrated his own spiritual question through his training! And even less, how can any present-day trainees who are descendants of Zen veteran Sōkō possibly understand the words 'awakening to one's True Self'?

Hence, the word 'self' and the word 'other' as used by the Buddhas and Ancestors refer to the Body and Mind of the Buddhas and Ancestors: they are the Eye of the Buddhas and Ancestors. And because they are the Bones and Marrow of the Buddhas and Ancestors, they transcend what 'getting the skin' would mean to those of ordinary mind.

Delivered to the assembly in Kippō-ji Temple in Echizen Province on the twenty-ninth day of the second lunar month in the second year of the Kangen era (April 8, 1244).

Copied by me whilst in the quarters of the Abbot's assistant at the foot of Kippō-ji Peak in Echizen Province on the twelfth day of the fourth lunar month of the same year (May 20, 1244).

Ejō

73

On the Great Practice

(Daishugyō)

Translator's introduction: 'The Great Practice' refers to the training and practice of someone who is following the Greater Course and is functioning as a morally good spiritual friend and guide for others, a fully perfected Master who is doing the Great Practice. By contrast, 'a wild fox' refers to someone who gives false teaching.

This discourse is one of the more difficult ones to follow, in part because Dogen spends a considerable amount of time in refuting the many ways in which others have interpreted the story that he is commenting on. In addition, he calls into question the accuracy of various aspects of the story.

This particular story has been the center of much controversy. The core question is whether or not someone who has realized fully perfected enlightenment and is doing the Great Practice is freed from causality or is still subject to cause and effect. Dogen will ultimately argue that both views, though seemingly contradictory, are accurate. That is, someone who has realized fully perfected enlightenment is not subject to causality because such a person is living in total accord with the Precepts, and at the same time, such a person, as a sentient being, is subject to the causal consequences of being a sentient being.

Something that is not explicitly stated but is implied by Dogen's commentary is that the old man in the story may be one of Hyakujō's past lives, the karma from which Hyakujō cleanses by helping the old man turn his thinking around.

Hyakujō Ekai was a Dharma heir of Baso. Whenever people came to hear him give a public Dharma talk, there was an old man who always came into the Dharma Hall immediately following those in the monastic assembly. He always listened to the Dharma talk and then, when the monks would leave the hall, he would leave at the same time. Then one day, he lingered behind. Thereupon, the Master asked him, "You who are standing here, who are you?"

The old man replied, "To speak truly, I am a non-human being. Long ago during the eon of Kashō Buddha,[1] I dwelt upon this mountain as Abbot. Then, one day, a trainee asked me, 'Is even the one who does the Great Practice still subject to cause and effect?' I replied that such a one is no longer subject to cause and effect. After that, as a consequence, I was reduced to being reborn as a wild fox for five hundred lives. I now beseech you, O Venerable Monk, say something that will turn me around, for I long to rid myself of this wild fox's attitude of mind."

Thereupon, he asked the Master, "Is even someone who does the Great Practice subject to cause and effect?"

The Master replied, "Such a one is not blind to causality."

Upon hearing these words, the old man had a great awakening. Prostrating himself before the Master, he said, "Since I have already shed the outer trappings of a wild fox, I have taken to dwelling on the far side of this mountain. Dare I ask the Venerable Abbot to perform for me a monk's funeral service?"

The Master had the senior monk who supervises the Meditation Hall strike the wooden gong to signal the monks to assemble so that he might tell them that, after their meal, there would be a funeral service for a deceased monk. The whole assembly was at ease with this, though they wondered about it, since there was no sick person in the temple infirmary. After the meal, the Master simply led the assembly up to the base of a rock on the other side of the mountain, where they saw him use his traveling staff to point out the corpse of a wild fox. They cremated the remains in accordance with the appropriate procedure.

At nightfall, the Master went to the Dharma Hall where he gave the monks a talk on the preceding events. His Dharma heir

---

1. Among the Seven Buddhas, the One whose eon directly preceded that of Shakyamuni Buddha.

Ōbaku then asked him, "In the past, the man said the wrong thing to turn his disciple around and, as a consequence, was reduced to being a wild fox for five hundred lives. Suppose he had not made this mistake, what would have become of him?"

The Master said, "Come up close and I will tell you."

Thereupon, Ōbaku went on up and gave the Master a slap.

The Master clapped his hands and laughed, saying, "I've always thought that the beards of foreigners were red, and here is a red-bearded foreigner."

The spiritual question that is arising here in this story is precisely what the Great Practice is all about. Just as the old man had said, during the eon of Kashō Buddha there was an Abbot of Mount Hyakujō in Hungchou Province, and in the eon when Shakyamuni Buddha existed there was an Abbot of Mount Hyakujō in Hungchou Province. These are key phrases in describing what has occurred. Although this is the case, the Abbot of Mount Hyakujō in the past during the eon of Kashō Buddha and the Abbot of Mount Hyakujō during the present eon of Shakyamuni Buddha are not one and the same person, nor are they different from each other, nor are they 'three and three before that, or three and three after that'.[2] The one who became the Abbot of Mount Hyakujō in the past did not become the Abbot of Mount Hyakujō later on, any more than the later Abbot of Mount Hyakujō was the preceding Abbot of Mount Hyakujō during the eon of Kashō Buddha. Even so, there is the old man's spiritual question of 'having dwelt upon this mountain as Abbot'. What he said for the benefit of his disciple is like what Hyakujō was now saying for the benefit of the old man. And the question that the disciple asked is like the question the old man was now asking. While setting forth one explanation, we cannot set forth a second, for if we let pass what is primary, we will get all involved with what is secondary.

---

2. That is, instances of people fully realizing their Buddha Nature are beyond count, so awakened people can only see just so many around them, just so many having come before them, and just so many coming after them.

The trainee in the long past is asking, "Is even 'that one' on Mount Hyakujō who is doing the Great Practice still subject to cause and effect?"[3] Truly, this question cannot be readily or easily grasped. And what is the reason for that? For the first time since the Buddha Dharma advanced eastwards during the Chinese Yung-p'ing era in the Later Han dynasty,[4] and since our Ancestral Master Bodhidharma came from the West during the Chinese P'u-t'ung era of the Liang dynasty, we are now able to hear the question of that trainee of the past due to what that old wild fox said. It is a condition that did not exist previously. So we can assert that it was rarely heard of.

When we search for, and find, the Great Practice, this will be the Great Cause and Effect. Because this Cause and Effect is invariably the full perfection of the cause and the complete fulfillment of the effect, there is nothing to debate concerning 'being subject to' or 'not being subject to', and there is nothing to discuss concerning 'being blind to' or 'not being blind to'. If 'not being subject to cause and effect' is a mistaken view, then 'not being blind to cause and effect' might also be a mistaken view. Even if we were to say that this is adding a mistake atop a mistake, still there was the old man's being reduced to the life of a wild fox and there was his dropping off of the life of a wild fox. It may appear reasonable that, even though 'not being subject to cause and effect' may have been a mistaken view in the past during the eon of Kashō Buddha, it may not be a mistaken view in the present during the eon of Shakyamuni Buddha. And it may also appear reasonable that, even though 'not being blind to cause and effect' during the present Shakyamuni Buddha's eon may have rid the old man of the attitude of a wild fox, it would not necessarily have done so during Kashō Buddha's eon.

In the old man's saying that he had been reduced to being reborn as a wild fox for five hundred lives, how, pray, did such a thing come about? There is no evidence that there was a wild fox who was enticing the earlier Abbot of Hyakujō and thereby causing him to be reduced to such a state, nor could there have been a former Abbot of Hyakujō who was a wild fox all along. It would be non-Buddhist to assert

---

3.   'That one' refers to the enlightened Abbot of Mount Hyakujō in the long past.

4.   This time period is concurrent with the introduction of Buddhist Scriptures into China.

that the spirit of the former Abbot of Hyakujō came out and jumped into the skin bag[*] of a wild fox. And a wild fox could not have come along and swallowed up the former Abbot of Hyakujō. If we were to say that the former Abbot of Hyakujō had once more become a wild fox, he would have had to rid himself of the body of a former Abbot of Hyakujō, so that he could subsequently reduce himself to the state of a dead wild fox. An Abbot of Mount Hyakujō cannot turn himself into the body of a wild fox! How could 'cause and effect' possibly be like that? Cause and effect is not something inherent, nor is it something that someone initiates, nor is cause and effect something idly awaiting the action of some person.

Now, let's deal with the old man's response, "Such a one is no longer subject to cause and effect." Even though he was mistaken, he would not necessarily have been reduced to the state of a wild fox for that. If being reduced to the state of a wild fox was the inevitable consequence of answering a trainee's question inaccurately, then how many thousands of myriad times would the Rinzais and Tokusans of more recent times, along with their disciples, have been reduced to being wild foxes as a consequence? And apart from them, senior monks who have made mistakes over the past two or three hundred years would certainly have become innumerable foxes. Yet, we have not heard of their having been reduced to being wild foxes as a consequence. If there had been many, then there would have been more than enough for us to encounter or hear about them. Even though you might well say that they have not made such a serious mistake, there are many indeed who have given even more dubious responses than "Such a one is not subject to cause and effect." And there have been many monks whom we cannot place even on the outskirts of the Buddha Dharma. You need to spot them by using the Eye of your training and practice, for if your Eye is not yet functioning, you may well not be able to discern them. So, you need to know that we cannot assert that someone who answers badly turns himself into a wild fox, whereas someone who answers well is not reduced to being a wild fox. In this story, it does not say what it is like after someone has rid himself of the attitude of a wild fox, but no doubt it will be that of a real gem of a trainee doing his best within a bag of skin.

---

[*] See *Glossary.*

As a rule, those who have never encountered or heard about the Buddha Dharma say, "After he had completely rid himself of the wild fox, he returned to the ocean of his Original Nature. Even though he was reduced to being a wild fox for a while due to his delusion, after he had had a great awakening, he shed being a wild fox and returned to his Original Nature." They mean by this that he returned to some innate, unchanging self which non-Buddhists speak of. Furthermore, this is not the Buddha Dharma. If they were to say that a wild fox is devoid of Original Nature or that a wild fox has no innate enlightenment, such would not be the Buddha Dharma. Were they to say, "When a person has a great awakening, such a one has let go of the mental attitude of a wild fox and has rid himself of it," then it would not have been the wild fox's great enlightenment, and being a wild fox would have served no purpose. So, do not assert such things.

You need to be clear about the point that the wild fox, which the former Abbot of Hyakujō had been for five hundred lives, forthwith dropped off being a wild fox by virtue of the triggering words concerning causality spoken by the later Abbot of Hyakujō. If you were to say, "When someone who was a bystander spoke a triggering phrase concerning causality, that freed another from the mind of a wild fox," well, the great earth with its mountains and rivers has already been giving forth innumerable triggering expressions concerning causality and is continually doing so. But even so, the old man had not yet dropped off the mind of a wild fox in the past, and he only dropped it off due to the later Abbot's triggering words concerning causality. This was the old man's killing off his doubt. If you were to say that the great earth with its mountains and rivers has never yet given expression to the triggering words concerning causality, then the later Hyakujō ultimately might not have been able to open his mouth.

Further, there are many old worthies who have contended that saying 'not being subject to' and 'not being blind to' are essentially the same, but they have not yet directly experienced how 'not being subject to' and 'not being blind to' are related. Consequently, they have not explored through their training the skin, flesh, bones, and marrow of falling into the body of a wild fox, nor have they explored through their training the skin, flesh, bones, and marrow of dropping off the mind of a wild fox. If you don't get the beginning right, you'll never get the end right. In the old man's remark, "I was reduced to being reborn as a wild fox for five hundred lives," what is it that was reborn and what was that reduced to? At the very moment when he was reborn as a wild fox, what form did his previous universe now take on? How is the phrase 'not being subject to causality' related to his being reborn five hundred times? And where did the pelt that was now lying beneath a rock on the other side of the mountain come from? He was reborn as a wild fox for giving another the phrase 'not subject to causality' and he dropped off the mind of a wild fox upon hearing the words 'not being blind to causality'. Even though there was a 'being reduced to' and a 'dropping off of', they were still the causal consequences of his being a wild fox.

At the same time, some of old have said, "Because the old man answered, 'Not subject to causality', he seemed to be denying causality." This assertion is beside the point and is something that people who are in the dark say about causality. Even if there had once been a former Abbot of Hyakujō who said that he was not subject to being a wild fox, he could not possibly deceive someone of the Great Practice, since such a one will not deny causality. On the other hand, there are those who say, "Not being blind to cause and effect means not being blind to causality, and because the Great Practice is transcendent Cause and Effect, such a trainee has dropped off the mind of a wild fox." This is truly eighty or ninety percent of the Eye for exploring the Matter.*⁵ Be that as it may, the old man might well have said in verse:

> *In the eon of Kashō Buddha*
> *I dwelt on this mountain,*
> *In the eon of Shakyamuni Buddha*
> *I dwell there now.*

> *My former self and my present self,*

---

5. This is Dogen's way of confirming the validity of someone's statement. Such statements are described as being eighty or ninety percent, which means that there are still other ways of saying exactly the same thing, since there is no single, absolute way of stating the Truth.

Face of Sun and face of Moon,
Intercept the wild fox's ghost
And reveal the wild fox's spirit.

How could a wild fox have possibly known of its five hundred lives? If you say that it knew of its five hundred lives by using the wiles of a wild fox, well, the wiles of a wild fox did not yet fully know the whole of the wild fox's life, and its whole life had not yet been stuffed into a wild fox's hide. The wild fox certainly knew that he had been reduced to being reborn for five hundred lives, because those lives were the manifesting of his spiritual question. But it did not fully know the whole of its life: there is that which it knew and that which it did not know. Unless what it knew arose and departed simultaneously with its body, it could not have calculated what 'five hundred lives' was. Since it could not make such a calculation, the words 'five hundred lives' must be a fabrication. Were you to say that the wild fox knew it by using information other than what the wild fox knew directly, then it would not have been something that the wild fox personally knew to be so. But over the generations, who could have known this on the wild fox's behalf? Without having any clear path through what we know and what we don't know, we cannot say that the old man was reduced to being a wild fox. If he was not reduced to being a wild fox, there could not be any dropping off of the mind of a wild fox. If there were neither a 'being reduced to' nor a 'dropping off of', there could not have been a former Hyakujō, and if there were no former Hyakujō, there could not be a later Hyakujō. Do not treat this lightly, for it needs careful study. Grasping this underlying principle, you need to see through and expose the mistaken opinions which have been voiced over and over again throughout the Liang, Chen, Sui, T'ang, and Sung Dynasties.

To return to the story, the old non-human being said to the later Hyakujō, "Dare I ask the Venerable Abbot to perform for me a monk's funeral service?" He should not have spoken like this. Since Hyakujō's time, a number of virtuous spiritual friends and guides have had no doubt about these words nor have they been surprised by them. But the main point is this: how could a dead fox become a dead monk, since it has never taken the Precepts, or attended a summer retreat, or kept to the everyday behavior of a monk, or held to the principles of a monk? If such a creature may arbitrarily undergo the funeral ceremony for a dead monk, then any dead person who has never left home life behind would have to be accorded the funeral rites of a dead monk too. If there were any male or female lay Buddhists who had requested it upon their demise, they, like the dead wild fox, would have to be accorded the funeral rites of a dead monk. When we look for an example of someone being accorded these rites, there is none, nor do we hear of one. Such a rite has never been Transmitted in Buddhism. Even if we thought we should do it, it should not be done.

Now there is the statement that Hyakujō cremated the remains in accordance with the appropriate procedure. This is not clear. Perhaps it is a mistake. You need to keep in mind that all the funeral rites for a dead monk are prescribed, from our efforts upon entering his sick room to our practicing the Way upon reaching the burial garden—nothing is done arbitrarily. Even though the former Hyakujō referred to himself as a dead fox at the base of a rock, how could this possibly be the usual way great monks behave? How could it have been the bones and marrow of an Ancestor of the Buddha? Who is there to prove that it was the former Hyakujō? Do not treat with arrogance the Dharma standards of the Buddhas and Ancestors by vainly taking as real the transformations of the spirit of some wild fox. As offspring of the Buddhas and Ancestors, you should treat with importance the Dharma standards of the Buddhas and Ancestors. Never leave matters up to what others request, as Hyakujō did. It is hard enough encountering the One Great Matter and the whole of the Dharma. Do not be hauled about by worldly desires or dragged hither and yon by human sentimentality.

As for here in our nation of Japan, it has been difficult to encounter the standards of the Buddhas and Ancestors or even to hear of them. Nowadays, hearing about them or encountering them is rare indeed, so we should prize them more deeply than the jewel that the king of old took from his topknot.[6] Those who lack our good

---

6. An allusion to a passage in the "Conduct That Eases the Way" chapter of the *Lotus Scripture,* in which a king bestows upon his servant the Jewel of the Dharma. One translation of this can be found in *Buddhist Writings on Meditation and Daily Practice,* (Shasta Abbey Press, 1994), pp. 18-20.

fortune have hearts that are irreverent and shallow in their trust. Sad to say, this is due to their never having known what is or is not important in their affairs. They lack the wise discernment of the past five hundred years or so. Be that as it may, we should be industrious with ourselves and should help others go forward. If you receive the genuine Transmission of even one prostration or one meditation period from an Ancestor of the Buddha, you will feel such joy at having encountered that which is difficult to encounter. Folks lacking this attitude of mind will not be able to obtain any merit or even a single benefit, though they may have encountered a thousand Buddhas after having left home life behind. They will simply be non-Buddhists who have vainly latched onto the Buddha Dharma. Although they may claim to be learning the Buddha Dharma, they cannot genuinely expound the Buddha Dharma in their own words.

So, if someone who has not yet become a monk—even if it were a ruler of a nation or one of his ministers, even if it were Brahma or Indra—comes and requests that you perform the funeral rites of a deceased monk for his sake, do not permit it. Tell him that he should come back after he has left home life behind, accepted the Precepts, and become a full monk. Those in the three worlds of desire, form, and beyond form who so crave rewards for their deeds that they do not seek after the venerable status of the Triple Treasure of Buddha, Dharma, and Sangha, may come bringing you a thousand corpses to bury as monks, thereby seeking to defile and act contrary to the funeral rites for deceased monks, but such an action on their part would merely be a serious transgression. It would certainly not produce any merit. If they wish to form good links to the merits of the Buddha Dharma, then, in accord with the Buddha's Teaching, they will need to be quick to leave home life behind, to accept the Precepts, and thereby to become full monks.

At nightfall, the Master went to the Dharma Hall where he gave a talk on the preceding events.

The underlying principle of this account is extremely dubious. Just what is it getting at? Hyakujō seems to be saying that the old man had already brought five hundred lives to an end and had now rid himself of his former body as a fox. Are the five hundred lives that are being spoken of here to be reckoned as they would be in the world of humans, or should they be counted as a wild fox would experience them, or are they to be counted as a Buddha would refer to them? And what is more, how could the eyes of an old wild fox possibly have caught sight of what a Hyakujō is? Those who have been spotted by a wild fox must have the spirit of a wild fox; those who have been spotted by a Hyakujō are Ancestors of the Buddha. This is why Meditation Master Koboku Hōjō composed the following verse:

> *Hyakujō once had a face-to-face encounter with a wild fox*
> *Who sought instruction from him because the Master was*
> *one with a tough-talking mind.*
> *So now I dare ask each of you trainees,*
> *"Have you also spit out all of your fox drivel?"*

So, the wild fox was the Eye with which Hyakujō had his face-to-face encounter. Even if you spit out half your fox drivel, it will be your sticking out your long, broad tongue to say a word that will transform others.[7] At the very moment when you do this, you will get free of the body of a wild fox, free of the body of a Hyakujō, free of the body of an old, non-human being, and free of the body of the whole universe.

> Ōbaku then asked Hyakujō, "In the past, the man said the
> wrong thing to turn his disciple around and, as a consequence, was
> reduced to being a wild fox for five hundred lives. Suppose he had
> not made this mistake, what would have become of him?"

Now, this question is a manifestation of what Buddhas and Ancestors ask. Among the venerable senior monks in the lineage of Nangaku, there is none like Ōbaku, either before or after him. At the same time, the old man never said that his response to his disciple was inaccurate, nor did Hyakujō ever say that the old man's response was

---

7.   A long, broad tongue is one of the thirty-two distinguishing marks of a Buddha.

inaccurate. So, why did Ōbaku arbitrarily say that the old man gave the wrong response which produced this transformation? If Ōbaku is asserting that Hyakujō is saying that it all depends on what the mistake is, then Ōbaku has not yet been able to grasp Hyakujō's greater intent. It would be as if Ōbaku had not thoroughly explored not only responses that are wrong but also responses that go beyond being right or wrong, which are what the Buddhas and Ancestors articulate. You need to learn through your explorations with your Master that in this particular story neither the former Hyakujō nor the later Hyakujō said that it was an inaccurate response.

Rather, by using five hundred wild fox pelts, each three inches thick, he kept dwelling on this mountain, speaking for the sake of his disciples. In that the stubble of a wild fox's coat had fallen away, the later Hyakujō had the stinking skin bag of a human being, which, when we take the measure of it, is half a wild fox's skin striving to get free. There is the former Hyakujō's being reduced to a certain mental state and there is the later Hyakujō's getting free of it. And also, there is the cause and effect that comes about through a Master's words turning things around for others, and doing so without making a mistake. Beyond question, these are the Great Practice.

Were Ōbaku to come here now and ask, "Suppose he had not made a mistake and was able to turn things around for his disciple, what would have become of him?" I would reply, "He would still have been reduced to being reborn as a wild fox." If Ōbaku were then to ask, "Why so?" I would reply, "O you embodiment of a wild fox's ghost!" And even then, it would not be a matter of Ōbaku having made a mistake or not having made a mistake. Do not concede that Ōbaku's question is the correct one to ask. And also, when Ōbaku asked, "What would have become of him?" I could answer, "Are <u>you</u> able to grope about for <u>your</u> hide and face yet?" And also, I could say, "Have <u>you</u> been reduced to being reborn as a wild fox yet?" And also, I could say, "Would you have replied to that disciple that <u>you</u> are not subject to cause and effect?"

However, Hyakujō's saying, "Come up close and I will tell you," already embraces the issue of what would have become of him. Ōbaku came up, dead to the past and oblivious to the future.[8] His giving Hyakujō a slap is his doing a bit of foxy transformation.

> The Master clapped his hands and laughed, saying, "I've always thought that the beards of foreigners were red, and behold, here is a red-bearded foreigner."[9]

This way of putting It does not capture the spirit one hundred percent, but is, in effect, a mere eighty or ninety percent of it. Even if we were to concede that it was eighty or ninety percent of it, it would still not be eighty or ninety percent accurate. And even if we were to concede that it was a hundred percent accurate, still it is something that is not eighty or ninety percent accurate.[10] Though this is the way things are, I would express it as follows:

> *What Hyakujō said permeates the whole universe.*
> *And even so, he had not yet left the wild fox's den.*
> *Ōbaku's feet were on solid ground,*
> *And even so, he still seems attached to the*
> *   mantis's way.*[11]
> *With a slap on the face and a clap of the hands there*
> *   is the one of them, not the two of them:*
> *The beards of foreigners are red, and a red-bearded*
> *   one is a foreigner.*

---

8.   That is, Ōbaku had dropped off everything and was living fully in each moment.

9.   That is, 'the beards of foreigners are red' and 'there are red-bearded foreigners' are two ways of saying the same thing.

10. That is, even if a way of putting the Matter is right on target one hundred percent, it is not the only way of putting the Matter, and hence is less than one hundred percent, or even eighty or ninety percent.

11. That is, Ōbaku has his feet on the ground, but he still tended to be cautious—like the movements of a praying mantis preparing to strike—as if fearful of making a mistake.

Delivered to the assembly at the old temple of Kippō-ji in Echizen Province on the ninth day of the third lunar month in the second year of the Kangen era (April 17, 1244).

Copied by me in the quarters of the Abbot's assistant in the same temple on the thirteenth day of the third lunar month of the same year (April 21, 1244).

Ejō

74

On Conferring the Face-to-Face Transmission
(Menju)

Translator's Introduction: This discourse is divided into three parts, the first two having their own postscripts. This suggests that Dōgen added material later based on questions from his disciples that he felt needed further clarification, particularly concerning the ways in which doing one's training, having a kenshō (that is, the experience of one's Buddha Nature), being Transmitted, and being certified as a Dharma heir interrelate.

In addition, there is a seeming contradiction in this discourse which may perplex some readers. Early on, where Dōgen describes how the Face-to-Face Transmission had been passed on through the generations from Shakyamuni Buddha down to Dōgen himself, he seems to imply that the Transmission can only occur between a disciple and his or her Master while the Master is still alive. Later, he cites several cases where there is a claim of monks' having been transmitted in some sense, but not physically face-to-face with the one who was his Master. However, as Dōgen makes clear towards the end of the discourse, the bottom line is that whatever someone may feel has been either a kenshō or a Face-to-Face Transmission, the experience must be confirmed by a living Master, either the monk's own or another's.

At the time when Shakyamuni Buddha was with His assembly atop the Divine Vulture Peak in India, and while amidst the millions gathered there, He plucked an udumbara flower and held it aloft, His eyes atwinkle. At that moment, the countenance of the Venerable Makakashō broke out into a smile. Shakyamuni Buddha said, "Since I too possess the Treasure House of the Eye of the True Teaching which is the Wondrous Heart of Nirvana, I have conferred It upon Makakashō."

This is the very principle of Buddha after Buddha and Ancestor after Ancestor conferring the Face-to-Face Transmission of the Treasure House of the Eye of the True Teaching. Having been genuinely Transmitted by the Seven Buddhas,[*] It came down to the Venerable Makakashō. Through twenty-eight Transmissions from the Venerable Makakashō, it came down to the Venerable Bodhidharma. The Venerable Bodhidharma himself came to China and gave the Face-to-Face

---

[*]   See *Glossary.*

Transmission to the Venerable Eka, who is a Great Ancestor of our authentic tradition and a Fully Enlightened Great Master. Through five more Transmissions, It came down to Great Master Daikan Enō of Mount Sōkei. Through seventeen more conferrings, It came down to my late Master, the Old Buddha Tendō Nyojō of Mount Tendō in Keigen Prefecture in Great Sung China. On the first day of the fifth lunar month in the first year of the Pao-ch'ing era in Great Sung China (June 8, 1225), I, Dōgen, offered incense in the Abbot's quarters and bowed in respect to my Master, the Old Buddha of Tendō, who is now deceased. This Old Buddha who was my former Master met me for the first time. At that time, he led me by the hand through the Teaching and gave me the Face-to-Face Transmission, saying:

> I have revealed to you the Dharma Gate of the Face-to-Face Transmission which Buddha after Buddha and Ancestor after Ancestor has conferred. This is the holding aloft of the flower on the Divine Vulture Peak. It is Eka on Mount Sūzan realizing Bodhidharma's Marrow. It is Daiman Kōnin's Transmitting the robe. It is Tōzan's conferring the Face-to-Face Transmission. These are the Buddha's Ancestors conferring the Treasure House of the Eye of the True Teaching through a Face-to-Face Transmission. It exists only within our monastic family and is something that others have not yet encountered even in their dreams.

When it comes to the principle underlying this conferring of the Face-to-Face Transmission, because Kashō Buddha personally gave the Face-to-Face Transmission to Shakyamuni Buddha when He was in that Buddha's assembly, and because Shakyamuni safeguarded It, It is the very face of an Ancestor of the Buddha. Had there been no Face-to-Face Transmission from the face of the Buddha, there would not have been all the various subsequent Buddhas. It is intimately connected with Shakyamuni Buddha's personal encounter with the Venerable Makakashō. Although Ananda was His cousin and Rahula was His son, neither attained the intimate connection with Him that Makakashō had. Even though there were various great bodhisattvas[*] in His assembly, none attained the intimate connection with Him that Makakashō had, nor could they sit in the Venerable Makakashō's seat. That the World-honored One and

Makakashō arrived at sitting in the same seat and wearing the same kesa* is taken to be the behavior of Buddhas of one and the same generation. The Venerable Makakashō had personally received the Face-to-Face Transmission of the World-honored One. This was the conferring of His Face, the conferring of His Mind, the conferring of His Body, the conferring of His Eye. Makakashō made alms offerings in veneration and prostrations in homage to Shakyamuni Buddha. Who knows how many thousands of myriad transformations He had been through, breaking His bones and shattering His body to bits in His efforts? His own Countenance is beyond face and eyes, for He had been given the Face and Eyes of a Tathagata for a countenance. Shakyamuni Buddha looked directly at the Venerable Makakashō, and the Venerable Makakashō looked directly at the Venerable Ananda, and the Venerable Ananda personally bowed in respect to the Buddha Countenance of the Venerable Makakashō, for this was his Face-to-Face Transmission. The Venerable Ananda resided in, and kept to, this Face-to-Face Transmission, and, having connected with Shōnawashu, gave him the Face-to-Face Transmission. The Venerable Shōnawashu, while directly attending on the Venerable Ananda out of respect, experienced the Face on his own, together with all Faces, as the conferring of the Face-to-Face Transmission and the accepting of the Face-to-Face Transmission.

In this way, Ancestral Masters, as successive heirs for generation after generation, have passed on the Face-to-Face Transmission. This was done in accord with a disciple being 'seen' by a Master and the Master 'recognizing' the disciple.[1] If even one Ancestor, or one Master, or one disciple had failed to confer the Face-to-Face Transmission, there would not be Buddha after Buddha or Ancestor after Ancestor. For instance, by letting the waters of many rivers gather and irrigate the roots, They have caused the branches of our tradition to grow long. And by Their keeping the Light going, Its brightness has been made constant. And by Their having done so in millions of billions of ways, the trunk and its branches are one and the same. And there have also been swift and nimble moments as mother hen and chick,

---

1. That is, the person occupying the position of Master sees that the one occupying the position of disciple appears as 'a vessel for the Dharma' and is therefore 'such a person', one suitable for Transmission.

the one without and the other within, cheep and peck the eggshell open. As a consequence, keeping true to Shakyamuni Buddha as though He were right before Them, They have let the days and nights throughout Their life pile up, and letting Themselves be illumined by the countenance of the Buddha, They have let the days and nights of Their whole life accumulate. We do not know for how many eons beyond measure this has gone on. Just quietly thinking about this should fill us with heartfelt gratitude.

By bowing down in respect to the Face of Shakyamuni Buddha and by transferring the Eye of Shakyamuni Buddha to our own eyes, we will have transferred our eyes to the Eye of Buddha. Ours will be the very Eye and Face of Buddha. Without even one generation's break, that which has been conferred face-to-face right up to the present by the mutual Transmission of this Buddha Eye and Buddha Face is this very Face-to-Face Transmission. These successive heirs over some dozens of generations are instances of face after face being the Face of Buddha, for they have received the Face-to-Face Transmission from the original Buddha Face. Their bowing down in respect to this conferring of the Face as the genuine Transmission is their respectful bowing down to the Seven Buddhas, including Shakyamuni Buddha, and it is their bowing in respect and making venerative offerings to the twenty-eight Indian Ancestors of the Buddha from Makakashō on down. This is what the Face and Eye of an Ancestor of the Buddha is like. To encounter this Ancestor of the Buddha is to meet Shakyamuni Buddha along with the other Seven Buddhas. It is the very instant when an Ancestor of the Buddha personally confers the Face-to-Face Transmission upon himself: it is a Buddha of the Face-to-Face Transmission conferring the Face-to-Face Transmission upon a Buddha of the Face-to-Face Transmission. Using that which entwines like the vines of kudzu and wisteria, He confers the Face-to-Face Transmission as an entwining, without any disruption. Opening his Eye, he confers the Eye-to-Eye Transmission and receives the Eye-to-Eye Transmission. Revealing his Face, he confers the Face-to-Face Transmission and receives the Face-to-Face Transmission. The conferring of the Face-to-Face Transmission is both receiving and giving from the place of the Face. When it comes to explaining Mind, He confers the Mind-to-Mind Transmission by means of Mind. When it comes to manifesting Body, He confers the Body-to-Body Transmission by means of Body. In other places and in other nations, such a one as this is treated as the Original Ancestor. In China and eastwards, the conferring and receiving of the Face-to-Face Transmission exists only in our monastic family of the Buddha's authentic Transmission. Moreover, it is the mutual passing on of the Genuine Eye with which we see the Tathagata.

When I bow in respect to the Face of Shakyamuni Buddha, I, as one in the fifty-first generation, do not stand side-by-side with the Seven Buddhas and the Ancestors of our tradition, nor do I stand in a line with Them; rather, a conferring of the Face-to-Face Transmission takes place with all of us at the same moment. If someone does not encounter a Master even once in a lifetime, that person is not a disciple: if someone does not encounter a disciple, that person is not a Master. When they have finally met each other and recognized each other, and when the conferring of the Face-to-Face Transmission and the passing on of the Dharma to the successor have taken place, that is the manifesting of what is called the conferring of the Face-to-Face Transmission in our Ancestral tradition. This is why their faces have taken on the radiance associated with that of the Tathagata. Accordingly, no matter how many thousands or tens of thousands of years or how many hundreds or millions of eons may pass, this conferring of the Face-to-Face Transmission is what is meant by Shakyamuni Buddha's conferring the Face-to-Face Transmission right here and now before our very eyes.

When this state of manifesting as an Ancestor of the Buddha in the here-and-now has been realized, it is a transformation of the World-honored One, of Makakashō, of the fifty-one generations, and of the seven founding Ancestors of our tradition, all of which is done for the sake of helping sentient beings. It is the Light manifesting before our very eyes, and it is Body manifesting before our very eyes, and it is Mind manifesting before our very eyes, and it is what comes from the ends of our toes to the tip of our nose. Even though not a single word has been grasped nor half a sentence understood, yet the Master has already seen the back of the disciple's head, for the disciple has already bowed his head in respect to the Master: this is a conferring of the Face-to-Face Transmission, which is the genuine Transmission. We should deeply respect a conferring of the Face-to-Face Transmission done in this manner. Merely leaving traces of one's mind on the mind field of another is hardly a greatly respected or valuable way to live. The changing of one's countenance or the turning of one's head whilst the Face-to-Face Transmission is being conferred may be a matter of the skin of one's Face being three inches thick or the skin of one's Face been ten feet thin. And this very skin of one's Face may well be the Great Round Mirror of the Buddhas. Because the Great Round Mirror is taken to be the skin of the Face, neither inside nor outside have any flaws, nor is the Face blurred over. And Great Round Mirrors have customarily conferred the Face-to-Face Transmission to Great Round Mirrors.

Those who have truly had Transmitted to them the Eye of the True Dharma with which they personally see a Shakyamuni Buddha appearing before them will have a more intimate connection with that Dharma than with Shakyamuni Buddha Himself. Sharp of eye, they will see innumerable Shakyamuni Buddhas appearing, lined up both in front of them and behind them. Accordingly, those who esteem Shakyamuni Buddha, who have lost their heart to Shakyamuni Buddha, should esteem and revere this genuine Face-to-Face Transmission and should bow down in deepest respect to that which is hard to come by, hard to encounter. It is their bowing down in reverence to the Tathagata: it is their having the Face-to-Face Transmission conferred on them by the Tathagata. Moreover, when those who are reverently exploring the True Transmission through their training are fortunate enough to encounter the Tathagata who is conveying the Face-to-Face Transmission, they will be loath to be apart from this Self and will protect and keep to It, whether the Tathagata is the Self that they think of as their own True Self or as the Self of another.

In speaking of the Genuine Transmission in our monastic family, those who bow in respect to the eight stupas* are delivered from hindrances resulting from their wrongdoings and come to realize the fruition of the Way.[2] These stupas mark the route that Shakyamuni Buddha took in His life. They were erected at such places as where He was born, where He first turned the Wheel of the Dharma, where He realized the Way, and where He entered nirvana. Another reliquary remains at Kanyakubja and

---

2.　The eight stupas are the places where Shakyamuni's ashes, which were divided into eight parts, are said to have been enshrined.

one was kept in Ambapāli Grove. Yet another became the Great Earth while the eighth became the vast Great Sky. And by our doing reverential bows to whatever has been treated as a stupa—based on some sound, smell, taste, touch, substance, palpable form, or the like—the fruition of the Way manifests before our very eyes. Reverentially bowing at these eight stupas is a diligent practice throughout India, and householders as well as monks, crowds of those of lofty position as well as crowds of ordinary people, vie to make reverential bows and venerative alms offerings. This is a veritable scroll of Scripture: it is just the way it is in Buddhist Scriptures. And what is more, by Shakyamuni Buddha's using thirty-seven methods as His training and practice,[3] and thereby bringing the Way to Its fruition in every moment of His life, the ever-present traces of His practice and discipline can be seen scattered about here and there along the pathways of old. And because He made these traces plain enough to see, we can realize the Way.

Keep in mind that the frosts and flowers have returned ever so many times to these multi-storied eight stupas. The winds and rain, time and again, have encroached upon them, yet they have put their mark in space and they have put their mark in form.[4] The spiritual benefits which they lavish upon people of the present day have not diminished. And when we now attempt to make the roots, strengths, realizations, and paths of these thirty-seven methods into our training and practice, even though defiling passions exist along with the hindrances created by our delusions, nevertheless, as we train and experience an awakening, the power of these methods will still be like new today.

The spiritually beneficial activity of Shakyamuni Buddha was no different. What is more, the present conferring of the Face-to-Face Transmission today should not be compared with those stupas and methods. The thirty-seven ancillary methods for realizing enlightenment have as their source the Buddha Face, the Buddha Mind, the Buddha Body, the Buddha Speech, the Buddha Brightness, the Buddha Tongue,

---

3.   Dōgen discussed these methods in detail in Discourse 70: On the Thirty-seven Methods of Training for Realizing Enlightenment (*Sanjushichihon Bodai Bumpo*).

4.   That is, despite erosion from wind and rain over time, enough remains of them that they can still be seen towering into the sky, and their form as stupas is still recognizable.

and so on. The mass of meritorious virtues of those eight stupas also have as their foundation the Buddha Face, and so forth. Now, when we, as fellow explorers of Buddhahood, conduct ourselves day-by-day in accord with the Absolute Path to liberation, we should, in the calmness and tranquility of our days and nights, make the effort to consider these matters deeply, and should take pleasure in, and cherish, the opportunity to do so.[5]

The 'Country' we call ours surpasses all others for our Way alone is unsurpassed. In other places, there are many who are not like us. I speak of our Country and our Way as being unsurpassed and solely held in veneration because, even though the multitudes who had assembled on the Divine Vulture Peak went forth and instructed others throughout the ten directions, only Bodhidharma, the authentic successor at Shōrin-ji Temple, was truly the religious head in China, and the descendants of Daikan Enō of Mount Sōkei have passed on the Face-to-Face Transmission right up to the present day. Today is a good time for the Buddha Dharma to once again 'be taken into the mud and into the water'.[6] If you have not realized a genuine fruition by this time, at what time will you realize a genuine fruition? If you have not cut off your delusions by this time, at what time will you cut them off? Should you not have become Buddha by this time, at what time will you become Buddha? Should you not be sitting as a Buddha at this time, at what time will you practice being a Buddha? Do your utmost to examine this in detail.

When Shakyamuni Buddha graciously conferred the Face-to-Face Transmission upon the Venerable Makakashō, He said, "Since I possess the Treasure House of the Eye of the True Teaching and the Wondrous Heart of Nirvana, I have conferred them upon Makakashō." While in the assembly on Mount Sūzan, the Venerable Bodhidharma pointed directly to the Second Ancestor and said, "You have realized what my Marrow is."

---

5. 'The Absolute Path' is a translation of a Buddhist technical term for the spiritual path of training that not only takes us to the point of realizing our True Nature but also takes us through the remainder of our life.

6. 'To be taken into the mud and into the water' is a common Zen Buddhist metaphor for going to whatever lengths are necessary to help sentient beings realize the Truth.

Be very clear about it: when someone Transmits face-to-face the Treasure House of the Eye of the True Teaching by saying, "You have realized what my Marrow is," this is plainly an instance of conferring the Face-to-Face Transmission. At that very moment when you let go of your everyday notions of what 'bones and marrow' means, there will be the Face-to-Face Transmission of the Buddhas and Ancestors. The Face-to-Face Transmission of the great Full Enlightenment and the Mind seal[*] will involve a particular moment in a definite place. Even though it may not be the Transmission of everything, do not probe into your training with the assumption that something is still lacking.

In summary, the Great Way of the Buddhas and Ancestors is simply one face conferring and one face accepting, the accepting of the Face and the conferring of the Face, and further, there will be nothing in excess and nothing lacking. We should take the opportunity to delight in, and have confidence in, the countenance of someone who has encountered this Face-to-Face Transmission, proffering our services to that person.

On the first day of the fifth lunar month of the Pao-ch'ing era in Great Sung China (June 8, 1225), I, Dōgen, for the first time bowed in deepest respect to my late Master Tendō, the Old Buddha, who conferred on me the Face-to-Face Transmission. I was then permitted to enter his private chambers. I had barely dropped off body and mind before returning to Japan and, since then, I have maintained and relied upon this Face-to-Face Transmission.

Given to the assembly in the training hall of Kippō-ji Temple in Yoshida Prefecture, Echizen Province, on the twentieth day of the tenth lunar month in the first year of the Kangen era (December 3, 1243).

Among those people who have never encountered or heard about, or explored through their training with a Master the principle that the Face-to-Face Transmission of the Way of the Buddha is like this, there was one called Meditation Master Jōko of Sempuku-ji Temple, who was alive during the Chinese Ching-yü era (1034-1037) in the reign of the great Sung emperor Jen-chung.[7] Upon entering the Lecture Hall, he said the following:

> The Great Master Ummon Bun'en is actually present here right now. Do all of you also see him? If you are able to see him, then you are a fellow trainee, one who is the equal of this mountain monk. Do you see him? Do you see him! You need to pierce directly to the bottom of this matter, then, straight off, you will realize what is true and right, and will no longer be able to delude yourselves.
>
> Let us consider for the moment the case of Ōbaku of olden days. Upon hearing his Master, the monk Hyakujō, relate the story of his own Master, Great Master Baso, giving forth with a sudden shout to startle and awaken his disciples, Ōbaku appeared to have entered a state of deep reflection, so Hyakujō asked him, "From now on, don't you wish to be an heir of the Great Master?" Ōbaku replied, "Although I know of the Great Master, to put it simply, I did not meet the Great Master. I dare say I would gladly forfeit having descendants of my own, if only I could have heard the Great Master name me as his heir."
>
> O members of this great assembly here, not five years had gone by since Great Master Baso had passed on, yet Ōbaku said of himself that he had never met the Great Master. You should by all means realize that Ōbaku's viewpoint had not fully matured; in short, he still possessed only one eye.
>
> This mountain monk is not like that. I have not only been able to know about Great Master Ummon, I have been able to see Great Master Ummon, and safe to say, I have heard Great Master Ummon name me as an heir of his. Yet given that it is already a

---

7. Sempuku Jōko (dates unknown) resided near the stupa of Meditation Master Ummon Bun'en (864-949). Though already a Meditation Master, Jōko, upon reading the recorded sayings of Ummon, felt he had finally fully awakened and consequently claimed that he was Ummon's Dharma heir.

hundred or more years since Ummon entered nirvana, how can I possibly make the assertion that the two of us had an intimate encounter? Safe to say, those who are sophisticated in the ways of the world and those who can see beyond surface appearances will attest to my having the radiance of direct experience, whereas those who are cynical or small-minded will give rise in their minds to doubts and criticisms. Those who have been able to see do not talk about it, and those who have not yet seen, should they not look right now? Since you have been standing here for some time without asking any questions, I now wish that you may take good care of yourselves.[8]

Now Jōko, even if you had known all about Great Master Ummon and had seen Great Master Ummon, has Great Master Ummon seen you? If Great Master Ummon has not met you, it would not be possible for you to hear Great Master Ummon name you as an heir of his. Because Great Master Ummon has not yet certified you, even you yourself dare not assert, "Great Master Ummon has met me." It is obvious that you and Great Master Ummon have never met each other. Among the Seven Buddhas, along with all the other Buddhas of the past, present, and future, is there any Ancestor of the Buddhas who has been heir to the Dharma without Master and disciple having met each other?

Jōko, do not assert that Ōbaku's viewpoint had not fully matured. How can you possibly gauge Ōbaku's daily behavior or fathom Ōbaku's words and phrases? Ōbaku was an Old Buddha. His exploration of inheriting the Dharma was thorough. You have not even seen, or heard, or dreamt of, much less studied through your training what the principle of being heir to the Dharma is. Ōbaku inherited the Dharma from his Master, and he held to and relied upon our Ancestor Baso. Ōbaku had an audience with his Master and saw his Master. You, Jōko, have not seen the Master, nor have you known the Ancestor, nor did you know your Self, much less have you met your Self. There is no Master who met you, nor have you ever experienced the

---

8. This statement is a typical way in which a Zen Master might bring a meeting of the assembly to an end.

Eye of a Master being opened. The truth of the matter is that you are the one whose viewpoint has not matured: it is your inheritance of the Dharma that is not complete.

Didn't you know in what sense Great Master Ummon really is a Dharma descendant of Ōbaku?[9] How could you possibly sound the depths of what Hyakujō and Ōbaku were talking about? You still haven't fathomed what Great Master Ummon was talking about. Those who have explored through their training with a Master what Hyakujō and Ōbaku were talking about will pick up on it; those who have reached the place where everything has dropped off, which is what is being directly pointed to here, will be able to fathom it. You, Jōko, have not explored the Matter* with a Master, nor have you reached the place where everything has dropped off, so you cannot understand it or gauge its depths.

You have said, "Not five years had gone by since Great Master Baso had passed on, yet Ōbaku said of himself that he had never met the Great Master." Truly, that is not worth a laugh. Someone who is capable of being an heir to the Dharma can inherit the Dharma even after countless eons. Were there someone who was incapable of inheriting the Dharma, that person could not inherit the Dharma even in half a day or half a minute. Jōko, you are someone in the dark, befuddled and ignorant, one who has not seen the Face of the Sun and the Face of the Moon which Buddhas speak of.

You say that even though it was already some one hundred years earlier that Great Master Ummon had entered nirvana, you had heard him name you as an heir of his. Is it due to some formidable power of yours that you have heard Ummon name you as an heir? You are more whimsical than a three-year-old child! People a thousand years from now who hope to inherit the Dharma from Ummon may well have abilities ten times yours.

We will all come to your rescue by exploring with you for a bit the account of Hyakujō and Ōbaku. Hyakujō's remark, "From now on, don't <u>you</u> wish to be an

---

9.   Dōgen's question is rhetorical, not literal. Ummon was a Dharma heir of Seppō and
       Tokusan, whereas Ōbaku's lineage goes back to Nangaku. Ōbaku died in 850 and
       Ummon was born in 864, so there was no physical interaction between them. Dōgen will
       explain what he means in the ensuing sentences.

heir of the Great Master?" is not saying, "Go inherit the Dharma from Great Master Baso." While taking a bit of time to explore the topic of a lion, in all fury, dashing off after some prey and the topic of a black turtle climbing a tree backwards, you should also thoroughly investigate progressing along the Absolute Path step-by-step.[10] You have the ability to explore through your training this step-by-step approach to inheriting the Dharma. Ōbaku's words, "I dare say I would gladly forfeit having descendants of my own," have all proved beyond your grasp. Do you know what he meant by 'my own' and who his descendants are? You needed to explore this carefully through your training. Ōbaku has fully stated the principle, concealing nothing and revealing all.

However, a certain Meditation Master named Bukkoku Ihaku, out of ignorance of how the Buddhist Ancestors inherit the Dharma, listed Jōko among Ummon's Dharma heirs.[11] This is surely a mistake. As trainees of a later time, do not imagine, out of ignorance, that Jōko may also have been doing his training with a Master.

Copied by me in the quarters of the Abbot's assistant at Kippō-ji Temple in Echizen Province, on the seventh day of the sixth lunar month in the second year of the Kangen era (July 13, 1244).

Ejō

Jōko, if, as you claim, it is possible to inherit the Dharma by relying on written words, then do all those who have given rise to enlightenment by reading Scriptures inherit the Dharma from Shakyamuni Buddha Himself? That is never the case. An enlightenment experience brought about by encountering Scriptural writings always requires certification by a genuine Master.

---

10.   That is, find the middle way in your training by progressing step by step, rather than by trying to dash ahead or by poking behind, thus doing your training the hard way.

11.   Bukkoku helped in the preparation of one of the records of Zen monastic practitioners and Dharma heirs.

Jōko, you have still not read the records of Ummon's sayings, as you have claimed. Only those folks who have truly read Ummon's words have inherited the Dharma from Ummon. You have never seen Ummon with your own eyes, nor have you seen Ummon with Ummon's eyes, nor have you seen yourself with Ummon's eyes. There are many things like this that you have not thoroughly explored through your training. And what is more, you will need to buy new straw sandals time and again should you go seeking for a genuine Master from whom to inherit the Dharma. Do not say that you have inherited It from Great Master Ummon. If you go around claiming such things, then you will just be a type of non-Buddhist. Even if Hyakujō himself were to speak as you have done, it would be a huge mistake.

75

On The Unbounded

(Kokū)

Translator's Introduction: While the title of this discourse may be translated as 'space', 'emptiness', or 'the void', these renderings tend to imply something that is negative, whereas *kokū* is a technical Buddhist term for That which is devoid of any obstructions: the Unbounded.

This was apparently the first formal talk that Dōgen gave in his new temple, originally called Daibutsu-ji and later renamed Eihei-ji.

Because right here is where the What exists, It causes Buddhas and Ancestors to find ways to express It. And because the ways that the Buddhas and Ancestors have expressed It have naturally been passed on from Dharma heir to Dharma heir, They have made their whole being their Master's Skin and Flesh, Bones and Marrow, so that it hangs suspended within the Unbounded. That which is Unbounded transcends categories such as the twenty types of emptiness. For, altogether, how could the Unbounded be limited to a mere twenty types of emptiness, since there are at least eighty-four thousand types of emptiness? And indeed there may be many more.

Meditation Master Shakkyō Ezō of the Fuchou region once asked Meditation Master Seidō Chizō, "Coming back to the topic, do you know how to grab hold of Space?"

Seidō replied, "Of course I know how to grab hold of space."

The Master said, "And just how do you grab hold of Space?"

Seidō made a gesture with his hand as if gathering up a handful of something.

The Master said, "You do not know how to grab hold of Space."

Seidō responded, "My elder monastic brother, you who are a Master, just how do you grab hold of space?"

Thereupon, the Master grabbed hold of Seidō's nose and gave it a yank.

Trying to suppress a yelp, Seidō exclaimed, "How awful of you! Pulling a person's nose like that! Fortunately, I've been able to get free, quick enough." [1]

The Master said, "If you could have grabbed hold of me like this, you would have grasped It right from the start."

Shakkyō's question, "Coming back to the topic, do you know how to grab hold of Space?" is asking, "Is your whole being, through and through, hands and eyes?" [2]

Seidō's reply, "Of course, I know how to grab hold of space," meant for him that Space was like a lump of something. But once It is understood in that way, It becomes stained, and after Space has become stained, It is brought down to earth. [3]

Shakkyō's saying, "And just how do you grab hold of Space?" meant "As soon as you call that Reality, it has already completely changed. But even so, by going along with change, you are going towards Reality, following the Tathagata."

The statement, "Seidō made a gesture with his hand as if gathering up a handful of something," meant that even though he might know how to ride the tiger's head, he did not yet know how to grab hold of the tiger's tail. [4]

Shakkyō's saying, "You do not know how to grab hold of Space," was not simply a matter of his stating that Seidō did not have an intellectual understanding of what 'grabbing hold of Space' meant, for Seidō was at a place where he had not yet

---

1.   That is, he awoke to the Truth.

2.   The second question here is a reference to the kōan story in Discourse 32: On Kannon, the Bodhisattva of Compassion *(Kannon)*.

3.   That is, once the Unbounded is thought as being some thing, It becomes tainted with intellectualizing and is reduced to a worldly understanding.

4.   That is, even though Seidō might know how to do the training, he still had not grasped the Essential Matter.

encountered the Unbounded even in his dreams. Even though that was the way things were with Seidō, Shakkyō did not want to end up trying to describe It to him.

Seidō's asking, "My elder monastic brother, you who are a Master, just how do you grab hold of space?" meant "My elder brother, express what it is in a verse or a word. Do not leave it totally up to me to get it."

Thereupon, Shakkyō grabbed hold of Seidō's nose and gave it a yank. We need to explore this through our training: Shakkyō has stuck his whole being up Seidō's Nose and Seidō fully revealed that he had been grabbed by the Nose. Even though this was how things were, the Unbounded is of a whole and It is 'stones bumping up against stones'.[5]

Seidō, trying to suppress a yelp, said, "How awful of you! Pulling a person's nose like that! Fortunately, I've been able to get free, quick enough." Earlier he had wished to encounter a True Person, but what he suddenly encountered was his True Self. At the same time, it was not that he could not have stained his True Self, it is that he had to train himself.

Shakkyō said, "If you could have grabbed hold of me like this, you would have grasped It right from the start." Well, it is not impossible that Seidō could have grasped It right from the start. Even so, Shakkyō did not lend his own strength to Seidō, because Seidō could not have grasped It by Shakkyō's extending a helping hand to Shakkyō, nor could he have grasped It by the Unbounded's extending a helping hand to the Unbounded.[6]

To put the matter in broader terms, the universe has no gaps to put 'space' into. Even so, this one account has long made Space resound with Its thunder. Since the time of Shakkyō and Seidō, there have been many trainees who have called themselves masterly teachers within the five traditional families—Sōtō, Ummon, Rinzai, Hōgen, and Igyō—but few of them have encountered, or heard of, much less fathomed, what Space is. Before and after Shakkyō and Seidō, there has been the

---

5.   That is, even though the Unbounded is totality, It is not static.

6.   That is, Seidō had to rely on doing his own training, rather than depend on the Master or the Buddha Nature to do the training for him.

occasional one who has played around with what Space is, but few have grabbed hold of what It is.

Shakkyō had taken hold of It, but Seidō had not caught sight of It. As Abbot of Daibutsu-ji Temple, I would like to have said to Shakkyō, "At that time when you grabbed hold of Seidō's nose, if you had wanted to grab hold of Space, you should have grabbed hold of your own Nose. And you should have understood how to grab hold of your Fingertips with your fingertips." Even so, Shakkyō knew a bit about a monk's everyday behavior of grabbing hold of Space. Even if you are a good hand at grabbing hold of Space, you need to explore through your training with your Master the ins and outs of Space. And you need to explore through your training the killing off of 'Space' and the revitalizing of It, and you need to know the relative importance of 'Space'. You need to preserve and rely upon the grasping of Space, which is, namely, your doing your utmost to train in the Way, your giving rise to the intention to realize that one's training and enlightenment are identical, and your listening to what Buddha after Buddha and Ancestor after Ancestor have put forth.

My late Master, the Old Buddha of Tendō, once said the following, "My whole being is like the mouth of a bell suspended in empty space."[7] Clearly, you need to recognize that the whole body of space hangs in Space.

The eminent scholar, Abbot Seizan of Hungchou Province, once paid a visit to Baso. Baso asked him, "What Scripture do you lecture on?"

Seizan replied, "The *Heart Scripture*."

Baso then asked him, "And what do you use to lecture on It with?"

---

7.   The opening line of a poem by Tendō Nyojō, quoted in Discourse 2: On the Great Wisdom That Is Beyond Discriminatory Thought (*Makahannya-haramitsu*).

Seizan replied, "I use my mind with which to lecture on It."

Baso then said, "The mind is like the starring actor, our will is like its supporting player, with the six senses playing the accompanying cast. How can these possibly comprehend how to lecture on a Scripture?"

Seizan responded, "Were the mind unable to give a lecture, surely empty space could hardly do it!"

Baso said, "On the contrary, it is Space that is able to give a lecture."

With a dismissive swish of his sleeve, Seizan departed.

Baso called after him, "Learned monk!" Seizan turned his head around. Baso said, "From birth to old age, It is ever thus."

Thereupon, Seizan caught It. Eventually, he went into hiding on Mount Seizan,—whence his name—and nothing more was heard from him.[8]

Accordingly, Buddhas and Ancestors alike are persons who expound the Scriptures and They invariably use Space in expounding these Scriptures. Were it not for Space, They would not be able to expound even one Scripture. Whether They expound on the mind as Scripture or expound on the body as Scripture, in either case They do the expounding by means of Space. By means of Space, They manifest what They are deliberately thinking about as well as what goes beyond deliberate thought. Not only have They achieved the wise discernment from having a Master and the wise discernment that goes beyond having a Master, They have also developed Their innate intelligence, as well as Their learned intelligence, for all of these are due to Space. Their becoming Buddha and Their becoming an Ancestor must likewise have been due to Space.

---

8. When someone who is erudite has an awakening, it is not uncommon for such a one to drop off his addiction to learning and 'disappear from public sight'.

Our Twenty-first Ancestor, the Venerable Bashubanzu, once said the following, "Our physical being is the same as the realm of Space, and this proclaims the Teaching that it is equal to Space. When someone is able to awaken to Space, there is no 'absolutely right' nor is there any 'absolutely wrong' way." To be precise, at the very moment when there is the mutual encountering and mutual recognition between a person facing the wall and the Wall facing a person. the realm of Space can be described as the mind of 'fences and walls' and the mind of 'a withered tree'. For those who need to be saved in accord with their own bodily form, Avalokiteshvara[*] will forthwith manifest in that form and give expression to the Dharma for the sake of that person. This is what is meant by pointing to the principle of 'being like Space'. For those who need to be saved in accord with some other bodily form, Avalokiteshvara will forthwith manifest in that form and give expression to the Dharma for the sake of that person. This too is what is meant by pointing to the principle of 'being like Space'. Whether you are being controlled by the twenty-four hours of any day or are in control of the twenty-four hours of any day, in either case, they are both times when you can awaken to the Unbounded.

When a stone is large, it is large just as it is, and when a stone is small, it is small just as it is. This is the principle of things being beyond 'right' and 'wrong'. This is simply the way, at this very moment, to thoroughly explore the Unbounded as the Treasure House of the Eye of the True Teaching, which is the Wondrous Heart of Nirvana.

Delivered to the assembly on the sixth day of the third lunar month in the third year of the Kangen era (April 4, 1245) at Daibutsu-ji Temple in Echizen Province.

Copied by me on the seventeenth day of the fifth lunar month in the second year of the Kōan era (June 27, 1279), while at Zenkō-ji Temple in the same land.

Giun

---

* See *Glossary.*

76

On a Monk's Bowl

(Hatsu'u)

Translator's Introduction: 'A monk's bowl' *(hatsu'u)* refers not only to the physical object that is given to novices upon their being ordained and which is to serve as their mealtime bowl from then on, but also to the monk's willingness to accept of whatever is placed in one's 'bowl', be it physically or spiritually. It is therefore a symbol of the practice of all-acceptance.

Prior to the Seven Buddhas,* there was the Essential Matter* which was genuinely Transmitted to the Seven Buddhas. It was genuinely Transmitted from each of the Seven Buddhas down through each of the Seven Buddhas, so that It was genuinely Transmitted from the Seven Buddhas as a whole to the Seven Buddhas as a whole. It was genuinely Transmitted from the Seven Buddhas down through twenty-eight generations of Indian Ancestors. The twenty-eighth generation Ancestral Master, our Founding Ancestor Bodhidharma, personally went to China and genuinely Transmitted It to the second Ancestor in China, our great Ancestor Eka. It passed on through six generations from Bodhidharma until It reached Enō. What has been passed on from India through the Eastern lands for a total of fifty-one Transmissions is the Treasure House of the Eye of the True Teaching,[1] which is the Wondrous Heart of Nirvana: It is a monk's kesa* and a monk's bowl. Buddhas of the past have taken great care to genuinely Transmit them to other Buddhas of the past. This is the way that Buddha after Buddha and Ancestor after Ancestor have accurately Transmitted them.

At the same time, each and every one of Them has had Their way of expressing what Skin and Flesh, Bones and Marrow mean, as well as Fist and Eye, which They employed to explore through Their training what Buddhas and Ancestors

---

*   See *Glossary.*

1.   There are fifty-one Transmissions counting from Makakashō through Dōgen.

are. Some have explored through Their training that a monk's bowl is the trusting heart of the Buddhas and Ancestors. And some have explored through Their training that a monk's bowl is a receptacle for what nourishes Buddhas and Ancestors. And some have explored through Their training that a monk's bowl is the very Eye of Buddhas and Ancestors. And some have explored through Their training that a monk's bowl is the very luminosity of Buddhas and Ancestors. And some have explored through Their training that a monk's bowl is the True Body of the Buddhas and Ancestors. And some have explored through Their training that a monk's bowl is the Treasure House of the Eye of the True Teaching, which is the Wondrous Heart of Nirvana. And some have explored through Their training that a monk's bowl is the place where Buddhas and Ancestors have turned Themselves around. And some have explored through Their training that the Buddhas and Ancestors are the rim and bottom of a monk's bowl. The principle underlying the exploring that such monastics do is expressed by each in his or her particular way, <u>and</u> there is something deeper to be explored.

On the day in the first year of the Pao-ching era of Great Sung China (1225), when my late Master, the Old Buddha of Tendō, assumed the role of Abbot of Tendō, he entered the Dharma Hall and said the following:

> I remember a story. A monk once asked Hyakujō, "What is this thing about something being miraculous?" Hyakujō replied, "It is your sitting all by yourself on Daiyū Peak." [2]
>
> You in this great assembly should not be disturbed by this. Just let the Old Fellow kill Himself with sitting! If someone here today should suddenly ask me what a miracle is, I would simply say to that person, "What is miraculous in the first place?" Ultimately,

---

2. Daiyū Peak was the site of Hyakujō's temple.

what else is there? I have brought my monk's bowl with me from
Jinzu Temple to eat my meals from.[3]

You need to know that what is miraculous is done for the sake of those who are already miraculous. For that which is miraculous, you need to use a miraculous tool, since this is a miraculous occasion. Accordingly, what manifests as something miraculous is the miraculous bowl of a monk. Thereby, you should call on the Four Guardian Kings to protect it and the various dragon lords to defend it, since this bowl is what we dedicate to the Buddhas and Ancestors and what They have entrusted to us.

Those folks who do not explore the Matter through their training within the private quarters of an Ancestor of the Buddha are given to saying that a Buddhist monk's kesa is something that is made of silk, or of cotton, or of some other spun material, or to saying that a Buddhist monk's bowl is something made of stone, or of porcelain, or of metal. They talk like this because they are not yet equipped with the Eye for training with a Master. The Buddha's kesa is a kesa for a Buddha. Further, you should not look upon it as being of silk or cotton. Considering it to be of such things as silk or cotton is an outmoded perspective. A Buddhist monk's bowl is a bowl for a Buddhist monk. Again, do not speak of it as being of stone or porcelain, or of metal or wood.

To speak more generally, a Buddhist monk's bowl is not something that is manufactured, nor is it something that arises only to later pass away, nor is it something that comes or goes, nor is it something subject to gain or loss. It does not span the new and old, nor is it connected with what is of the past or of the present. Even if the robe and bowl of the Buddhas and Ancestors have been brought into existence by the collective efforts of novices, they are beyond the delusions that snare and entrap novices, and even if they are brought into existence by the springing up of myriad helpful laity, they are beyond the delusions that snare and entrap lay folk. The underlying principle of this is that water is water as a result of its bringing together a varied assembly, and clouds, in turn, are clouds as a result of their bringing together

---

3.   Before being invited to be Abbot of Tendō, Nyojō was serving as Abbot of Jinzu Temple.

a varied assembly.[4] What brings together clouds are 'clouds' and what brings together water are 'waters'. A monk's bowl is one that is simply composed by a varied assembly, a bowl that is simply composed of all their hearts, a bowl that is simply composed of Emptiness, a bowl that is simply composed of monks' bowls. A monk's bowl is restricted by 'a monk's bowl'; a monk's bowl is tainted by 'a monk's bowl'.[5]

The monk's bowl that novices now receive is the monk's bowl that the Four Guardian Kings offered to the Buddha. If the monk's bowl were not that which the Four Guardian Kings offered, it would not be the one that appears right before our eyes. The monk's bowl that has now been genuinely Transmitted everywhere by the Buddha's Ancestors who have received the Buddha's Treasure House of the Eye of the True Teaching is the monk's bowl that is beyond past and present. As a consequence, now that we have spotted, and broken free from, the old views held onto by men of iron will, we no longer need to be wedded to the opinion that this monk's bowl of ours is simply something made of wood. And we have gone beyond the view that it is something constructed from the bits and pieces that our sense organs pick up. And it does not hinder the mind that distinguishes rocks from jewels. Do not speak of it as being of jade or of tile.[6] Do not speak of it as being but a bit of carved wood. By not speaking thus, we affirm what a monk's bowl really is.

Given to the assembly at Daibutsu-ji Temple in Echizen Province on the twelfth day of the third lunar month in the third year of the Kangen era (April 10, 1245).

---

4. There is a word play here that is lost in translation. Novices were known as *unsui*, literally 'water and clouds', because they would flow like water or drift about like clouds, going from monastery to monastery in search of the teacher they would come to regard as their Master. Coming into a monastery—particularly during the summer retreat period—they would bring their assembled talents into action by taking up collective projects, such as making bowl sets and monastic robes.

5. That is, if we think in terms of something called 'a monk's bowl', we tend to limit its meaning to its most literal sense.

6. 'Jade and tile' is a metaphor for what is polishable and what is not polishable.

Copied by me in the office of the Abbot's assistant at Daibutsu-ji Temple on the twenty-seventh day of the seventh lunar month in the third year of the Kangen era (August 20, 1245).

Ejō

77

On the Summer Retreat

(Ango)

Translator's Introduction: This discourse, dated at the end of summer, puts forth the purpose and methods of holding a ninety-day summer retreat, as Dōgen had just conducted it at Eihei-ji, his new temple in Echizen Province.

Whereas some who have studied the writings of Dōgen have understood certain of his remarks in Discourse 81: On Leaving Home Life Behind *(Shukke)* as rejecting lay and female discipleship, Dōgen is unequivocal about the issue in the latter part of this discourse, where he says, "Keep in mind that male and female lay trainees can also do the retreat," a retreat that Dōgen considered fundamental to the practice of a Buddhist monastic.

My late Master, the Old Buddha of Tendō, once recited a poem of his during an informal session at the beginning of a summer retreat:

> *Set your bones upright upon level ground,*
> *And to seclude yourself, scoop out a cavern in space.*
> *Pass forthwith beyond the gate of dualities,*
> *Only taking with you a darkness as dark as a black-*
> *lacquered pail.*

Accordingly, since you already have that nose ring of yours in place and have not avoided eating food, stretching out your legs, or taking a snooze, you will remain so for the rest of your life.[1] Since this is the way things are, you have not slackened and wasted your time by putting down your tools. Those tools include the ninety-day summer retreat, which is the very crown and countenance of Buddha after Buddha and Ancestor after Ancestor, all of Whom have continually experienced it intimately in Skin and Flesh, Bones and Marrow. Taking up the Eye and the head crown of the Buddhas and Ancestors, we make them into the days and months of ninety days of summer. One summer retreat is therefore something equivalent to Buddha after

---

1. 'The nose ring in place' is a reference to having learned how to train oneself, just as one goes about domesticating a water buffalo.

Buddha and Ancestor after Ancestor. The summer retreat, from beginning to end, is what an Ancestor is. Beyond this, there is not a single additional inch of ground, nor is there a great earth.

The gatepost for the summer retreat is beyond the new and beyond the old, and it is beyond coming and beyond going. The measure of this retreat is measured by the Fist, and its form has been in the form of a nose ring. Even so, because we began a summer retreat, it came, filling all space, without excluding anything in all the ten quarters. And because we ended the summer retreat, it has gone, having torn asunder the whole universe, until not an inch of ground remains. For this reason, when the summer retreat began, it resembled your giving rise to your spiritual question. And when it came to an end, it resembled your having torn asunder the nets and cages of your delusions. Even though this is how it was, there are some of you who may well have personally experienced it as hindering you from beginning to end. Well, for ten thousand miles there has not been an inch of grass, so come on, pay me back for ninety days' board!

The venerable monk, Ōryū Shishin, once said, "For thirty-some years I have tread the mountain paths as a mendicant monk. With ninety days I make me a summer. I cannot add even a single day to that, nor can I subtract one either." So, what the Eye of a wanderer of thirty-some years has penetrated is simply that a summer retreat is comprised of ninety days. Were he to add a single day, the other days would vie to be that extra day, and were he to fall one day short, his other days would vie not to be that missing day. Furthermore, he was unable to leap free from his cavernous snare of delusion. This leaping free is simply a springing up from this ninety-day pit by using one's own hands and feet.

Treating a single summer as comprised of ninety days is a tool among us, but because this is not something that was first concocted by some Ancestor of the Buddha all on His own, it has come down to us this very day as a natural endowment from Buddha after Buddha, Ancestor after Ancestor, and Dharma heir after Dharma heir. Hence, to do a summer retreat is to see Buddhas and Ancestors, as well as to meet Them, for a summer retreat has, for ever so long, created Buddhas and Ancestors.

Even though this worldly, temporal measurement of 'one summer is comprised of ninety days' is a measurement that the mind thinks up, it is not simply one eon or ten eons, nor is it simply hundreds of thousands of immeasurable eons. Ordinary times are used up by hundreds of thousands of immeasurable eons, whereas these ninety days of a summer retreat use up hundreds of thousands of immeasurable eons. As a result, even though immeasurable eons resemble the ninety days wherein you meet a Buddha, these ninety days do not necessarily depend on there being any eons. Thus, you should explore through your training that the one summer comprised of ninety days is simply a measurement of one's Eye. This is how one who attends the retreat in both body and mind is.

Both making use of acting freely and leaping beyond making use of acting freely have their origins and their foundations. Even so, <u>our</u> summer retreat has not come from some other place or from some other time, nor has it arisen just in this particular place at this particular time. When we get hold of what the origin of these ninety days is, they immediately come forth, and when we grope for what the foundation of 'ninety days' is, it immediately comes forth. Ordinary folk, as well as the saintly, treat them as a comfortable cave for them to reside in, but these ninety days go far, far beyond the realm of the ordinary and the saintly. These ninety days cannot be reached by thinking about them, nor can they be reached by not thinking about them, nor are they simply something that is unreachable by thinking about or not thinking about them.

When the World-honored One was residing in the country of Magadha, He once gave a Dharma talk for those assembled. At that time, He was intent on performing a pure summer retreat. Accordingly, he spoke to Ananda, saying, "If I am continually giving expression to the Dharma, my senior disciples, as well others in the four classes—male and female monastics and male and female laity—will not give rise to respect for It. So I am now going to enter Shakrendra's Cave and sit for the ninety days of summer.[2] When people suddenly show up and ask for Teaching, say to them on My behalf, 'All thoughts and things are beyond arising, and all thoughts and things are beyond decay.'" Having spoken thus, He concealed Himself within the cave and sat in meditation.

Since then, two thousand ninety-four years have already passed—it being now the third year of the Japanese era of Kangen. Many of His descendants who did not have entry into the private quarters of their Master would see the Buddha's sequestering Himself as a form of expressing the Dharma without using words. That wrong-minded bunch today merely think:

> The Buddha went into the cave and to meditate for the summer because using words to express It is not completely the Truth but is merely a virtuous expedient means. To reach the Truth, one cuts oneself off from using the spoken word and lets the intellective function die out. This is because going beyond words and going beyond intellect are how one reaches the Truth, since having words and having thoughts is entirely different from the Truth. This is why the Buddha cut Himself off from human beings during the ninety summer days that He sat within the cave.

What these folks are saying runs counter to the World-honored One's intention as a Buddha. If such people are going to say that His intention was to cut off speech and let the mind's functions die out, then all productive human activities and undertakings would involve cutting off speech and letting the mind's functions die out. To speak of 'cutting off speech' means all speech, and to speak of 'letting the mind's functions die out' means all functions of the mind. And what is more, this account about Him was never given for the sake of esteeming the absence of words. In all earnestness, He dragged His whole being through mud and water, and went amidst the weeds that had sprouted up, never shrinking from giving voice to the Dharma in order to help human beings reach the Other Shore, never failing to turn the Wheel of the Dharma to help

---

2.   Shakrendra's Cave is a cave on Vulture Peak that was used as a place for meditation.

rescue them. If any of the bunch of you who call yourselves His offspring were to say that His sitting through the ninety days of the summer was advocating silence, then I must say to you, "Give me back the ninety days that you spent sitting here this summer!"

The Buddha enjoined Ananda to say on His behalf, "All thoughts and things are beyond arising, and all thoughts and things are beyond decay." Do not lightly pass over what the Buddha was doing. In short, how could His sequestering Himself in a cave and sitting in meditation for the summer possibly be beyond speaking or beyond expressing the Teaching? Let's suppose for the moment that Ananda had asked the World-honored One, "How am I to express the meaning of 'All thoughts and things are beyond arising, and all thoughts and things are beyond decay'? Even were I to try to express It like this, how am I to go about doing so?" Having spoken thus, he would have listened carefully to the World-honored One's reply. Speaking more generally for the moment, the Buddha's behavior is the foremost expression of turning the Wheel of the Dharma. It is not the paramount evidence of silence. Further, do not take it to be evidence of wordless Teaching. Should you take It to be wordless Teaching, you would be just like Mr. To, who, sad to say, mistook the three-foot Dragon Spring Sword for a weaving shuttle and hung it on the wall of his humble abode.

Accordingly, the ninety-day summer sitting is the ancient turning of the Wheel of the Dharma and it is the ancient practice of Buddhas and Ancestors. In the present account, there is the phrase, "At that time, He was intent on performing a pure summer retreat." Keep in mind that what He practiced was ninety days of sitting in a summer retreat. Those who try to evade this are non-Buddhists.

To speak more generally, when the World-honored One was in the world, He sometimes did a ninety-day summer retreat in the Trayastrimsha Heavens and sometimes He did it in the quiet caves on Vulture Peak along with five hundred monastics. Throughout all five nations of India where the Buddha and His retinue traveled, when the time was ripe, without discussing where, they would do a pure summer retreat, which was their carrying out a ninety-day summer retreat. It is what Buddhas and Ancestors of the present carry out as the One Great Matter,* for it is the

---

*   See *Glossary.*

unsurpassed Way of unifying training and enlightenment. In the *Scripture of Brahma's Net* there is mention of a winter retreat, but how it was done has not been passed on; only the method for performing the ninety-day summer retreat has been passed on. It has been accurately Transmitted to me personally in the fifty-first generation.

In the *Procedures for Cleanliness in a Zen Temple*, it says the following, "If monks on pilgrimages wish to begin their summer retreat at a particular monastery, they should settle in half a month before the opening day. What is important is that they not be hurried in making their tea offerings and paying their respects." 'Half a month before' means 'during the last ten days of the third lunar month'. Accordingly, you should arrive and get settled in during the third lunar month. From the first day of the fourth lunar month on, monks are not to go outside the confines of the monastery. The doors of the reception rooms in various quarters, as well as those to the rooms for temporary lodging of itinerant monks are all locked. Accordingly, from the first day of the fourth lunar month on, itinerant monks will be making the retreat within the confines of the temple buildings or they will have settled into a monk's hut. Some may do the retreat in the residence of a lay Buddhist, for which there is a precedent. All these are rules of the Buddhas and Ancestors, so you need to do the practice and training out of a desire to emulate the ancient ways. Once the Fists and Noses have all taken up residence in the halls of the monastery, they hang up their traveling bag in their place for the duration of the retreat.

Despite this, that band of demons say, "The perspective of Mahayana* is what is important. The summer retreat is a practice of Hinayanists of the Lesser Course,* so by all means, do not engage in the practice of it." Such folks have never encountered, much less heard of, the Buddha Dharma. Supreme, fully perfected wisdom is synonymous with doing meditation throughout the summer at a ninety-day retreat. Even though the Ultimate is to be found in both the Greater and the Lesser Courses, Its branching, leafing out, flowering, and fruiting emerge from the ninety-day retreat.

First off, after breakfast on the third day of the fourth lunar month, the following ceremony is performed. Prior to the first day of the fourth lunar month, the senior monk in charge of the trainees within a Meditation Hall has already prepared the notice boards announcing the ceremony of *kairō*.[3] Right after breakfast, he hangs up these boards in front of the halls where the monks are residing. That is, he hangs them outside the latticed window which is to the left of the front entrance. He hangs them after breakfast and removes them after the bell is rung at the end of the day's practice. These are hung from the third day through the fifth day. The times to hang them and to take them down remain the same.

There is a set style and order for signing in on these boards. The order is not according to one's general position in the hierarchy of the retreat temple as 'temple officer' or 'senior monk', but just according to the date when the monk first took the monastic preceptual vows. Those who may be senior monks or temple officers elsewhere should sign in as Chief Junior or Prior or whatever.[4] Those who have served in various offices should write their highest office. Anyone who has ever served as an Abbot puts down 'So-and-so of the Western Hall'.[5] Although someone may have served as Abbot of a small temple, this may not be known by other monks, so, as often as not, he may choose not to write this title. When a monk of the Western Hall stays in the training assembly of his Master, there are examples where such a one does not follow the custom of the Western Hall and simply refers to himself as Veteran Monk So-and-so. There are many excellent examples of such a monk taking a nap in the common room of the Abbot's attendants who take care of their Master's robes and monk's bowl. Also, there is an old tradition of such a veteran monk serving as the attendant in charge of the Master's robe and bowl, or as the attendant responsible for handling incense offerings, or what is more, in any other office that is assigned at the discretion of the Master. In a large temple, when someone else's disciples come to the

---

3.   *Kairō* is a ceremony in which monks enter their name in a registry along with the number of years since their ordination, that is, since taking the preceptual vows of a monastic.

4.   That is, they should register in accordance with the specific position held in their own temple.

5.   'So-and so of the Western Hall' refers to the retired head monk of another temple, one who is staying in the guest quarters on the west side of the monastery. The Western Hall is also the place where retired monks in their Master's assembly are sequestered.

retreat, even if they served the Abbot of a small temple, it is a reliable precedent for them to be given a title for the ninety-day retreat, such as Chief Junior, Clerical Officer, Chief Supervisory Officer, or Prior, for instance. Those who use their title from some minor post in a small temple cause laughter among those in the monastery. A sensible person who has been even the Abbot of a small temple will sign himself without using that title.

The board is set up in the following style:

Such-and-such Temple on Such-and-such Mountain in Such-and-such District of Such-and-such Province is holding a summer retreat this summer. For the Sangha attending, the number of years that each has passed since taking the monastic Precepts is as follows:

The Venerable Kaundinya[6]
The Venerable Abbot

<u>Precept recipients in 1st year of the Kempō era:</u>

So-and-so Veteran	So-and-so Librarian
So-and-so Veteran	So-and-so Veteran

<u>Precepts recipients in 2nd year of Kempō era:</u>

So-and-so of Western Hall	So-and-so Trainees' Supervisor
So-and-so Chief Junior	So-and-so Guestmaster
So-and-so Veteran	So-and-so Bathhouse Monk

<u>Precepts recipients in 1st year of Kenryaku era:</u>

So-and-so Grounds Supervisor	So-and-so Abbot's Assistant
So-and-so Chief Junior	So-and-so Chief Junior
So-and-so Chief Cook	So-and-so Meditation Hall Head

6.   Ajnyata Kaundinya was Shakyamuni Buddha's first disciple.

<u>Precepts recipients in 2nd year of Kenryaku era:</u>

So-and-so Clerical Officer	So-and-so Veteran
So-and-so of Western Hall	So-and-so Chief Junior
So-and-so Veteran	So-and-so Veteran

The preceding is respectfully offered. If there are any errors, please point them out. Respectfully written.

Respectfully submitted by So-and-so Supervisor of Trainees on the third day of the fourth lunar month in such-and-such an era.

This is how it should be written. We write it on white paper. We write it in the standard, non-cursive style. We do not use the cursive grass style or the seal style. To hang a board, attach a cord about the width of two rice grains to the top of the board from which to hang it, just like we do with a rattan blind or a vertical tablet. It is taken down on the fifth day of the fourth lunar month after the bell is rung at the end of the day's practice.

On the eighth day of the fourth lunar month, the community celebrates the birth of the Buddha.

After the midday meal on the thirteenth day of the fourth lunar month, the monks assemble in their own common room where a tea ceremony is performed, followed by a Scripture recitation. The Dormitory Heads perform these tasks. It is their duty to provide hot water and to burn incense. A Dormitory Head sits in the innermost part of the monks' common room, seated to the left of the saintly image of the hall's bodhisattva.*[7] Monks such as the Chief Juniors and the senior monks do not participate in the Scripture recitation; it is only done by the monks staying in that particular hall.

---

7. Such a 'saintly image' *(shōsō)* will most likely be that of the Buddha, Manjushri, Maitreya, or Avalokiteshvara.

Towards evening, a senior monk prepares an offering of incense and flowers at the shrine of the Guardian of the Field, placing it before the shrine's tablet.[8] The monks then assemble before the shrine to perform the ceremonial recitation.

The Method for Doing the Recitation

After all the monks have assembled, the Abbot makes an incense offering, followed by the administrative monks and monastic managers of the monastery, all in the same manner in which incense is offered during the ceremony of bathing the Buddha's image. Next, the Supervisor of Trainees gets up from his place and, going to the front, bows with hands in gasshō,* first to the Abbot and then before the shrine of the Guardian of the Field. Then, while facing north—that is, facing the shrine—he conducts the mindful recitation, saying the following:

> Balmy breezes fan over the fields and the emperor of heat rules everywhere. This is a time when, in obedience to the Lord of the Law, we take not a step from the temple. These are the days for protecting the lives of the Buddha's disciples. We have assembled the whole community in all humility and respectfully visit your sacred shrine. We recite the names of the great Buddhas of myriad virtues and offer the merit therefrom to you, the Guardian Deity of all the monastic halls. We pray for your divine protection that we may be able to accomplish this retreat; out of respect we take refuge in the Holy Sangha. Now let us invoke the names of the Ten Buddhas:

---

8.   The Guardian of the Field Shrine is dedicated to whatever spiritual beings might have already inhabited the grounds upon which the temple was erected. A shrine is built for them and they are respectfully asked to serve as guardians of the temple.

> The completely pure Buddha, Vairochana* Buddha,
> Dharma Itself,[9]
> The complete Buddha Who has been rewarded for His
> previous training,
> Shakyamuni Buddha, one of the many Buddhas who
> have appeared in the many worlds,
> Maitreya* Buddha Who will appear in the future,
> All the Buddhas in all directions and in the Three Worlds,
> Holy Manjushri* Bodhisattva;
> The great and wise Samantabhadra* Bodhisattva,
> The great and kind Avalokiteshvara,*
> All the Bodhisattvas and Ancestors,
> The great Prajñāpāramitā.[10]

We offer the merits of this recitation to the Guardians of the Field—the dragons and the celestial hosts—and to all who protect and preserve the true Dharma. Bowing, we pray that your spiritual light will aid all of us to manifest the merits of our deeds, and that your pure light will flourish and confer upon us selfless joy. Once again, let us join together to recite:

> All the Buddhas in all directions and in the Three Worlds,
> All the Bodhisattvas and Ancestors,
> The great Prajñāpāramitā.

Then the drum sounds and the whole assembly of monks immediately go to their sitting places in the Cloud Hall for a serving of sweetened hot water. The preparation of sweetened water is a responsibility of the officers who oversee the Kitchen. The assembly goes to the Cloud Hall and circumambulates the hall in seniority order, Upon arriving at their own place, they each sit facing outwards. One of the senior

---

9.   A gong is struck before each name is recited.

10.   This is a reference to the Bodhisattva who is the personification of Great Wisdom. She is regarded as the mother who gives birth to all the Buddhas.

administrative officers does the prescribed ceremony, that is, he or she makes an incense offering, and so forth. In the *Procedures for Cleanliness in a Zen Temple,* it says, "Originally, the Prior would perform this ceremony, but according to circumstances, the Supervisor of Trainees may act on the Prior's behalf."

It is proper that, before the Mindful Recitation, a notice should be copied onto an announcement board and presented to the Chief Junior. The administrative officer, upon seeing the Chief Junior wearing a kesa* and carrying his or her bowing mat, performs the ceremony of twice offering to spread one's mat and then doing three bows.[11] The Chief Junior responds with bows of his or her own, done in the same manner. A novice monk then presents the Chief Junior with a box containing the notice board wrapped in a cloth. The Chief Junior accepts it and then sees the officer off.

The form of the notice is as follows:

> This evening, on behalf of the Chief Junior, the Kitchen Hall officers are offering green tea and cakes in the Cloud Hall for the benefit of the community. We humbly inform you of this ceremony to celebrate the opening of the retreat, and respectfully pray that you, the community, will honor us with your illustrious presence.

> Respectfully presented on this 14th day of the 4th lunar month in the 3rd year of the Kangen era (May 11, 1244) by So-and-so of the Kitchen Hall.

This is signed with the first name of the presiding officer of the kitchen. After presenting the board to the Chief Junior, the officer asks the novice to post it up in front of the Cloud Hall, to the left of the hall's front entrance.

On the outside wall to the south of the front entrance there is a lacquered board on which the notice is to be posted. There is a leather envelope to the side of

---

11. This ceremony entails a monk's beginning to spread his or her bowing mat in preparation for doing three bows, but each time they are signaled with a gesture by the monk who is being honored that such formal bowing is unnecessary, whereupon the monk ends up by simply doing three standing bows without spreading his or her mat.

this board. It is aligned with the right edge of the board and fastened with a bamboo peg. This board is made according to a set method. The writing is in small characters about half an inch high; they should not be too big. The message on the front of the envelope is as follows:

> An invitation to the Chief Junior, along with all the other
> monks of the community, enclosed with respect from the monks of
> the Kitchen Hall.

After the ceremony of green tea and cakes, the board is taken down.

Before breakfast on the fifteenth day, the temple officers and senior monks, as well as the Abbot's disciples and fellow monks, first enter the Abbot's quarters to pay their respects. But if, on the previous day, the Abbot had excused them from performing this courtesy, they should not visit the Abbot's quarters at all. 'Being excused from performing this courtesy' means that the Abbot has had someone paste up a notice board on which he has written a verse or some words of Teaching. This is posted either on the east side of the entrance to his quarters or in front of the Cloud Hall.

After breakfast on the fifteenth, the Supervisor of Trainees hangs on the east wall that is in front of the Meditation Hall a single *kairō* board that he had prepared in advance. He hangs it above the front hall, that is, between the pillars to the south of the front entrance. In the *Procedures for Cleanliness in a Zen Temple,* it says that the senior monk in charge of the Meditation Hall puts up a *kairō* board and makes an alms offering of incense and flowers. (He puts this board up in front of the Meditation Hall.) After the midday meal on the fifteenth day of the fourth lunar month, a board announcing a Mindful Recitation ceremony is hung in front of the Meditation Hall.[12] Similar boards are also hung up outside other temple buildings.

Also on the fifteenth day, after the Abbot has given his Dharma talk, he comes down from the Dharma seat and stands before its steps. He then steps onto the

---

12.   The Mindful Recitation ceremony consists primarily of the recitation of the Names of the
       Ten Buddhas.

north corner of the bowing seat and stands facing south.[13] A temple officer approaches him and performs the ceremony of twice offering to spread one's mat and then doing three bows. After the first offering, he says the following:

> On this occasion of our being sequestered during the summer retreat, we are able to serve you with a towel and water jug. We pray that, due solely to the strength of your Dharma, O Venerable Monk, we shall meet with no impediments.

As his next offering, he expresses the compliments of the season by wishing for the cold weather to warm and then does three informal bows.[14] Once he has finished paying the compliments of the season and has done his three bows, he picks up his mat and continues, saying the following:

> How fortunate we are that the early summer is finally warming up. Reflecting upon this period when our Dharma Lord has opened this summer retreat, I am humbled by the thought that our gratitude is not equal to the thousand blessings that you, our Venerable Monk who is the Head of our Hall, bestow upon us lowly trainees.

After this, the temple officer responds by placing his mat on the ground and then doing three more informal bows. Saying nothing, the Abbot and all others respond with three informal bows.

The Abbot then responds, as follows:

> It is likewise my great good fortune to be able to carry out a summer retreat here with all of you. And I earnestly desire that you, So-and-so the Chief Junior, and you, So-and-so the Prior, along

---

13. The bowing seat *(haiseki)* is a bowing mat that lies in front of the altar. During ceremonies, it is the customary place where a celebrant stands or spreads his bowing mat to do his prostrations.

14. The most common style of doing informal bows is by placing one's folded bowing mat on the ground and doing a prostration with one's forehead touching one's mat.

with all you others, will assist me, through the strength of your Teaching, to go beyond all impediments.

The Chief Junior, along with the whole community, then follows the same procedure of making three informal bows. At this time, the Chief Junior, along with the whole community, including the officers, all face north and bow. Only the Abbot faces south, standing in front of the stairs to his Dharma seat. The Abbot then spreads his bowing mat upon the bowing seat.

Next, the Chief Junior and the rest of the assembly perform the ceremony of twice offering to spread their mat and then doing three bows before the Abbot. At this time, the Master's disciples, his attendants, his Dharma relatives,[15] and the novices remain standing to one side; they should not blindly follow the rest of the assembly in paying their personal respects. 'To remain standing to one side' means 'to stand along the eastern wall of the Dharma Hall'. If the screened-off area for donors is at the east wall, then the aforesaid monks should stand near the Dharma drum or along the western wall.

When the assembly has finished their prostrations, they return to the temple kitchen led by the administrative officers, who stand at the right side.[16] Next, the Chief Junior leads the rest of the assembled monks to the kitchen to pay their respects to the Kitchen Officers, that is, they do three informal bows to them. At this same time in the Dharma Hall, the Abbot's disciples, his assistants, his Dharma relatives, and the novices do their prostrations to him. His Dharma relatives should do the ceremony of twice offering to spread one's mat and then doing three bows, with the Abbot returning these bows. The Abbot's disciples and his assistants each do nine prostrations; the Abbot does not return these bows. The novices do either nine or twelve prostrations, which the Abbot receives whilst just holding his hands in gasshō.

Next, the Chief Junior goes in front of the Monks' Hall and, to the right of the entrance, on a level with the southern end of the administrative officers' meditation

---

15. One's Dharma relatives—Dharma brothers and sisters—are monks who share the same Master as oneself.

16. The administrative officers are the Chief Supervisory Officer, the Prior, the Treasurer, the Supervisor of Trainees, the Chief Cook, and the Grounds Maintenance Officer.

seats—that is, in front of the Cloud Hall and facing south—stands before the monks. The assembled monks face north and do three informal bows while turned towards the Chief Junior. The Chief Junior then leads the assembled monks into the Monks' Hall. In order of monastic seniority, the monks circumambulate the hall and stand before their own place. The administrative officers enter the hall and do three bows, spreading their mats before the main image in the hall. Next, they do three informal bows to the assembly, to which the assembled monks bow in response. The six administrative officers then do one circumambulation of the hall and, according to rank, stand by their place, their hands in shashu.*

The Abbot enters the hall, offers incense before the main image, does three full prostrations, and then rises. During this time, his disciples stand out of the way, behind the main image, whereas his Dharma relatives follow the other monks. Next, the Abbot does three informal bows to the Chief Junior. That is, the Abbot remains standing in his place and does these bows while facing west. The Chief Junior, along with the community, bows in response, as before.

The Abbot then circumambulates the hall and departs. The Chief Junior, leaving by the south side of the front entrance, sees the Abbot off. After the Abbot has departed, all the monks, from the Chief Junior down, spread their bowing mats and perform three full bows, facing outwards from their sitting place, and then recite in unison, as follows:

> How fortunate we are to be doing this retreat together. I
> fear lest my acts of body, speech, and mind should not prove to be
> good, and I pray that I will show benevolence and compassion
> towards all.

The prostrations following this are done thrice with one's bowing mat spread out fully. Having completed this, the Chief Junior, the Clerical Officer, the Chief Librarian, and the other department heads each return to their quarters. Those who are staying in the monks' common quarters,[17] from the Head of the Quarters on down, all do three informal bows to each other, reciting the same verse that was recited in the Main Hall.

---

17.   As distinct from the resident monks who stay in the Meditation Hall.

After this, the Abbot makes his rounds of the various offices, beginning with the Kitchen Hall. The monks follow after the Abbot in sequence, accompanying him to his quarters and then withdrawing. That is to say, the Abbot goes first to the Kitchen Hall. Once he has paid his respects to the Kitchen Officers and departs, he continues making his rounds, with the Kitchen Officers following behind him. Following after the Kitchen Officers are those who are staying in or around the Eastern Quarters. At this time, the Abbot does not enter the Infirmary, but turns west from the Eastern Quarters, passing by the Temple Gate and continuing on his rounds of the various quarters. Those who are residing near the Temple Gate join the procession. From the south, the Abbot goes around to visit the quarters on the west side. At this time, while he is traversing the west side, he is facing north. By this time, the elderly retired monks, retired officers, retired assistant officers, those over one hundred years old, and veteran monks who live in private quarters as well as the monk in charge of the toilets, among others, will have joined the procession. The Supervisor of Trainees and the Chief Junior, among others, will follow behind them. Following them are the monks from the common quarters. The quarters are circumambulated according to the convenience of their location. This is what we call "the monks' escort".

Thence, the Abbot goes up the western stairs to his quarters and then, positioning himself directly in front of his quarters, he faces south with hands in shashu. The whole assembly, from the administrative officers on down, face north and make monjin* to the Abbot. This monjin should be especially deep. The Abbot makes monjin in response. The assembly then withdraws.

My late Master did not lead the assembly to his quarters; when he reached the Dharma Hall, he stood before the stairs of the hall, facing south with hands in shashu. The assembly made monjin and then retired. This was the traditional ceremony from ancient times. After this, the monks in the assembly would pay their respects to each other, as they pleased. They paid their respects by doing bows to each other. For instance, those from the same home district—even dozens of them—would exchange prostrations, some in the Hall of Illumination and others in some convenient place in the corridors,[18] and they would offer to each other the congratulatory verse on attending the retreat together. At the same time, there are some whose words resemble those spoken formally in the Main Hall, and there are also personal ways some have of expressing their feelings. And there are also Masters who have brought their disciples. In that case, the disciples will invariably offer their bows, doing nine full prostrations. Those who are Dharma relatives of the Abbot do the ceremony of two offerings and three bows or do three full prostrations. The prostrations of any Dharma relative of anyone in the assembly should be the same. And there will be prostrations to the younger and elder brothers of one's Master. Those who sit and sleep next to each other in the Meditation Hall all do prostrations to each other, as well as to those who are mutually acquainted or have done a retreat together in the past. Those who are veteran monks living in private quarters, as well as the Chief Supervisory Officer, the Prior, the Supervisor of Trainees, the Chief Cook, the Grounds Maintenance Officer, the monks of the Western Hall, and the Teacher of the Female Trainees should all visit each other's quarters or visit each other's sitting place in the Meditation Hall and do their bows and greetings. When we go to visit someone and find the entryway to their quarters too crowded to enter, we write out a card and attach it beside their entrance. The card is written on white paper an inch or so high and about two inches wide. The style of writing is as follows:

So'un, Eshō, and others.
Congratulations, with three bows!

or

So-and-so.
Salutations and congratulations!

or

So-and-so of Such-and-such Hall.
Congratulations, with three bows!

or

---

18. The Hall of Illumination is a small room next to the Monks' Hall, which is used by the Chief Junior to give Dharma talks to novice monks when the Abbot is unable to perform that duty.

So-and-so bows.

Congratulations!

or

So-and-so

Humbly offering prostrations.

The styles of writing are many, but these give the general idea. So, a large number of these cards can be seen beside entrances. They are not attached to the left of an entrance, but to the right of it. These cards are taken down after the midday meal by the person in charge of the quarters. On that day the rattan blinds are raised on the entryways of all halls and quarters.

There is a custom that the Head of a Temple, his or her administrative officers, and the Chief Junior, in succession, offer tea and cakes. However, this can be abridged, or dispensed with, for those on a remote island or deep in the mountains, as they simply do what is within their means. Retired senior monks, as well as monks who are serving as temporary Chief Juniors for the duration of the retreat, offer tea and cakes in their quarters, especially for the various temple officers.

Having thus opened the summer retreat, we do our utmost in practicing the Way. You may well have been pursuing the Way and keeping to the Precepts, but if you have not done a summer retreat, you are not an offspring of the Buddhas and Ancestors, much less a Buddha or Ancestor. By virtue of a summer retreat, Jetavana Park and the Divine Vulture Peak will fully manifest themselves for you. The training ground of a summer retreat is the realm of the Mind seal* of the Buddhas and Ancestors and is the dwelling place of all Buddhas.

The Closing of the Summer Retreat

As it says in the *Procedures for Cleanliness in a Zen Temple*, "On the thirteenth day of the seventh lunar month, the serving of tea and cakes and the reciting of Scriptures in the Common Room is once more the responsibility of the one who is the head of the Common Room for that month."

The mindful recitation of the names of the Buddhas on the evening of the fourteenth, as well as the attending of a Dharma talk, the paying of one's respects, the circumambulating of the quarters, and the serving of tea and cakes, are all, one after the other, the same as at the opening of the retreat. Only the wording of notices is different. The notice for the kitchen staff's offering of tea reads as follows:

> The kitchen staff will offer tea and cakes in the Cloud Hall this evening, especially for the benefit of the Chief Junior and the community. We will perform a small closing ceremony. We humbly pray that you will be so kind as to join in. Spoken in respect, So-and-so, the monks of the Kitchen Hall.

The words for the mindful recitation before the Shrine of the Guardian of the Field are as follows:

> Golden breezes fan over the fields and the emperor of frost rules everywhere. The time is as that when the Buddha, Lord of Enlightenment, commenced the monks' retreat. It is the day of our being a whole year older in the Dharma. Three months have passed without disaster and the whole Community is at ease. We recite the names of the great Buddhas of myriad virtues as we humbly report to you, the Guardian Deity of all the monastery halls, out of respect for you. We take refuge in the Holy Sangha as we all recite Their names.

The mindful recitation from here on is the same as at the opening of the summer retreat.

After the formal talk in the Dharma Hall, the administration officers, along with the other officers, recite the following in unison:

> Humbly, we rejoice that the Dharma year has been fulfilled without difficulties. This is undoubtedly due to the protective strength of the Master's Dharma. We cannot fully express our deep gratitude.

The Abbot then responds with these words:

> Now that the Dharma year has been fulfilled, we all offer
> our thanks to So-and-so Chief Junior and to So-and-so Prior, among
> others, for sharing with us the strength of their Dharma. I cannot
> fully express my deep gratitude.

The Chief Junior and staff of the Hall, as well as the Dormitory Heads of the various
quarters and their staff, say the following:

> During the ninety days of the summer retreat, we have
> relied upon each other, but I fear lest my acts of body, speech, and
> mind have not proved to be good, and I humbly pray that you will
> show benevolence and compassion towards me.

The administrative officers, along with the other officers of the temple, then make the
following announcement:

> We ask those brothers and sisters who are planning to
> travel on to remain with us for tea before departing. This, of course,
> does not apply to those who have some pressing engagement.

This ceremony of the ninety-day summer retreat is fundamental to us since
time immemorial—from before to after the Age of the Lords of Awe-inspiring Voices.
The Buddhas and Ancestors have placed great emphasis on just this ceremony alone.
And the non-Buddhists and the demon hordes have yet to corrupt this one ceremony.
Not a single one who is an offspring of the Buddhas and Ancestors within the three
nations of India, China, and Japan has ever failed to perform it, but those outside the
Way have never studied it. Because of the long-cherished desire of the Buddhas and
Ancestors for the One Great Matter, from the morning of Their entering the Way until
the evening of Their entering nirvana, what They proclaim is simply the underlying
principle of the summer retreat. Even though there are differences among the five
monastic families in India, they are alike in observing the ninety-day summer retreat,
inexorably practicing the Way of enlightenment. Of the nine monastic families in

China, not even one has ever violated the rule of the summer retreat. Those who have never done a ninety-day summer retreat should never be called a monk who is a disciple of the Buddha. This means that we should not only do this practice during the bodhisattva stages for awakening, but we should also continue the practice of a summer retreat after having awakened. The Great Awakened, World-honored One performed the practice of a summer retreat throughout His life, not missing a single summer. Keep in mind that it was what the Buddha realized as the ultimate fruition.

At the same time, although you may laugh at one who has not done a ninety-day summer retreat and yet calls himself an offspring of the Buddhas and Ancestors, such a foolish person is not even worth a laugh. Do not listen to the words of that bunch who talk like that. Do not get into discussions with such people. Do not sit with them. Do not even walk the same path with them. For, in the Buddha Dharma, we handle such wicked people by using the method of Brahma's rod of silence.

You should simply understand the ninety-day summer retreat as the Buddhas and Ancestors have done, and rely upon it, and preserve it. It has been genuinely Transmitted from the Seven Buddhas* down to Makakashō. It was genuinely Transmitted by Dharma heir after Dharma heir through the twenty-eight Indian Ancestors. When the Twenty-eighth Ancestor came to China, he genuinely Transmitted It to our Great Ancestor, the Second Chinese Ancestor, Great Master Eka. From the Second Ancestor, It was genuinely Transmitted by Dharma heir after Dharma heir and has been genuinely Transmitted down to this very day. When I went to China, I directly received the genuine Transmission from within the assembly of an Ancestor of the Buddha, and I am doing the genuine Transmission in Japan. Now that you are within an assembly where the genuine Transmission exists and have done the ninety-day summer retreat within that assembly, you have already had the Way of the summer retreat genuinely Transmitted to you. Because I am of the genuine Transmission and you are doing the summer retreat while residing here together with me, it will be a true summer retreat. Because the summer retreat has been conferred face-to-face to Dharma heir after Dharma heir, starting with the summer retreats held when the Buddha was in the world, the countenance of both a Buddha and an Ancestor has been genuinely Transmitted to you right before your very eyes, and the body and mind of the Buddhas and Ancestors has personally awakened you to the promise of full enlightenment. This is why it is said that to encounter the summer retreat is to encounter Buddha, to experience the summer retreat is to experience Buddha, to practice the retreat is to practice Buddha, to hear the retreat is to hear Buddha, and to model oneself after the retreat is to learn Buddha.

In sum, it is the Teaching that all the Buddhas and Ancestors never went counter to the summer retreat, or beyond it. Thus, lordly humans, lordly Shakras, lordly Brahmas, and so on, should do the summer retreat and become monastics, even if it is only for a single summer, for that would be their encountering Buddha. Ordinary people, persons in lofty positions, and erudite 'dragons' should do the summer retreat and become monastics—be they male or female—even if only for a single period of ninety days, for this would be their encountering Buddha. To join the community of an Ancestor of the Buddha and do a ninety-day summer retreat is to encounter Buddha forthwith. It is your good fortune that, before the dewdrop of your life has fallen, you have already done one summer's retreat, be it as an ordinary lay person or as someone in a lofty position, so that you are now someone who has exchanged your skin and flesh, bones and marrow for the Skin and Flesh, Bones and Marrow of the Buddhas and Ancestors. Because the Buddhas and Ancestors come and do the retreat through us, each person's practice of the retreat is the retreat's practicing each of us. Because this is the way things are, those who have done the retreat are described simply as 'a thousand Buddhas and myriad Ancestors'. If you were to ask why, the reason is because the retreat is the Skin and Flesh, Bones and Marrow, conscious mind and physical body of those who are Ancestors of Buddha. It is the Crown of their head and their Eye, it is their Fist and their Nose, it is their Buddha Nature fully perfected, it is their hossu* and traveling staff,* it is their lacquered, ceremonial bamboo sword and their meditation cushion. A summer retreat is not something brought forth as newly made. At the same time, it is not something that is merely making use of something old.

The World-honored One once addressed the Bodhisattva Whose Enlightenment is Fully Perfected, along with the great assembly and all sentient beings, saying, "When the summer begins and you go into retreat for the three months of the rainy season, you should let the immaculate bodhisattvas stop and abide with you in your sanctuary. In your hearts, you should stay clear of those who merely come to listen but do not train, because the community of disciples is not a sometimes thing. Upon arriving for the opening day of the summer retreat, you should say something like the following before the Buddha or His image, 'I, the monk or lay person So-and-so, being seated in the vehicle of bodhisattvahood, will cultivate tranquility and freedom from my defiling passions so that I too may enter the Truth of Immaculacy and abide therein. I take the great Fully Perfected Enlightenment to be my true monastery and sanctuary, with my body and mind, equally, both dwelling peacefully within the spiritual knowledge of Buddha Nature. Because the True Nature of nirvana is without ties or attachments to anything, I now pray respectfully that I may not rely solely on listening to the voicing of the Dharma, but may spend this three-month retreat with the Tathagatas of all the ten quarters and with the great bodhisattvas. Also, for the sake of the Great Cause for which we cultivate the supreme and wondrous awakening of a bodhisattva, I will not let myself be distracted from the purpose of the retreat through entanglements with my fellow trainees.' O My fine disciples, I call this the dwelling at ease which a bodhisattva displays during a summer retreat."

Thus, whenever the monks and laity arrive for the three months of the retreat, they put into practice the Important Matter of the supreme and wondrous enlightenment of the bodhisattvas. Keep in mind that male and female lay trainees can also do the retreat. The place of this retreat is great, fully perfected enlightenment. This being so, Jetavana Park and the Divine Vulture Peak are both temples of the Tathagata's great fully perfected enlightenment. You should carefully listen to, and take to heart, the World-honored One's teaching that the Tathagatas and great bodhisattvas in all ten quarters did the practice and training of the three months' summer retreat.

Once when the World-honored One was doing the ninety-day summer retreat somewhere, on the final day, when the ceremony of public repentance was held,[19] Manjushri suddenly appeared in the assembly, whereupon Makakashō asked him, "Where did you do your retreat this summer?" Manjushri replied, "This summer I did the retreat in three other places." At this, Makakashō assembled the community, intending to have Manjushri expelled by striking the wooden fish.[20] But just as he had raised the hammer to strike the wooden fish, he suddenly saw innumerable Buddhist temples appearing. He could see that there was a Buddha with a Manjushri at each place and a Makakashō at each place, his hand raising a hammer to expel Manjushri, whereupon the World-honored One spoke to Makakashō, saying, "Which Manjushri do you wish to expel now?" Makakashō was immediately dumbfounded.[21]

Meditation Master Engo, in commenting on this account, once said the following:

If a bell is not struck, it does not ring; if a drum is not struck, it does not resound. Makakashō had already grasped the essential function of a summer retreat; Manjushri had rid himself of all duality by means of his doing his meditation throughout the ten quarters. This very moment in the story is an excellent one, for it expounds the functioning of the Buddha's Teaching. How

---

19. This is the ceremony where the participants ask their fellow trainees to have compassion on them for their poor training during the retreat.

20. The wooden fish is a wooden gong in the shape of a fish. It traditionally hangs just outside the Meditation Hall. Regulations for monks stipulate that a monastic must do the summer retreat in only one place. Breaking this regulation is considered a serious enough infraction to entail expulsion from the monastic Sangha.

21. Quoted from the *Great Far-reaching Scripture That is a Veritable Treasure Chest*.

regrettable to have missed such a move! As our dear Master Shakyamuni was about to say, 'Which of the Manjushris do you wish to expel now?' just imagine, what if Makakashō, right off, had given the fish a good whack! What mass annihilation would he have then created?

Meditation Master Engo added a verse to this commentary of his:

> *A great elephant does not play about in the narrow path*
> > *that a rabbit makes,*
> *And what could a little bird know of a great wild swan?* [22]
> *It was just as if Makakashō had created a new way of*
> > *putting the Matter whilst staying within the rules*
> > *and regulations;*
> *It was just as if Manjushri had grabbed a flying arrow*
> > *within his teeth, having already broken the target.*
> *The whole universe is one with Manjushri;*
> *The whole universe is one with Makakashō.*
> *Face-to-face, each is solemn in his authority.*
> *Makakashō raised his hammer, but in which place will he*
> > *punish Manjushri?*
> *Manjushri did It with one fine prick of his needle;*
> *Makakashō s ascetic practices rid him of all hindrances.*

So, the World-honored One's doing the summer retreat in one place is equivalent to Manjushri's doing it in three places, and neither is not doing the summer retreat. If someone is not doing the retreat, then such a one is not a Buddha or a bodhisattva. There is no account of any offspring of the Buddhas and Ancestors not doing a summer retreat. You should realize that those who do a summer retreat are offspring of the Buddhas and Ancestors. Doing a summer retreat is the body and mind of the Buddhas and Ancestors. It is the Eye of the Buddhas and Ancestors, the very

---

22. 'A great elephant' is an allusion to Manjushri. 'A great wild swan' is a reference to Makakashō.

life of the Buddhas and Ancestors. Those who have not done a summer retreat are not the offspring of the Buddhas and Ancestors: they are neither a Buddha nor an Ancestor. We now have Buddhas and bodhisattvas, be They as humble as clay and wood, as precious as silk and gold, or as wondrous as the seven precious jewels.* All of Them have performed the retreat of sitting in meditation through the three months of the summer. This is the ancient custom of abiding within, and maintaining, the Treasures of Buddha, Dharma, and Sangha. In short, those who reside within the house of the Buddhas and Ancestors must, by all means, do the practice of sitting in retreat for the three months of a summer.

Delivered to the assembly at Daibutsu-ji Temple in Echizen Province, on the thirteenth day of the sixth month, during the summer retreat in the third year of the Kangen era (July 8, 1245).

Copied by me in the same province at Shinzenkō-ji Temple in Nakahama on the twentieth day of the fifth month, during the summer retreat in the second year of the Kōan era (June 30, 1278).

Giun

78

On Reading the Minds and Hearts of Others

(Tashintsū)

Translator's Introduction: This discourse is Dogen's reworking of his commentary on a section in Discourse 18: On 'The Mind Cannot Be Grasped' *(Shin Fukatoku)* concerning the encounter between the National Teacher Echū and a Tripitaka Master named Daini. 'National Teacher' is a Chinese imperial title often posthumously conferred upon a monk whose devotion to spiritual life was exemplary. Such a monk customarily served as the emperor's personal spiritual advisor. 'Tripitaka Master' is a secular title which might be comparable to the present-day academic 'Professor of Buddhology'; it does not imply that the person was necessarily a monk or even a practicing Buddhist.

National Teacher Echū of the Temple of Luminous Residence in the Western Capital was a man from Chuchi in the Yüeh-chou District. His family name was Zen. After having received the Mind seal,* he went to reside on Mount Poyai in Tangtsu Valley in the Nang-yan District. For forty years he did not go out from the monastery's gate, yet his reputation for practicing the Way was well-known throughout the country, not only in the towns and villages but also in the imperial court. In the second year of the Chinese Shang-yüan era (761 C.E.), Emperor Su-tsung of the T'ang dynasty privately dispatched his messenger, Sun Ch'ao-chin, to convey to the monk an invitation, summoning him to come to the capital. The emperor attended on the monk with all the courtesies due a Master, and had him take up residence in the Western Meditation Cloister of the Temple of a Thousand Blessings. When Emperor T'ai-tsung ascended to the throne after Su-tsung, he too sent his messenger to the monk, and now had him sequestered in the Temple of Luminous Residence. During his sixteen-year stay

---

*   See *Glossary.*

1051

there, Echū gave voice to the Dharma in accordance with the capabilities of his audience. Then, one day, a person arrived at the capital from India, calling himself Tripitaka Master Daini. He claimed that he possessed the Eye that is keen enough to read people's minds. The emperor summoned the National Teacher Echū to test this person. No sooner had the Tripitaka Master caught sight of the National Teacher than he did a full prostration and then stood to the left of the National Teacher.

The National Teacher asked him, "Do you have the ability to read minds?"

The Tripitaka Master answered, "I would not dare to make such a claim."

The National Teacher then said, "You, say! Where is the old monk right now?"[1]

The Tripitaka Master replied, "The reverend monk is indeed the teacher of this nation, so why does he go to the Western River and watch people racing about in their boats?"[2]

The National Teacher then asked a second time, "You, say! Where is the old monk right now?"

---

1.   'The old monk' is an ambiguous term. On the one hand, it is a conventionally humble way for older senior monastics to refer to themselves, which is how the Tripitaka Master would have understood it. On the other hand, as 'the Old Monk', it can be understood as the National Teacher referring to his Buddha Nature, something which the Tripitaka Master would not have picked up on. In the latter sense, what the National Teacher asked could also be taken to mean, "Where is your Buddha Nature?"

2.   The Western River flows through the Western Paradise. The Tripitaka Master is saying, in effect, "Why do you, who are so saintly that you are already in the Western Paradise, bother to pay any attention to us ordinary people who are engaged in worldly, competitive pursuits?"

The Tripitaka Master replied, "The reverend monk is the teacher of this nation, so why does he go to Tientsin Bridge and watch people playing with their pet monkeys?"[3]

The National Teacher asked a third time, "You, say! Where is the old monk right now?"

Although the Tripitaka Master remained there for quite a long time, he did not know what to say.

The National Teacher said, "O you wild fox spirit, where is your ability to read minds now?"

The Tripitaka Master still had no response.[4]

Concerning this story, there was a monk who once asked Jōshū, "Why didn't the Tripitaka Master see where the National Teacher was the third time?" Jōshū replied, "He did not see where the National Teacher was because he was right on the tip of the Tripitaka Master's nose."

Also, there was a monk who once asked Gensha Shibi, "Since the National Teacher was already right on the tip of the

---

3.   'Tientsin Bridge' literally means 'the bridge that leads into the Harbor of Heaven'. The Tripitaka Master is saying, in effect, "Why do you, who are standing on the very Bridge of Heaven, concern yourself with us worldly people who are preoccupied with playing around with our everyday minds?" Both this and the Tripitaka Master's previous statement are offering seemingly flattering but spiritually meaningless remarks in response to the National Teacher's deeply spiritual question, all the while still hinting that he could, indeed, read the minds of others.

4.   Evidently, the Tripitaka Master realized that what he was being asked for required something beyond 'parlor Zen' responses, but because he did not know what the True Mind of the National Teacher was, he was unable to reply. 'A wild fox spirit' here refers to a clever and manipulative person who gives teachings that are false and misleading.

Tripitaka Master's nose, why didn't he see him?" Shibi replied, "Simply because he was just much too close."

A monk once asked Kyōzan, "Why didn't the Tripitaka Master see the whereabouts of the National Teacher the third time, since he was there a rather long time?" Kyōzan replied, "The first two times, the National Teacher's mind was in the realm of externals. He then entered the meditative state of delight in the Self, so the Tripitaka Master was unable to perceive his whereabouts."

Kaie Shutan once said, "If the National Teacher was right on the tip of the Tripitaka Master's nose, why was he having such difficulty seeing it? After all, he did not recognize that the National Teacher was right inside the Tripitaka Master's Eye."

Also, as if rebuking the Tripitaka Master, Shibi once remarked, "You, say! Did you even see It the first two times?" About this, Setchō Jūken once said, "Seen through the first time! Seen through the second time!"

From ancient times, there have been many senior monks who have commented on or tried to explain this story concerning National Teacher Echū's testing of Tripitaka Master Daini, but these five venerable Fists are noteworthy.[5] And though I do not deny the insight and appropriateness of the remarks of these five esteemed veteran Masters, there are several points where the commentators have not spotted the way that the National Teacher was behaving. If we ask why this is, it is because all concerned, in both the past and present, have been of the opinion that the first two times the Tripitaka Master correctly knew where the National Teacher was residing. This was the common error of our Ancestors and, as present-day trainees, you need to recognize it.

Now there are two reasons why I have doubts about these five esteemed veteran Masters. First, they did not recognize the underlying intention in the National

---

5. When referring to a Master, the term 'Fist' refers to someone who has gone beyond conceptualizing and verbalizing in order to express the Buddha Dharma.

Teacher's testing of the Tripitaka Master. Second, they did not appreciate the body and mind of the National Teacher.

To begin with, I have said that they did not appreciate the body and mind of the National Teacher because the first time the National Teacher said, "You, say! Where is the old monk right now?" his underlying intention was to test whether the Tripitaka Master had the Eye to see and hear the Buddha Dharma; he wished to test whether the Tripitaka Master had the ability to read the minds and hearts of others, which is part of the Buddha Dharma. At that moment, if the Tripitaka Master had been equipped with the Buddha Dharma, then when asked, "You, say! Where is the old monk right now?" he would have been in possession of a path for going beyond the discriminatory, of an expedient means for putting the Matter* in his own personal way. The National Teacher's saying "Where is the old monk right now?" is equivalent to asking, "What is the Old Monk?" His question, "Where is the Old Monk right now?" is his asking, "What occasion is 'right now?'" His saying, "Where is..." is his asserting "This is the place where the What resides." It has the underlying principle of referring to 'the What' as 'an old monk'. The National Teacher is not the whole of what the Old Monk is, but the Old Monk is certainly the National Teacher's Fist. Even though Tripitaka Master Daini had come from India, he did not know the heart of this, for he had not learned what the Buddha Dharma is and had just vainly studied the paths of non-Buddhists and those of the two Lower Courses.*

The National Teacher then asked a second time, "You, say! Where is the old monk right now?" And here, again, the Tripitaka Master gave a pointless reply. Again the National Teacher asked, "You, say! Where is the old monk right now?" This third time, even though the Tripitaka Master took a considerable amount of time, he was in a daze and gave no respectful reply. The National Teacher now rebuked the Tripitaka Master, saying, "O you wild fox spirit, where is your ability to read minds now?" Even though the Tripitaka Master was rebuked in this way, he was without a respectful reply and had no way out of his predicament.

However, in regard to the National Teacher rebuking the Tripitaka Master, all of the five Ancestors were of the opinion that the latter knew the whereabouts of the National Teacher the first two times and only failed to see it the third time, and because he did not see it then, he was rebuked by the National Teacher. This is a huge mistake. The National Teacher's rebuke of the Tripitaka Master was, from the first, a rebuke for not having encountered the Buddha Dharma even in his dreams. He does not rebuke him, as some have thought, for not having understood the third time even though having understood the first two times. He rebukes him for having styled himself as one who knew how to read minds when he did not know how to read minds at all.

The National Teacher is, first off, testing the Tripitaka Master by asking him, in effect, whether the ability to read minds exists within the Buddha Dharma. By his answering, "I would not dare to make such a claim," he implies that it does exist. After that, the National Teacher is apparently of a mind that thinks, "If we say that the ability to read minds exists in the Buddha Dharma and if we obtain the ability to read minds during our practice of the Buddha Dharma, then things are as they should be, but if what is expressed by words is not a full offering of the Teaching, then it cannot be the Buddha Dharma." Even if the Tripitaka Master was at a point where he could have managed to express a small bit of the Teaching the third time, if it was anything like the first two times, it would not be a genuine expression through words and the National Teacher should rebuke him on principle. In asking his question three times, the National Teacher was trying to see again and again whether the Tripitaka Master could understand the question, which is why he asked his question three times.

Second, none of the ancient worthies could fully appreciate the Body and Mind of the National Teacher. What I have called 'the Body and Mind of the National Teacher' is something that is beyond the reach of scholastic teachers of Scriptures like the Tripitaka Master, who could not see It, much less comprehend It. Among the bodhisattvas,[*] even the 'thrice wise and ten times saintly'[*] have not reached It, nor is It something that those who will be reborn as Buddhas have clarified. Scholars who are students of Scriptures are ordinary, unenlightened people, so how could they possibly comprehend the National Teacher's Whole Being? By all means, you need to be certain about this underlying principle. To say that the Body and Mind of the National Teacher can be known or seen by a scholar of Scriptures is to insult the Buddha Dharma. To believe that his Body and Mind are on a par with those of scholarly commentators on Scriptures is the utmost height of lunacy. Do not teach yourself that someone who may be able to read the worldly intentions of others must surely know where the National Teacher is existing.

Now and again, as a cultural custom, there have been those in India who have succeeded in developing the ability to read minds. But I have never heard an example of anyone attaining the ability to read minds without, at the same time, relying on the Mind that has given rise to the intention to realize Buddhahood and without relying on the Right Views of the Greater Course.* A person like this, after attaining the ability to read minds, has genuinely mastered the Buddha Dharma. On the other hand, if an ordinary lay person has attained the ability to read minds, and then later gives rise to the intention to realize Buddhahood and therefore undertakes the training and practice, that person can, quite naturally, realize enlightenment in the Buddha's Way. If one could comprehend the Buddha's Way merely by having attained the ability to read the minds of others, then all the saintly ones of the past would have, first off, trained themselves to read the minds of others and then used that ability to realize the fruits of Buddhahood. But this has yet to be the case, even though thousands of Buddhas and myriad Ancestors have come into the world. I must ask, if someone has not already come to know the Way of the Buddhas and Ancestors, what is one to do, for such a person is of no use to the Way of the Buddhas? Someone who has attained only the ability to read minds and some ordinary, everyday person who cannot read minds are surely equals. When it comes to maintaining and relying upon one's Buddha Nature, someone who can read minds and some ordinary, everyday person may well be the same.

You who are studying what Buddha is must never think that those who possess the five or six spiritual abilities—be they non-Buddhists or those of the two Lesser Courses—are in any way superior to an ordinary, everyday person. There is simply the Mind that seeks the Way—the Mind of one who is truly studying the Buddha's Teaching—which will surpass the five or six spiritual abilities, just as the song of the kalavinka bird, even in its egg, surpasses that of all other birds. Furthermore, what is called in India 'the ability to read the minds of others' should be called 'the ability to know the concerns of others'. Even though one with such an ability may have some affinity with the thoughts and feelings that arise in someone else, they are so vague as to be laughable. What is more, Mind is not necessarily thoughts and feelings, nor are thoughts and feelings necessarily what Mind is. When one's mind becomes entangled with thoughts and things, one cannot know how to read the minds of others, and when thoughts and things become entangled in the mind, that mind cannot know how to read the thoughts of others.

Thus, the five or six abilities of India cannot come up to mowing down weeds and tending the fields in this country of ours. Such abilities are ultimately of no use. Accordingly, all the previous virtuous ones in China and the lands east of India had no taste for practicing the five or six abilities, because they had no need for them. Even a foot-wide jewel may still have some value, but there is no value in the five or six abilities. Even a foot-wide jewel is not the Treasure, but every inch of time is precious. How could anyone who attaches any importance to moments of time waste them by dabbling with the five and six abilities? In short, you need to be decisive in affirming the principle that the ability to read the mind of another is outside the bounds of the wise discernment of a Buddha. Also, all five of the veteran Masters were greatly mistaken in having thought that the Tripitaka Master knew the whereabouts of the National Teacher the first two times. The National Teacher was an Ancestor of the Buddha, whereas the Tripitaka Master was an ordinary, everyday person, so how can anyone possibly take him to be the National Teacher's equal in any spiritual discussion?

First off, the National Teacher is saying, "You, say! Where is the Old Monk right now?" There is nothing that is hidden in this question; what he said clearly expresses It. The Tripitaka Master was not at fault in that he did not recognize this, but it was a serious mistake that the five veteran Masters did not pick up on this and failed to see it. The National Teacher had already said, "You, say! Where is the Old Monk right now?" He did not say, "You, say! Where is the old monk's mind now?" nor did he say, "Where are the old monk's thoughts now?" Rather, what he said is something which is vital to hear, and recognize, and inquire into. But the veteran monks neither recognized nor saw it. They did not hear or see what the National Teacher was saying. As a result, they did not know what the Body and Mind of the National Teacher was. One who has a way of explaining what a National Teacher is saying is called a National Teacher. If someone does not have a way of putting It, such a person cannot be a teacher of one's nation. What is more, a person like this will not know that the Body and Mind of the National Teacher is beyond being something great or something mediocre, beyond being oneself or being someone else. It is as if this person had completely forgotten that he had a Crown upon his head or that he had a Nose on his face. Since the National Teacher had no break from his daily practice, how could he possibly have in mind the goal of becoming a Buddha! Therefore, we should not await our meeting up with him, waiting to meet a 'Buddha'.

The National Teacher already has the Body and Mind of a Buddha, but we cannot take measure of It by employing spiritual abilities or by realizing what It is through practice, nor can we be prepared to say what It is by suppressing thought or by being oblivious to karmic* conditions, for It is not something that can be successfully talked about or not talked about. The National Teacher is not one who possesses a Buddha Nature, and he is not one who lacks Buddha Nature, and he is not one whose being is vast space. The Body and Mind of such a National Teacher is something that is completely unknown. In our lineage from Daikan Enō of Sōkei on down, apart from Seigen and Nangaku, only National Teacher Echū is such an Ancestor of the Buddha.

I now wish to test each of the five veteran Masters and will attempt to go them one better.

Jōshū said that the Tripitaka Master did not see where the National Teacher was because he was right on the tip of the Tripitaka Master's nose. This remark lacks validity. How could the National Teacher possibly be right on the tip of the Tripitaka Master's nose when the latter still lacked a Nose?[6] If we grant that the Tripitaka Master did have a Nose, then the National Teacher would have had a spiritual encounter with him. Even if we grant that the National Teacher had a spiritual encounter with the Tripitaka Master, this would simply be one Nose facing one Nose but, to put it simply, the Tripitaka Master was unable to have a mutual encounter with the National Teacher.

Shibi said that it was simply because he was just much too close. The phrase, 'being much too close', may have some truth to it, but it still does not hit the mark. Just what is this 'being much too close'? Shibi may well have still not known what

---

6.   That is, he still lacked an awakened Buddha Nature.

'being much too close' means, for he may not have encountered being much too close. If you were to ask why, it is because he only knew that a mutual encounter is never too close. He did not know that a mutual encounter is being ever too close. We can say that when it comes to the Buddha Dharma, he was the farthest of the far. If we say that being ever too close only applies to the third time, then it must be that there was a being ever too close which existed before the first two times. I should like to ask Shibi at this time, "What are you calling 'being too close'? Do you call it a Fist? Do you call it the Eye?" In the future, don't you trainees go around saying that nothing you see is ever too close!

Kyōzan said that the first two times the National Teacher's mind was in the realm of externals, and that he then entered the meditative state of delight in the Self so that the Tripitaka Master was unable to perceive his whereabouts. While you were living in China, Kyōzan, you were honored in India as having the reputation of a lesser Shakyamuni, but even so, what you are saying now contains a great error. The mind that is in the realm of externals and the mind that enters the meditative state of delight in the Self are not two different minds. Therefore, you should not say that the Tripitaka Master is unaware the third time because the mind in the realm of externals and the mind taking delight in the Self are different. So, even though you come up with a reason based upon a difference between taking delight in the Self and being in the realm of externals, that assertion of yours is still not a true assertion. Were you to say that when someone enters the meditative state of taking delight in the Self, others cannot 'see' that person, then taking delight in the Self could not realize taking delight in the Self, and there could be no practice that is synonymous with enlightenment.

Kyōzan, if you gathered that the Tripitaka Master truly saw the whereabouts of the National Teacher the first two times, then you are not yet one of those who has learned what Buddha is. In short, it was not just the third time that the Tripitaka Master Daini failed to see the whereabouts of the National Teacher, he also failed to see it the first two times as well. And if your understanding was as I have just stated it, then I would have to say that not only did the Tripitaka Master not know the whereabouts of the National Teacher, but you too, Kyōzan, did not know the whereabouts of the National Teacher. Right now I would like to ask Kyōzan, "Where is the National

Teacher at this very moment?" And if, at this time, you should deign to open your mouth, I would let out such a yell!

Shibi, as a reproach to the Tripitaka Master, questioned whether he had even seen the National Teacher the first two times. Now this one statement, "Had you even seen the National Teacher the first two times?" sounds as if he is saying what needs to be said. But Shibi needs to study his own words. This sentence is fine as fine goes, but if we just look at it, it is as if he was saying, "He saw and he didn't see." Therefore, it is not accurate. Upon hearing this, Setchō Jūken said, "Seen through the first time! Seen through the second time!" When we see Shibi's words as true, we should also say this, but when we do not see Shibi's words as true, we should not say this.

Kaie Shutan said, "If the National Teacher was right on the tip of the Tripitaka Master's nose, why was the latter having such difficulty seeing it? After all, he did not recognize that the National Teacher was right inside the Tripitaka Master's Eye." This statement also only deals with the third time. He did not reprimand the Tripitaka Master, as he should have, for failing to see the first two times, so how could he possibly recognize that the National Teacher was on the tip of the Tripitaka Master's nose or inside his Eye? If he talks like this, we can say that he has not yet heard what the National Teacher is saying, for the Tripitaka Master did not have the Nose or the Eye for it. But even should the Tripitaka Master have maintained and relied upon an Eye and a Nose of his own, if the National Teacher penetrated that Nose and Eye, both the Tripitaka Master's Nose and Eye would immediately have been ripped open. Once they had been ripped open, they would not be the niches and baskets that a National Teacher needs to stay in.[7]

None of the five veteran monks really knew the National Teacher. He was the Old Buddha of his generation and the Tathagata for his world. He had clarified the Matter and had received the genuine Transmission of the Buddha's Treasure House of

---

7. That is, if the Eye of the Tripitaka Master were to open, even though he would then be one who had awakened to the Truth, the National Teacher, who was already more spiritually advanced, would not need to depend on the Eye and Nose of the Tripitaka Master to accurately point out the Old Monk's whereabouts.

the Eye of the True Teaching. And he was undoubtedly preserving, and relying upon, his Eye, which was as black as a nut from a bo-tree.[8] He genuinely experienced the Transmission within his own Buddha Nature and he genuinely Transmitted It to the Buddha Nature of others. He was as a fellow trainee with Shakyamuni Buddha and, at the same time, he thoroughly explored the Matter with the Seven Buddhas.* And he acted like a fellow trainee with all the Buddhas of the three temporal worlds. He awoke to the Way that came before the Lord of Emptiness,* and awoke to the Way that came after the Lord of Emptiness, and awoke to the Way as a fellow trainee at the very time of the Buddha Who is the Lord of Emptiness. Right from the start, the National Teacher treated our ordinary, everyday world of suffering as his native land, and at the same time, this world of suffering was not necessarily within his Dharma world or within the whole of his universe in all ten directions. And Shakyamuni, as Lord of this world of suffering, never usurped or hindered the National Teacher's native land, which is just like each of the former and latter Buddhas and Ancestors who had innumerable awakenings to the Truth, but without interfering with or hindering each other's experience. And it is like this because the awakening to the Truth by former and latter Buddhas and Ancestors was unique to each of Them based on how it is that They awoke to the Truth.

Based on the evidence that Tripitaka Master Daini did not understand the National Teacher, the underlying principle should be clearly evident that folks like the shravakas* and pratyekabuddhas* of the Lesser Two Courses do not recognize even the periphery of Buddhahood. You should clarify through your training the National Teacher's intention in censuring the Tripitaka Master. That is, if the National Teacher had reprimanded him for knowing his whereabouts the first two times, and then reprimanded him for not knowing it the third time, this would lack validity. To know two thirds is to know the whole. So if it were this way, the National Teacher should not have reprimanded him. If he is reprimanded, it is not for being ignorant of the whole, but because the Tripitaka Master's attitude was insulting to the National

---

8. The black nut from the bo-tree resembles the pupil of an eye. The reference is to the Eye, which unlike ordinary eyes does not function as one of the thieving sensory organs.

Teacher.[9] If the latter had reprimanded the Tripitaka Master simply for failing to know the third time, who could trust the National Teacher's judgment? On the grounds of the Tripitaka Master knowing the first two times, the Tripitaka Master would be justified in reprimanding the National Teacher.

The National Teacher's intent in censuring the Tripitaka Master is as follows: He reprimands him because, right from the start, he failed all three times to recognize where the National Teacher was, what he was thinking, and what his Body and Mind were. He reprimands him for never having encountered or heard the Buddha Dharma, much less having studied It. Because this was the National Teacher's purpose, from the first time through the third, he asked his question using the same words. The first time the Tripitaka Master answered, "The reverend monk is indeed the teacher of this nation, so why does he go to the Western River and watch people racing about in their boats?" Spoken to in this way, the National Teacher did not reply, "Yes, Tripitaka Master, you have truly grasped the Old Monk's whereabouts." He simply repeated his question two more times. For several centuries since the time of the National Teacher, monks of long standing in all quarters, failing to grasp and clarify this point, have irresponsibly brought forth their commentaries and expounded their theories. The comments made by these individuals of the past lack the original intent of the National Teacher, and none accords with the Buddha Dharma. How sad that these veteran monks of the past have tripped up over this!

Now, if we say that, within the Buddha Dharma, there is the ability to see into someone's mind, then there must surely be an ability to see into someone's body, an ability to see into someone's Fist, and an ability to see into someone's Eye. If that is the way things are, then we ought to have the ability to see into our own mind and our own body. In that things are already like this, you certainly must have the ability to use your own mind right at this very moment to see into your own mind. To state more clearly what is being said, you undoubtedly have the ability to see into the minds of others, for this arises spontaneously from your own mind.

---

9. The Tripitaka Master's two responses were insulting because, despite his feigning humility and his using flowery language, he is actually accusing the National Teacher of engaging in behavior that is improper for a monk.

Let me ask you right now: which is better, to use your ability in order to see into the minds of others or to use it to see into your own mind? Answer! Quick! Quick! Putting this aside just for the moment, let me say that Bodhidharma's remark, "You have gotten what my Marrow is," is what 'seeing into the Mind of another' is all about.

Delivered to the assembly at Daibutsu-ji Temple in Echizen Province on the fourth day of the seventh lunar month in the third year of the Kangen era (July 28, 1245).

79

On 'The King Requests Something from Sindh'

(Ō Saku Sendaba)

Translator's Introduction: The term *sendaba* (Skt. *saindava*), 'something from Sindh', refers to products from the Indus River area, which were held in great esteem throughout India. Thus, asking for something from Sindh is equivalent to asking for the very best someone can offer that is appropriate to the situation. Dōgen views such acts of asking by one and offering by another as a model for the Master-disciple relationship.

> *Being possessed of words is having gone beyond words,*
> *As a wisteria vine is to a tree:*
> *The one feeds a donkey and the other feeds a horse,*
> *The one dives into water and the other passes through clouds.*[1]

Because this is the way matters already are, in the *Great Scripture on the Buddha's Parinirvana,* the World-honored One is quoted as saying the following:

> For instance, it is like the great king who would bid his ministers supply him with something from Sindh. The single term 'something from Sindh' had four references. The first was to salt, the second was to a goblet, the third was to water, and the fourth

---

1. This poem describes various aspects of the Master-disciple relationship. To paraphrase the poem on one level, just as a tree supports a wisteria vine, so the Master's having gone beyond words supports his verbal teaching. Hence, there are times when the Master uses words and times when he does not. The use of verbal instruction nourishes those who are plodding along nicely, doing their training, 'the donkeys' who have not yet awakened, whereas those who have awakened are like horses who do not need words but, upon seeing only the shadow of the trainer's riding crop, know which way to go. As a result, the trainee who is like a donkey is led to dive into the water of training and practice, whereas the one who is like a horse flies up, penetrating anything that obscures his view of the unbounded sky, which corresponds to That which he has awakened to.

was to a horse. These four goods were alike in having one and the same term of reference. Astute ministers were quite familiar with this term. At the king's bath time, should he ask for something from Sindh, they would accordingly offer him water. At the king's mealtime, should he ask for something from Sindh, they would accordingly offer him salt. When the king had finished eating and wished for something to drink, should he ask for something from Sindh, they would accordingly offer him a goblet. Should the king wish to make an excursion, he would ask for something from Sindh, and they would accordingly offer him a horse. In this way astute ministers understood well the king's four hidden meanings.

The sayings, "The king asked them for something from Sindh" and "The ministers offered him something from Sindh," have come to us from the distant past. They have been passed down to us just as the Eye of the Dharma has. Because the World-honored One had inevitably taken them up as a topic for the Dharma, His descendants have often taken them up too. I suspect that those who have become accustomed to being in step with the World-honored One make 'something from Sindh' their way of treading the Path. If their practice is not in step with that of the World-honored One, they should buy straw sandals and go in search of a Master, for such trainees need but advance one step in that direction and they will get it right off. The 'something from Sindh' that was already within the house of the Buddhas and Ancestors has quietly leaked out, so that 'something from Sindh' is to be found within the households of great kings.

The Old Buddha Wanshi of Mount Tendō in the Great Sung Chinese prefecture of Ch'ing-yüan, in addressing his assembly in the Lecture Hall, once said the following:

> To begin with, a monk asked Jōshū, "When a king asks for something from Sindh, what is it?"

Jōshū bowed, his hands in shashu.[*]

Setchō, picking up on this, has commented, "When the one asked for salt, the other offered him a horse."

Master Wanshi went on to say:

> A hundred years ago, Setchō was an excellent trainer of disciples. And Jōshū was an Old Buddha who lived to be a hundred and twenty. If Jōshū is right, then Setchō is simply otherwise; if Setchō is right, then Jōshū is simply otherwise.[2] Now, at this very moment, say! What ultimately is It? I, Wanshi, cannot avoid adding a comment to this, for if you are a hair short of It, you have missed It by ten thousand miles.

> > *To simply comprehend my words is to beat about in the*
> > *grass and thereby startle some snake*
> > *And not to comprehend them is to burn funeral money*
> > *and thereby attract some demon.* [*]
> > *Old Gutei showed no preferences among his uncultivated*
> > *fields,*
> > *He just reached out and took whichever one came to*
> > *hand.*[3]

---

[*] See *Glossary.*

2. Although the conventional expectation of what would follow the statement 'if Jōshū is right' would be that 'Setchō is therefore wrong', Wanshi does not say that Setchō is wrong, but asserts that what he is talking about is 'simply otherwise'. That is, each has expressed the whole of the Truth, hence the action by Jōshū and the statement by Setchō in no way contradict or stand against each other.

3. To paraphrase this poem, to content oneself with an intellectual understanding of Wanshi's Teaching is to beat around in the bushes and thereby run the risk of meeting up with something poisonous to one's training. On the other hand, not to have a clue as to what that Teaching is about is like mechanically going through the ritual of burning 'hell

When the Old Buddha who was my former Master was giving Teaching in the Lecture Hall, he would customarily refer to 'my Old Buddha Wanshi'. At the same time, only the Old Buddha who was my late master personally encountered the Old Buddha Wanshi as an Old Buddha. In Wanshi's time, there was a certain Sōkō, known as Meditation Master Daie of Mount Kinzan, who was supposed to have been a distant descendant of Nangaku. The whole realm of Great Sung China apparently thought Daie to be at least the equal of Wanshi, and some even thought him to surpass Wanshi as 'such a person'.* This error had arisen because, in that their eyes for the Way were not yet clear, both monks and laity in Great Sung China were negligent in their learning, they lacked clarity in recognizing what people were, and they were weak in knowledge of themselves.

In what Wanshi was recommending there was a genuine giving rise to the will to train. You need to explore through your training the principle of the Old Buddha Jōshū's bowing with hands in shashu. At the very moment of his doing it, was this the king asking for something from Sindh? Or was it the offering of something from Sind? You need to explore through your training the import of Setchō's saying, "When the one asked for salt, the other offered him a horse." Both 'asking for salt' and 'offering a horse' together are the king's asking for something from Sindh and the minister's offering something from Sindh. It is the World-honored One asking for something from Sindh and Makakashō's face breaking out into a smile. The First Chinese Ancestor asked for something from Sindh and his four disciples offered him a horse, salt, water, and a goblet. You need to learn that, when a horse, salt, water, and a goblet from Sindh are asked for, this is the pivotal point for the offering of a horse and the offering of water.

❀

One day, Nansen saw Tō Impō coming towards him and,
pointing at a jar, said to him, "The jar is a vessel and there is water

---

money' at a funeral only to attract devilish obstructions to one's training. When the great Meditation Master Gutei trained his disciples, he showed no preferences among them but would work with whichever disciple happened to come nearest to hand.

inside the jar. Without disturbing the vessel, please fetch me the water."

Accordingly, Impō fetched the water in the jar and, turning to face Nansen, poured it over Nansen's head. Nansen remained still.

Actually, in Nansen's asking for water, the sea dried up to its very bottom; in Impō's offering a vessel, the jar leaked out its contents which sank into a pond. Even though this is the way things were, you need to explore through your training that there was Water in the vessel and a Vessel in the water. Impō had not yet done anything to disturb the Water, nor had he yet done anything to disturb the Vessel.

Great Master Kyōgen Chikan was once asked by a monk, "What in the world is this 'king asking for something from Sindh' all about?"

Kyōgen replied, "Just come over here."

The monk went over to him.

Kyōgen said, "Your noodle-headed act could get someone killed!"

Now, let us ask, is the basis of Kyōgen's remark, "Come over here," his asking for something from Sindh or is it his offering something from Sindh? Please, I beg of you, try to answer! Was the monk's having gone over to him based on Kyōgen's asking for something or based on Kyōgen's offering something? Or was either of these even Kyōgen's original intention? If neither was his original intention, he could not have said, "Your noodle-headed act could get someone killed!" If either was his original intention, such a noodle-headed act could not kill anyone. Even though one may say that what Kyōgen has expressed is the full force of a whole lifetime, he still did not escape the disintegration of his body and the loss of his life. He is, for instance, like the general of a defeated army who still talks about his military prowess. In sum, from the Crown of his head and from his Eye, Kyōgen gave voice to what is yellow and spoke of what is black, which is his most meticulous asking for, and offering of, something from Sindh.[4] Who can say that they do not understand the taking up of the traveling staff* and the raising of the hossu?* Even so, these are not the criteria of folks that play a *koto* with its bridge glued down.[5] Because these folks don't even know that they are playing a *koto* with its bridge glued down, they are beyond having such criteria.

> One day, the World-honored One ascended the Dharma Seat. Manjushri,* having then rapped upon the signal block with his mallet, said, "When we clearly see what the Dharma of the Lord of Dharma is, the Dharma of the Lord of Dharma is just like this," whereupon, the World-honored One came down from His Dharma seat.

Meditation Master Setchō Jūken commented on this by saying:

> *As any skilled Master among the sacred ranks of those in*
> *the forest grove knew,*
> *"The Teaching of the Lord of Dharma is <u>not</u> just like this."*
> *If, in the Buddha's assembly, there had been any trainee*
> *from Sindh,*
> *Why would Manjushri possibly have needed to sound even*
> *one single clap?*

---

4. In China, yellow and black are traditionally viewed as opposites or complements: the earth is yellow by day, the sky is black by night. In Chinese Buddhist texts, 'giving voice to what is yellow' is associated with the positive teaching of the Precepts and Buddhist training, whereas 'speaking of what is black' is associated with the pointing out of acts that are contrary to the Precepts and to training.

5. The *koto* is a traditional Japanese stringed musical instrument. The bridge of a *koto* needs to remain flexible and to 'give' according to the way it is being played; hence, to glue the bridge down would be analogous to holding onto rigid views.

Accordingly, Setchō is saying that if one clap is as though one's whole being is flawless, then whether the block has already been struck or has not yet been struck, it would be one's dropping off of 'being flawless'. If it were like this, then one clap would be something from Sindh. If there were already 'such a person', that one would be a trainee from Sindh who was among the sacred ranks within the forest grove. Hence, the Dharma of the Lord of Dharma is just like this. To make good use of all the hours of a day is to ask for something from Sindh. We should ask for the Fist and offer the Fist: we should ask for the hossu and offer the hossu.

Even so, of the so-called senior monks in all the various monasteries in Great Sung China, none have ever seen something from Sindh even in their dreams. Painful, oh how painful, that the Way of the Ancestors has so declined! Do not shirk from hard training and, beyond question, you <u>will</u> inherit the lifeline of the Buddhas and Ancestors. For instance, someone asks, "What <u>is</u> Buddha?" and the Master asserts, "Your very mind is Buddha!" What does this mean? Would this assertion not be 'something from Sindh'? You need to explore in detail through your training with your Master who it really is that says, "Your very mind is Buddha!" Would any of you know that it is striking, and being struck by, something from Sindh?

Given to the assembly at Daibutsu-ji Temple in Echizen Province on the twenty-second day of the tenth month in the third year of the Kangen era (November 12, 1245).

80

On Instructions for Monks in the Kitchen Hall

(Jikuin Mon)

Translator's Introduction: The text of this discourse would have been placed in the kitchen for the Chief Cook and the other kitchen monks to read and refer to.

When Hangyō Kōzen prepared the first published version of the *Shōbōgenzō* in 1690, he added this chapter, along with Discourse 1: A Discourse on Doing One's Utmost in Practicing the Way of the Buddhas (*Bendōwa*) and Discourse 5: On Conduct Appropriate for the Auxiliary Cloud Hall (*Jūundō Shiki*), to the other versions of the *Shōbōgenzō* that he found in Eihei-ji.

On the sixth day of the eighth lunar month in the fourth year of the Kangen era (September 17, 1246), I expounded on the following for the assembly, "The method of training for monks who are responsible for preparing meals is to have them make reverence their underlying principle." After the Tathagata's entering parinirvana, the Dharma has been accurately Transmitted from far off India and to China, and during that time, celestial beings have made spiritual offerings to the Buddhas and Their disciples. Rulers of nations have also made alms offerings of royal food to the Buddhas and Their disciples. In addition, the households of wealthy and ordinary lay folk have respectfully made food offerings, and there have even been laborers and servants who have done the same. These alms offerings were accompanied with deep respect and cordiality. Among persons in lofty positions, as well as among ordinary folk, were those who made offerings of food and other things in a most respectful way, accompanied with highly courteous bows and with the most polite forms of speech, because of the depth of their intentions. Now, even though we are deep within remote mountains, we should personally receive the authentic Transmission of polite acts and respectful words from those who serve in the Kitchen Hall of our temple, for this is how those in lofty positions, as well as ordinary folk, have pursued their study of the Buddha's Dharma.

For example, when speaking of the breakfast gruel, you should take the time to say, 'our revered gruel' or 'our morning gruel', but not just 'the gruel'.[1] When speaking of the midday meal, you should take the time to say 'our revered midday meal' or 'our lunchtime', but not just 'lunch'. You should take the time to say, "Would you please prepare some white rice for me?" and not just, "Pound me some rice!" As to washing rice, you should take the time to say, "Would you please wash some rice for me?" and not spend your time saying, "Wash me some rice!" You should take the time to say, "Would you please select some vegetables for our stir-fry dish?" and not, "Get me some veggies!" You should take the time to say, "Would you please prepare a nice broth for our meal?" and not, "Make us some broth!" You should take the time to say, "Would you please prepare some nice hot soup for our meal?" and not, "Make us some soup!" You should take the time to say, "The lunchtime meal—or the morning gruel—has been prepared ever so nicely."

Be sure to treat all the utensils used to prepare the midday meal and the morning gruel with similar respect. Disrespect invites calamity; it is never accompanied by anything meritorious.

While the midday meal and the breakfast gruel are being prepared, no one should breathe all over the rice and vegetables, or any other food items. Do not let the sleeve of your robe brush against even dry food items. If your hand has come in contact with your head or face, do not handle any utensils or food until you have washed it. From the time of sorting the rice until the cooking of it to make a broth, should you happen to scratch yourself, by all means you should wash your hands.

In places where the midday meal and the morning gruel are being prepared, you should recite lines from Buddhist Scriptures or passages spoken by the Ancestral Masters. Do not engage in worldly talk or use crude speech. As a principle, you should

---

1.   'Our revered gruel' and similar phrases are somewhat heavy-handed English translations. In Japanese, the respectful form for 'gruel' is made simply by adding the prefix 'o-' to the Chinese-derived word *shoku* to form *o-shoku*. The word for 'morning gruel' is *chōshoku*, which again is a reading derived from the Chinese. Dōgen contrasts these with the colloquial Japanese word for gruel: *kayu*.

take the time to use polite word forms when speaking of such things as rice, meals, salt, and soy sauce. You should not use your time saying, "There's rice," or "There's veggies."

When senior monks and novices pass by the place where the midday meal or the morning gruel is being conducted, they should respectfully bow with hands in gassho.*

If there are any spilt vegetables or spilt rice, they should be made use of after the meal.[2]

To the extent that the morning or midday meals have not concluded, you should not intrude upon them.

You should take care to preserve the utensils used for preparing meals and not use them for other purposes. Do not let them be handled by lay folk who have come from home until they have washed their hands. Such foodstuffs as vegetables and fruit which have come from lay folk and which have not yet been cleansed should be rinsed, incensed, and left to dry by the fire, and then respectfully offered to the Three Treasures and to the monks of the assembly. In the mountain retreats and the temples of Great Sung China today, if lay folk bring such things as dumplings, dairy cakes, and steamed cakes, they should be reheated before being served to the monastic community. This will purify them. Do not serve them without reheating them.

These are but a few points among many. O you who are in charge of the Kitchen Hall, you need to understand their great import and put them into practice. Within all your myriad duties, do not act contrary to these standards.

These items are the lifeblood of the Buddhas and Ancestors and the Eye of patch-robed monks. Non-Buddhists know them not: celestial demons cannot endure them. Only the disciples of Buddha have been able to Transmit them. O you who are senior officers of the Kitchen Hall, discern them well and do not let them be lost!

Displayed here by Dōgen,
the Founding Monk of this temple.

---

*   See *Glossary.*

2.   That is, fed to animals or used for compost.

I, as Master of Eihei-ji Temple, now address the Chief Officer: If it is already past noon when a donor makes an offering of cooked rice, you should keep it in storage until the next day. But if it is something like cakes, fruit, or some kind of gruel, or the like, even though it is already evening, serve it as a medicine meal for the assembly of the Buddhas and Ancestors.[3] And what is more, such a meal is an excellent trace left by those in Great Sung China who realized the True Way.

The Tathagata always permitted monks living in the Himalayas to wear underclothing. We on this mountain also permit such medicine during the times of snow.

Kigen, the Founding Monk of Eihei.[4]

---

3. Traditionally, only two meals are served to the monastic community, one in the morning and another before noon. Because monks, particularly those who are ill or are engaged in heavy physical labor, may need more nourishment than these two meals provide, an evening meal may be offered as a form of 'medicine' to provide additional nourishment for the body.

4. Kigen was one of Dōgen's names.

81

On Leaving Home Life Behind

(Shukke)

Translator's Introduction: The term *shukke*, 'leaving home life behind', has a double meaning. Figuratively, it refers to letting go of worldly values; literally, it refers to someone entering a monastery to become a monk.

Some of Dōgen's readers have taken this discourse as evidence that he had completely rejected the idea of lay discipleship. But if that were the case, it is difficult to explain why he would be giving this talk to his assembly of monastic disciples rather than to the relatively few lay disciples who were present at Eihei-ji. It seems more likely that some of his monks were having difficulties with the harshness of monastic training in such an isolated locale, and Dōgen was trying to get some starch into their backbones by insisting that only through sticking with their commitment to leave home life behind, in both senses of the term, and to live in accord with the Precepts could they realize That which they had come there to find.

In the *Procedures for Cleanliness in a Zen Temple* it says the following:

All Buddhas in the three temporal worlds—past, present, and future—affirm that to leave home life behind is to realize the Truth. The twenty-eight Indian Ancestors and the six Chinese Ancestors, all of whom Transmitted the Buddha's Mind seal,* were, each and every one of them, monastics. Most likely, it was because they strictly observed the monastic regulations that they were able to become outstanding models for those in the three worlds of desire, form, and beyond form. Thus, in practicing meditation and inquiring of the Way with their Master, they made the Precepts and the monastic regulations foremost. Had they not distanced themselves from their faults and guarded against misdeeds, how could they have realized Buddhahood and become an Ancestor?

---

*   See *Glossary.*

As to the method for doing the ordination ceremony of Taking the Precepts, three types of kesas* and a set of mealtime bowls, along with fresh, clean robes, are provided for the one to be ordained. If new robes are not available, be sure to launder old ones, but you must not use borrowed kesas or a borrowed bowl set to put on the altar when doing the ceremony of Taking the Precepts. Concentrate wholeheartedly and take care not to get distracted by side issues. Assuming the form of a Buddha, being provided with the Precepts and the monastic regulations, and acquiring what the Buddha received and made use of are, by no means, small matters, so how could you possibly treat them lightly? Were you to borrow someone's kesas or bowl set, and then go up to the altar to take the Precepts, you would not really be obtaining the Precepts. Should you never receive the Precepts, you will be a person devoid of the Precepts for the whole of your life as you vainly cross over the threshold of empty scholasticism, meaninglessly accepting alms given in good faith. Those entering the path with a beginner's mind may not as yet have memorized the rules and regulations. Should their Master offer no guidance, they will lapse into error. What I am saying here is stern advice indeed. Dare I hope that you will engrave it on your heart? If you have taken the monastic Precepts, by all means you should also take the Bodhisattva* Precepts, for They are foremost for those who would enter the Teaching.[1]

Clearly understand that the full perfecting of the innate enlightenment of all the Buddhas and all the Ancestors has been nothing other than Their leaving home life behind and Their accepting the Precepts. And the vital line of Transmission of all the Buddhas and Ancestors is nothing other than Their leaving home life behind and accepting the Precepts. Those who have not yet left home life behind are also not

---

1. The Bodhisattva Precepts can be found in the *Scripture of Brahma's Net*. One translation of this appears in *Buddhist Writings on Meditation and Daily Practice* (Shasta Abbey Press, 1994), pp. 55-188

Buddhas or Ancestors. Meeting up with a Buddha and meeting up with an Ancestor is what leaving home life behind and accepting the Precepts is all about.

Makakashō, in following the World-honored One, was intent on leaving home life behind, as he desired to help all beings to cross to the Other Shore. The Buddha said, "Welcome, good monk." Thereupon, the hair on Makakashō's head naturally came off and a kesa enveloped his body. When someone learns what a Buddha is and drops off whatever that person is holding onto, such a one is, in this way, an excellent example of leaving home life behind and accepting the Precepts.

In the third fascicle of the *Great Scripture on Wisdom* it says the following:

The World-honored Buddha once said, "If a bodhisattva-mahasattva[*] were to think thus: 'Were I, at some time, to abandon my position in our nation, then on the very day that I realized supreme, fully perfected wisdom I would, also on that day, turn the Wheel of the Wondrous Dharma in order to help sentient beings beyond count to distance themselves from their defiling passions and to depart from their delusions, as well as help them bring to life their pure Eye for the Dharma. I would also help sentient beings beyond count bring their delusive, evil deeds to an end, and help them set free the Wisdom within their heart. And I would also help sentient beings beyond count realize the state where they neither regressed nor turned away from their supreme, fully perfected Wisdom.' If this bodhisattva-mahasattva were to desire such things, then he or she should, by all means, study the *Great Scripture on Wisdom*."

Generally speaking, our supreme enlightenment is fulfilled at the time of our leaving home life behind and accepting the Precepts. Were there no day on which we left home life behind, then it would not be completely fulfilled. Thus, making use of the day on which we leave home life behind, we bring about the day on which we realize supreme enlightenment, and we pick out the day on which we will realize supreme enlightenment, which is the day on which we leave home life behind. This leaving home life behind turns us upside down. It is the turning of the Wheel of the Dharma. Accordingly, leaving home life behind helps innumerable beings keep from regressing or turning away from supreme enlightenment. Keep in mind that what is meant by fulfilling 'what benefits oneself benefits others' and by not regressing or turning away from fully perfected enlightenment is leaving home life behind and accepting the Precepts. On the other hand, the day of leaving home life behind is the day of realizing what Wisdom truly is. And beyond doubt, you need to realize that the day of leaving home life behind goes beyond sameness or difference.

On the day of leaving home life behind, we experience through our training innumerable eons of time. And on the day of leaving home life behind, we dwell within an unbounded ocean of time, turning the wondrous Wheel of the Dharma. And the day of leaving home life behind should not be thought of as comparable to 'a time to eat', nor is it sixty seconds, but it goes beyond the three periods of past, present, and future, for one has dropped off temporal boundaries. The day of leaving home life behind transcends 'the day of leaving home life behind'. Be this as it may, when we have broken open the nets and cages of our delusions, the day of leaving home life behind will be <u>our</u> day of leaving home life behind. The day for manifesting the Truth will be <u>our</u> day of manifesting the Truth.

In the thirteenth section of Nāgārjuna's *Commentary on the Great Scripture on Wisdom*, there is the following:

> Once when the Buddha was at Jetavana Park, an intoxicated Brahman came to where the Buddha was and asked to become a monk. The Buddha requested that some of his monks shave the Brahman's head and clothe him in a kesa. After the effects of the liquor had worn off, the Brahman was astonished and frightened upon seeing that his bodily form had changed into that

of a Buddhist monk, whereupon he ran away forthwith. The monks respectfully asked the Buddha why He had allowed the drunken Brahman to become a monk only to have him run back home. The Buddha answered, "For eons beyond measure, this Brahman did not have the heart to leave home life behind, but now, while under the influence, he gave rise to a bit of courage. Due to this, he will, later on, leave home life behind."

There are all sorts of stories like this one. The breaking of the Precepts by one who has left home life behind is far better than the keeping of the Precepts by one who has remained in home life, because others do not rid themselves of their delusions and spiritual suffering due to a lay person's keeping of the Precepts.

The principle underlying the Buddha's instructions concerning the Brahman is quite clearly recognizable. Within the Teaching being given here by the Buddha, what is fundamental is simply leaving home life behind. Not yet freeing oneself from home life is not the Buddha's Way.[2] While the Tathagata was in the world, whenever non-Buddhists discarded their false views and took refuge in the Teaching of the Buddha, invariably they sought, first off, to leave home life behind. Either the World-honored One Himself would personally greet such persons, saying, "Welcome, good monk!" or He would have His monks shave them, and then have them formally leave home life behind and take the Precepts. In either case, the means for leaving home life behind and taking the Precepts were immediately supplied.

You need to keep in mind that once the Buddha's Teaching envelops our body and mind, the hair on our head naturally falls away and a kesa clothes our body.

---

2. This sentence has been understood in different ways. Some believe that Dōgen is saying everyone must become a monastic, whereas others assert that Dōgen's view is that everyone needs to free oneself from worldly values and worldly ways of thinking and behaving. Perhaps the deciding question is for whom did Dōgen intend this talk? Was he trying to encourage the lay Buddhists who were working at Eihei-ji or otherwise supporting the monastery to let go of such values, thinking, and behaving? Or was he upbraiding monks who were disinclined to give up their pursuit of worldly interests?

If the Buddhas had not yet given Their approval, our hair would not have been shaved off, nor would a kesa have been wrapped around our body, nor would we have been able to take the Buddha's Precepts. So, our leaving home life behind and accepting the Precepts is our personally receiving from the Buddhas and the Tathagata the affirmation of our ultimate enlightenment.

In the *Lotus Scripture*, Shakyamuni Buddha once said the following:

> My virtuous sons! Upon seeing sentient beings who are low in moral character and sunk deep in delusion taking pleasure in trivialities, I, the Tathagata, instruct them by saying, "While still young, I left home life behind and realized supreme, fully perfected enlightenment. And the time since I truly realized Buddhahood has been ever so long." I give instruction in this manner, but only as a skillful means for teaching sentient beings that they too may enter the Buddha's Way.

So, His realizing the Truth long ago was synonymous with His having left home life behind while still young, and His realizing supreme, fully perfected enlightenment was also synonymous with His having left home life behind.

By the Buddha's putting forth the statement, "While still young, I left home life behind," those human beings who are low in moral character and sunk deep in delusion, and who therefore take pleasure in trivialities, also come to realize that they too, though still young, may leave home life behind. At any point where we can encounter, or hear about, and learn through practice the Teaching contained in "While still young, one may leave home life behind," we encounter the Buddha's supreme, fully perfected enlightenment. When He rescued those human beings who were taking pleasure in trivialities, He taught them, "While still young, I left home life behind and realized supreme, fully perfected enlightenment." Though He expressed the Essential Matter[*] like this, were someone ultimately to ask me, "Just how much merit is there in leaving home life behind?" I would reply, "It is worth your very head!"

Delivered to the assembly at Eihei-ji Temple in Echizen Province on the fifteenth day of the ninth lunar month in the fourth year of the Kangen era (October 25, 1246).

82

On the Spiritual Merits of Leaving Home Life Behind

(Shukke Kudoku)

Translator's Introduction: 'Leaving home life behind' has a double meaning. In one sense, it refers to someone who becomes a monk upon taking the monastic Precepts. In another sense, it refers to the renouncing of the mundane values of worldly society, and as such, would apply not only to monks but also to those who have accepted the lay Precepts while remaining in lay life. Which meaning Dōgen intends seems to shift back and forth, and context does not always make clear whether he is referring to the literal or figurative meaning, or both simultaneously. And there is a third aspect to leaving home life behind which Dōgen brings up later in relation to a quotation from Rinzai.

While Dōgen insists most emphatically throughout this discourse that leaving home life behind is a prerequisite for realizing full Buddhahood, there is no place where he openly rejects being involved with sincere, practicing lay Buddhists. Indeed, in Dōgen's Zen Buddhist tradition, when lay persons formally take all ten Great Precepts, there is a symbolic shaving of the head, and they are given a wagesa, which is a token kesa, along with a certificate containing the bloodline of the Buddhas and Ancestors from Shakyamuni Buddha down to the present ordinand.

The bodhisattva* Nāgārjuna once said the following:

> Someone once asked me, "If we are able to be reborn in some celestial world, realize the Way of bodhisattvas, and realize nirvana by just keeping to the lay Precepts, of what use are the Precepts that a monastic takes?"[1]
>
> In reply, I said, "Both lay people and monastics can reach the Other Shore, but even so, each way has its difficult and its easy aspects. Those in lay life have all manner of duties and occupations.

---

*   See *Glossary.*

1.   The laity in the Theravadin tradition customarily take five Precepts. In the Mahayana tradition, the laity take those five plus five more. Monastics in both traditions take Precepts that number in the hundreds.

If they should wish to concentrate on pursuing wholeheartedly the Path to full awakening, then their family duties will fall by the wayside, and if they should wholeheartedly fulfill the responsibilities of family life, then matters that pertain to pursuit of the Way will be abandoned. They would need to be able to practice the Dharma without selecting one way and abandoning the other. And this is what I would describe as 'taking on what is difficult'. In leaving lay life behind, we sever ourselves from pursuing worldly profits and from indulging in dislikes and wrangling, as we devote ourselves wholeheartedly to practicing the Way, which is what I would describe as 'taking on what is easy'. Also, there is the noise and bustle of a home, with its many affairs and many duties, all of which are the roots of entanglements and the storehouse of wrongdoings. This is what is described as 'taking on what is extremely difficult'. When we leave home, we are, for instance, like someone who has departed to reside somewhere where the lands are empty and there is no one else about. In that way, our heart is as one, being beyond intentions and beyond fear. Our expectations have already been removed. And our wayward ways have also departed. It is like what is being expressed in the following poem:

> *I sit at ease within the forest grove.*
> *Tranquilly, my human failings are overthrown.*
> *Through being impartial, I attain a singleness of mind,*
> *The pleasure of which surpasses the pleasures of celestial worlds.*

> *Others may seek to gain wealth and honor,*
> *Or fineries of dress or comfortable abodes,*
> *But such pleasures lack true peace,*
> *Since for one in pursuit of gains, there is no satiety.*

Adorned in my patched robe, I go forth begging my food,
Whether moving or standing still, I am always at one within
      my heart.
With my very own Eye of wise discernment,
I fathom the True Nature of all thoughts and things.

Within the sundry gates to the Dharma,
I enter, only to see that all are just alike,
So this Heart that understands the Why of things is tranquil,
For there is nothing that can surpass It within the triple
      world.[2]

"Thus, by this poem we know that leaving home life behind, living by the Precepts, and doing the practice as a monk is 'taking on what is extremely easy'.

"Further, leaving home life behind and practicing the Precepts gain for us good moral rules and regulations beyond measure, all of which we possess to the full. For this reason, a white-robed one like you should leave home life behind and accept the full Precepts.[3]

"Further, within the Buddha Dharma the Teaching of leaving home life behind is the most difficult to practice. The young Brahman Jambukadaka once asked Shariputra, 'Within the Buddha Dharma what is the most difficult thing to do?'

"Shariputra responded, 'Leaving home life behind is the most difficult to achieve.'

"The Brahman then asked, 'What are the difficulties in leaving home life behind?'

"Shariputra replied, 'In leaving home life behind, contentment is the most difficult to achieve.'

---

2.   The triple world consists of the worlds of desire, form, and beyond form.

3.   'A white-robed one' is a common reference to a lay person.

"The Brahman then asked, 'When one has attained contentment, what then is the most difficult to attain?'

"Shariputra responded, 'Putting good ways into practice is what is difficult. For this reason, by all means you should leave home life behind.'

"Further, when someone leaves home life behind, the Lord of Demons, taken aback, sorrowfully says, 'This person has scarcely any entanglements or delusions left. Such a one will certainly realize nirvana and enter the ranks of the Sangha Treasure.'

"And also, it says the following in the story concerning the female monastic Utpalavarna:

"If people who have left home life behind to be within the Buddha Dharma break the Precepts and lapse into impure ways, once they have brought their impure ways to an end and obtained liberation from them, they will be like the female monk Utpalavarna.

"While the Buddha was in the world, this female monk attained the six spiritual abilities and realized arhathood.* She once entered the house of a member of the nobility and, continually extolling the Dharma of leaving home life behind, she admonished the wives and daughters of the noble, saying, 'My sisters, you should leave home life behind and become monastics.'

"The noblewomen all replied, 'We are young and our bodies are comely; for us to keep to the Precepts would indeed be hard, and we would surely beak them on occasion.'

"The monk replied, 'If you break the Precepts, then you break them. Just leave lay life behind!'

"They then asked her, 'If we break the Precepts, then we shall certainly fall into some hellish state, so why would you have us break them?'

"She replied, 'If you fall into some hell, then you fall into some hell.'

"All the women broke out in laughter and said, 'In a hell we will receive the consequences of our defiling deeds, so why would you have us fall into such a state?'

"The monk replied, 'In recalling my own past lives, there was a time when I had become a prostitute. I dressed up in all sorts of clothes and told the age-old licentious stories. One day, I dressed up as a female monk, just as a joke. As a direct result of this, I became a female monk in Kashō Buddha's time. After a while, I took to depending on my aristocratic demeanor and gave rise to pride and arrogance, thereby breaking monastic prohibitions as well as Precepts. Because of the defilement from breaking monastic prohibitions and Precepts, I fell into a hellish state where I suffered the consequences of my various defiling acts. After I had suffered these consequences, I met Shakyamuni Buddha and left home life behind, ultimately obtaining the six spiritual abilities and realizing arhathood. Due to this, I have come to know that if we leave home life behind and take the monastic Precepts, even though we later break Precepts, we <u>will</u> realize arhathood because of the karmic[*] effect of the Precepts. If I had merely done bad things, without having received any effects from the Precepts, I would not have realized the Way. In times long past, I had fallen into hellish states generation after generation, getting out of some hell only to become a wicked person. When that wicked person died, again a hell was entered and nothing whatever had been gained. Now because of this, I have come to realize that if someone leaves home to be a monastic and takes the Precepts, even though that person breaks the Precepts, because of having taken them, that person <u>will</u> obtain the fruits of the Way.'

"Also, once when the Buddha was at Jetavana Park, an intoxicated Brahman came to where the Buddha was and asked to become a monk. The Buddha requested that some of his monks shave the Brahman's head and clothe him in a kesa.* After the effects of the liquor wore off, the Brahman was astonished and frightened upon seeing that his bodily form had changed into that of a Buddhist monk, whereupon he forthwith ran away. The monks respectfully asked the Buddha why He had allowed the drunken Brahman to become a monk only to run back home. The Buddha answered, 'For eons beyond measure, this Brahman did not have the heart to leave home life behind, but now, while under the influence, he gave rise to a bit of courage. Due to this, he will, later on, leave home life behind.'

"In various stories like these, the benefit from leaving home life behind is described as producing spiritual merit beyond measure. Even though one who is garbed in white may have the five Precepts, such a one does not know what leaving home life behind is like."

Thus the World-honored One let the intoxicated Brahman hear about leaving home life behind and taking the Precepts, thereby planting the first seeds for realizing the Way. Clearly, you need to know that, from ancient times, human beings who still lack the merits of having left home life behind have not been able to realize the fully awakened state of Buddhahood. Because the Brahman was in his cups, he gave rise to a bit of courage, and by having his head shaved and his taking the Precepts, he became a monk. Though it was not long before he sobered up, the principle that he will preserve the merits of this act and will increase his good roots for realizing the Way is to be found in the World-honored One's golden words of Truth, for this was the Tathagata's original wish, which led Him to come forth into the world. All sentient beings—be they of past, present, or future—should clearly trust in this principle and put it into practice. Truly, giving rise to the intention to realize the Way is something that one establishes moment by moment. The merits from this Brahman's momentarily leaving home life behind are just like this. And what is more, how could the merits of your leaving home life behind and taking the Precepts during your present lifetime be inferior to those of an intoxicated Brahman!

The saintly Wheel-turning Lords* emerged more than eighty-thousand years ago and ruled over the four continents, having been supplied with the seven royal treasures.[4] At that time, these four continents were all like Pure Lands. The delight of these Wheel-turning Lords goes beyond words to express. It is said that there were some of these Wheel-turning Lords who ruled over three-thousandfold worlds. Distinctions have been made among those whose Wheel was of gold, silver, copper, or iron. Those with these Wheels ruled over the first, second, third, and fourth continents, respectively. And their whole being was positively free from the ten evils.[5] Though these saintly Wheel-turning Lords enjoyed their delights in abundance, as soon as a single white hair appeared on their head, they would turn their office over to the crown prince and forthwith leave home life behind. They would don a kesa and go off into the mountains or forests to do their spiritual training, so that when they came to the end of their life, they would undoubtedly be reborn in Brahma's Heaven.[6] They would place their white hair in a golden coffer to be stored in the royal palace and passed on to the next Wheel-turning Lord. When the hair of the next Wheel-turning Lord turned white, he would do the same as the previous Lord. The length of a saintly Wheel-turning Lord's life after leaving home life behind far surpasses that of people today. It is said that the life of a Wheel-turning Lord is more than eighty thousand years and his body is endowed with the thirty-two physical marks, which surpass those of people today.[7] Be that as it may, when such Wheel-turning Lords saw their white hair, they awoke to impermanence and invariably left home life behind to train in the Way in order to fully realize the merit of practicing untainted deeds. Rulers today cannot match the saintly Wheel-turning Lords. If today's rulers were to waste precious time just chasing after their greeds and ultimately failed to leave home life

---

4.   The seven are the Golden Wheel, wise elephants, swift horses, the divine Pearl, able ministers, women as precious as jewels, and loyal generals.

5.   The ten evils are the ways in which one acts contrary to the ten Mahayana Precepts.

6.   The heaven ruled over by Lord Brahma, the lowest of the four meditational heavens in the world of form, one that is free of sexual desires.

7.   According to ancient Indian traditions, both Buddhas and Wheel-turning Lords were born with the thirty-two marks of a great being.

behind them, they might well come to regret it in future ages. And what is more, in small nations in remote lands, there are rulers in name only, for they lack the virtues of a Wheel-turning Lord and are unable to bring their greeds to a halt. But if they were to leave home life behind and practice the Way, many celestial beings would be glad to offer them their protection, dragon spirits would respectfully guard them, and the Eye of Buddhas would joyfully confirm their awakened state.

During her past as a prostitute, Utpalavarnā put on the robe of a female monastic, not with a sincere heart but for the sake of making a joke out of it. More than probably, she was committing a wrong deed by making light of the Dharma, but the power of her having put this robe upon her body brought her face-to-face with the Buddha Dharma in a second generation. The female monastic's robe refers to a kesa. As a result of her having previously donned the kesa as a joke, she met Kashō Buddha in a second lifetime. She left home life behind, took the Precepts, and became a female monastic. As the result of her having broken the Precepts, she fell into a hellish state as the consequence of her misdeeds. But, due to the merits of the kesa not having crumbled away, she ultimately met Shakyamuni Buddha, and upon meeting the Buddha and hearing His Teaching, she gave rise to the intention to devote herself to the training, leaving the triple world far behind her and ultimately becoming a great arhat, one possessed of the six spiritual abilities and the three kinds of spiritual insights. Without doubt, she must have realized the supreme Truth.

Therefore, when you straightaway and in all earnestness commit your innately immaculate heart of faith to realizing supreme enlightenment and accept the kesa in trust, the spiritual merit of this will increase faster than the spiritual merit of that prostitute. And what is more, when you give rise to the heart that seeks enlightenment, leave home life behind, and accept the Precepts, all for the sake of supreme enlightenment, the spiritual merit of this will be beyond measure, for without a human body, it is rare indeed for any being to realize this spiritual merit.

In India and China, there have been many monks and lay people who have been bodhisattvas and Ancestral Masters, but none is the equal of our Ancestral Master Nāgārjuna. Only our Ancestral Master Nāgārjuna has offered us stories like those of the intoxicated Brahman and the prostitute in order to encourage us human beings to leave home life behind and accept the Precepts.

This is what our Ancestral Master Nāgārjuna recorded of the golden speech of the World-honored One:

> The World-honored One once said, "In the southern continent of Jambudvipa,* there are four kinds of preeminent events: first is encountering a Buddha, second is hearing the Dharma, third is leaving home life behind, and fourth is realizing the Truth."

You need to clearly recognize that these four kinds of preeminent events surpass anything in the northern continent of Uttarakura or in the celestial abodes.[8] Being drawn along through the power of our long-accumulated good roots, we have now acquired the peerless body of a human being. We are people who can joyfully, and with deepest gratitude, leave home life behind and accept the Precepts. Do not treat this preeminently good body lightly and leave our dew-like life to the mercy of the winds of impermanence. By piling up life after life of leaving home life behind, we will be amassing merit and accumulating virtue.

> The World-honored One once said, "The karmic recompense that results from having left home life behind in order to be within the Buddha Dharma is mind-boggling. Even if someone were to erect a seven-jeweled stupa* that was high enough to reach the thirty-third heavenly world, the merit gained from such a deed would not equal that from leaving home life behind. And why is this so? Because a seven-jeweled stupa can be demolished by foolish people acting from their greed and wickedness, but there is nothing

---

8.   Uttarakura is the realm of those who are in a state of continual, blissful ignorance.

that can destroy the merits of leaving home life behind. Thus, if someone instructs both men and women about leaving home life behind, and if they then set their servants free to do so, or if they let the populace at large do so, or if they themselves leave home life behind and enter the Way, the merits of that are immeasurable."

The World-honored One clearly knew the amount of merit involved, and so He evaluated it in this manner. Shrīvaddhi, whose name means 'he whose wealth is ever increasing', on hearing this Teaching of the Buddha, felt compelled to leave home life behind and take the Precepts, even though he had already reached the advanced age of a hundred and twenty years.[9] He sat in the rear of the assembly alongside the young novices, polishing his training. He ultimately became a great arhat.

Keep in mind that having a human body in this lifetime is something temporary, comprised as it is of the four elements[*] and the five skandhas.[*] It is always subject to the eight forms of pain.[10] And what is more, its arising and vanishing goes on uninterruptedly moment by moment. It is said that during one click of our fingers, sixty-five of these moments of time arise and disappear, but we are in the dark about this, due to our lack of awareness. Within the period of a single day and night, there are over sixty-four hundred million of these moments during which our five skandhas arise and disappear, but we are unaware of this. How sad that even as we arise and vanish, we ourselves are unaware of it! This measure of the arising and vanishing of a moment has been known only by the World-honored Buddha and Shariputra. Not even the saintly have known it. In accord with this principle of the appearance and disappearance of each moment, human beings fashion their good or wicked deeds, and give rise to their intention to realize both Buddhahood and the Way. Ours is a body that appears and disappears in this manner, so even though we treasure it, it does not remain unchanging. Since time immemorial, there has never been a single person who,

---

9. When Shrīvaddhi asked if he could become a monk, Shariputra told him he was now too old, but the Buddha intervened and ordained him.

10. The eight are being born, aging, sickening, dying, being separated from loved ones, having to associate with those one dislikes, chasing after what is unobtainable, and suffering the ills that afflict the five skandhas.

through prizing the body, has kept it from changing. In this sense, this human body does not belong to us. But if we make use of it to turn ourselves around so that we may leave home life behind and accept the Precepts, then we may realize the supreme, fully perfected enlightenment of the Buddhas of the three temporal worlds, as well as the fruits of Buddhahood, which are as indestructible as a diamond. What sage person would not be delighted to seek for them?

According to the *Lotus Scripture,* the eight disciples of the Buddha Whose Guiding Light Is as Luminous as the Sun and Moon all renounced their previous lordly positions in which they held dominion over the four earthly continents and left home life behind. And the sixteen disciples of the Buddha Whose Universal Wisdom Is Unsurpassed had, all together, left home life behind as well. Then, when the Buddha of Universal Wisdom entered eternal meditation, they gave voice to the *Lotus Scripture* for the sake of His assembly and have now become Tathagatas in the ten quarters. Eighty trillion people under the governance of their paternal lord, who was a saintly Wheel-turning Lord, upon seeing the sixteen princes leave home life behind, also sought to leave home life behind, whereupon the Wheel-turning Lord forthwith granted it. And the two sons of His Majesty the Lord of Wondrous Splendor, along with their father and mother, all left home life behind. Keep in mind that whenever great saintly ones have appeared in the world, they have invariably viewed leaving home life behind to be what the True Teaching is. You must not go around saying that these people left home life behind because they were confused; if you realize that they left home life behind out of wisdom, you should consider doing the same. During the time of Shakyamuni, our Buddha of the present, His son Rahula and His cousin Ananda, among others, left home life behind, along with a thousand of the Buddha's Shakya clan on one occasion and twenty thousand on another. We should consider them to be excellent examples. From the time when His first five monks left home until the time when Subhadra, at the end of the Buddha's life, also did so, all those who were converted to the Buddha's Teaching left behind their worldly ways. You need to know that this is what we call 'immeasurable merit'.

Thus, if worldly people have compassion for their offspring, they should forthwith let them leave home life behind. If they have compassion for their parents, they should let them leave home life behind as well. For this reason, there is a poem which says the following:

> *If there were no past ages,*
> *There could not have been Buddhas in the past.*
> *If there were no Buddhas in the past,*
> *There could be no leaving home to accept the full Precepts.*

This poem is one for all Buddhas and Tathagatas. It annihilates the non-Buddhist assertion that there were no past ages. Thus, you should know that leaving home to accept the full Precepts is the Teaching of the Buddhas of the past. Fortunately, we are living in a time when leaving home life behind and accepting the full Precepts is the wondrous Teaching of the Buddhas; were we to vainly fail to leave home and accept the Precepts, it would be difficult indeed to fathom what the obstacle is. By relying upon this most modest physical existence of ours, we may well realize the most exalted merit, for it can be the greatest merit within Jambudvipa and its three worlds of desire, form, and beyond form. While this human body in Jambudvipa has not yet disappeared, we should, by all means, leave home life behind and accept the Precepts.

An ancient holy one—Master Bashumitsu—once said:

> Even though someone who has left home life behind may act counter to the Precepts, nevertheless, that person surpasses one who has kept to the Precepts while remaining in lay life. Thus, it is difficult to repay the benevolence of one who humbly gives voice to the Scriptures that encourage people to leave home life behind. Further, the one who encourages others to leave home life behind is simply someone who is encouraging the practicing of the most venerable of deeds. The karmic recompense that results from this surpasses even that of Lord Yama, a Wheel-turning Lord, or the guardian deity Shakrendra. Thus, it is difficult to repay the benevolence of one who humbly gives voice to the Scriptures that

encourage people to leave home life behind. There is no case where Scriptures encourage people to accept just the Precepts of a lay follower, hence that practice is not substantiated by the Scriptures.

Keep in mind that once you have left home life behind, even if you then act counter to one of the restrictive Precepts, your practice surpasses remaining in home life and not acting counter to the lay Precepts. By taking refuge in the Buddha, leaving home life behind, and accepting the Precepts, you will invariably excel. The recompense from leaving home life behind surpasses that of a Lord Yama, a Wheel-turning Lord, and a Shakrendra. Even had you been a peasant or an untouchable in India, if you left home life behind, you would surpass those of the warrior caste, as well as surpass a Lord Yama, a Wheel-turning Lord, or a Shakrendra. The Precepts of those who remain in home life are not like this, therefore you should leave home life behind. Keep in mind that what the World-honored One taught cannot be fully measured, even though His teachings were collected from far and wide by the World-honored Master Bashumitsu, along with his five hundred arhats. Truly, you need to keep in mind that when it comes to the Buddha's Dharma, you must be clear about Its fundamental principles. Mundane teachers of recent times have not been able to fathom the wisdom from the three spiritual insights and six spiritual abilities of a single saintly person, much less that of the five hundred saintly arhats![11] These saintly ones knew what mundane teachers of recent times do not know, they have seen what these teachers have not seen, and they have realized what these others have not realized. There is nothing that mundane teachers know that was unknown to these saintly ones. So, do not compare the ignorant and foolish explanations of mundane teachers with the insightful words of the saintly.

---

11. The three spiritual insights are the recognition of universal impermanence, universal suffering, and the universal absence of any permanent, unchanging self. Dōgen discussed the six spiritual abilities in detail in Discourse 24: On the Marvelous Spiritual Abilities *(Jinzū)*.

It says in the 120th fascicle of the *Vibāshā Commentary*, "Even one who has given rise to the intention to realize Buddhahood and then leaves home life behind is already called a saintly one. How much more so is one who has attained awareness of the Four Noble Truths!" Keep in mind that one who has given rise to the intention to realize Buddhahood and then leaves home life behind is already called a saintly one.

Among Shakyamuni Buddha's five hundred great vows, number 137 is as follows:

> In the future, after I have fully realized true enlightenment, if there are any who desire to leave home life behind to be within the Dharma, I vow that they will know no obstacles due to physical weakness, loss of memory, emotional distress, pride, lack of reverence, being foolish, lacking wise discernment, being entangled in many defiling passions, or being mentally distracted. Should it be otherwise, then I have not realized true enlightenment.

His vow number 138 is as follows:

> In the future, after I have fully realized true enlightenment, if there are any women who desire to leave home life behind to study My Teaching and take the Great Precepts, I vow to help them accomplish the Way. Should it be otherwise, then I have not realized true enlightenment.

His vow number 314 is as follows:

> In the future, after I have fully realized true enlightenment, if there are human beings whose good roots are few, but who give rise to feelings of love for their good roots and delight in them, I will help them leave home life behind to study the Way within the

Buddha Dharma, and I will help them dwell peacefully within the ten immaculate Precepts. Should it be otherwise, then I have not realized true enlightenment.

Keep in mind that the good sons and daughters who have left home life behind have all received assistance from the strength of His great vows made long ago in the past, and thus have been able, unhindered, to leave home life behind and accept the Precepts. Through His vows, the Tathagata has already been helping us to leave home life behind. Clearly, He is saying that leaving home is the most venerable, unsurpassed great merit.

The Buddha once said:

Moreover, if there are any who follow My example by shaving their head, putting on a kesa, and accepting the Precepts, then anyone who makes alms offerings to them will ultimately succeed in entering the fortress that is free from fear of temptations. Because this is the way things are, I teach in this manner.

Even if someone with a shaven head dons a kesa but does not take the Precepts, anyone who makes an alms offering to that person will enter the fortress that is free from fear of temptations.[12] The Buddha also said the following:

And further, if there is someone who, for My sake, has undertaken leaving home life behind and has donned a kesa, but has not yet taken the Precepts, should someone who is devoid of the Teaching torment or harm this person, even going so far as to undertake to destroy the Dharma Body and the Reward Body of a

---

12.   That is, the person making the alms offering may not know whether the monk has taken the Precepts or not and will, therefore, still receive the merit of their offering.

Buddha of the three temporal worlds,[13] it will be because they are fully committed to the three evil worlds of existence."[14]

If there are any human beings who, for My sake, have left home life behind, shaved their head, and donned a kesa, even though they have not kept to the Precepts, they are already stamped with the Nirvana seal.[15] Further, if they have left home life behind but do not keep to the Precepts, should anyone who is devoid of the Teaching then speak ill of them, humiliate them, or insult them, or should strike, bind, or cut them by using a hand, a sword, or a stick, or if that person should steal their kesa or their monk's bowl, or steal from them their various monastic necessities, then such a one acts to harm the real Reward Body of the Buddhas of the three temporal worlds and offends the eyes of all humans, both the ordinary and the lofty. Because this person wants to hide the seeds of the true Teaching and the Three Treasures which Buddhas possess, and because this person is interfering with the ability of both the lofty and the worldly to receive the benefits of these seeds, it will cause such a one to fall into some hellish state because this person, out of his conceit, is broadening the roads to the three evil worlds of existence.

Keep in mind that when people shave their heads and dye their robes a monkish color, even though they may not keep to the Precepts, they are still stamped with the supremely great Nirvana seal. If someone worries them, that person aims at injuring

---

13. The Reward Body is the *Sambhogakaya*, the second of the three Bodies of the Buddha. The first is the Truth Body *(Dharmakaya)*, which represents Absolute Truth or Buddha Mind Itself. The Reward Body represents the blissful reward of Buddhist training. The third is the Transformation Body *(Nirmanakaya)*, which is the physical body of the Buddha as it appears in the world.

14. That is, they are acting like a savage beast, a hungry ghost, or a power-mad asura.

15. The Nirvana seal is associated with the stillness that derives from the keeping to the Noble Eightfold Path.

the Reward Body of the Buddhas of the three temporal worlds, which is equivalent to a traitorous wrongdoing. Clearly keep in mind that the merits of leaving home life behind go hand-in-hand with the Buddhas of the three temporal worlds.

The Buddha also once said:

> Now then, those who leave home life behind ought not give rise to evil acts. Should they give rise to evil acts, then they have not left behind worldly ways. The body and speech of those who have left home life behind are in accord. When they are not in accord, then there is no leaving home life behind. When I left home life behind in order to explore the Way, I gave up parents, brothers, wife and child, relatives, and acquaintances. It was a time when I was accumulating meritorious insights; it was not a time for accumulating non-meritorious insights. 'Meritorious insights' means having compassion for all living beings as if they were one's own offspring. 'Non-meritorious insights' are altogether different from these.

Based on this, what is inherent in leaving home life behind is having compassion for all living beings as if they were one's own offspring. This means not giving rise to evil acts, and our body and speech being in mutual accord. Since this is what one's leaving home life behind is like, its merit will be like what the Buddha also said:

> Furthermore, Shariputra, if bodhisattvas and mahasattvas[*]
> wish to realize supreme, fully perfected enlightenment, then on that
> very day when they leave home life behind, they should wish to turn
> the Wheel of the Dharma, because immeasurably great numbers of
> sentient beings have not been able to accept the whole of the
> Dharma. When they turn the Wheel of the Dharma, if they desire to
> free their own minds from the taint of delusions and enable
> immeasurably numerous sentient beings to realize supreme, fully

perfected enlightenment without regressing or turning away from it, then they should learn the *prajñāpāramitā*, which is the wisdom needed to help ferry all sentient beings to the Other Shore."

The bodhisattvas who have learned the *prajñāpāramitā* are our Ancestors, one after the other. At the same time, supreme, fully perfected enlightenment is invariably brought to maturity on the very day when one leaves home life behind. Even so, as students of the Way, you need to know that when bodhisattvas do the practice that is identical with enlightenment for three eons of indefinite length or for immeasurable eons of indefinite length, they do not taint that practice with notions of its being limited or unlimited.

If a bodhisattva-mahasattva were to think, "At some point in time, I will undoubtedly relinquish my position in our country and leave home life behind. On that day I will realize supreme enlightened wisdom. And on that day I will turn the wondrous Wheel of the Dharma, whereupon I will help immeasurable, countless living beings depart from the spiritual dust and dirt of life, and produce the immaculate Eye of the Dharma. Also, I will help immeasurable, countless living beings completely bring to an end all the taint from their delusions and set free the Wisdom in their heart. Also, I will be able to help immeasurable, countless living beings keep from regressing or turning aside from their supreme enlightenment." Then, this bodhisattva-mahasattva should, by all means, study the *Wisdom Scriptures.*

This describes the merit of the Buddha's coming into existence in a royal palace as a bodhisattva embodied for the final time, and of His relinquishing His position in His country in order to realize genuine enlightenment and turn the Wheel of the Dharma to help all sentient being reach the Other Shore.

There is a biography of the Buddha that has the following account:

> Prince Siddhārtha took from His charioteer Chandaka's side a sword whose hilt was encrusted with the seven precious jewels* and other gems. Grasping the sword with His right hand, He drew it from its scabbard. With His left hand, He then took hold of His shell-shaped topknot, which was the deep blue color of a water lily, and with His right hand He cut it off. Then with His left hand, He dedicated it before discarding it by throwing it into the sky. At that moment, there arose in the Celestial Lord Indra a great joy, something that he was not accustomed to feeling. He caught hold of the Prince's topknot and, not allowing it to touch the ground, he wrapped it in a wondrous celestial robe for safe keeping. Then all manner of celestial beings made their most excellent offerings to it out of respect.

This is how the Tathagata Shakyamuni, whilst still a prince, came to climb over the walls of the palace in the middle of the night and, with the coming of the morning, went into the mountains and cut off the hair from His own head. At that time, the celestial beings from the Heaven of Pure Abiding came down to shave His head and offer Him the kesa.[16] This is undoubtedly an auspicious sign of a Tathagata emerging in the world and is the usual way with World-honored Buddhas.

Not even one Buddha, at any place or at any time, has ever realized Buddhahood whilst remaining in home life. Because there have been Buddhas in the past, the merit of leaving home life behind and taking the Precepts exists. A sentient being's realizing the Way invariably depends on leaving home life behind and accepting the Precepts. In short, because the merits of leaving home life behind and accepting the Precepts are the customary way of Buddhas, the merits of these acts are

---

16. The Heaven of Pure Abiding is the highest of the celestial abodes that comprise the world of form.

beyond measure. Some people are of the opinion that one may realize Buddhahood whilst holding onto lay life, and likewise, some think that one may realize Buddhahood whilst holding onto distinctions based on gender, but these views are not accurate.[17]

During the time of our Fourth Indian Ancestor, the Venerable Ubakikuta, there was a certain rich man's son by the name of Daitaka. He came to the Venerable One and, bowing low, sincerely sought to leave home life behind. The Venerable One said, "Are you leaving home life in body, or are you leaving home life in mind?"

Daitaka responded, "I have come to leave home life behind, but it is not for the sake of my body or my mind."

The Venerable One then asked him, "If it is not for the sake of your body or your mind, well then, who is it that is leaving home life behind?"

Daitaka responded, "Well, those who leave home life behind do so because there is no 'I, me, my, or mine'. Because they have no 'I, me, my, or mine', their Mind is not subject to arising and passing away. The Mind's not arising and passing away is the normal procedure. And it is normal for Buddhas, as well; Their mind has no characteristic form, and it is the same with Their body."

The Venerable One then said, "You will undoubtedly have a great awakening, and your mind will quite naturally fully comprehend the Matter.* Well and good. Through your devotion to Buddha, Dharma, and Sangha, you will inherit Their saintly seeds and help Them flourish." He then had Daitaka leave home life behind and receive ordination.

---

17. Dōgen's views on gender-based distinctions are clearly enunciated in the second half of Discourse 10: On 'Respectful Bowing Will Secure for You the Very Marrow of the Way' *(Raihai Tokuzui)*.

Well, now, to meet the Dharma of the Buddhas and leave home life behind is the foremost form of excellent karmic recompense for good deeds done in the past. That process is not done for the sake of 'me', nor for the sake of 'mine', nor for the sake of 'my body and mind', for it was not Daitaka's body and mind that left home life behind. It is no different from the underlying principle that what leaves home life behind is not an 'I' or a 'mine'. When it is not a matter of 'me' and 'mine', it will be the process of Buddhas, for it is simply a Buddha's customary way. Because it is a Buddha's customary way, it is not only beyond 'I' or 'mine', it is also beyond 'my body and mind'. It is beyond comparison with those in the three worlds of desire, form, and beyond form. Because this is the way things are, leaving home life behind is the supreme method. It is beyond sudden and gradual, beyond certainty and uncertainty, beyond something that comes and something that goes, beyond what has been ever-abiding and what is newly fashioned, beyond what is broad and what is narrow, beyond the large and the small, and beyond what is dependent on circumstances and what is independent of circumstances. There has never been a case of an Ancestral Master of the genuine Transmission of the Buddha Dharma failing to leave home life behind and accept the Precepts. The underlying principle of Daitaka's present encountering of the Venerable Ubakikuta for the first time and seeking to leave home life behind was no different. He left home life behind, received ordination, trained under the Venerable Ubakikuta, and ultimately became our Fifth Ancestral Master.

Our Seventeenth Indian Ancestor, the Venerable Sōgyanandai, was the son of Ratnavyūha, the King of Koshala, who dwelt in the capital city of Shravasti. No sooner had he been born than he could speak, constantly praising Buddhist matters. By the age of seven he had lost interest in worldly pleasures and, speaking in verse, he announced the following to his parents:

> *Prostrating myself before you, my most wise father,*
> *And bowing to you, mother of my bones and blood,*
> *I now desire to leave home life behind,*
> *Praying for your happiness for the compassion you*
> *have shown me.*

His parents firmly forbade this, whereupon he stopped eating that very day. Because of this, they permitted him to leave home life behind while continuing to stay in their home. They give him the name of Sōgyanandai and appointed a monk named Zenrita to be his teacher.[18] By his nineteenth year, he had still not regressed or lost interest in his training. This Venerable One kept saying to himself, "My body resides in a royal palace, so how can that be 'leaving home?'" One night, a bright light poured down from the heavens and Sōgyanandai saw that it illumined a broad, level pathway. Without thinking, he slowly walked down it for some ten miles until he arrived before a huge grotto. There was a stone cavern, which he entered, settling down in its quietude. His father had, by that time, discovered the loss of his son. Thereupon, he sent Zenrita from the palace out into the countryside to search for his son, but he did not find the young man's whereabouts. After ten years had passed, the Venerable One realized the Dharma and received the confirmation. He then traveled to the kingdom of Madai, teaching as he went.

The terms 'remaining in home life' and 'leaving home life behind' were first heard of at this time. An excellent example of this is Sōgyanandai's finding the broad road within the celestial light. As a result of the help received from his good deeds in past lives, he was finally able to leave the royal palace and arrive at the stone cavern.

---

18.   Zenrita is the Japanese reading of the Chinese characters used to spell out the monk's name in Sanskrit, but it is not certain what the actual Sanskrit equivalent is.

Those who have no interest in worldly amusements and who deplore the dust and dirt of defiling passions are saintly ones. Those who crave the stimulation of their five senses and give no thought to freeing themselves from the tyranny of the senses are truly foolish and confused. The T'ang dynasty emperors T'ai-tsung and Su-tsung often associated with monastics, but they still coveted their royal position and never cast it aside. Daikan Enō, while still a layman, had already left his mother, becoming our Sixth Ancestor due to the merits of his having left home life behind. Layman Hō'on cast aside his worldly treasures, but he did not cast aside his defiling passions, which can be called the height of folly.[19] Daikan Enō's strength in the Way and Hō'on's method of practice are not to be compared. Those who are clear about the Matter invariably leave home life behind, whereas those who are in the dark end up at home, which creates the causes and conditions that produce misfortunate karmic recompense.

One day, Meditation Master Nangaku Ejō spontaneously came out with this laudatory remark:

> Well now, leaving home life behind is done for the sake of
> the Dharma, which goes beyond anything that arises. There is
> nothing that surpasses It in the heavens above or among humankind.

His phrase, 'the Dharma, which goes beyond anything that arises' refers to the Tathagata's true Teaching, which is why nothing surpasses It in the heavens above or among humankind. 'In the heavens above' refers to the six heavens in the world of desire, the eighteen heavens in the world of form, and the four heavens in the world beyond form, yet none of them can compare with the way of leaving home life behind.

---

19. A lay person who originally studied under Sekitō Kisen, but who went on to become a lay disciple of Baso Dōitsu.

Meditation Master Banzan Hōshaku once said:

> O my virtuous meditative monks, the practice of the Way
> that hits the bull's-eye resembles the earth holding aloft a mountain
> without realizing that it is a solitary peak, or it is like a stone in
> which a jewel is embedded without the stone realizing how flawless
> the jewel is. Whoever is like this is called one who has left home
> life behind.

The true Teaching of the Buddhas and Ancestors is not necessarily concerned with
realizing or not realizing something. Because leaving home life behind is the true
Teaching of the Buddhas and Ancestors, its spiritual merit is evident.

Meditation Master Rinzai Gigen in Chienchou Province once said:

> Well now, those who have left home life behind should be
> able to correctly discern what a normal, reliable view is. They
> should be able to distinguish between a Buddha and a demon,
> between the true and the false, between the worldly and the saintly.
> If someone is able to discern things in this way, we call that one
> someone who has left home life behind. If someone cannot
> distinguish a demon from a Buddha, we invariably call such a
> person someone who leaves one home only to enter another home
> and who thereby creates karma. We cannot consider such a person
> to be one who has genuinely left home life behind.

What he calls 'a normal, reliable view' means having such things as a deep conviction
in cause and effect, and a deep faith in the Three Treasures. What he calls
'distinguishing a Buddha' means being clear in realizing what the merits of a Buddha
are, both as to their cause and as to their result. It is being able to clearly distinguish

between the genuine and the fake, the mundane and the saintly. When it comes to demons and Buddhas, if you are not clear about the difference, you will sacrifice your practice of the Way, regressing or turning away from it. If you detect the doings of demons and do not pursue those activities, then you will not be regressing from your ability to discern the Way. We consider this to be the method of someone who has truly left home life behind. There are many who vainly consider the doings of demons to be the Buddha Dharma. It is the mistake of modern times. You who are learning should quickly recognize demons, be clear about Buddhas, and practice the Way, which is enlightenment itself.

At the time of the Tathagata's entering His parinirvana, the bodhisattva Makakashō said to the Buddha, "O World-honored One, since a Tathagata is equipped with the ability to know what someone's spiritual conditions are, You surely must have known that Sunakshatra would sever his good spiritual roots. What conditions caused You to allow him to leave home life behind?"[20]

The Buddha responded, "O My good disciple, in the past when I first left home life behind, my younger half-brother Nanda, along with my cousins Ananda and Devadatta, as well as my son Rahula, among others in My clan, all followed Me in leaving home life behind in order to train in the Way. Had I not allowed Sunakshatra to leave home life behind, he would ultimately have inherited the royal position of king. Had he been free to exert that power, he might have destroyed the Buddha Dharma. Because of this condition, I allowed him to leave home life behind and practice

---

20. Sunakshatra is said to have been one of Prince Siddhārtha's close relatives who, as a monk, served as a personal attendant to the Buddha. Though he was well informed in all the Buddha's Teachings, he later returned to lay life where he reviled the Three Treasures. As a result, he is said to have fallen into a state of hellish suffering during his lifetime.

the Way. O My good disciple, had Sunakshatra not left home life behind to become a monk, he would still have severed his good roots and, for untold generations, he would have had no spiritual benefits at all. Now, after someone has left home life behind, were that person to cut off his good spiritual roots, he would still be able to keep to the Precepts by donating his services, as well as showing his respect, to those who were long-time monks, greatly experienced monks, and virtuous persons, and by practicing the four stages of meditation. These are called good causes that can give rise to good ways. If people have already given rise to good ways, they will be practicing and learning the Way. If they are already practicing and learning the Way, they can realize supreme, fully perfected enlightenment. This is why I let Sunakshatra leave home life behind. O My good disciple, if I had not let Sunakshatra leave home life and take the Precepts as a monk, then I could not be called a Tathagata possessing the ten abilities.[21] O My good disciple, a Buddha recognizes whether a human being is possessed of virtuous or non-virtuous ways. Even though this man Sunakshatra possessed both these ways, in time he succeeded in severing all his good roots until he possessed only non-virtuous roots. And why? Because such human beings have no close friends who are spiritually good, they do not pay attention to the True Teaching, they do not think of what is spiritually good, and they do not act in accord with the Dharma.

---

21.   The ten abilities of a Tathagata are (1) recognizing what is right or wrong under any circumstances; (2) recognizing what everyone's karma is in past, present, and future; (3) comprehending the various forms of meditation; (4) recognizing the superior or inferior qualities of others; (5) recognizing the desires of others; (6) recognizing the spiritual lineage of others; (7) recognizing which of the six worlds of existence someone is headed for; (8) knowing the past lives of others; (9) recognizing everyone's patterns of birth and death; and (10) knowing how to destroy all delusions within oneself and others.

This is why they sever all their good roots until they possess only non-virtuous roots.

Keep in mind that the World-honored Tathagata was quite aware that there were human beings who might cut off their good roots; still, out of His great benevolence and great compassion, He let them leave home life behind in order to give them a cause to be virtuous. The causes of cutting off one's good roots are due to failing to associate with virtuous friends, failing to listen to the true Teaching, failing to think about what is good, and failing to act in accord with the Dharma. You who are now learning the Way must keep close to morally good friends and be on intimate terms with them. What we call 'a good friend' is someone who asserts that Buddhas do exist and teaches us that there is wrongdoing, as well as happiness. One who does not deny cause and effect is considered a good friend and a good counselor. What such a one gives expression to is the true Teaching. To think about this principle is to think about what is good. To act in this way will be to act in accord with the Dharma. Thus, regardless of whether people choose to be our intimates or not, you should simply recommend that they leave home life behind and take the Precepts. Do not pay attention to whether or not they later regress, and do not worry about whether they do the practice or not, for this is doubtless the true Teaching of our Venerable Shakyamuni.

The Buddha, in instructing His monks, once said, "By all means, you need to keep in mind that Lord Yama gave the following teaching,[22] 'Some day I shall be free of this suffering of mine. I shall be reborn among those in the world of humans. Obtaining a human body, I will be able to leave home life behind, have my head shaved, receive the kesa of the Three Treasures, and learn the Way as one who has left home life behind.' Even a Lord Yama had these thoughts. And what is even more, you now have received the body

---

22.   Lord Yama is the Lord of the Dead.

of a human being and have had the opportunity to become monks! Because of this, my monks, you should consciously work on the actions of your body, speech, and mind, and do not allow faults to exist in them. By all means, you need to eliminate the five fetters and put into practice the five good roots.[23] Monks like you should certainly do just such training."

At this time the monks, having heard what the Buddha expressed through words, were filled with joy and devotedly undertook to act upon them.

It is clear that the desire to be reborn within the human world is something longed for even by a Lord Yama. Once someone has been reborn as a human being, he or she should forthwith have their head shaved, don the kesa of the Three Treasures, and take up the study of the Way of the Buddha. These are the merits of being within the world of humans, which surpasses the other five worlds of existence. But to be born in the human world and then to wantonly seek out the path to political power or some other worldly career, vainly spending one's life as a toady to ministers and kings, wrapping oneself up in fantasies and dreams, only to proceed in later times towards pitch darkness without anything to rely upon, that is folly indeed! Not only have you received the body of a human being, which is hard to come by, but you have also encountered the Buddha Dharma, which is hard to encounter. You should forthwith cast aside all your involvements and quickly leave home life behind in order to study the Way. Rulers and ministers, along with their wives and children, their relatives and households, are encountered everywhere, but the Buddha Dharma, like the rare udumbara blossom, is hard to meet up with. In short, when impermanence suddenly arrives, there is no ruler or minister, friend or relative, spouse or child, or any precious treasure that will save us, for each of us simply returns to death's Yellow Spring

---

23. The five fetters are covetousness, hate, arrogant pride, envy, and mean-spiritedness. The five good roots are faith, diligent effort, mindfulness, meditative contemplation, and wise discernment.

alone.[24] What follows along with us is simply our good and bad karma. When we are about to lose our human body, our feelings of regret for our human body may well be deep indeed! So, while we still have our human body, we should quickly leave home life behind. Just this alone will be the true Teaching of the Buddhas of the three temporal worlds.

For those who have left home life behind in order to put the Dharma into practice, there are four things called 'the four necessities'.[25]

> *The first is to go so far in one's fleshly life as to sit*
> *beneath a tree.*
> *The second is to go so far in one's fleshly life as to wear*
> *robes made of discarded cloth.*
> *The third is to go so far in one's fleshly life as to beg*
> *for one's food.*
> *The fourth is to go so far in one's fleshly life as to take*
> *the long-abandoned, old-fashioned remedies,*
> *when physically ill.*[26]

---

24. The Yellow Spring is the Chinese equivalent of the River Styx, the river in Greek mythology that one crosses at death.

25. That is, the four necessities for sustaining life: shelter, clothing, food, and medicine.

26. The passage that Dōgen is citing comes from a seventh century text describing the ideal for a Mahayana monk. The four examples given represent the extremes to which a monk should be willing to go in order to continue on as someone who has left home life behind. All four represent practices that, in the Buddha's time, could sustain a monk's existence without requiring him or her to return to lay life. The long-abandoned, old-fashioned remedies alluded to include the ancient Indian medical practice of using the urine and dung of cattle for sterilization as well as for a variety of internal and external ailments.

If you practice all these methods, you may indeed be called one who has left home life behind and, in being given that name, you have become a member of the Sangha. If you do not practice these, you have not become what we call a member of the Sangha. For that reason, these four are called the practice of the Dharma by those who have left home life behind.

Now, what the Buddhas and Ancestors in India and China have authentically Transmitted is leaving home life behind in order to put the Dharma into practice. Those who spend their life without leaving the monastery even once are supplied with these four necessities so that they may put the Dharma into practice. This is what I call 'practicing the four necessities'. Should someone alter this by trying to establish a fifth necessity, you need to know that this is a false teaching.[27] Who could accept it in good faith? Who could bear to hear such a thing? What the Buddhas and Ancestors have correctly Transmitted, that is the true Teaching. Accordingly, those human beings who have left home life behind are supremely fortunate and most worthy of our veneration. For this reason, Nanda, Ananda, Devadatta, Aniruddha, Mahānāma, and Bhadrika, all of whom were grandsons of King Simhahanu and were of the most noble in the warrior caste in India, quickly left home life behind, which should be an excellent example for succeeding generations.[28] Those who are not warriors today should not regret who they are. For those who may well not be princes, what can there possibly be to regret? The noblest of families in Jambudvipa ended up as the noblest in the human realms, that is, they left home life behind. Rulers of lesser nations, like those of the Licchavi multitudes, were wont to prize that which is not worth prizing, to flaunt what is not worth flaunting, to confine themselves to what is not worth

---

27. The so-called 'fifth necessity' is sex.

28. Simhahanu was Siddhārtha's grandfather on his father's side.

abiding with, <u>and</u> not to leave home life behind.[29] Who could fail to see that they were bunglers? Who could fail to see that they were foolish people?

The Venerable Rahula was the son of the Bodhisattva.[30] And he was the great-grandson of King Simhahanu, who would have bequeathed the throne to him were it not for the World-honored One's influencing him to leave home life behind. You need to know that the Dharma of leaving home life behind is the most venerated. As the disciple foremost in keeping to the Precepts, Rahula has yet to enter nirvana. Even to this day, as an arhat he helps human beings to abide in this world as in a cultivated field of happiness.

Among our Indian Ancestral Masters to whom the Buddha's Treasure House of the Eye of the True Teaching was Transmitted, there has been an abundance of princes who left home life behind. Our first Ancestor in China, Bodhidharma, was the third son of the King of the Indian state of Kōshi. Not taking his royal position as something of importance, he received the Transmission of the true Teaching and held to It. It should be clear to you that he held leaving home life behind in greatest veneration. While he may not have held a station that was the equal of those other princes, he was in a position where he was able to leave home life behind. So why would he not hasten to do so? What kind of tomorrow should he have waited for? Were he to leave home life behind right off, not waiting to inhale and exhale a single breath, that would be wise indeed. Also, keep in mind that our Master, one who has left home life behind and accepted the Precepts, is due the same gratitude and appreciation which we owe to our parents.

It says in the first fascicle of the *Procedures for Cleanliness in a Zen Temple:*

All Buddhas in the three temporal worlds—past, present, and future—affirm that to leave home life behind is to realize the

---

29. The Licchavis were thought to be among the earliest supporters of the Buddha, but not to the extent that they left home life behind.

30. The Bodhisattva here is Prince Siddhārtha prior to his enlightenment.

Truth. The twenty-eight Indian Ancestors and the six Chinese Ancestors, all of whom Transmitted the Buddha's Mind seal,* were, each and every one of them, monastics. Most likely, it was because they strictly observed the monastic regulations that they were able to become outstanding models for those in the three worlds of desire, form, and beyond form. Thus, in practicing meditation and inquiring of the Way with their Master, they made the Precepts and the monastic regulations foremost. Had they not distanced themselves from their faults and guarded against misdeeds, how could they have realized Buddhahood and become an Ancestor?

Even if one's monastery has become subject to the winds of decay, it may still be a grove of fragrant trees in full bloom, a grove that has not fallen to the level of ordinary trees or commonplace sproutings. Then again, it may be like milk diluted with water. When we want to make use of milk, we should use this milk that has been diluted with water, but we should not use any other substance.[31]

Thus, what is most revered is the genuine Transmission of what all Buddhas in the three temporal worlds teach as the Dharma of leaving home life behind. Furthermore, there has never been a single Buddha of the three temporal worlds who failed to leave home life behind, for this is the Treasure House of the Eye of the True Teaching, which is the Wondrous Heart of Nirvana and supreme enlightenment, as accurately Transmitted from Buddha to Buddha and from Ancestor to Ancestor.

A day during the summer retreat in the seventh year of the Kenchō era (1255).

Copied here on the sixth day of the eighth lunar month in the third year of the Enkyō
    era
(August 30, 1310).

---

31.   That is, even though milk may be diluted with water, it is still milk. This is a metaphor for the Dharma. Undiluted milk refers to the Dharma in its purest form. Diluted milk refers to the Dharma that has been simplified to make it more accessible to people, but it is still the Buddha Dharma.

83

On Receiving the Precepts

(Jukai)

Translator's Introduction: In this discourse, Dōgen presents the ceremony of taking the Mahayana Precepts. In the Sōtō Zen tradition, the form of these Mahayana Precepts derives from the *Scripture of Brahma's Net*. They are traditionally given to the laity when they decide that they wish to live their lives as Buddhists, to those who are being ordained as novice monks, and to a novice monk as part of the ceremonial associated with Transmission. These Bodhisattva Precepts are distinct from the 250 preceptual regulations for male monastics and the 348 preceptual regulations for female monastics, which address everyday problems that may arise for those living in a monastic or hermetic setting.

In the *Procedures for Cleanliness in a Zen Temple* it says the following:

All Buddhas in the three temporal worlds—past, present, and future—affirm that to leave home life behind is to realize the Truth. The twenty-eight Indian Ancestors and the six Chinese Ancestors, all of whom Transmitted the Buddha's Mind seal,* were, each and every one of them, monastics. Most likely, it was because they strictly observed the monastic regulations that they were able to become outstanding models for those in the three worlds of desire, form, and beyond form. Thus, in practicing meditation and inquiring of the Way with their Master, they made the Precepts and the monastic regulations foremost. Had they not distanced themselves from their faults and guarded against misdeeds, how could they have realized Buddhahood and become Ancestors?

As to the method for doing the ordination ceremony of Taking the Precepts, three types of kesas* and a set of mealtime bowls, along with fresh, clean robes, are provided for the one to be ordained. If new robes are not available, be sure to launder old ones,

---

*   See *Glossary.*

but you must not use borrowed kesas or a borrowed bowl set to put on the altar when doing the ceremony of Taking the Precepts. Concentrate wholeheartedly and take care not to get distracted by side issues. Assuming the form of a Buddha, being provided with the Precepts and the monastic regulations, and acquiring what the Buddha received and made use of are, by no means, small matters, so how could you possibly treat them lightly? Were you to borrow someone's kesas or bowl set, and then go up to the altar to take the Precepts, you would not really be obtaining the Precepts. Should you never receive the Precepts, you will be a person devoid of the Precepts for the whole of your life as you vainly cross over the threshold of empty scholasticism, meaninglessly accepting alms given in good faith. Those entering the path with a beginner's mind may not as yet have memorized the rules and regulations. Should their Master offer no guidance, they will lapse into error. What I am saying here is stern advice indeed. Dare I hope that you will engrave it on your heart? If you have taken the monastic Precepts, by all means you should also take the Bodhisattva* Precepts, for They are foremost for those who would enter the Teaching.

In India and China, whenever an Ancestor of the Buddha passed on the Transmission, without fail, the Precepts were accepted as the first act of entering the Dharma. Unless we accept the Precepts, we are not yet a disciple of the Buddhas, nor are we an offspring of our Ancestral Masters, because They have considered one's departing from error and resisting wrong to be synonymous with practicing meditation and inquiring of the Way. The words, "They have made the Precepts foremost," are already precisely what the Treasure House of the Eye of the True Teaching is. Realizing Buddhahood and becoming an Ancestor have invariably been based on receiving and preserving the Transmission of the Treasure House of the Eye of the True Teaching. Ancestral Masters who have authentically Transmitted the Treasure House of the Eye of the True Teaching have invariably received and preserved the Buddha's Precepts. There cannot be an Ancestor of the Buddha who has not received and preserved the

Precepts. There are Those who received and preserved them in compliance with the Tathagata, and there are Those who received and preserved them in compliance with a disciple of the Buddha, all of whom received the bloodline thereby.

The Buddhist Precepts, which have now been authentically Transmitted from Buddha to Buddha and from Ancestor to Ancestor, were Transmitted only by our Ancestral Founder Bodhidharma, the Abbot of Mount Sūzan, until They came down through five Transmissions in China to our Founding Ancestor of Mount Sōkei, Daikan Enō. Although the genuine Transmission of Seigen Gyōshi and Nangaku Ejō and beyond has been conveyed to us of the present day, there are those senior monks who have never recognized the Precepts and could care less. Oh, how extremely pitiful they are!

As has been said, we should receive and accept the Bodhisattva Precepts, for this is how we reach the entryway into the Dharma. This is something that we need to know in our exploration through our practice with our Master. This procedure of receiving and accepting the Bodhisattva Precepts has invariably been correctly Transmitted to those of us who have explored the Matter* through our long-standing training within the private quarters of an Ancestor of the Buddha. It is not something that those who are lazy or indifferent achieve. This procedure invariably involves lighting incense and doing prostrations before our Ancestral Master Bodhidharma, and then asking if we may receive the Bodhisattva Precepts. Once we have been given permission, we bathe that we may purify ourselves. We then put on clean, new robes. Or, we may wash our previous robes, strew flowers, burn incense, and perform prostrations to show our reverence, after which we put those robes on. We respectfully bow to the altar images, to the Three Treasures, and to our venerable Ancestors, ridding ourselves of any obstructions. Thereby we can purify our body and mind. This procedure has been accurately Transmitted for ever so long from within the private quarters of Ancestors of the Buddha. After this, the presiding teacher of the Monks' Training Hall invites the ordinand to make a prostration and then recite the following refuges, while kneeling upright with hands in gasshō:*

> *I humbly take refuge in the Buddha,*
> *I humbly take refuge in the Dharma,*
> *I humbly take refuge in the Sangha.*

> *I humbly take refuge in the Buddha, the most venerated among humans,*
> *I humbly take refuge in the Dharma, the most venerated among those who have forsaken their passions,*
> *I humbly take refuge in the Sangha, the most venerated among those in our assemblies.*

> *I have taken refuge in the Buddha,*
> *I have taken refuge in the Dharma,*
> *I have taken refuge in the Sangha.*

(Repeat the above refuges three times.)

Ordinand: "The Truth of the supreme, fully perfected enlightenment which was realized by the Tathagata is my great Teacher, in which I will take refuge from now on. From now on, I shall not seek refuge in the demons of heresy or in those outside the Way, because I shall have His compassion and benevolence."

(Repeat the above words three times. After the third time, repeat three more times the line "I shall have His compassion and benevolence.")

Preceptor: "Good disciple, you have discarded past evils and been converted to the Truth. The Precepts have already embraced you. Now you are about to receive the Three Pure Precepts.

"The first is the Precept of Ceasing from Evil. From this present state of yours to that of becoming Buddha, will you keep this Precept or not?"

Ordinand: "I will."

(Asked three times, answered three times.)

> Preceptor: "The second is the Precept of Doing Only Good. From this present state of yours to that of becoming Buddha, will you keep this Precept or not?"
> Ordinand: "I will."

(Asked three times, answered three times.)

> Preceptor: "The third is the Precept of Doing What Is Good for the Sake of All Sentient Beings. From this present state of yours to that of becoming Buddha, will you keep this Precept or not?"
> Ordinand: "I will."

(Asked three times, answered three times.)

> Preceptor: "You must not violate the preceding Three Pure Precepts. From this present state of yours to that of becoming Buddha, will you keep these Precepts or not?"
> Ordinand: "I will."

(Asked three times, answered three times.)

> Preceptor: "This is how you must keep Them."

The ordinand then does three prostrations, ending by kneeling straight up with hand in gasshō.

> Preceptor: "Good disciple, you have already received the Three Pure Precepts. Now you are about to receive the Ten Great Precepts. These are the Great Immaculate Precepts of all Buddhas and Bodhisattvas.
> "The first is 'Do not kill.' From this present state of yours to that of becoming Buddha, will you keep this Precept or not?"
> Ordinand: "I will."

(Asked three times, answered three times.)

Preceptor: "The second is 'Do not steal.' From this present state of yours to that of becoming Buddha, will you keep this Precept or not?"

Ordinand: "I will."

(Asked three times, answered three times.)

Preceptor: "The third is 'Do not covet.' From this present state of yours to that of becoming Buddha, will you keep this Precept or not?"

Ordinand: "I will."

(Asked three times, answered three times.)

Preceptor: "The fourth is 'Do not say that which is untrue.' From this present state of yours to that of becoming Buddha, will you keep this Precept or not?"

Ordinand: "I will."

(Asked three times, answered three times.)

Preceptor: "The fifth is 'Do not sell the wine of delusion.' From this present state of yours to that of becoming Buddha, will you keep this Precept or not?"

Ordinand: "I will."

(Asked three times, answered three times.)

Preceptor: "The sixth is 'Do not speak against others, be they laity or monastics.' From this present state of yours to that of Buddha, will you keep this Precept or not?"

Ordinand: "I will."

(Asked three times, answered three times.)

Preceptor: "The seventh is 'Do not be proud of yourself and devalue others.' From this present state of yours to that of becoming Buddha, will you keep this Precept or not?"

Ordinand: "I will."

(Asked three times, answered three times.)

Preceptor: "The eighth is 'Do not be mean in giving either Dharma or material possessions.' From this present state of yours to that of becoming Buddha, will you keep this Precept or not?"

Ordinand: "I will."

(Asked three times, answered three times.)

Preceptor: "The ninth is 'Do not be angry.' From this present state of yours to that of Buddha, will you keep this Precept or not?"

Ordinand: "I will."

(Asked three times, answered three times)

Preceptor: "The tenth is 'Do not defame the Three Treasures.' From this present state of yours to that of becoming Buddha, will you keep this Precept or not?"

Ordinand: "I will keep It."

(Asked three times, answered three times.)

Preceptor: "The preceding Three Refuges, Three Pure Precepts, and Ten Great Precepts are what all Buddhas receive and keep to. From this present state of yours to that of becoming Buddha, will you keep these Precepts or not?"

Ordinand: "I will."

(Asked three times, answered three times.)

Preceptor: "These are what you should keep to."

The ordinand does three prostrations, coming back to kneeling straight up with hands in gasshō. The Preceptor and the ordinand together then chant the following verse in Sanskrit:

We live in the world as if in the sky,

Just as the lotus blossom is not wetted by the
water that surrounds it.

The mind is immaculate and beyond the dust.

Let us bow to the highest Lord.

When this is finished, they recite the following:

Homage to the Buddha,

Homage to the Dharma,

Homage to the Sangha.

The ordinand then leaves the Training Hall.

This ceremony of receiving the Precepts is what the Buddhas and Ancestors have, beyond question, correctly Transmitted to us. Such trainees as Yakusan Igen's disciple Tanka Tennen, as well as his novice Kō, both received and kept to Them. Even though there have been Ancestral Masters who did not take the two hundred and fifty monastic precepts, there has never been an Ancestral Master who failed to take these Bodhisattva Precepts, which the Buddhas and Ancestors authentically Transmitted. And it is These that we invariably receive and preserve.

84

On the Spiritual Merits of the Kesa

(Kesa Kudoku)

Translator's Introduction: One element that is markedly different between this discourse and Discourse 12: On the Transmission of the Kesa *(Den'e)* is that the present discourse has several extensive quotes from Chinese translations of Scriptural writings which Dōgen uses to clarify and support his points.

The robe and the Teaching which Buddhas have directly passed on to Buddhas, and Ancestors to Ancestors, were, beyond doubt, correctly Transmitted to China by Bodhidharma, our noble Ancestor of Mount Sūzan, and by him alone. This noble Ancestor was of the twenty-eighth generation from Shakyamuni Buddha. In India, he was the twenty-eighth in line to have legitimately received the Transmission, and, as the Twenty-eighth Ancestor, he came to China where he became known as the First Chinese Ancestor. Those of Chinese nationality made five Transmissions until coming to Daikan Enō, who became the thirty-third generation Ancestor, and was called the Sixth Chinese Ancestor. Known as the Thirty-third Ancestor Meditation Master Daikan Enō, he received the genuine Transmission of the robe and the Teaching in the middle of the night whilst on Mount Ōbai. He watched over and protected the robe for the rest of his life, and it is still enshrined in Hōrin-ji Temple on Mount Sōkei.

Successive generations of Chinese emperors have respectfully requested that this robe be brought to their court so that they might make offerings and reverently bow to it. They are persons who, as spiritual guardians, have protected it. During the T'ang dynasty, the emperors Chung-tsung, Su-tsung, and T'ai-tsung repeatedly had it brought back to court so that they might make offerings to it. Whenever they requested it or had it sent back, they would have an emissary accompany it and would issue an edict to that effect. On one occasion, Emperor T'ai-tsung, in returning the Buddha's robe to Mount Sōkei, issued the following edict, "I am now pleased to entrust to Commander General Liu Chung-ching, Pacifier of Our Nation, the returning of this robe with all courtesies. We declare this robe to be a national treasure. Venerable

1123

Abbot, I pray that you will safely enshrine it in your temple, placing it under the rigorous care and protection of those monks of your community who have personally received from you the tenets of our religion, never letting the robe fall into neglect."

Truly, it would be better than having sway over the three-thousand great-thousandfold worlds—which are as countless as the sands of the Ganges—just to have the opportunity, as ruler of some small, present-day country, to actually see the Buddha's robe and make venerative offerings to it, for such would truly be a good life within one's cycle of birth and death; it would, indeed, be the ultimate in one's life.

Surely, nowhere within the three thousand worlds in which the influence of Buddhism has extended has the kesa* been absent. Be that as it may, the only one to receive the Buddha's kesa that had been passed on from person to person, from successor to successor, was our Ancestor of Mount Sūzan in times long gone. The Buddha's kesa was not accorded to any other, subsidiary disciple. Even though the Transmission through the Bodhisattva* Bhadrapala, a subsidiary descendant of the Twenty-seventh Ancestor, was, beyond doubt, extended to Dharma Teacher Jō in the fifth century, the genuine passing on of the Buddha's kesa was not involved. Likewise, the Fourth Chinese Ancestor, Great Master Daii Dōshin, ferried Meditation Master Hōyū of Mount Gozu to the Other Shore, but he did not pass the Buddha's kesa on to him. Well, even though someone may not have received Transmission from a direct heir, nevertheless, the Tathagata's genuine Dharma is never devoid of spiritual merit, so for thousands, nay, myriads of eons, Its benefits will be great and far reaching. And, obviously, anyone who has not been Transmitted is not to be considered comparable to someone who has been Transmitted by a direct heir.

Thus, if commoners or those of more lofty status were to accept and keep to a kesa, they would need to have passed on to them the genuine Transmission which the Buddhas and Ancestors have passed on. In India and China, during those periods of the genuine and the superficial teaching of the Dharma, householders still kept to the kesa that they had accepted. But now, in these weak and degenerate times in a remote land like ours, those who shave their heads and beards and call themselves disciples of the Buddha do not keep to the kesa that they have received. Alas, they still

---

* See *Glossary.*

do not believe, or know, or clearly understand that they should keep to what they have accepted, to say nothing of their lack of knowledge about its materials, colors, or measurements, much less of the ways to wear one.

The kesa, from ancient times, has been called 'the garment of liberation', for it can free us from all our obstructions, be they from the karmic* effects of our past deeds, from our defiling passions, or from the effects of our rebirth in one of the six worlds* of existence. Should a dragon be able to obtain a single thread from a kesa, it will be delivered from its three forms of burning pain.[1] Should an ox be able to touch a kesa with even one horn, its past defilements will spontaneously disappear. Upon realizing Buddhahood, every Buddha, without exception, was wearing a kesa, which is obviously why wearing one is described as the most venerable and highest of spiritual merits.

True, we have been born in a remote country and have been exposed to the Dharma in Its final days, sad to say, but even so, in that we have encountered the robe and the Teaching as received by Buddha after Buddha for generation after generation, what greater joy could there be? Which other tradition has correctly Transmitted both the robe and the Dharma of the Venerable Shakyamuni as we have straightforwardly Transmitted them? Even if, in the space of a single day, we were to renounce our physical life for times as countless as the sands of the Ganges, we should still humbly make offerings to both the robe and the Dharma. Indeed, we should vow that, upon encountering them in life after life, for generation after generation, we will humbly raise them above our head, make offerings to them, and venerate them.

Even though we are separated from the Buddha's native land by more than a hundred thousand leagues of mountains and seas too difficult to traverse, nevertheless, spurred on by our good deeds in some past life, these mountains and seas do not stand as obstacles blocking our way, nor have we ever been dismissed or shunned as muddle-headed, ignorant provincials. Having respectfully encountered this genuine

---

1. Namely, suffering from fiery heat, from fierce desert winds, and from being devoured by a garuda bird.

Teaching, we put It into practice day and night to the best of our ability; keeping to this kesa which we have respectfully accepted, we guard and protect it, constantly taking joy in it. How could this possibly be due to the cultivation of spiritual merits under the tutelage of just one or two Buddhas? It must be due wholly to the cultivation of all kinds of spiritual merits under the tutelage of Buddhas as numerous as the sands of the Ganges. Even if it were due to our own efforts, we should feel respect for the robe and the Dharma and should enjoy heartfelt gratitude. We should cordially show our gratitude to the ancestral Masters for their profound kindness in Transmitting the Dharma to us. Since even animals repay kindliness, how could humans fail to understand kindness? If people do not recognize kindness, they must be even denser than animals.

When it comes to the spiritual merits of this Buddha robe and this Buddha Dharma, if there had not been Ancestral Masters who Transmitted the Buddha's True Dharma, then the rest of us would not yet be able to clarify, much less comprehend, what these merits are. If you are able to take delight in seeking out the trail left by the Buddhas, you will enjoy this Dharma all the more.

Even after a hundred thousand myriad generations, people will be able to recognize this genuine Transmission as the genuine Transmission. This <u>will</u> be the Buddha Dharma; the proof of Its authenticity will undoubtedly be evident.

Do not liken the Transmission to adding water to milk, since It more closely resembles a crown prince ascending to the throne. When we do make use of milk, even though it is that which has been diluted with water, we should still go ahead and use it if there should happen to be no other milk than that. Even if we have not added water to it, we should not use oil in its place, or lacquer, or wine.[2] The genuine Transmission may also be likened to this analogy. Even though someone is a run-of-the-mill disciple of a mediocre teacher, if there is a genuine Transmission, it will be a suitable time to 'make use of milk'. But the genuine Transmission of Buddha to

---

2.   Because milk is still milk even in a diluted form.

Buddha and Ancestor to Ancestor is more like the enthronement of a crown prince. Even the secular Confucian teachings admonish us not to wear clothing which differs from that officially worn during the time of the previous ruler, so why would a disciple of the Buddha wear any type of robe other than that which the Buddha wore?

Starting in the tenth year of the Eihei era (67 C.E.), during the reign of the Later Han dynasty emperor Hsiao-ming, monks and lay disciples went back and forth between India in the west and their homelands in the east, ceaselessly following on the heels of their predecessors, as they say. Even so, none of them reported encountering in India an Ancestral Master of the genuine Transmission from Buddha to Buddha and from Ancestor to Ancestor; none of these travelers had a record of the lineage of the Face-to-Face Transmission direct from the Tathagata. They just attended on teachers of Scriptures and Scriptural commentaries, and brought back copies of Scriptures and scholarly texts written in Sanskrit. Among them, none spoke of having met an Ancestral Master who was a genuine heir of the Buddha Dharma, nor did anyone report the existence of an Ancestral Master who had passed on to them the Buddha's kesa. It is quite clear that they had not crossed the threshold into the deeper significance of the term 'Buddha Dharma'. People like these have not clearly grasped the import of the phrase 'the genuine Transmission of the Buddhas and Ancestors'.

When the Tathagata Shakyamuni conferred on Makakashō the Dharma of Supreme Wisdom—which is the Treasure House of the Eye of the True Teaching—He passed on to him at the same time the kesa that Kashō Buddha had directly Transmitted to Him. It is the kesa that generation after generation of genuine heirs received down to Meditation Master Daikan of Mount Sōkei, who was the thirty-third heir. The material, color, and dimensions of that kesa have been passed on first-hand. Since then, the Dharma descendants of Seigen and Nangaku have directly Transmitted the Dharma in person, employing the ways taught by the Ancestors for wearing a kesa, and following the methods taught by the Ancestors for constructing them.[3] If someone has not learned the deeper meaning behind the method for washing and cleansing a kesa, as well as the procedure for accepting and keeping to one—both of which have been conferred face-to-face through the generations of successors—there is no way for that person to know of them.

The kesa is said to be of three types: the five-paneled robe, the seven-paneled robe, and the large robe of nine or more panels. Even those whose practice is the very finest accept just these three robes; they do not hoard additional robes. They use just these three robes, which are sufficient for their bodily needs.

When conducting daily business or attending to daily duties within the monastery, or when going outside to see to large or small matters, we wear a five-paneled robe. Upon our entering among the Sangha to engage in all manner of good spiritual acts,[4] we wear a seven-paneled robe. To help inculcate respect and trust whilst giving Teaching to both commoners and those in lofty positions, we should, by all means, wear a large robe of nine or more panels. Also, when alone in our quarters, we wear the five-paneled robe; when coming together with the Sangha, we wear the seven-paneled robe; when we enter a ruler's residence or go into a populous area, we should, by all means, wear the large robe. Further, in accord with times of warm weather, we wear the five-paneled robe; when the weather turns cold, we add the seven-paneled robe; and when the cold becomes intense, we also add on the large robe.

Once, in days long gone, as a mid-winter night came on, the weather turned so cold that it cracked open the bamboo. At eventide, the Tathagata was wearing a five-paneled robe. As the night grew more and more chill, He added a seven-paneled robe. In the final hours of the night, the cold weather had grown ever more intense, so

---

3.   Seigen and Nangaku were both direct Dharma heirs of Daikan Enō, thereby forming two branches within the Zen tradition.

4.   A reference to one's joining with fellow members of the Sangha for formal meditation periods and religious ceremonies.

He added on His large robe. The Buddha immediately had the thought, "In the generations yet to come, all good disciples who find the cold unbearable will be able to wrap themselves up sufficiently with these three robes."

The Methods for Wearing the Kesa

The usual method is to keep the right shoulder bare. There is a method of wearing the kesa over both shoulders, which was a custom of the Tathagata and of the more elderly and senior monks.[5] Although it is described simply as 'covering both shoulders', there are times when the chest is exposed, and times when the chest is covered. The covering of both shoulders is a time for wearing a large kesa of at least sixty pieces.[6]

When wearing an ordinary kesa, we bring both upper corners together at the left arm and shoulder, placing one atop the other. We bring the left edge to the front, letting it ride atop the right vertical edge which has been tucked in between the left arm and the torso; the left edge is draped over the left arm.[7] With a large kesa, we put the front corner over the left shoulder and drape it so that it hangs down in back. In addition to these methods, there are various other methods for wearing a kesa, which you should look into as part of your training and practice.

During the centuries of the Chinese Liang, Ch'en, Sui, T'ang, and Sung dynasties, many of the scholars of both the Greater* and the Lesser Courses* abandoned their preoccupation with lecturing on Scriptures, realizing that this was not the ultimate goal. Faring on, they strove to explore the Teaching of the genuine Transmission of the Buddhas and Ancestors, at which time they invariably discarded their previous worldly clothing and took on the kesa that the Buddhas and Ancestors

---

5.   The word Dōgen uses for 'elderly' implies age fifty and over.

6.   The sixty-piece robe refers to a fifteen-paneled kesa.

7.   Dōgen gives a somewhat more detailed description of this method in the preceding Discourse 12: On the Transmission of the Kesa *(Den'e)*.

had correctly passed on. This was truly their abandonment of what was false and their return to what was upright.

The True Teaching of the Tathagata originated in India, as we all know. Many past and present teachers have held to the shallow views of common folk, which are colored by emotionalism and narrow-mindedness. Because the Realm of Buddha and the realms of sentient beings are beyond such notions as 'having limits' or 'being without limits', the Teachings, practices, and reasoning of both the Greater and Lesser Courses will not fit within the narrow-minded thinking of common folk today. And, at the same time, there are those in China who absurdly argue that India was not the source, but that China was, and they put forth this parochial view as their own bright new idea, taking it to be Buddha Dharma. As a consequence, if those today who have awakened to their Buddha Nature are determined to accept and keep to the kesa, they should accept and keep to the genuinely Transmitted kesa; they should not accept or keep to some kesa fashioned according to someone's 'bright new idea'.

The 'genuinely Transmitted kesa' refers to the one genuinely Transmitted from Shōrin-ji Monastery through Mount Sōkei, and it is the one that has been received by generation after generation of the Tathagata's successors without missing even a single generation.[8] What those disciples of the Dharma and their Dharma disciples wore is, precisely, the genuinely Transmitted kesa. What has been newly fashioned in China is not of the genuine Transmission. Now, the members of the monastic assembly who came from India all wore the same style of kesa as that which was genuinely Transmitted by the Buddhas and Ancestors; not even one of those monks ever wore a kesa like those new-fangled Chinese ones which were fashioned by that bunch who devote themselves to a scholarly study of the monastic regulations. Ill-informed folk may trust the kesa of scholastics; those who are clear-minded toss it aside.

---

8. Shōrin-ji Monastery is associated with Bodhidharma and Mount Sōkei with Daikan Enō.

Broadly speaking, the spiritual merits of the kesa—which was passed on from Buddha to Buddha and Ancestor to Ancestor—are clear, and these merits are easy to accept and trust in. The kesa's genuine Transmission has been duly inherited; its original form has been personally handed down, and it actually exists here and now. The practice of accepting and keeping to it has come down to the present, along with the inherited Dharma. The Ancestral Masters who have received and kept to it, as both Masters and disciples, are all ones who have realized the same Truth and Transmitted Its Dharma. As a consequence, we should construct our kesas according to the methods correctly passed on by the Buddhas and Ancestors, because Their method alone is of the genuine Transmission. This is what everyone has long come to know and understand, be they everyday folk or saintly ones, commoners or lofty ones, dragons or deities.

The kesa came into being to accord with the dissemination of the Dharma. Once it has been wrapped around a body and accepted, and is being kept to for a second—or even a flash of a moment—it will become a veritable amulet, safeguarding us in our resolve to realize Supreme Wisdom.[9] Should we imbue our trusting heart with a single line of Scripture or with the whole of the kesa verse, It will be a seed for our bright-mindedness for lengthy eons to come, and will ultimately take us to Supreme Wisdom. Moreover, if we infuse our body and mind with a single Teaching or a single good practice, the result will be the same. The thoughts in our mind arise and disappear moment after moment, yet nary a one permanently abides; our body is being born and is ceasing moment after moment, yet nowhere is there a place where it permanently abides. Nevertheless, the spiritual merits of our practice will undoubtedly have their time of fruition, which will liberate us. So the kesa is not simply a manufactured thing, nor is it something that spontaneously arises in nature,

---

9.   Dōgen is not asserting that the kesa has some inherent magical property which wards off evil; rather, it protects the wearer by serving as a constant reminder of the purpose for which he or she donned the robe in the first place, as well as serving as an outer sign to others of the wearer's spiritual commitment.

nor is it something that has always existed somewhere, nor is it something that exists nowhere: it is That which Buddhas, and Buddhas alone, all ultimately realize. Be that as it may, the spiritual merits from what is realized by practitioners who accept and keep to the kesa will undoubtedly come to full fruition, and will undoubtedly take them to the Ultimate. As to those who have sown no good seeds previously, even if they were to undergo one or two lifetimes more, up through immeasurable lifetimes, they would not be able to see a kesa, or wear a kesa, or accept a kesa with a trusting heart, or clearly understand what a kesa really is. If we look at China and Japan today, we will see that there are people unable to do so, but not because they are rich or poor, nor because they are dim-witted or sharp. Clearly, the wearing of a kesa is due to the sowing of good seeds in the past.

As a consequence, those who accept and keep to the kesa should rejoice in their having sown good seeds in the past, and should not doubt that they have piled up merits and accumulated virtues. Those who have not yet acquired a kesa should aspire to one and, right away in this life, busy themselves with planting good seeds. Those who are unable to accept and keep to it due to some spiritual impediment, should, out of shame and remorse, admit their failings to all the Buddhas and Tathagatas, as well as to the Triple Treasure of Buddha, Dharma, and Sangha. How sentient beings in other countries must wish that the Tathagata's robe and Dharma had been directly Transmitted to them in the same way as They were Transmitted in China, and that They were now present in their country too! What a deep sense of embarrassment they must feel; what sorrow and regret they must have that there has been no genuine Transmission in their country. Through what good fortune have we encountered the Teaching whereby the World-honored Tathagata directly Transmitted the robe and the Dharma? Surely, it is due to the agency of great spiritual merits accumulated from past lives that were spent in training to realize True Wisdom.

In this present-day, degenerate world when the Dharma is in Its last phase, some feel no shame for themselves that they lack the genuine Transmission, while others envy or resent those who have received the genuine Transmission. I suspect that these people may well be a gang of hellions. The way things are for them now and the state in which they now dwell have sprung from their previous deeds and are not what is truly real. Were they to turn themselves around and simply respect the genuine Transmission of the Buddha Dharma, then this would be to really take refuge in learning what Buddha is.

Broadly speaking, we must realize that the kesa is what all Buddhas revere and devote themselves to. It is the Body of Buddha; it is the Mind of Buddha. It is called 'the garment of liberation'; it is called 'the robe that is a fertile field of blessings'; it is called 'the formless robe'; it is called 'the unsurpassed robe'; it is called 'the robe of patient forbearance'; it is called 'the robe of a Tathagata'; it is called 'the robe of great benevolence and great compassion'; it is called 'the robe that is the banner of victory'; it is called 'the robe of supreme, fully perfected enlightenment'. Truly, in these ways we should accept it, keep to it, and humbly raise it above our heads. Because it <u>is</u> as it is spoken of, it is not something to be altered to make it conform to some personal fancy.

As to the material for a robe, we use silk or cotton cloth, as it suits us. Cotton is not necessarily 'pure', any more than silk is 'impure'. And to choose silk because you look down on cotton is unwarranted, laughable even. The usual approach of the Buddhas has been, beyond doubt, to consider a robe made from waste cloth as the best.

There are ten types of waste cloth, four of which are charred cloth, cloth that has been chewed by an ox, cloth that rats have gnawed on, and cloth that was previously used for a shroud. People in all five regions of India discard such types of cloth in back alleys and barren fields. Since they are considered the same as bodily waste, they are called 'waste cloth'. Trainees collect them, wash and dye them, then sew them together and use the robe for furbishing their body. Among these are various scraps of silk and cotton. Trainees should abandon any discriminatory notions about silk and cotton, and concentrate on the meaning of 'discarded waste material'. Long ago, when the Buddha was in one of His past lives, He was washing a robe of just such waste cloth in Lake Anavatapta. The dragon who was the lord of the lake praised Him, rained flowers down upon Him, and respectfully bowed to Him. In addition, there are some among the Scriptural teachers of the Lesser Course who hold to the theory of transformed thread,[10] a view which has no foundation and at which persons of the Greater Course must smile, for what thread is not the product of some form of transformation? O you ancient scholarly teachers, even though you may believe your ears when you hear the word 'transformation', you doubt your eyes when you actually see a transformation.

Obviously, when you are picking up waste material, it may include cotton that resembles silk and silk that resembles cotton. Regional customs differ in myriad ways, so that there is no telling how something was manufactured, for it is not something that the naked eye can readily determine. Once we have obtained such material, we should not argue over whether it is silk or cotton, but should refer to it as discarded waste. Even though ordinary humans or lofty beings may 'continue to exist' as waste matter after death, they will not be sentient beings, they will simply be waste matter. Even though a dead pine tree or chrysanthemum should 'continue to exist' as waste matter, they will not be non-sentient beings, they will just be waste matter. O you ancient scholarly ones, when you accept and trust in the principle that waste material does not mean silk or cotton, or gold or silver, or jade or jewels, waste material will be what manifests before your very eyes. Since you had not yet let go of your opinions about silk and cotton, waste material was something you had not even dreamt of.

A certain monk once asked the ancient Buddha Daikan Enō, "Is the robe passed on to you on Huang-mei Mountain in the middle of the night one made of cotton or one made of silk? Pray, tell me, what on earth is it made of?"

---

10.   An ancient Indian view that silk is thread which is created by a living creature; it is not naturally occurring of itself.

The ancient Buddha replied, "It is not cotton, nor is it silk."

Understand that a kesa is neither silk nor cotton. This instruction on the Buddha's Way is profound and difficult to grasp.

The Venerable Shōnawashu ('He of Hempen Clothing') was the Third Indian Ancestor connected with the Treasure House of the Dharma. From the time he was born, he spent his whole life inseparable from his robe. This robe was, to be sure, a conventional garment whilst he was still at home, but when he left home to become a monk, it became a kesa.

Also, once the female monk Shukra ('She Who is Spotless') had taken her Bodhisattva vows and put on the cotton robe, then, life after life, even during the periods between lives, she was inseparable from the robe. On that very day when she met Shakyamuni Buddha and left home to become a monk, the ordinary robe that she had acquired at birth was immediately transformed into a kesa, the same as with the Venerable Shōnawashu.

Be very clear about this: a kesa is beyond being silk or cotton or any other type of cloth. Moreover, the spiritual merits of the Buddha Dharma transform all thoughts and things, physical and mental, just as in these examples. The principle is unambiguous: when you leave home to take the Precepts and become a monk, whatever your body and mind experience as objective or subjective is transformed. It is only because you are confused or ignorant that you do not realize this. None of the Buddhas ever taught that this principle applied only to Shōnawashu and Shukra, and therefore does not apply to you. So, have no doubts about the many spiritual benefits that <u>you</u> receive. Obviously, you should assiduously explore such a principle as the one just described.

The kesa that someone dons when taking the Precepts is not necessarily of cotton or of silk, for indeed the Buddha's edifying influence is difficult to comprehend. The precious Jewel within is beyond anything that those who calculate grains of sand are capable of finding.[11] So, we should probe deeply to clarify what has dimensions and what is beyond measurement, as well as what has a form and what is beyond form. This is what our Ancestral Masters who traveled to and from India and China investigated and correctly Transmitted. Should a person encounter and listen to someone who is doubtlessly making clear the genuine Transmission of the Ancestors, and then vainly refuse to accept the genuine Transmission from this Ancestral Master, such a person's attitude would be hard to condone. It must be due to a lack of trust as a result of befuddled and foolish thinking. Such a person is one who discards what is true in order to pursue some fabrication, one who forsakes the Source in a desire for trifles. This may well take the form of a belittling contempt for the Tathagata.

Folks who would give rise to Supreme Wisdom should always accept the Transmission passed on to them by an Ancestral Master. Not only have we encountered the Buddha Dharma, which is so hard to come by, but also, as the Dharma descendants of the genuine Transmission of the Buddha kesa, we have the opportunity to experience It directly, to explore and learn from It, to accept It, and to keep to It. This, accordingly, is our encountering the Tathagata; it is our hearing the Buddha give voice to the Dharma; it is our letting the Buddha's radiance shine forth; it is our experiencing what the Buddha experienced; it is our directly Transmitting Buddha Mind; it is our reaching the very Marrow of Buddha; it is our putting on the kesa of Shakyamuni Buddha, which is before our very eyes, and it is Shakyamuni Buddha right before our very eyes, entrusting the kesa to us. Through our devoutly following the Buddha, we have humbly accepted the kesa.

The Methods for Washing the Kesa

Put the unfolded kesa into a clean washtub and leave it to soak for about four hours in boiling hot water that has been incensed. Another method is to immerse it in clean boiling water and wait until the water has cooled down. Nowadays, we

---

11.   A reference to scholars who are unrelenting in their involvement with making distinctions over terms and their meanings.

customarily use hot ash-water. Here in Japan, ash-water refers to hot water containing lye. When the ash-water has cooled down, rinse the kesa in clean, fresh, hot water several times, but do not scrub it with your hands or tread on it with your feet. Continue in this manner until the dirt and grease have been removed. Then, rinse it in cold water in which some incense, such as aloes or sandalwood, has been mixed. After that, hang it on a clean clothes pole to dry. After it has completely dried, fold it, put it on a high place, burn incense and strew flowers,[12] circumambulate it to the right several times, and respectfully bow to it. Make three, six, or nine full bows, hands in gasshō,* then kneel with hands in gasshō and, holding the kesa in both hands, recite the kesa verse. After this, stand up and respectfully put the kesa on in the usual manner.

The World-honored One, in advising His great assembly, said:

> In the ancient past when I was in the presence of Ratnagarbha Buddha—the Buddha Who is the Storehouse of the Treasure—I was the Bodhisattva of Great Compassion. At that time, as the Bodhisattva-Mahasattva* of Great Compassion, I made the following vow before Ratnagarbha Buddha, saying, "World-honored One, when I have finally become a Buddha, there may be sentient beings who have entered into My Teaching and, leaving home to become monks, have donned a kesa. They may include monks or laity, male or female, who show a lack of faith by breaching grave Precepts, putting false views into practice, or acting contemptuously towards the Triple Treasure, thereby accumulating for themselves all sorts of heavy defilement. But if they give rise to

12. Whether Dōgen intended the conventional phrase referring to incense and flowers to be taken literally is uncertain. 'Strewing flowers' is sometimes understood to mean 'reading Scriptures'. Burning incense and strewing flowers is also associated with the offering of one's training. For more about the metaphoric meaning of these phrases, see "Bodhidharma's Discourse on Pure Meditation" in *Buddhist Writings on Meditation and Daily Practice,* (Shasta Abbey Press, 1994), pp. 369-71.

a feeling of respect for even the span of a single thought, so that they regard the large patchwork robe with esteem, or if they give birth to a feeling of respect so that they regard the World-honored One, or the Dharma, or the Sangha with esteem, then, O World-honored One, I declare that, if even one among such sentient beings in any of the Three Courses* is incapable of receiving confirmation of ultimate Buddhahood, and, as a result, that person regresses or completely turns away, then I have deceived and misled all present-day Buddhas within all worlds everywhere for countless, limitless, immeasurable eons, and I will surely fail to realize supreme, fully perfected enlightenment.

"World-honored One, after I have become a Buddha, should any being—be it a dragon or a demon, human or non-human—be able to don this kesa, revere and make offerings to it, reverence and praise it, then should that being be able to catch sight of the smallest bit of this kesa, he or she will be able to keep from regressing from within the Three Courses.¹³

"If there are sentient beings pressed by hunger and thirst— be they spirits who are violent because of their dire poverty, or persons of humblest birth, or beings who act like hungry ghosts*— should they acquire a bit of a kesa, even four inches square, then they will be able to have their fill of what they thirst and hunger for and will be able to realize fully what they have prayed ever so long for.

"When there are sentient beings who are acting with each other in offensive ways, stirring up malicious and hostile thoughts

---

13. That is, after having reverently accepted a kesa and put it on, some may become so accustomed to wearing it that they forget that they have it on, but should they then catch sight of even a bit of it, this will remind them of why they donned the kesa in the first place, which will enable them to keep from regressing in their training and practice.

and intentions, and keeping things roiling until a fight breaks out— whether any of those engaged in such fighting be dragons, fierce spirits, gandharvas, asuras, garudas, kinnaras, mahoragas, kumbandhas, or pishachas, human or non-human[14]—should any of them call this kesa to mind, then, due to the influence of the kesa, they will give rise to a heart that is compassionate, a heart that is soft and flexible, a heart that is free of malice and hostility, a heart that is tranquil and devoid of defiling passions, a virtuous heart that is well-tamed and subdued, and thereby be able to return to a state of immaculacy.

"Should there be someone who is in the midst of an armed conflict, a civil litigation, or a criminal prosecution, and should this person, whilst holding onto a fragment of this kesa, go among those involved and, for self-protection, make offerings to it, show reverence for it, and venerate it, this person and others like him will lose the inclination to injure others through aggression, to coerce them, or to treat them with ridicule and scorn. Constantly being able to surpass others in this regard, such a person will come through all such difficulties as these.

"World-honored One, if my kesa were unable to fulfill the saintly merits of such acts as these aforementioned five, then I have deceived and misled all present-day Buddhas within all worlds everywhere for countless, limitless, immeasurable eons, and will surely fail to realize supreme, fully perfected enlightenment in the future and to do the work of a Buddha. Moreover, having strayed from the virtuous Dharma, I would certainly be incapable of exposing and destroying whatever leads others off the Path."

---

14. 'Dragons...pishachas' comprise a list of quasi-mythical beings who were originally given to violent or seductive acts but who, upon conversion to Buddhism, became spiritual guardians, each type having governance over some protective function. Hence, they may manifest as some human or non-human being fulfilling that function.

O my good disciples, the Tathagata Ratnagarbha then extended His golden-hued right arm and, rubbing the crown of the head of this Bodhisattva of Great Compassion, said warmly, "Well put, well put, my splendid disciple! What you have said is a great, precious treasure that is both wise and virtuous. You will ultimately realize supreme, fully perfected enlightenment. This kesa garment will be able to fulfill these five saintly merits and create great benefits."

O my virtuous disciples, as the Bodhisattva-Mahasattva of Great Compassion, having heard the Buddha's praise, I felt a joy arising in My heart that made it dance beyond measure. It then happened that the Buddha extended His golden-hued arm, its hand with its long, webbed fingers as soft and supple as a heavenly robe. Once He had rubbed My Bodhisattva head, My Bodhisattva body was immediately transformed, resembling the figure of a young man of twenty.

O my good disciples, the great crowd in that assembly, all the various creatures, such as the dragons, the celestial beings, the gandharvas, both the human and the non-human, put their hands in gasshō as an offering, bestowing many kinds of blossoms on Me as the Bodhisattva of Great Compassion, and they danced and made music, offering this as well. After they had praised Me in these various ways, they dwelt in silence.

From the time that the Tathagata was in the world up to this very day, whenever bodhisattvas and monks search through the Scriptures and monastic regulations for the merits of the kesa, without fail, they take these five merits to be the principal ones.

Truly, the kesa is the Buddha robe for all Buddhas in the three temporal worlds of past, present, and future. Though we say that its spiritual merits are beyond measure, to attain the kesa amidst the Teaching of Shakyamuni Buddha must surpass the attaining of a kesa amidst the Teaching of any other Buddha. Should you ask why, well, long ago when Shakyamuni Buddha, as the Bodhisattva-Mahasattva of Great Compassion, was in a state conducive to His realizing Buddhahood, He made five hundred great vows in the presence of Ratnagarbha Buddha, in particular taking solemn vows like the five just mentioned on the spiritual merits of the kesa. These merits, moreover, must surely be limitless and beyond the mind's ability to grasp. Consequently, what we call 'the genuine Transmission down to today of the Skin and Flesh, Bones and Marrow of the World-honored One' is the kesa robe. The Ancestral Masters who genuinely Transmitted the Treasure House of the Eye of the True Teaching have invariably made a proper Transmission of the kesa. Sentient beings who have kept to this robe when it was passed on to them and who have humbly placed it atop the crown of their head as an act of respect have invariably realized the Way within two or three lifetimes. Even if someone were to put one on as a joke or for some personal profit, this act will be a cause for his or her realizing the Way.

Our Ancestral Master Nāgārjuna once said:

> If people who have left home to be within the Buddha Dharma break the Precepts and lapse into impure ways, once they have brought their impure ways to an end and obtained liberation from them, they will be like the female monk Utpalavarna ('She Who Has the Hue of a Lotus Blossom') in the Jataka Scripture on past lives. While the Buddha was in the world, this female monk attained the Six Transcendent Abilities[15] and realized arhathood.* She once entered the house of a member of the nobility, and, continually extolling the Dharma of leaving home to become a monk, she admonished the wives and daughters of the noble, saying, "My sisters, you should leave home and become monks."

---

15.   Dōgen will explain what these are later in this discourse.

The noblewomen all replied, "We are young and our bodies are comely. For us to keep to the Precepts would indeed be hard, and we would surely break them on occasion."

The monk replied, "If you break the Precepts, then you break them. Just leave lay life behind!"

They then asked her, "If we break the Precepts, then we shall certainly fall into some hellish state, so why would you have us break them?"

She replied, "If you fall into some hell, then you fall into some hell."

All the women broke out in laughter and said, "In a hell we will receive the consequences of our defiling deeds, so why would you have us fall into such a state?"

The monk replied, "In recalling my own past lives, there was a time when I had become a prostitute. I dressed up in all sorts of clothes and told the age-old licentious stories. One day, I dressed up as a female monk, just as a joke. As a direct result of this I became a female monk in Kashō Buddha's time. After a while, I took to depending on my aristocratic demeanor and gave rise to pride and arrogance, thereby breaking monastic prohibitions as well as Precepts. Because of the defilement from breaking monastic prohibitions and Precepts, I fell into a hellish state where I suffered the consequences of my various defiling acts. After I had suffered these consequences, I met Shakyamuni Buddha and left home to become a monk, ultimately obtaining the Six Transcendent Abilities and realizing arhathood. Due to this, I have come to know that if we leave home and take the Precepts, even though we may later break Them, we will realize arhathood because of the karmic effect of the Precepts. If I had merely done bad things without having any effects from the Precepts, I would not have realized the Way."

Nāgārjuna then continued with Utpalavarna's narrative:

"In times long past, I had fallen into hellish states for
generation after generation, getting out of some hell only to become
a wicked person once again. When that wicked person died, again
a hell was entered, and nothing whatsoever had been gained. Now,
because of this, I have come to realize that if someone leaves home
to be a monk and takes the Precepts, even though that person later
breaks the Precepts, because of once having taken Them, that
person will obtain the fruits of the Way."

The first cause for this female monk, who had the hue of a lotus blossom, to
realize the arhat's way was not something meritorious on her part, but just her having
donned a kesa as a joke, and, due to the merits of that, she had now realized the Way.
In a second lifetime, she met Kashō Buddha and became a female monk. In a third
lifetime, she met Shakyamuni Buddha and became a great arhat, equipped with the
Three Insights and the Six Transcendent Abilities. The Three Insights are the
awareness of what is really transpiring within us, the awareness of what has brought
about the karmic effects from our past lives, and the awareness of whether or not our
defiling passions have truly come to an end. The Six Transcendent Abilities are the
ability to freely deal with external situations or circumstances as needed, the ability to
know what is really on the minds of others, the ability to see what is really transpiring
with others, the ability to hear what others are really saying, the ability to grasp what
is really causing people to behave the way they do, and the ability to determine
whether or not someone has truly brought his or her defiling passions to an end. Truly,
when she was just a person who was doing wicked deeds, she would die only to enter
a hellish state. Emerging from that hellish state, she would again become someone
doing wicked deeds. But when she felt the impact of the Precepts, even though she
would fall into some hellish state due to her breaking of the Precepts, nevertheless,
They were ultimately the cause of her realizing the Way. Now, anyone who may put
on a kesa as a joke will still be able to realize the Way by his or her third go-round.
How, then, could anyone who put on a kesa with a pure and trusting heart for the sake
of Supreme Wisdom fail to fully realize its spiritual merits, to say nothing of the
spiritual merits realized by one who respectfully accepts and keeps to it during his

lifetime and humbly raises it atop the crown of his head, for such merits are indeed so vast as to be immeasurable.

Whoever gives rise to the Mind that seeks the Way will undoubtedly accept and keep to the kesa, humbly raising it atop the crown of his or her head. To have encountered such a fortunate existence and yet fail to sow the seeds of one's Buddhahood, how pitiful that would be! To have received the body of a human being in the Southern Continent of Jambudvipa,* to have met with the Dharma of Shakyamuni Buddha by being born in proximity to an Ancestral Master who is in the direct line of inheritors of the Buddha Dharma, and then, to no profit, to pass up accepting a kesa that has been directly Transmitted from person to person, a kesa that points directly to one's Buddha Nature—could there be anything more pathetic?

Now, as to the genuine Transmission of the kesa, a genuine Transmission from an Ancestral Master is, in and of itself, the genuine inheritance. It is not something that any other teacher can equal. And even the spiritual merits from accepting and keeping to the kesa whilst following a teacher who has not been Transmitted will be exceedingly profound. How much more, then, will merit accrue to us from our accepting and keeping to a kesa that we received from a genuine teacher, one who had legitimately been given a kesa personally by someone in the Transmission line! Certainly, we will then be a child or grandchild of the Tathagata, for we will have had correctly Transmitted to us the Skin and Flesh, Bones and Marrow of the Tathagata. In sum, the kesa has come to be legitimately Transmitted by all Buddhas everywhere, at all times, without interruption. It is what all Buddhas, bodhisattvas, shravakas,* and pratyekabuddhas* alike, everywhere and at all times, have come to safeguard and protect.

In constructing a kesa, take coarse cotton cloth as your base. When you do not have coarse cotton cloth, use a fine cotton cloth. If you have neither coarse nor fine cotton, use raw silk cloth. If you have neither silk nor cotton cloth, then use, say, a wool twill or a thin silk gauze, all of which the Tathagata endorsed. In a country that does not have any variety of silk, cotton, or twill, the Tathagata also permitted leather kesas.

Speaking in general terms, when dyeing a kesa, we should use blue-green, yellow, red, black, or purple. Whichever color we choose, it should be a loaded color.[16] The Tathagata always wore a flesh-colored kesa, for this is the color of the Kesa. The Buddha's kesa that the First Ancestor passed on to succeeding Ancestors was blue-black in color, and its cloth was of Indian cotton. It is now on Mount Sōkei. In India, it was passed on twenty-eight times, and in China, five times. Now, the descendants of the ancient Buddha Daikan Enō have all had Transmitted to them the ancient custom of the Buddha's robe and have kept to it, which is something that is beyond other monks.

Generally speaking, there are three types of kesa. The first is a waste cloth robe, the second a fur robe, and the third a refurbished robe. 'Waste cloth' refers to what was discussed earlier. A fur robe is made from the fur and down of beasts and birds. Should trainees be unable to obtain waste cloth, they may gather this down and make it into a robe. A refurbished robe refers to one whose worn spots and tears have been patched and which is then presented to a trainee. We do not wear worldly finery.

The venerable monk Upali asked the World-honored One, "O World-honored One of Great Virtue, how many panels does a sanghati robe have?"[17]

The Buddha responded, "There are nine types. And what are these nine? They are referred to as nine-paneled, eleven-

---

16.   That is, not a pure, intense, primary color, but one whose brightness has been toned down by mixing some other color in with it.

17.   These are the large robes Dōgen spoke of earlier. The meaning of the Sanskrit term sanghati, as well as other similar technical names for robes, is explained later in the text.

paneled, thirteen-paneled, fifteen-paneled, seventeen-paneled, nineteen-paneled, twenty-one-paneled, twenty-three-paneled, and twenty-five-paneled robes. The first three of these large monastic robes have two long segments and one short segment in each panel, and we should keep to this style. The panels of the next three types have three long segments and one short segment, whereas the final three have four long segments and one short segment. Any panel that has more segments than these would be one whose tears have been repaired."

Upali once again addressed the World-honored One, saying, "O World-honored One of Great Virtue, how many sizes of sanghati robes are there?"

The Buddha replied, "There are three, namely, large, medium, and small. A large one is three hasta long and five hasta wide.[18] A small one is two and a half hasta long by four and a half hasta wide. Anything between these two is called 'medium.'"

Upali then addressed the World-honored One, saying, "O World-honored One of Great Virtue, how many panels does an uttarasangha robe have?"

The Buddha replied, "It has just seven panels, with each having two long segments and one short segment."

Upali then addressed the World-honored One, saying, "O World-honored One of Great Virtue, how many sizes does this seven-paneled robe have?"

The Buddha replied, "It has three, namely, large, medium, and small. A large one is three by five hasta, and a small one is a half hasta shorter on each side. 'Medium' refers to anything between these two."

---

18. A hasta is an Indian measure of variable length. One hasta is the distance from the intended wearer's elbow to the tip of his or her fist or index finger, generally ranging between sixteen and twenty inches.

Upali then addressed the World-honored One, saying, "O World-honored One of Great Virtue, how many panels does an antarvasa robe have?"

The Buddha replied, "It has five panels, each composed of one long and one short segment."

Upali again addressed the World-honored One, saying, "How many sizes does an antarvasa robe have?"

The Buddha replied, "There are three, namely, large, medium, and small. A large one is three by five hasta, with a medium and a small being the same as before, that is, reduced up to a half hasta on each side."

The Buddha added, "The antarvasa robe has two additional types. And what are these two? The first is two hasta long and five hasta wide. The second is two hasta long and four hasta wide."

The term 'sanghati' translates as 'double-layered robe'. The term 'uttarasangha' translates as 'uppermost robe'. The term 'antarvasa' translates as 'innermost robe', and is also called 'the lower robe'. It is also said that the sanghati robe is called 'the large robe', or 'the robe for entering royal palaces', or 'the robe for giving Teaching'. The uttarasangha robe is referred to as 'the seven-paneled robe', or 'the middle robe', as well as 'the robe for entering amongst the assembly'. The antarvasa robe is called 'the five-paneled robe', or 'the small robe', as well as 'the robe for going about on one's daily paths', and 'the robe for carrying out one's temple duties'.

We should safeguard and protect these three robes. Further, among the sanghati robes there is a sixty-paneled kesa that we also must not fail to accept and hold to.

It is generally held that the measurements of a body depend on the span of a lifetime, ranging from eighty thousand years down to a hundred years. Some say that 'eighty thousand years' and 'one hundred years' are different; others say that they are equal. Between these two views, the one which says that they must be equal corresponds to the genuine Transmission. The dimensions of a Buddha's Body and that of a human are far distant: a human body can be measured, but ultimately a Buddha's Body is beyond measure. This is why, the moment a Shakyamuni Buddha of the present dons the kesa of Kashō Buddha, it will be something that is neither long nor wide. The moment the Tathagata Maitreya* dons the kesa of a present Shakyamuni Buddha, it will be something that is neither short nor narrow. We must clearly perceive, unequivocally resolve, fully comprehend, and infer in detail the principle of a Buddha's Body being something that is neither tall nor short. Lord Brahma resides high in the world of form, yet he does not see the crown of the Buddha's head. Moggallana may have reached all the way to the distant World Whose Banner Signpost Is the Bright Light, yet he has not thoroughly investigated what the Buddha has voiced. It is truly beyond our minds to imagine or grasp that the form and voice of Buddha are one and the same, whether seen or heard from near or far. All the spiritual merits of the Tathagata are like this, so we should humbly keep these merits in mind.

When it comes to cutting out and sewing a kesa, there is the separate piece robe, the pleated robe, the gathered robe, and the plain robe.[19] All of these are proper methods of construction. We should accept and keep to those robes that we have.

---

19.   The separate piece robe consists of trimmed pieces of cloth (segments) sewn into vertical panels, which are then joined together and bounded by strips of the base cloth. The pleated robe is made from an uncut piece of base cloth folded in vertical pleats and then sewed to form the appearance of panels. The gathered robe is made from an uncut piece of base cloth folded in vertical pleats, between which panels made of separate segments of cloth are then sewed together. The plain robe is a hemmed piece of uncut cloth.

The Buddha once said, "The kesa of Buddhas in any of the three temporal worlds is invariably backstitched." [20]

In obtaining material for these robes, again, we consider what is immaculate to be best. We consider the robe of waste material to be the most immaculate. All the Buddhas in all the three temporal worlds, without exception, consider this material to be immaculate. In addition, a robe given as an alms offering by one with a trusting heart is also immaculate. And one purchased in the marketplace with untainted money is also immaculate. Even though the time within which a robe is to be made has been set by tradition, we are now in the decadent final days of the Teaching, living in a region remote from the original source, so in our accepting and keeping to the kesa, it would probably be best for us to do our cutting and sewing when we have aroused our trusting heart.

The best key to understanding the Greater Course is that the laity—whether commoners or those in lofty positions—also accept and keep to the kesa. Both Lord Brahma and Lord Shakra have now accepted and keep to the kesa, and they are excellent models in the worlds of sensual desire and form. And among humans, the number of excellent examples cannot be calculated. Lay bodhisattvas have all accepted and keep to it.

In China, both Emperor Wu of the Liang dynasty and Emperor Yang of the Sui dynasty accepted and kept to the kesa. Both Emperor T'ai-tsung and Emperor Su-tsung of the T'ang dynasty wore the kesa, trained and studied amidst the monastic

---

20. A form of hand sewing in which one first sews one stitch backward on the front side of the fabric, and then sews one stitch forward of double length on the reverse side to form a solid line of stitching on both sides.

family, and accepted and kept to the Bodhisattva Precepts.[21] Other folks—such as lay disciples and their wives—who have accepted the kesa and taken the Precepts have been excellent models in both the past and the present.

In Japan, Crown Prince Shōtoku accepted and kept to the kesa, and, whilst giving Dharma talks on various Scriptures, such as the *Lotus Scripture* and the *Scripture on the Lion's Roar of Queen Shrimala*, he experienced the auspicious sign of jeweled flowers raining down from the heavens. After that, the Buddha Dharma spread throughout our country. Although the prince is regarded as the nation's imperial regent, he was, in fact, a spiritual guide and teacher for commoners as well as for those in lofty positions. As an emissary of the Buddha, he was a father and a mother to sentient beings. In our country today, even though the materials, colors, and measurements of kesas have been misunderstood and have become corrupted, that we have even heard the word 'kesa' is due simply to the influence of Crown Prince Shōtoku. How sad it would be today if he had not shattered what was false and set up what is genuine during his time. Later, Emperor Shōmu likewise accepted and kept to the kesa, and he also took the Bodhisattva Precepts as well. Therefore, whether we are of imperial rank, or whether we are ministers or subjects, we should not delay in accepting and keeping to the kesa, as well as in taking the Bodhisattva Precepts. There can be no greater joy and good fortune for any being in human form.

Someone once said, "The kesa that a lay person accepts and keeps to is called either 'a single-stitched robe' or 'a secular garment'.[22] That is, the backstitch was not yet used in sewing one." It has also been said, "When laity pay a visit to a training

---

21. At that time in China, it was usual for the laity to take only the first five of the Ten Great Precepts. To take the Bodhisattva Precepts is to take all ten of these Great Precepts, as well as the forty-eight Less Grave Precepts. These Precepts can be found in the *Scripture of Brahma's Net.* One translation of this appears in *Buddhist Writings on Meditation and Daily Practice* (Shasta Abbey Press, 1994), pp. 55-188

22. Single stitching consists of alternating stitches of the same length, one on the front of the fabric and one on the back.

hall, they need to bring with them the three Dharma robes, a willow twig toothpick, water for rinsing the mouth, food utensils, and a meditation mat. They should train and practice in precisely the same pure manner as monks do."

Such is the legacy of some ancient worthy. However, what is now passed on directly by the Buddhas and Ancestors is that kesas are all backstitched, whether conferred on rulers, ministers of state, lay disciples, or ordinary folk. A good example of this is the Sixth Chinese Ancestor Enō who had already received the genuine Transmission of the Buddha's kesa while he was still the temple servant known as Lu.

Speaking in general, the kesa is the badge and banner of a Buddhist disciple. If we have completely accepted and are keeping to the kesa, then every day we should humbly raise it above our heads. Then, with it placed upon the crown of our head and with our hands in gasshō, we should recite the following verse:

> *How great and wondrous is the robe of enlightenment,*
> *Formless and embracing every treasure!*
> *I wish to unfold the Buddha's Teaching*
> *That I may help all sentient beings reach the Other Shore.*

After this recitation, we then put on the kesa. While robed in the kesa, we should think of it as our teacher and look upon it as a stupa.* We also recite this verse when we place it on our head after having laundered it.

The Buddha said, "When you shave your head and don the kesa, you receive the protection of all the Buddhas. When any of you leave home behind, both the lofty and the humble will make venerative offerings to sustain you." Be clear in your thinking: once you have shaved your head and put on a kesa, you <u>will</u> be aided and protected by each and every single Buddha. By relying on the help and protection of all these Buddhas, you <u>will</u> be able to experience the spiritual merits of Supreme Wisdom. Both the assemblies of lofty beings and the masses of commoners <u>will</u> make offerings to sustain such a one as you.

The World-honored One, in advising the monk Jnanaprabha ('He Whose Wise Discernment is Radiant'), spoke thus:

The Dharma robe, based on its material, color, and dimensions, acquires ten superb benefits.

First, because it blankets your body well, it keeps feelings of shame or embarrassment at bay and shields you with a sense of modesty, so that you may train with the good Dharma and put It into practice.

Second, because it keeps off heat and cold, as well as mosquitoes, vicious creatures, and poisonous insects, you can train in the Way with a feeling of peace and tranquility.

Third, it makes manifest the look of one who has left home to be a monk, so that those who see you will feel delight and stay far away from evil thoughts and feelings.

Fourth, the kesa has the appearance of a veritable jeweled banner to persons of both ordinary and lofty positions, and those who honor and esteem it will be able to be reborn in Brahma's heavenly world.

Fifth, when we wear a kesa, it gives rise to thoughts of a precious banner which can extinguish whatever is bedeviling sentient beings and can produce all manner of happiness and virtue.

Sixth, right from the beginning, when we construct a kesa we should dye it with a loaded color, thereby avoiding thoughts of greed engendered by the five senses, and without arousing feelings of covetousness or lust.

Seventh, the kesa is the immaculate robe of the Buddha, which permanently cuts off defiling passions because it transforms them into fertile fields for good.

Eighth, when you put a kesa on your body, it wears away the karma from your defiling acts and, moment by moment, promotes your treading the path of good deeds by keeping to the Ten Precepts.

Ninth, the kesa also resembles a fertile field because it promotes the good and virtuous Bodhisattva Way.

Tenth, the kesa also resembles armor because it is able to protect you from being harmed by the poisonous arrows of defiling passions.

O Jnanaprabha, you surely realize that whenever Buddhas, as well as pratyekabuddhas, shravakas, and immaculate monks, put the kesa upon their body, as a result of the causal effects of these ten benefits, these three holy types alike will sit upon the precious platform of liberation.[23] Wielding the Sword of Wisdom, they will defeat the demons of defiling passion, and these holy types, together as equals, will enter the various realms of nirvana.

The World-honored One, then wishing to express this in verse, said:

> *O My monk Jnanaprabha, listen well to what I say,*
> *The robe that is so vast a field of blessings has profits ten.*
> *Worldly clothing increases the taint of desire,*
> *But not so the Tathagata's Dharma attire.*
> *The clothes of Dharma hinder well the shame and blush*
> *of those with worldly minds,*
> *Filling all with modest thoughts that bring to fruit*
> *the fertile fields of happiness.*
> *Cold, and heat, and insect's poisonous sting it keeps at bay,*
> *And firms the heart that seeks the Way, till to the Ultimate you*
> *come.*

---

23. The three holy types are Buddhas, lay trainees, and monks.

Making clear your leaving home, it parts you from your greeds
    and lusts,
And severs you from the false views five, that you may train
    and practice in the proper way. [24]
The kesa is as a precious flag whose sight inspires respect;
Whoever humbly bows to it will gain Lord Brahma's joyful
    gifts.
When, as the Buddha's child, you spread your kesa wide, bow
    as before a stupa you would bow,
For then will such joy arise that all defiling thoughts will
    disappear, making the hearts of the lofty and the
    common to be moved.
When you refrain from putting on proud airs and come to deep
    respect, you are a monk in truth,
And all you do will become free of worldly dust and cares.
All Buddhas praise the kesa as a good and fertile field,
As unsurpassed in profit and delight for sentient
    beings all.
Wondrous beyond belief are the kesa's powers
    and strengths;
It helps you to train so that your actions plant the
    Bodhi seeds.
Their sproutings of the Truth will be as seedlings
    in the spring,
Their wondrous fulfilling of enlightenment like autumn's
    fruits.
Truly is the kesa a suit of armor, diamond hard,

---

24. The five false views are: 1) attachment to self or other, 2) belief in the existence of a self, whether eternal or not, 3) denial of cause and effect, 4) to hold that the preceding three views constitute the Truth, 5) belief that only strict adherence to the Precepts leads to enlightenment.

Impregnable against the harm from passion's poisoned
 darts.
So brief have I now praised these profits ten;
Had I all eons to expound them, never could I exhaust
 what they enfold.
Were a dragon to wrap about his body but a single kesa
 thread,
Then from a lordly garuda's feasting could he escape.
Should some human whilst crossing the open sea but hold
 this robe,
He need have no fear of woe from monstrous fish or any
 hungering thing.
Though thunder roar and through an angry sky the
 lightning flash,
The one who wears a kesa need have no fear.
Should a layman, clothed in white, hold this robe aloft,
All wicked, hungering beings will never dare draw nigh.
Should such a one arouse the will to train and seek to
 leave domestic life behind
So that, now wearied of all worldly things, he may pursue
 the Buddha's Way,
All devilish mansions everywhere will tremble and
 quake,
As this person, arrow swift, comes to truly know the Body
 of the Dharma Lord.

These ten superb benefits have broadly encompassed all the spiritual merits of the Buddha's Way. It would be good for you to explicitly explore and apply all the merits and virtues described in these sentences and verses. Do not scan them and then hastily put them aside, but look at each and every line and consider its import at length. These superb benefits are simply what the spiritual merits of the kesa are; they are not strengths arising from some trainee's lengthy and fierce pursuit of spiritual benefits.

The Buddha said, "The spiritual strengths of the kesa are beyond all imaginings and conceptions." So, any attempt by ordinary persons, as well as by the wise or saintly, to understand these benefits by conjecture will be in vain. In more general terms, immediately upon our realizing the Body of the Dharma Lord, we will indeed be wearing the Kesa. There has never been anyone from ancient times onwards who realized the Body of the Dharma Lord and was not wrapped in the Kesa.

The most immaculate material for a robe is waste cloth. Its spiritual merits are evident throughout the three divisions of the canon—the Scriptural Discourses, the monastic regulations, and the commentaries—of both the Greater and the Lesser Courses, so we would do well to make inquiries of those who have explored them extensively. We also need to clarify in detail what other materials may be used for making a robe. This is something that Buddha after Buddha and Ancestor after Ancestor have made abundantly clear and have correctly Transmitted to us, and They are persons unsurpassed by any others.

In the *Middle Āgama Scripture*, the Buddha said:

> O all you discerning ones, let us suppose that there is someone whose physical behavior is unstained, but whose manner of speaking and intentions are tainted. If an astute person should see this, and then feel any hostility arising, this feeling must, by all means, be dispelled. O all you discerning ones, let us further suppose that there is someone whose bodily actions are tainted, but whose speech and intentions are unstained. If an astute person should see this and then feel any hostility arising, this feeling too must, by all means, be dispelled. And just how should such a one dispel this feeling?
>
> O you discerning ones, such a person should be like the hermit monk living in a forest who gathers up pieces of waste cloth. He discards from this waste material whatever part he sees is

shabby, or soiled with excrement, or stained with urine, nasal mucus, or any other unclean substance. After he has spotted such a cloth, he picks it up with his left hand and stretches it out with his right. If there are any parts free from stain of excrement, urine, mucus, or any other unclean substance, or any part not riddled with holes, he then tears that part off and takes it.

In like manner, O you discerning ones, if there is someone whose bodily actions are stained while his speech is untainted, do not think about that person's tainted bodily behavior. Simply keep in mind the purity of his speech. If astute people feel hostility arising at what they see, by all means they should dispel it in this manner.

This is the method by which hermit monks of the forest handled waste cloth.

There are four kinds and ten types of waste cloth. When gathering waste cloth, first, take those parts that have no holes. Next, reject those parts too deeply or too long stained by feces or urine so that they cannot be washed clean. You may take those parts that are washable.

The Ten Types of Waste Cloth

First, cloth chewed by an ox.

Second, cloth gnawed by rats.

Third, cloth singed by fire.

Fourth, menstrual cloth.

Fifth, cloth discarded from childbirthing.

Sixth, cloth abandoned at a wayside shrine for
      birds to peck apart.

Seventh, cloth from a dead person's clothing
      abandoned at a grave site.

Eighth, cloth from abandoned prayer flags.

Ninth, cloth from robes discarded by officials
upon their advancement to higher rank.
Tenth, burial shrouds discarded by those
returning from a funeral.

These ten types of cloth are what people discard; they are not something that people in general make further use of. We pick these up and make them into the immaculate material of a kesa. They are what all Buddhas at all times have sung the praises of and have come to make use of. This waste cloth robe is therefore what the ordinary and the lofty, as well as dragons and other such beings, hold in great esteem, protect, and defend. Gather these pieces of cloth and make them into a kesa, for they are indeed the foremost of pure materials: they are the foremost in immaculacy.

In Japan today, such waste cloth robes do not exist. Though you may try to seek them out, you will be unable to come across them. How sad that our country is so small and remote! Instead, we need to use the clean materials that donors have given us as alms-cloth. Or, we may make into kesas some cloth bought in the marketplace by persons whose money comes from an untainted livelihood. Such waste material as this, as well as what has been earned through an untainted livelihood, is, indeed, neither silk nor cotton, neither gold nor silver cloth studded with pearls or jade, nor patterned cloth or silk gauze that is brocaded or embroidered: it is simply waste cloth. This waste material is not for the sake of humble dress, nor for the sake of beautiful raiment: it is simply for the sake of the Buddha Dharma. Using it for clothing is precisely the genuine Transmission of the Skin and Flesh, Bones and Marrow of all Buddhas at all times. It is the genuine Transmission of the Treasure House of the Eye of the True Teaching. Moreover, we should not ask commoners or lofty ones about the virtues of this, but should learn of them through training with the Buddhas and Ancestors.

Whilst I was in Sung China doing my training on the long bench in the Meditation Hall, I noticed that every morning following the striking of the wake-up block, the monks who sat on either side of me would raise their folded kesa in a gesture of offering, place it atop their head, respectfully make gasshō, and recite a verse to themselves. What they were saying in that verse was:

> *How great and wondrous is the robe of enlightenment,*
> *Formless and embracing every treasure!*
> *I wish to unfold the Buddha's Teaching*
> *That I may help all sentient beings reach the Other Shore.*

On the occasion when I learned of this, a feeling I had never experienced before welled up in me. A joy filled my body to overflowing; tears of gratitude, stealing from my eyes, rolled down my cheeks and wet the collar of my robe. The reason for this was that I had been reading the *Āgama Scriptures* shortly before, and though I had seen the passage on humbly offering up the kesa above one's head, I was not clear about the ceremonial procedure. Now I was personally witnessing it and was filled with such joy and worshipful admiration at being able to see manifest before me its deeper intent. When I was in my native land, there had been no teacher to instruct me in this, nor any good spiritual companion. How could I not regret the days and years I had so vainly spent or not grieve their passing? But upon seeing and hearing what was now before me, I was able to rejoice because of some good deed done in a past life. If I had vacantly remained in my homeland, how could I possibly have sat shoulder-to-shoulder with these Treasures of the Sangha who had received and actually donned the kesa of a Buddha! My joy and sorrow were not unmixed, as my myriad tears issued forth.

Then, in silence, I took a vow: no matter how, be I ever so incompetent, I <u>will</u> become an inheritor of the Buddha Dharma, I <u>will</u> correctly Transmit the True Teaching, and, out of pity for the sentient beings in my homeland, I <u>will</u> help them see and hear the Teaching concerning the robe that the Buddhas and Ancestors have genuinely Transmitted. The vow that I took then has now proved not to be in vain. The lay and monastic bodhisattvas who have accepted and keep to the kesa are many, for which I rejoice. These companions who have accepted and keep to the kesa, without fail, humbly raise their kesa above their head each morning and evening, since the spiritual merits of this will be unsurpassed. The practice of reading or listening to a single line from Scripture or the whole of this kesa verse was prevalent everywhere throughout all the highways and byways of China, and was as common as trees and stones. And even if the spiritual merits from the genuine Transmission of the kesa were encountered for only a scant day and night, they would still be pre-eminent and unsurpassed.

In Great Sung China during the tenth lunar month of the seventeenth year of the Chia-ting era (November 1223), two Korean monks came to Ch'ing-yüen Prefecture. One was called in Chinese Chi-hsüen, and the other was called Ching-yün. These two incessantly talked about the meaning of Buddhist Scriptures, for they were scholarly men of letters, and, though they were also monks, they had neither kesa nor alms bowl and resembled those who wander through life in ignorance. Sad to say, they had the superficial form of monks but lacked the Dharma of monks. This may have been due simply to their being from a small, remote nation. When those from Japan who have the superficial form of monks travel to other countries, they too resemble those like Chi-hsüen.

Shakyamuni Buddha, before His enlightenment, humbly raised the kesa above His head, never ignoring it for some twelve years. You are already His distant descendants, so train well with this practice. Turn away from bowing to celestial beings, spirits, rulers or their ministers, since all such acts are done in the vain pursuit of fame and gain. Instead, offer them the spiritual merit from your humbly raising the Buddha's kesa above your head, for that will be joy indeed!

Given to the assembly at Kannondōri in Kōshōhōrin-ji Temple on the first day of winter in the first year of the Ninji era (October 17, 1240).

85

On Giving Rise to the Enlightened Mind

(Hotsu Bodai Shin)

Translator's Introduction: This discourse was given on the same day as was Discourse 67: On Giving Rise to the Unsurpassed Mind *(Hotsu Mujō Shin)*. Because of the nature of its content, it may have been intended primarily for monastics.

Generally speaking, there are three types of mind. "The first is the mind of *chitta*, which we call the discriminative mind. The second is the mind of *hridaya*, which we call the mind of grass and trees. The third is the mind of *vriddha*, which we call the True Mind." Among these, we invariably employ the discriminative mind to arouse *bodhichitta*, the enlightened Mind. *Bodhi* is an Indian word which we call the Way, or what is True. *Chitta* is an Indian word which we call the discriminative mind. Without this discriminative mind we could not give rise to the enlightened Mind. I am not saying that this discriminative mind is the enlightened Mind; rather, we give rise to the enlightened Mind by means of the discriminative mind.

Giving rise to the enlightened Mind not only means vowing to take all sentient beings across to the Other Shore before one has taken oneself across, but it also means actively engaging in the task. Though somebody may be considered lowly, when such a one gives rise to this Mind, that person is already a spiritual guide and teacher for all sentient beings.

This Mind is neither something innate nor something that suddenly rises up as new at this moment, nor is It something singular or something plural, nor is It something spontaneous or something planned, nor is It something within our physical body, nor is our body something within that Mind. This Mind is not something that has permeated the entire universe of thoughts and things, nor is It something of the past or something of the future, nor is It something that is present or something that is absent, nor is It something intrinsic or something produced by an external cause, nor is It something of a combined nature or something of a causeless nature. Even so, at that point when we have established a spiritual connection with a Master, we give rise to the Mind that aspires for enlightenment. It is not something that the Buddhas and bodhisattvas* confer upon us, nor is It something that we can do for ourselves. This Mind arises due to Its being established through a spiritual connection with our Master and, consequently, It is not something spontaneous.

Giving rise to the enlightened Mind occurs, by and large, in human beings in the southern continent of Jambudvipa.* Only on rare occasions does this event occur among those in the eight states where it is difficult to hear of Buddhism.[1] After giving rise to the enlightenment-seeking Mind, one does the training and practice for three asamkhyeya eons or for a hundred great eons.[2] In some cases, people train for immeasurable eons and then become a Buddha. In other cases, people train for immeasurable eons to help sentient beings reach the Other Shore, ultimately not becoming a Buddha but just continuing to help ferry sentient beings across, doing this solely for the benefit of sentient beings. They are pursuing the course that is the delight of bodhisattvas.

To speak more broadly, the Mind of enlightenment operates via the three modes of behavior—body, speech, and mind—without a moment's idleness, always helping sentient beings give rise to the Mind of enlightenment and leading them along the Buddha's Way. To waste one's time bestowing worldly pleasures on people does not benefit sentient beings. Giving rise to this Mind and giving rise to this training for the enlightenment of others go far beyond the outer bounds of delusion versus enlightenment. Having transcended the three worlds of desire, form, and beyond form, such persons have become preeminent among all beings, and have gone quite beyond shravakas* and pratyekabuddhas.*

---

*   See *Glossary*.

1.   The eight states where it is difficult to encounter a Buddha or hear His Teaching are: 1) being born in one of the hells; 2) being born as a hungry ghost; 3) being born as an animal; 4) being born in the Northern Continent of Uttarakuru where all is pleasant; 5) being born in one of the heavens where life is long and easy; 6) being deaf, dumb, and blind; 7) being an erudite scholar; 8) being born in the intermediate period between a Buddha and His successor.

2.   These time measurements may seem to be of inordinately long duration, but they are simply of indeterminate length: it takes just as long as it takes.

The bodhisattva Makakashō, wishing to pay homage to Shakyamuni Buddha, composed the following eulogy:

> *Awakening one's intention and arriving at the Ultimate,*
> *though two, are not separate.*
> *Of these two states of mind, the former is the more*
> *difficult to arrive at,*
> *So when those who have not yet arrived at the Ultimate*
> *first lead others to arrive,*
> *I, for that reason, bow to their first giving rise to their*
> *intention.*
>
> *With Your first arising, You were already a Teacher for*
> *humans and gods,*
> *Surpassing those who merely listen and those who seek*
> *the Goal only for themselves.*
> *The arising of such an intention as Yours has surpassed*
> *the triple world,*
> *And therefore we call it the supreme state above all.*

The arising of the intention means giving rise, right off, to the intention to help others reach the Other Shore, even though you yourself have not yet reached that Place. We call this giving rise to the enlightened Mind for the first time. Once you have given rise to this Mind, you will then encounter Buddhas to whom you should make alms offerings, and you should hearken to Their Teaching. Further, should you then strive to give rise to the enlightened Mind, it would be like adding frost atop snow.[3]

The term 'the Ultimate' refers to the Wisdom that is the result of Buddhahood. Were we to compare the state of supreme, fully perfected enlightenment with the state of giving rise to the enlightened Mind for the first time, it is like

---

3. That is, having once given rise to the enlightened Mind there is no need to strive after It as if it had not yet arisen.

comparing the universal, all-consuming conflagration of the final age with the light of a firefly. Even so, when you give rise to the heart that helps others reach the Other Shore, even though you yourself have not yet reached that Place, there is no difference between the two. As the Tathagata said in the *Lotus Scripture,*

> *I constantly make this My intention:*
> *How may I help living beings*
> *Enter the Unsurpassed Way*
> *And quickly realize Buddhahood?*

This is what is meant by the immeasurable life of the Tathagata. Giving rise to the intention, doing the training and practice, and awakening to the fruits of Buddhahood are the same for all Buddhas.

'To benefit all sentient beings' means helping sentient beings give rise to the heart that helps others reach the Other Shore even though they themselves have not yet reached that Place. Even though you yourself have not yet reached that Place, you should not reckon that you will become a Buddha simply on the basis of your ability to help others reach the Other Shore. Even if the ripening of your meritorious activities, which could turn you into a Buddha, were at its full, still you should offer this merit to sentient beings in order to help them realize Buddhahood and recognize the Truth.

This Mind is not ours, or someone else's, or something that comes to us, yet after this intention arises, whenever we raise aloft the Great Earth, everything turns into gold, and whenever we sprinkle the waters of the Great Ocean, they immediately turn into the sweet dew. After that, whenever we lay hold of soil or rocks, sand or pebbles, we make use of this enlightened Mind, and whenever we explore the gushing forth of water and the blazing up of fire, we are personally shouldering the enlightened Mind. Hence, to offer as alms one's nation and city, one's spouse and children, the seven treasures,* men and women, one's head and eyes, one's marrow and brains, one's body and flesh, or one's hands and feet, all are the hustle and bustle of an enlightened Mind; all are an enlightened Mind's playfulness, which is like a fish frolicking in a pool of water.

Chitta, our mind that is engaged in discriminating at this very moment, is neither close to us nor distant from us; it is neither ourselves nor someone else. Even so, if we use this mind to turn ourselves towards the principle of helping others awaken before we ourselves are fully awakened, without retreating or turning away from it, this is our giving rise to enlightened Mind. Thus, if we employ enlightened Mind in making an alms offering of grass and trees, tiles and stones, gold and silver, and rare treasures, which all sentient beings hold onto as if these things were their own possessions, how could this not be our giving rise to enlightened Mind?

Because Mind, as well as all thoughts and things, is beyond self and other, beyond both together, or beyond being without a cause, if we should give rise to this enlightened Mind, even for a split second, all the myriad thoughts and things will become Its additional effects.

Generally speaking, the arising of Mind and the realizing of Truth rely upon the instantaneous arising and vanishing of all things. If things did not arise and vanish instantaneously, previous moments of evil actions would not yet have passed. And if previous moments of evil action had not yet passed, later moments of good actions could not arise now. Only a Tathagata alone clearly knows the measure of this moment. The Teaching that our mind in any single moment can give rise to a single utterance and that an utterance in any single moment can express a single word is also true, but it is true only of a Tathagata alone; this is not something that those of the other two Courses are capable of. As a rule, there are sixty-five moments within the time it takes for someone to snap his fingers, during which the five skandhas[*]—that is, the five components of existence—arise and vanish, but ordinary, unawakened people have not noticed or recognized this though they may have sensed it. Based on the length of a tatkshana, which is comprised of a hundred twenty moments, in the passing of a single day and night there are sixty-four hundred million, ninety-nine thousand, nine hundred and eighty moments during each of which the five skandhas arise and vanish. Even so, ordinary, unawakened people have not taken notice of this, and because they have not taken notice of it, they have not given rise to the enlightened Mind. Those who do not know the Buddha Dharma or who do not trust the Buddha Dharma do not believe in the principle of the arising and vanishing of moments.

Anyone who has clarified what the Tathagata's Treasure House of the Eye of the True Teaching, which is the Wondrous Heart of Nirvana, is certainly believes in this principle of the arising and vanishing of moments. Now that we have encountered the Tathagata's giving expression to it in the Scriptures, we may seem to be experiencing it as if it had fully dawned on us, but if we are barely aware of it during the span of a tatkshana, we can only take on faith that this principle must be so. If we fail to clarify and understand through direct experience all of the Dharma that was expressed by the World-honored One, it will be as if we do not know what the length of a moment is. As trainees, do not be reckless and act proud or arrogant. Not only are we ignorant of the smallest of things but we are also ignorant of the largest. Should ordinary sentient beings rely on the power of the Tathagata's Truth, they too will see the whole of the three-thousandfold worlds that comprise the universe. In sum, as we pass from fully existing to intermediately existing, and from intermediately existing to fully existing again, everything moves on, moment by moment.[4] Thus, whatever our intentions, we are led by our deliberate actions, so that the cycle of birth and death rolls on without stopping even for a single moment. With our body and mind rolling on like this through the cycle of birth and death, we should immediately give rise to the enlightened intention of helping others reach the Other Shore, even though we ourselves have not yet reached that Place. As we simply give rise to enlightened Mind, even if we regret having a body and mind, they are what arises, ages, sickens, and dies, and ultimately they are not our possession.

Oh, how unceasingly and swiftly sentient beings go through life from arising to vanishing!

While the World-honored One was in the world, there was a monk who came to call on Him. The monk bowed, his head respectfully touching the Buddha's feet. He then arose and, out of deference, stood to the side and, addressing the World-honored

---

4. 'Intermediately existing' describes the period between one moment of existing and the next moment of existing.

One, said, "At what speed does the course of a living being's life—from its arising to its departing—go?"

The Buddha replied, "Although I could tell you, you would not understand."

The monk then asked, "Is there some example that could illustrate it?"

The Buddha said, "There is. And I shall tell it to you now, for your benefit. Consider, for example, four fine archers. Each takes up his bow and arrow, then the four, standing together back to back, prepare to shoot in the direction each is facing. Now, there is a nimble man who comes along and says to them, 'Now, if you will all shoot off your arrows at the same time, I will be able to catch them all before any of them touch the ground.' What do you think? Would such a one be nimble or not?"

The monk said to the Buddha, "He would be exceedingly swift, O World-honored One."

The Buddha then said, "The swiftness of that man is not as fast as that of an earth-dwelling yaksha.[5] And the swiftness of an earth-dwelling yaksha is not as fast as that of a sky-dwelling yaksha. And the swiftness of a sky-dwelling yaksha is not as fast as the swiftness of the Four Celestial Lords. And the swiftness of those Celestial Lords is not as fast as the swiftness of the two orbs of sun and moon. And the swiftness of the two orbs of sun and moon is not as fast as the swiftness of the resolute celestial children. It is they who pull the chariot whose wheels are the orbs of sun and moon. These celestial beings are swift at rolling things. The course of a living being's life—from its arising to its departing—passes swifter still. It rolls on in every moment, without the slightest pause."

---

5. A yaksha is a belligerent demon that enjoys stirring things up. After its conversion, it becomes a guardian of Buddhism.

The swiftness with which the cycle of arising and vanishing rolls on in every moment during the course of our life is like this. You who are doing the practice instant by instant, pray, do not forget this principle. While you are experiencing this swiftness with which the cycle of arising and vanishing rolls on in every moment during the course of your life, if you give rise to a single thought of helping others arrive before you yourself have done so, the Life that is eternal will manifest before your very eyes. All the Buddhas in the ten quarters during the three periods of time, along with the Seven Buddhas,* the twenty-eight Ancestors in India and the first six Ancestors in China, as well as all the other Ancestral Masters who have Transmitted the Buddha's Treasure House of the Eye of the True Teaching have maintained and relied on this enlightened Mind. Those who have not yet given rise to this enlightened Mind are not our Ancestral Masters.

Question 120 in the *Procedures for Cleanliness in a Zen Temple* states, "Have you awakened to enlightened Mind?" You clearly need to realize that what this is saying is that, in learning the Truth of the Buddhas and Ancestors, awakening to enlightened Mind is unquestionably foremost. This is the continual Teaching of the Buddhas and Ancestors. 'To awaken' means to have something fully dawn on you. This does not refer to the great, ultimate awakening of a Buddha. Even if someone has entirely experienced all ten stages of bodhisattvahood, that person is still a bodhisattva. The twenty-eight Ancestors in India and the first six Ancestors in China, as well as the other great Ancestral Masters, were bodhisattvas; they were not the Buddha, nor were they shravakas or pratyekabuddhas, or anything else. Among those who are exploring the Matter* in the world today, there is not even one who has clearly understood that the Ancestors are bodhisattvas, not shravakas. Such folks today carelessly describe themselves as patch-robed monks or patch-robed disciples. Since they do not yet understand this, they have recklessly created confusion. How sad that, in these degenerate days of ours, the words and ways of the Ancestors have died out.

Thus it is that even though there are those who remain in home life and those who have left home life behind, and even though there are those who are in lofty positions and those who are just ordinary folk, and even though there are those who say that they are suffering and those who say that they are happy, all should quickly give rise to the intention of helping others awaken before they themselves have fully awakened. Even though the world of sentient beings has its limits and is also beyond limits, we give rise, first off, to the intention of helping all sentient beings awaken, for this is what the enlightened Mind is.

When bodhisattvas who are but one stage away from realizing Buddhahood are about to descend to Jambudvipa, they offer the following as their final Teaching for the sake of those celestial beings in the Tushita Heaven: "The enlightened Mind is the bright gateway to Truth, for It does not separate Itself from the Three Treasures." You need to clearly understand what they are saying, namely, that not separating oneself from the Three Treasures is what comes after the arising of the enlightened Mind. After we have given rise to the enlightened Mind, we must not regress or wander off from It, but must steadfastly protect and defend It.

The Buddha once said, "How do bodhisattvas protect the One Great Matter, which is enlightened Mind? The bodhisattvas and mahasattvas* are always diligent in protecting enlightened Mind, which is like ordinary, conventional parents in the world protecting their child, or like a one-eyed person protecting his one remaining eye, or like someone protecting his guide when going through a wilderness. A bodhisattva's protecting enlightened Mind is just like this. Because bodhisattvas rely on safeguarding enlightened Mind in this way, they realize supreme, fully perfected enlightenment. Because they rely on realizing supreme, fully perfected enlightenment, they come equipped with certainty, bright-mindedness, self-worth, and freedom from defilement, which describes the unsurpassed great nirvana. For this reason, bodhisattvas protect this one Teaching."

Such are the Buddha's words concerning the safeguarding of enlightened Mind. The reason why we protect It and do not let ourselves regress or wander off from It is, as popular custom would put it, because It is like the three things that are born but do not reach maturity, namely, fish eggs, mangos, and bodhisattvas who have given rise to the intention.[6] Because, generally speaking, there are many who have regressed and thereby have forgotten enlightened Mind, I too once feared that I would regress and forget It. This is why I have protected enlightened Mind.

When bodhisattvas are beginners, many regress or wander off because they do not have a genuine Master. If they do not have a genuine Master, they do not hear the true Teaching, and if they do not hear the true Teaching, they are apt to deny causality, along with denying the end of suffering, the Three Treasures, and all thoughts and things in the three temporal worlds. Vainly craving the five fleeting desires of property, sexual involvement, food and drink, fame, and sleep in the present, they forget the merits of enlightenment in the future. Sometimes, in order to obstruct a trainee, bedevilers and tempters will take on the form of a Buddha or appear in the figure of one's parents or of one's Master, as well as of one's relatives or even of heavenly beings. Then, drawing near, they make up ever-worsening stories, saying, "The Buddha's Way is far, far off. You will soon enough experience many sufferings and deep sorrows. Better to free yourself from birth-and-death first and then help others awaken." The trainee, hearing these tales, regresses from enlightened Mind and backs away from the conduct of bodhisattvas. Further, you need to know that preachings like these are nothing but the mouthings of demons. O my bodhisattvas, know this and do not follow such teaching. Even more, you should not regress or wander away from your vow to practice helping others to awaken before awakening yourself.

Should you consider going against your vow to help others to awaken before you do, you must realize that this is the preaching of demons, the preaching of non-Buddhists, the preaching of wicked companions. So do not follow it.

---

6.   Many fish eggs are produced but few succeed in hatching. Mango trees produce many
     flowers, but few become mature fruit. Dōgen will explain the third.

There are four kinds of demons: first, the demons of disturbing passions; second, the demons of the five components of existence; third, the demons of death; and fourth, the celestial demons of desire.[7]

'The demons of disturbing passions' refers to the hundred and eight disturbing passions.[8] When these are analyzed in detail, they actually comprise eighty-four thousand hindering passions.

'The demons of the five components of existence' are the various ways in which whatever arises unites with some hindering passion. For instance, we have a body. The four basic elements of this body—earth, wind, water, and fire—along with whatever else is fashioned from these four elements,* such as what we see with our eyes, comprise what we call 'the component of physical form'. Whatever we perceive through our senses that unites with the hundred and eight disturbing passions, we call 'the component of perception'. Whatever distinctions our mind makes up—be they measurable or immeasurable—which unite with judgments, we give the name of 'the component of mentation, or of thought'. When, by giving rise to thoughts of pleasure or disgust, we then give rise to a disposition to be greedy or angry, we call this activity—be it proper or improper—'the component of conduct'. By uniting the six sense organs—eyes, ears, nose, tongue, body, and mind—with the six objects of the senses—color and shape, sound,

---

7.   'Demons' are not necessarily something in human form, but whatever bedevils the trainee by creating a feeling of being hindered in one's practice.

The first sentence of this quotation by Dōgen is from the *Great Scripture on the Buddha's Parinirvana*. The remainder is from a commentary on this sentence by our Indian Ancestor Nāgārjuna.

8.   These are the mental functions that disturb and pollute our mind and body.

odor, taste, touch, and thoughts—we give rise to the six kinds of mental functioning—seeing, hearing, smelling, tasting, feeling, and discerning; we call the immeasurable, boundless mind which unites with the judgments formed by these six kinds of mental functioning 'the component of consciousness'.

Because causes and conditions are impermanent, what we call 'the demon of death' interrupts the flow of the five components of existence, and because this completely removes the three elements of consciousness, heat, and life, we call it 'the demon of death'.

'The celestial demons' are the lords of the world of desire. Because they are deeply attached to worldly pleasures and engage in ulterior motives to gain them, they give rise to fallacious views. They despise and envy the words and ways taught by all the sage and saintly ones for realizing nirvana, which is why we call them 'the celestial demons'. In India, Māra is their name; in China, they are called those who can steal someone's very life. Although such demons of death can truly rob you of your life, other celestial demons can also produce the causes and conditions for your life being stolen, and they can also rob one of a life of wise discernment. Because of this, they are called 'killers'.

Someone once asked me, "The one category of the demons of the five components of existence embraces the other three types, so why do you separate them into four?" I replied, "Truly, there is but one demon, but in order to clarify what that one means, there are the four."

The preceding is what our Ancestral Master Nāgārjuna taught. You trainees should remember it and diligently study it. Do not regress or turn away from enlightened Mind, vainly concealing demons of fascination.

Delivered to the assembly at Kippō-ji Temple in Echizen Province on the fourteenth day of the second lunar month in the second year of the Kangen era (March 24, 1244).

Copied in the Master's hermitage on the ninth day of the fourth month in the seventh year of the Kenchō era (May 16, 1249).

Ejō

86

On Making Venerative Offerings to Buddhas

(Kuyō Shobutsu)

Translator's Introduction: The key term in this discourse is *kuyō*, translated in the title as 'making venerative offerings', and shortened in the text itself to 'making offerings' or some variation thereof. It refers not only to selflessly giving alms and expressing gratitude to the Buddhas but also to showing respect for the sacred objects associated with Them, such as the memorial monuments called stupas, which also serve as reliquaries for sacred relics. What is important is the attitude of mind behind the offering, and, when it is free of any tinge of self, the merit that returns to the giver thereby is, as Dōgen says, beyond measure.

The original text, which is still in draft stage, is one of twelve that Dōgen had not been able to complete before his death. It contains many excerpts, particularly from writings attributed to Nāgārjuna.

The Buddha once said the following in verse:

If there were no past ages,
There could not have been Buddhas in the past.
If there were no Buddhas in the past,
There could be no leaving home to accept the full Precepts.

Clearly you need to keep in mind that Buddhas invariably exist in the three temporal worlds. When it comes to the Buddhas of the past, do not assert that They had a beginning, and do not assert that They had no beginning. If you erroneously impose upon Them Their having or not having a beginning and an end, this is not something that you have learned from the Buddha's Teaching. Those who make offerings to Buddhas invariably become Buddhas, just as do those who leave home life behind and faithfully follow their Master. They become Buddhas due to the merit of their making offerings to Buddha. How could people who have never made alms offerings to even one Buddha ever become Buddhas themselves, since they lack a cause for becoming a Buddha?

In the *Scriptural Collection of the Past Deeds of the Buddha*, it says the following:

The Buddha once told Moggallana, "I recall from My past having planted good roots in places where there were immeasurable, unbounded World-honored Ones and having ultimately sought supreme, fully perfected enlightenment.

"O Moggallana, I recall from My past having taken on the body of a saintly Wheel-turning Lord* and having encountered thirty billion Buddhas, all sharing the same name of Shakya. I, the Tathagata, along with My assembly of disciples, out of our esteem for Them, sustained Them by respectfully making offerings to Them of the four necessities: namely, shelter, clothing, food, and medicine. At that time, those Buddhas did not foretell My future by saying, 'You will realize supreme, fully perfected enlightenment and become one who understands the ways of the world, who is a teacher for ordinary people as well as those in lofty positions, and who is the World-honored One, for at some future time You will indeed be able to realize True Wisdom.'

"O Moggallana, I recall from My past having taken on the body of a saintly Wheel-turning Lord and having encountered eight billion Buddhas, all sharing the same name of Dipankara, the One Who Sets the Lamplight Ablaze. I, the Tathagata, along with My assembly of disciples, out of our esteem for Them, sustained Them by respectfully making offerings to Them of the four necessities: namely, shelter, clothing, food, and medicine, along with banners and canopies, flowers and incense. At that time those Buddhas did not foretell My future, saying, 'You will realize supreme, fully perfected enlightenment and become one who understands the ways of the world, who is a teacher for ordinary people as well as those in lofty positions, and who is the World-honored One.'

"O Moggallana, I recall from My past having taken on the body of a saintly Wheel-turning Lord and having encountered three billion Buddhas, all sharing the same name of the One Who Nourishes. I, the Tathagata, along with My assembly of disciples, made offerings to Them, completely supplying Them with the four necessities. At that time, those Buddhas did not foretell My future, saying, 'You will certainly become a Buddha.'"

In addition, He made offerings to countless other Buddhas. While in the body of a saintly Wheel-turning Lord, He surely would have ruled over the four continents and his supplies for making offerings to Buddhas must truly have been abundant.[1] If He was a great, saintly Wheel-turning Lord, He would have been lord over a three-thousandfold world. His offerings to Buddhas at that time were beyond the estimation of ordinary people today. Even if the Buddha were to explain it to them, it would be difficult for them to comprehend.

In the eighth chapter, "Pure View", of the *Scripture That Is the Buddha's Treasure House*, it says the following:

The Buddha once told Shariputra, "I recall from My past, when I was chasing after supreme, fully perfected enlightenment, I encountered thirty billion Buddhas, all sharing the same name of Shakyamuni. I then became a saintly Wheel-turning Lord and, for the purpose of seeking after supreme, fully perfected enlightenment, I made offerings of shelter, clothing, food, and medicine to all of Them and to Their disciples. Even so, those Buddhas did not foretell My future, saying, 'You will certainly realize Buddhahood in some future lifetime.' And why was that? Because My giving had an ulterior motive.[2]

"O Shariputra, I recall from My past that I was able to encounter eight thousand Buddhas, all of whom were called One of Constant Radiance. I then became a saintly Wheel-turning Lord and, for the purpose of seeking after supreme, fully perfected

---

1. The four continents refer to the four regions that lay around the spiritual Mount Sumeru.

2. Namely, seeking to 'get' supreme enlightenment, as if it were something to be purchased by doing virtuous deeds. Also, there is no mention in the quotations in this discourse that He sought enlightenment for the sake of helping others to realize the Truth.

enlightenment, I made offerings of shelter, clothing, food, and medicine to all of Them and to Their disciples. Even so, those Buddhas did not foretell My future, saying, 'You will certainly realize Buddhahood in some future lifetime.' And why was that? Because My giving had an ulterior motive.

"O Shariputra, I recall from My past that I encountered sixty thousand Buddhas all of whom were called One Who Is the Brightness of the Light. I then became a saintly Wheel-turning Lord and, for the purpose of seeking after supreme, fully perfected enlightenment, I made offerings of shelter, clothing, food, and medicine to all of Them and to Their disciples. Even so, those Buddhas did not foretell My future, saying, 'You will certainly realize Buddhahood in some future lifetime.' And why was that? Because my giving had an ulterior motive.

"O Shariputra, I recall from My past My encountering three billion Buddhas, all of whom were called One who Nourishes. I then became a saintly Wheel-turning Lord and made offerings of the four necessities to all of Them, but none foretold My future because My giving alms had an ulterior motive.

"O Shariputra, I recall from My past a time when I succeeded in encountering eighteen thousand Buddhas, all of whom were called One Who Is a Lord of the Mountain and whose eon was called the Upper Eight. Within this assembly of eighteen thousand Buddhas, all of us shaved our head, donned a kesa,[*] and studied the practice of supreme, fully perfected enlightenment, but none foretold My future Buddhahood because of My having an ulterior motive.

"O Shariputra, I recall from My past My being able to meet five hundred Buddhas, all of whom were called One Who Is Atop the Lotus Blossom. I then became a saintly Wheel-turning Lord and made alms offerings to all of Them and to Their disciples, but none foretold My future Buddhahood because I had an ulterior motive.

"O Shariputra, I recall from My past having had the opportunity to meet five hundred Buddhas, all of whom were called One Whose Virtue Is Majestic. Although I gave alms to one and all, none forecast My becoming a Buddha because of My having an ulterior motive.

"O Shariputra, I recall from My past My being able to meet two thousand Buddhas, all of whom were called Kaundinya. I then became a saintly Wheel-turning Lord for the sake of Them all, giving alms to one and all, but none foretold My becoming a Buddha because of My having an ulterior motive.

"O Shariputra, I recall from My past My encountering nine thousand Buddhas, all of whom were called Kashō. I supplied Their assembly of Buddhas and disciples with alms in the form of the four necessities, but none predicted My future Buddhahood because of My offering having an ulterior motive.

"O Shariputra, I recall from My past that there was a period of ten thousand eons, during which no Buddha emerged. At that time, there were ninety thousand pratyekabuddhas* during the first five hundred eons. Throughout the whole of My lifetimes, I made alms offerings of clothes, food, bedding, and medicine to all of Them, without exception, while showing My respect by praising Them. During the next five hundred eons, I again made alms offerings of the four necessities to all of Them, without exception, while showing My respect by praising Them.

"O Shariputra, when these thousands of eons had completely passed, there were no more pratyekabuddhas. I then died in Jambudvipa* and was reborn in the Brahma Heaven, becoming its great Lord Brahma.[3] Tossing about like this for five hundred eons, I was then born again in the Brahma Heaven, being

---

3. The Brahma Heaven is the lowest of the four meditation heavens in the world of form. Its inhabitants are said to be without sexual desire.

reborn as its great Lord Brahma rather than being reborn in Jambudvipa. When these five hundred eons had completely passed, I was reborn down in Jambudvipa, over which I governed. When My life came to an end, I was reborn in the celestial world of the Celestial Guardian Rulers of the Four Quarters. When My life came to an end there, I was reborn as Lord Indra in the Trayastrimsha Heaven with the name Shakrendra.[4] Rolling on in this manner, I was reborn in Jambudvipa after completing five hundred eons and then reborn in the Brahma Heaven for five hundred eons, becoming its great Lord Brahma.

"O Shariputra, for nine thousand eons only once was I reborn in Jambudvipa, and for another nine thousand eons I was reborn only in celestial worlds. At the time of the conflagration that ends an eon, I was reborn in the celestial world called Luminous Sound. When the world was completely recreated, I was again reborn in the Brahma Heaven. For nine thousand eons I was not reborn within the world of humans.

"O Shariputra, during these nine thousand eons, there were no Buddhas or pratyekabuddhas. Human beings who fell into evil ways were many indeed!

"O Shariputra, when these ten thousand eons had come to an end, there was a Buddha who emerged in the world called the Tathagata Who Guards the Universe, the Arhat,* the One Who Is Fully Enlightened, the One Possessed of Wise Discernment Who Travels the Way, the One Who Has Attained Emancipation, the One Who Knows the Ways of the World, the Unsurpassed One, the Trainer of Ordinary People and Those in Lofty Positions, the Awakened World-honored One. At that time, when My life came to an end in that Brahma Heaven, I was reborn in Jambudvipa, where I became a great saintly Wheel-turning Lord by the name of the

---

4.   The Trayastrimsha Heaven is the second of the six heavens in the world of desire.

Lord of the Celestial Community and had a life span of ninety thousand years by human reckoning. I spent the whole of that lifetime making all manner of pleasant offerings to the Buddha and ninety thousand of His monks, while remaining intent upon chasing after supreme, fully perfected enlightenment during these ninety thousand years. The Buddha Who Guards the Universe also did not predict My future Buddhahood. And why? Because at that time I was not able to thoroughly penetrate what the True Nature of all thoughts and things is, and therefore indulged in the viewpoint of having a personal self with its ulterior motive.

"O Shariputra, during this eon, there were a hundred Buddhas who had left home life behind, each having a different name. At that time, I became a saintly Wheel-turning Lord for each of Them and spent My entire life making alms offerings to Them, along with Their disciples, with the intent of pursuing supreme, fully perfected enlightenment. However, because of My having an ulterior motive, those Buddhas likewise did not foretell My realizing Buddhahood.

"O Shariputra, I recall from My past My having been able to encounter a thousand Buddhas during seven hundred eons of indeterminate length, all of whom were called One Who Is as the Golden Sands of the River Jambu. During the whole of that life, I made offerings to Them of the four necessities, and still none foretold My realizing Buddhahood because of My having an ulterior motive.

"O Shariputra, I recall from My past My having been able to encounter six hundred twenty myriad Buddhas during those great seven hundred eons of indeterminate length, all of whom were called One Who Sees the True Form of All Things. At that time, I became a saintly Wheel-turning Lord and throughout My life made all manner of pleasant alms offerings both to Them and to Their disciples, but again, none foretold My future Buddhahood because I had an ulterior motive.

"O Shariputra, I recall from My past My having been able to encounter eighty-four Buddhas during those great seven hundred eons of indeterminate length, all of whom were called One of Imperial Form. At that time, I became a saintly Wheel-turning Lord and throughout My life made all manner of pleasant alms offerings both to Them and to Their disciples, but none foretold My future Buddhahood because I had an ulterior motive.

"O Shariputra, I recall from My past My having been able to encounter fifteen Buddhas during those great seven hundred eons of indeterminate length, all of whom were called One Who Is as Radiant as the Sun. At that time, I became a saintly Wheel-turning Lord and through my life made all manner of pleasant alms offerings both to Them and to Their disciples, but none foretold My future Buddhahood because I had an ulterior motive.

"O Shariputra I recall from My past My having been able to encounter sixty-two Buddhas during those great seven hundred eons of indeterminate length, all of whom were called One Whose Tranquility Is Spiritually Good. At that time, I became a saintly Wheel-turning Lord and throughout my life made all manner of pleasant alms offerings both to Them and to Their disciples, but none foretold My future Buddhahood, because I had an ulterior motive.

"I tossed about like this until I met Dipankara, the Buddha Whose Radiance Is Constant, whereupon I was immediately able to realize the non-arising of all thoughts and things. Because of this, Dipankara Buddha foretold My future Buddhahood, saying 'In the future, after the present eon has passed, You will be able to realize Buddhahood, and You will be called Shakyamuni the Tathagata, the Arhat, the One Who Is Fully Enlightened, the One Possessed of Wise Discernment Who Travels the Way, the One Who Has

Attained Emancipation, the One Who Knows the Ways of the World, the Unsurpassed One, the Trainer of Beings High and Low, the Awakened World-honored One.'"

From His initial encounter with thirty billion Shakyamuni Buddhas up to His meeting the Tathagata Dipankara, He constantly served as a saintly Wheel-turning Lord, spending His whole life offering Them alms. Wheel-turning Lords may well live for more than eighty thousand years. His was an alms offering of all manner of pleasant things during each lifetime of some eighty or ninety thousand years. The one He called Dipankara, the Buddha Whose Radiance Is Constant, is the one we know as Dipankara, the Buddha Who Sets the Lamplight Ablaze. In both Scriptures, the Buddha-to-be encountered thirty billion Shakyamuni Buddhas. What is voiced in the passages from the *Scriptural Collection of the Past Deeds of the Buddha* and from the *Scripture That Is the Buddha's Treasure House* is essentially the same.

During His first immeasurable eon, Shakya Bodhisattva* encountered seventy-five thousand Buddhas whom He served and to whom He gave venerative offerings. The first was called Shakyamuni, and the last was one called Ratnashikhin, the One Whose Topknot Contains the Jewel. In His second immeasurable eon, He encountered seventy-six thousand Buddhas whom He served and to whom He gave venerative offerings. The first one was Ratnashikhin, the One Whose Topknot Contains the Jewel, and the last was one called Dipankara, the One Who Sets the Lamplight Ablaze. In His third immeasurable eon, He encountered seventy-seven thousand Buddhas whom He served and to whom He gave venerative offerings. The first one was Dipankara, the One Who Sets the Lamplight Ablaze, and the last was one called Bibashi, He

Whose Reflections Are Excellent.[5] During the ninety-one eons while He was exploring the deeds done in the past for which He was receiving karmic[*] effects, He encountered the Six Buddhas, whom He served and to whom He gave venerative offerings. The first of the six was Bibashi Buddha and the last was one called Kashō Buddha.

Generally speaking, in making offerings to Buddhas during the three great eons of indeterminate length, He did not begrudge Them anything, beginning with His very life and including such things as His kingdom and cities, His wife and children, His seven royal treasures, and His male and female servants.[6] This is something that goes beyond the ken of ordinary people. Sometimes He made Them offerings of golden millet piled high in silver bowls. At other times He made Them offerings of the Seven Treasures[*] piled high in gold and silver bowls. And sometimes He made offerings of sweet beans, or of flowers taken from the water and the land, or of sandalwood, aloes, and other types of incense. And sometimes He made offerings to Dipankara Buddha of five-stemmed blue lotus flowers bought at the price of five hundred gold pieces. He even made an offering to Dipankara Buddha of His deerskin kesa.

When it comes to offerings for Buddhas, as a rule you need not make offerings of what you think must surely be important to Them, just hasten to make your offerings while you are still alive, without letting any time—day or night—pass by in vain. Of what value is gold or silver to a Buddha? Of what value are incense and flowers to a Buddha? Even so, Their accepting what is offered is due to Their great wisdom and great compassion in helping us human beings to increase our merit.

---

5.   Bibashi Buddha is the first of the Seven Buddhas, of whom Shakyamuni Buddha is the seventh.

6.   The seven royal treasures are the Golden Wheel, wise elephants, swift horses, the divine Pearl, able ministers, women as precious as jewels, and loyal generals.

In the twenty-second fascicle of the *Great Scripture on the Buddha's Parinirvana*, it says the following:

> The Buddha once said, "O My good disciples, I recall that immeasurable, unbounded eons ago, when the world at that time was said to be corrupt, there was a World-honored Buddha who was called the Tathagata, the Arhat, the One Who Is Fully Enlightened, the One Possessed of Wise Discernment Who Travels the Way, the One Who Has Attained Emancipation, the One Who Knows the Ways of the World, the Unsurpassed One, the Trainer of Beings High and Low, the Awakened World-honored One. For the sake of His assembly, He was going to give voice to a great Teaching on His passing, a Teaching like this present one. At that time, I turned away from where My friends were in order to hear what that Enlightened One was about to say to His assembly concerning His Great Passing. Having heard of this topic, My heart was filled with joy and I desired to supply Him with an alms offering, but I was so poor that I had no possessions to give Him. Although I wanted to offer My own body for sale, unfortunately it did not sell, so I decided to return home. On My way back home, I met a man on the road, and I asked him, 'I am desirous of offering my body for sale. Could you not buy it?' The man replied, 'The task that I have at my home is beyond what anyone could endure. But if you were able to do it, I would indeed buy it.' Accordingly, I asked him, 'What task is it that no one could endure to do?' The man, seeing My interest, replied, 'I have a dreadful illness, for which a good physician has prescribed that I must take two or three servings of human flesh a day. If you, good sir, could supply me with two or three servings of your flesh daily, I would by all means provide you with five gold coins.' When I had heard this, a joy arose in My heart. I then told

him, 'If you will supply me with the coins and allow me seven days to wind up my affairs, I will return to you.' The man responded, 'Seven days won't do. If you will do as I have asked, I can allow you one day.'

"O my good disciples, I then took those coins and returned to where the Buddha was and bowed before Him, My forehead touching His feet. I then took all that I had received and gave it to Him as an alms offering. After that, I listened to His Teaching with an earnest heart. But at the time I was dull-witted, so even though I heard His Teaching, I was only able to retain the following stanza:

> *The Tathagata awoke to what nirvana is*
> *And cut Himself free from birth and death forever.*
> *If you listen to this with a sincere heart,*
> *You will ever know joy beyond measure.*

"Having taken this verse in, I forthwith returned to the sick man's house.

"O My good disciples, after My return I gave the man two or three pieces of My flesh daily, but because of the karmic effect of My reciting that verse, I experienced no pain. Day after day, without ceasing, I completed a whole month.

"O My good disciples, due to the karmic effect of this, the man recovered from his illness and My body also returned to normal, leaving no wounds or scars behind. At that time, seeing the merit that My body had been so fully supplied with, I gave rise to the intention to seek supreme, fully perfected enlightenment, for if the strength of one of His verses was like this, how much more so were I to fully accept, preserve, and recite His whole Scripture! Seeing that this Scripture had such profit as this only strengthened My resolve, and I vowed that if I were able to realize Buddhahood at a future time, I would take the name of Shakyamuni.

"O My good disciples, because of the strength from the karmic effects of this one verse, I have given voice to the whole Scripture today for the sake of ordinary people as well as those in lofty positions within this great assembly.

"O My good disciples, because of these karmic effects you should know that this *Great Scripture on the Buddha's Parinirvana* is wondrous beyond comprehension, creating immeasurable, boundless merit. Accordingly, this Scripture is the Treasure House of Fully Awakened Tathagatas, of That which is the Profoundly Mysterious."

The bodhisattva who would sell his own body at that time was a cause from the past for the arising of our present-day Shakyamuni Buddha. When we search through other Scriptures, we learn that at the very beginning of the first eon of indeterminate length, there was a time when He made venerative offerings to a previous Shakyamuni Buddha. At that time, He was a tiler who went by the name of He Who Is a Great Radiance. When He gave alms to the previous Shakyamuni Buddha, along with His disciples, He made three kinds of offerings: namely, meditation cushions, sweetened water, and candles. At that time, He made a vow that His nationality, name, life, and disciples would be one and the same with those of this previous Shakyamuni Buddha.

The vow that He made has already been fulfilled today. Thus, when you consider making an offering to the Buddha, do not say that your body is insufficient or that your home is devoid of any value. This account of someone selling his own body in order to make an offering to the Buddhas is genuine Teaching by our present-day Great Master, the Venerable Shakyamuni. Who would not take delight in it? In this story, the Buddha describes someone who would cut off three pieces of his own bodily flesh day after day. Even if that person had been the sick man's good spiritual friend, it is not something that any friend could bear to do. Even so, aided by his profound desire to give alms to a Buddha, he performed the good deeds just described. We are now able to hear the True Teaching of the Tathagata because He was able to dispense with His fleshly body in ancient times. The four lines of the present stanza are beyond anything that can be bought with five gold coins. During your three immeasurable great hundred eons, do not forget your receiving and discarding of lives. Truly, there will be merit that will boggle the mind in your awakening to the Radiance, just as all the Buddhas have done. The disciples who inherit the Dharma should, in all humility, receive It upon the crown of their head and recite It from memory. The Tathagata has already stated that the power of a single verse can be like this, so immensely profound It is.

In the "Expedient Means" chapter of the *Lotus Scripture*, there is the following verse:

> *If people at stupas and shrines,*
> *And before bejeweled statues and their painted forms*
> *Make offerings of flowers and incense, banners and*
>   *canopies,*
> *And all with a reverent heart,*
> *Or have others make music*
> *By beating drums, blowing horns and conches,*
> *Playing panpipes and flutes, lutes and lyres,*
> *As well as harps and cymbals and gongs,*
> *And make all such wondrous sounds as these*
> *To be their offering,*
> *Or if, with a heart filled with joy,*
> *They sing the praises of the Buddha's merit,*
> *Though it be but a single small sound,*
> *All will realize the Buddha's Way.*
> *Even if people with a scattered mind*
> *Should make an offering to His painted form,*
> *Though it be but a single flower's bloom,*
> *They will, at length, meet Buddhas beyond count.*

> *Or if they bow in deepest respect,*
> *Or simply make gasshō**
> *Though it be with the raising of a single hand*
> *Or a slight nod of the head,*
> *And thereby make their offering to a pictured Saintly One,*
> *They too, at length, will meet Buddhas beyond count.*
> *And, personally realizing the Supreme Way,*
> *They will help countless beings reach the Other Shore.*

This is the very Countenance of the Buddhas in the three temporal worlds. It is Their very Eye, so you should strive with all diligence to meet those of wise discernment and emulate them. Do not let time vainly pass by. As Great Master Sekitō Kisen once said, "Do not waste time." Spiritually beneficial actions like these produce Buddhahood in every case and will do so in the past, present, and future. There cannot be two ways, or three ways.[7] Realizing the fruits of Buddhahood is due to one's making offerings to Buddhas.

Our Ancestral Master Nāgārjuna once said the following in verse:

> *In our seeking the fruits of Buddhahood,*
> *To extol a single verse,*
> *To recite a single 'Homage',*
> *To burn a single pinch of incense,*
> *To offer a single flower,*
> *Even such small deeds as these,*
> *Without fail, will enable us to realize Buddhahood.*

Even though this is what our Ancestral Master Nāgārjuna Bodhisattva put forth for himself, nevertheless we should dedicate our life to it. And what is more, it is something that our Great Master Shakyamuni Buddha expressed, and which our

---

7.　That is, there is only one way to realize Buddhahood in any time period.

Ancestral Master Nāgārjuna expressed and accurately Transmitted. What can be more wonderful than our being so fortunate as to obtain something so precious, as we now climb the Treasured Mountain of the Buddha's Way and enter the Treasured Ocean of the Buddha's Way?[8] Surely it must be due to the power from our making offerings to the Buddha over vast eons. You must not doubt that you will inevitably realize Buddhahood, for it is a foregone conclusion. It is precisely what the Buddha gave voice to.

Furthermore, there are instances when a small cause produces great fruit and a small karmic condition produces great recompense. In our pursuit of the Buddha's Way, if we extol a single verse, recite 'Homage to the Buddha' one time, or burn a single pinch of incense, without fail, we will be able to realize Buddhahood. And what is more, if, upon hearing the Teaching, we really know the True Form of all thoughts and things, which is beyond birth and beyond death, beyond non-arising and beyond non-perishing, then we will not likely lose sight of whatever karmic causes or conditions we are involved with.

It is clear from this passage that what the World-honored One voiced was authentically Transmitted to our Ancestral Master Nāgārjuna. His golden words, which are faithful to the Truth, are endowed with what he had inherited through the genuine Transmission. Even though they are indeed what our Ancestral Master Nāgārjuna voiced, they should not be judged by comparing them with what other Masters have taught. What can be a greater source of joy than our being able to encounter the genuine Transmission that has spread abroad what the World-honored One was

---

8. 'The Treasured Mountain' is an allusion to Mount Sumeru, which is associated with doing our training. 'The Treasured Ocean' is an allusion to the merit realized through doing that training.

pointing us to? So, do not compare these saintly Teachings with the arbitrary and meaningless preachings of ordinary teachers in China.

Our Ancestral Master Nāgārjuna once said, "Furthermore, it follows that, because Buddhas revere the Dharma, They make a venerative offering to the Teaching and take the Dharma as Their Master. And why is this? Because all Buddhas in the three temporal worlds make the True Form of all thoughts and things Their Master."

Someone then asked, "Why do They not make offerings to the Teaching that is within Their own being, but only make offerings to the Teaching in others?"

Nāgārjuna replied, "To make such offerings would be to follow worldly ways. If monks are desirous of showing veneration to the Treasure of Teaching, they do not make such an offering to the Teaching within their own being, but make it to others who are preserving the Teaching, who know the Teaching, who understand the Teaching. Buddhas are no different. Even though They have the Teaching within Their own being, still, They make venerative offerings to the Teaching in other Buddhas."

The person then asked, "Granted that monks, like Buddhas, are not seeking for good fortune or virtue, so why do they make venerative offerings?"

Nāgārjuna replied, "The Buddha had been cultivating all manner of meritorious deeds over immeasurably long eons, always doing what was good. Even so, He did not seek any manner of recompense. He made His venerative offerings out of His reverence for meritorious deeds.

"For instance, when the Buddha was alive, there was a blind monk who, nevertheless, was able to sew. One day, his needle came unthreaded. Thereupon, he asked, 'Is there someone who so longs for the merit from performing good deeds that he would thread this needle for me?' At that very moment, the Buddha had just arrived where the monk was and said to him, 'I am one who longs for the merit from performing good deeds, so I will come and thread your needle.' This monk, upon recognizing the Buddha's voice, immediately stood up, put on his kesa, and then prostrated himself before the Buddha's feet, saying, 'O Buddha, You are already filled to the brim with merit, so why do You say that You long for more?' The Buddha responded, 'Though I may already be filled with merit, I profoundly recognize My debt of gratitude for that merit, the effects and recompense from good deeds done in the past, and the power of meritorious actions. My having attained preeminence among all sentient beings is due to the merit from performing good deeds, which is why I long for it.' The Buddha, having finished His praise of meritorious actions, then gave an impromptu Dharma Teaching for the monk's sake. Having attained the Pure Eye, this monk's fleshly eyes were also made clear."

I heard this story a long time ago during an evening talk in my late Master's quarters. Later, I was able to check up on it, comparing it against the passage in the *Commentary on the Heart Scripture*. The instructive retelling by my late Master who had Transmitted the Dharma to me was clear, without anything left out. This passage is in the tenth fascicle of the *Commentary on the Heart Scripture*. It was clear from this that all Buddhas, without exception, take the True Form of all thoughts and things to be Their great Teacher. The Venerable Shakyamuni Buddha had also given witness to the eternal Truth of all Buddhas.

Taking the True Form of all thoughts and things to be one's great Teacher means making offerings out of deep respect for the Three Treasures of Buddha, Dharma, and Sangha. For immeasurable, indeterminately long eons, Buddhas have amassed meritorious deeds and good spiritual roots without seeking any recompense, but simply making offerings out of reverence for meritorious actions. Having arrived at the state of wise discernment, which is the fruition of Buddhahood, They are fond of doing small virtuous acts, such as threading a needle for a blind monk. If you desire to clarify what the meritorious actions are of someone who brought Buddhahood to fruition, the present story is certainly a precise account of it.

Therefore, meritorious actions that are based on both the wise discernment that is a fruit of Buddhahood and on the underlying principle of what the True Form of all thoughts and things is, are not something akin to what ordinary, everyday people in the world today would fancy them to be. What ordinary people think today is that the True Form of all thoughts and things refers to the manufacturing of evil, and that the wise discernment which is the fruition of Buddhahood simply means having an ulterior motive. False views like these, even though they are known to have existed for eighty thousand eons, have never been free of the eternalist view of past eons or of the nihilistic view of future eons.[9] So how could they possibly fully realize that the True Form of all thoughts and things is something that each and every Buddha has penetrated through and through? The reason for this is that each Buddha and every Buddha has thoroughly explored the True Form of all thoughts and things.

Generally speaking, there are ten types of venerative offerings:[10]

---

9.   The eternalist view is that there is something that continues through time as an unchanging, unchangeable essence. The nihilistic view is that there is a self which comes to an end at the time of death.

10.   Quoted by Dōgen from the *Writings on the Teachings of Mahayana (Daijōgi-shō)*.

First, making a venerative offering to the Buddha's Person;

Second, making a venerative offering to the shrine attached to His stupa;[11]

Third, making a venerative offering to a stupa, a shrine, or whatever else represents the body of that Buddha;

Fourth, making a venerative offering to that Buddha where there is no such representation;

Fifth, making a venerative offering by oneself;

Sixth, urging others to make venerative offerings;

Seventh, making a venerative offering of goods and money to the Buddhas or to Their shrines;

Eighth, making a venerative offering with a devout mind;

Ninth, making a venerative offering with a non-attached mind;

And tenth, making a venerative offering of one's devotion to Buddhist practice.

Among these, Number 1, making a venerative offering to the Buddha's Person, is explained in the commentary as: "Providing an alms offering to the physical body of a Buddha is called making a venerative offering to the physical body of a Buddha.

Number 2, making a venerative offering to the repository of a Buddha, is called making a venerative offering to the shrine attached to His stupa. It says in the *Code of Behavior for the Members of the Greater Sangha,* "That which houses relics we call a stupa, and that which contains no relics we call a shrine." Some say that both are called a *caitya.* Also, what is called a stupa in Indic languages is also called a pagoda. Also, what is translated here as 'shrine' is called a *caitya* in Sanskrit, which

---

11.   Stupa is a Sanskrit term for a pagoda-shaped structure, which customarily contains the funeral ashes of someone who is regarded as a Buddha. The shrine, or in Sanskrit *caitya,* is a ceremonial chapel which is attached to a stupa and which customarily does not contain relics.

in the *Āgama Scriptures* was pronounced 'shicha'. But it seems to make no difference whether we call it a stupa or a shrine. Even so, as the great Tendai Meditation Master Nangaku Eshi said in his commentary, *My Humble Explanation of the Meditative State That Is a Blossoming of the Dharma*: "Wholeheartedly do we respectfully bow to the relics of the Buddhas throughout the whole universe and to Their venerable portraits, to Their caityas and to Their stupas, to Them as Tathagatas of many treasures, and to the treasured stupa that is the whole body that They have discarded." Clearly, stupas and shrines, as well as relics and portraits, seem to be separate things.

The following account comes from the thirty-third fascicle of the *Code of Behavior for the Members of the Greater Sangha,* entitled "The Teaching Regarding Stupas":

> Once when the Buddha was wandering about while sojourning in the country of Koshala, He came upon a Brahman who was tilling the soil. Upon seeing the World-honored One passing by, he stuck his ox-goading staff into the ground as a prop and respectfully bowed to the Buddha. The World-honored One, having seen this, broke out in a smile.
>
> His monks said to Him, "We'd really like to hear what has caused You to smile."
>
> Thereupon, He told His monks, "This Brahman has just paid homage to two World-honored Ones."
>
> The monks then asked, "Which two Buddhas do you mean?"
>
> The Buddha then told the monks, "Under that very staff which he used when bowing to Me, there is the stupa of Kashō Buddha."
>
> The monks then said to the Buddha, "We pray that You will let us see the stupa of Kashō Buddha."

The Buddha then told the monks, "You must defer to this Brahman and ask him for this plot of land, along with its clod of earth."

The monks thereupon sought this from the Brahman. The Brahman forthwith offered it to them. The World-honored One then made the seven-jeweled stupa of Kashō Buddha appear. Its height was one yojana,* and the width of its face was half a yojana. When the Brahman saw this, he immediately said to the Buddha, "World-honored One, my family name is Kashō, and this is the stupa of our Kashō."

At that time when the World-honored One was fashioning the stupa for Kashō Buddha at that place, the monks asked the Buddha if the World-honored One would permit them to contribute the earth that they had received from the Brahman, to which the Buddha replied that they could. He thereupon gave voice to the following poem:

> *A hundred thousand loads of purest gold*
> *Are not the equal of a single lump of soil*
> *Used, with devoted mind,*
> *To fashion a Buddha's stupa.*

The World-honored One then personally erected Kashō Buddha's stupa. From its square base, which was bordered on all four sides with a railing, there arose two circular terraces, with ornamental tusk-like structures coming out from the base at its four corners. From the top, there arose a tall pole adorned with banners and ringed with parasols. The Buddha said, "This is how a stupa should be constructed." Once the setting up of the stupa was finished, the World-honored One Himself made prostrations to it out of respect for the past Buddha.

---

* See *Glossary.*

The monks then asked the Buddha. "World-honored One, may we too make prostrations to Him?"

The Buddha responded, "You may." He then composed the following poem:

> *Even hundreds of thousands of gold coins*
> *Brought here as people's offering of alms*
> *Do not equal the respect of someone of good*
> *heart*
> *Bowing before a Buddha's stupa.*

At that time, the local people, having heard of the World-honored One's constructing a stupa, brought incense and flowers as offerings to the World-honored One. Because the World-honored One had paid respect to a Buddha of the past, He forthwith accepted the flowers and incense and offered them to the stupa.

The monks then asked the Buddha, "May we too make offerings?" The Buddha replied, "You may." He then composed the following poem:

> *Even a hundred thousand carts filled with pure gold*
> *Brought here as an alms offering*
> *Do not equal an offering of flowers and incense*
> *By one of good heart.*

A great assembly then gathered like clouds. The Buddha then instructed Shariputra, "You should give voice to the Dharma for the sake of these people." Afterwards, the Buddha composed the following poem:

> *Even an alms offering of pure gold*
> *Enough to fill a hundred thousand Jambudvipas*
> *Does not equal one offering of Dharma*
> *That persuades others to pursue the practice and*
> *training.*

At that time, there were those sitting in the assembly who had realized the Way. The Buddha then composed the following poem for them:

> *Even an offering of pure gold*
> *Enough to fill a hundred thousand worldly realms*
> *Does not equal one offering of Dharma*
> *That leads others to see the Truth.*

At that time, a Brahman of unshakable faith set forth before the stupa a food offering for the Buddha and His monks. Then King Prasenajit,[12] hearing of the World-honored One's constructing a stupa for Kashō Buddha, ordered seven hundred carts to be loaded with tiles, then coming to where the Buddha was, he bowed, touching his forehead to the Buddha's feet. He then asked the Buddha, "World-honored One, I would like to enlarge this stupa. May I do so?" The Buddha replied, "You may."

The Buddha then told the great king, "In a past age, at the time of Kashō Buddha's passing away, there was a ruler named He of Good Fortune. He was desirous of constructing for Him a stupa made of the Seven Treasures, when one of his ministers said to the king, 'At some future time, there will be those who are opposed to the Dharma who will appear and will destroy this stupa, acquiring heavy wrongdoing. O Great King, I beg of you that you will simply construct it of tiles, which will then be covered in gold and silver. Even if the gold and silver are taken away, the stupa will still be as it was at first'. Thereupon, in accord with what the minister had said, the stupa was built of tiles, which were then covered over with a thin layer of gold foil. Its height was one yojana high and its front face was half a yojana wide. The railing was made of copper. It took seven years, seven months, and seven days to complete."

---

12.   The king of Koshala, who was a lay disciple of the Buddha.

King Prasenajit then told the Buddha, "That king had an abundance of merit along with rare treasures. I too will now build a stupa, though I am not that king's equal." When seven months and seven days had passed, the stupa was completed. Upon its completion the king made offerings to the Buddha and His monastic community.

The Method for Constructing a Stupa

The base is foursquare, with a railing around the perimeter. Two circular terraces rise up from the base, and four tusk-like structures emerge from its four corners. A tall spire adorned with banners and ringed with parasols arises from the top. If any say, "Even though the World-honored One may have freed Himself from greed, hatred, and delusion, He still has need for a stupa," they are harboring a violation of the Buddhist Precepts and, for ages, the retribution from that will be great indeed. The preceding is called 'the method for constructing a stupa'.

Matters Concerning Stupas [13]

When building a temple, first off, take a survey of land well-suited for erecting a stupa. The stupa is not to be located in the south or in the west. Rather, it should be located in the east or the north. Do not let the place where monks will reside encroach on the Buddha's land, and do not let the place where the Buddhas reside

---

13.   In this section, the term 'stupa' is being used as synonymous with 'temple' or 'monastery'.

encroach on the place for the monks.[14] If the stupa is close to a burial grove or if dogs were to desecrate this area by bringing in the remains of what they have been eating, by all means, construct a perimeter fence. When you construct monks' quarters, you should locate them in the west or in the south. You should build the stupa atop a high place, and not let water from the monks' land flow onto the Buddha's land, though water from the Buddha's land may be allowed to run onto the monks' land. Within the perimeter of the stupa, you are not to wash or dye your robes, set them out to dry, wear leather shoes, cover your head, or cover your bare shoulder. Nor should you hack and spit on the ground. Were you to say such a thing as, "If the World-honored One has rid Himself of greed, hatred, and delusion, what use does He have for this stupa?" you would be harboring wrongdoing that surpasses what has been spelled out in the monastic Precepts, and the karmic consequences will be heavy indeed! These things are what we call 'matters concerning stupas'.

Stupa Alcoves

At a time when King Prasenajit paid a visit to the Buddha, he bowed down, respectfully touching his forehead on the Buddha's feet, and asked the Buddha, "World-honored One, in making a stupa for Kashō Buddha, may we fashion alcoves?"

The Buddha replied, "You may. In a past generation, after Kashō Buddha had passed on into parinirvana, a ruler named He of Good Fortune raised a stupa for that Buddha. He constructed alcoves on its four faces. On their upper parts he fashioned images

14. That is, the monks' quarters (in particular, the Meditation Hall) should be kept separate from the Buddha Hall, which is to be reserved for ceremonial.

of lions and all sorts of painted ornamental patterns. In front of them he constructed railings. The alcoves were places for putting flowers. Inside the alcoves he hung banners and parasols.

"Should people say, 'The World-honored One has already rid Himself of greed, hatred, and delusion, so why does He still take pleasure in glorifying Himself?' they will be harboring wrongdoing that surpasses what has been spelled out in the monastic Precepts, and the karmic consequences of that will be heavy indeed! This is what we call 'methods for stupa alcoves.'"

It is evident that, above and beyond the wisdom from realizing Buddhahood, to erect a stupa for a past Buddha and to respectfully bow and make offerings to it is a customary practice of Buddhas. Although there have been many examples of actions such as these, for the present, I will just cite the preceding. As for the Buddha Dharma, the Sarvastivādin tradition is supreme,[15] and within that tradition, the *Code of Behavior for the Members of the Greater Sangha* is considered the most fundamental. The *Code of Behavior for the Members of the Greater Sangha* was first brought to China by Hōken after he had cleared a path to India through brambles and thorns and had climbed the Divine Vulture Peak. The Dharma that has been Transmitted by our Ancestors from one to another is in accord with the Sarvastivādin tradition.

Number 3, making a venerative offering to a stupa, a shrine, or whatever else represents the body of a Buddha, means making venerative offerings to something that is actually right before one's eyes, such as a Buddha in the flesh or a shrine.

---

15. The Sarvastivādin tradition, though associated with a scholastic Hinayana viewpoint, nevertheless shares a common viewpoint with the Mahayana Zen tradition: namely, that all thoughts and things have real existence, which thereby affirms the existence of this world.

Number 4, making a venerative offering to a Buddha where there is no such representation, means 'making a venerative offering when there is no Buddha or shrine right before us. That is to say, we make offerings not only to what is right before us but also to what is not right before us, be it a Buddha, a shrine, a stupa, or a tomb. Making offerings to what is right before our eyes earns great merit, and making offerings to what is not right before our eyes earns even greater merit, because the scope is ever so much broader. Those who make venerative offerings both to what is right before their eyes and to what is not right before their eyes earn the greatest amount of merit.

Number 5, making a venerative offering by oneself, means using our whole being to make venerative offerings to Buddhas and shrines.

Number 6, urging others to make a venerative offering to a Buddha or a shrine means that even though what someone has to offer is but something quite small, we should help that person not to be shy about offering it. That is, whether such an offering is actually made by oneself or by another, it is all the same. One's own making of the offering earns great merit, helping others learn to make offerings earns twice as much merit, and making offerings together with others earns the greatest merit.

With Number 7, making a venerative offering of goods and money to Buddhas or to Their shrines or stupas or relics, there are three types of offerings. The first is the offering of necessities, such as clothing and food. The second is the offering of venerative goods, such as incense and flowers. The third is the offering of ornamental objects, namely all other kinds of treasures and adornments.

With Number 8, making a venerative offering with a devout mind, there are three types of devotion. With the first, one simply makes various types of offerings. With the second, when we have a pure and trusting heart that has faith in the virtue of Buddha, then the underlying principle is in accord with what is offered. The third is the heart that transfers one's merit to others, which is the making of our offering from within a heart that seeks Buddha.

Number 9, as to making a venerative offering with a non-attached mind, there are two kinds. The first is the mind being untainted, by which we let go of all our mistakes. The second is the things offered being untainted, in which we let go of all the mistakes that we have made through our not conforming to the Dharma.

Number 10 is making a venerative offering that attains the Way. That is to say, what we call making a venerative offering that attains the Way is our doing venerative deeds that comply with the goal. Some call 'attaining the Way' by names like 'making an offering of the Dharma', and some call it 'making an offering of one's actions'. As to these, there are three types: The first treats making an offering that attains the Way as making offerings of material goods. The second treats making an offering that attains the Way as making an offering that complies with what is good. The third treats making an offering that attains the Way as making an offering of one's training and practice.

Making venerative offerings to the Buddha already encompasses these ten types of offerings. Similar categories also apply to the Dharma and the Sangha. That is to say, making venerative offerings to the Dharma is our making offerings to the principles that the Buddha taught, as well as to the methods of practice that He gave expression to, including the Scriptural texts. And making venerative offerings to the Sangha is our making offerings to saintly assemblies of all Three Courses,* as well as to their temples, along with their iconography and stupas, including monastics who have not yet fully awakened.

Next, there are six types of minds that make venerative offerings.

The first is the unsurpassed mind that produces good fortune like a field abundant with rice. It is the most excellent good fortune that arises within such an abundant field.

The second is the unsurpassed mind that recognizes the virtue of indebtedness, since all virtuous joys arise from the Three Treasures.

The third is the unsurpassed mind that arises within all sentient beings.

The fourth is the mind that is as hard to encounter as a flowering udumbara tree.

The fifth is the solitary, unique mind that is one with the three-thousand great-thousandfold universe.

The sixth is the mind that is fully equipped with dependable understanding of all realms and what lies beyond such realms.

In short, the Tathagata, who fully comprehends the ways of the world and the ways beyond the worldly, has been able to supply sentient beings with a reliable foundation. This is called 'being fully equipped with dependable understanding'. If you make venerative offerings to the Three Treasures with these six attitudes of mind, then even if your offerings are small, you will receive immeasurable, boundless merit. How much more so if your offerings were plentiful!

We should make such alms offerings with a sincere heart, for, without fail, it is how Buddhas have been accustomed to making offerings. Stories in Scriptures and monastic regulations about such alms offerings are plain to see, still, the Buddhas and Ancestors have customarily Transmitted this practice personally. Occasions for making venerative offerings abound in the days and months you spend attending on others and carrying out your work duties. The methods for placing images and relics, for making venerative offerings and respectfully bowing, for building stupas, and for constructing shrines have been authentically Transmitted only in the quarters of our Ancestors of the Buddha. If these methods had not descended from our Ancestors of the Buddha, they would not have been authentically Transmitted.

Also, if such methods have not been authentically Transmitted in accord with the Dharma, they will contradict the Dharma. When the ways of making offerings contradict the Dharma, they will not be genuine. When the ways of making offerings are not genuine, the merit therefrom will be negligible. Beyond question, you need to learn the methods for making venerative offerings that are in accord with the Dharma and authentically Transmit them. Meditation Master Reitō spent many years tending to Daikan Enō's stupa. The temple worker Ro spent his days and nights pounding rice as his alms offering for the assembly. Both of these are instances of methods for making venerative offerings that accord with the Dharma.[16] These are but a small sample of such instances, which I do not have the time to quote extensively. You should make your alms offerings in a similar manner to theirs.

On a day during the summer retreat in the seventh year of the Kenchō era (1255).

Copied in the Monks' Hall at Eihei-ji Temple on the twenty-third day of the sixth lunar month in the second year of the Kōan era (August 2, 1279).

---

16.   Reitō was a monk in Enō's monastery on Mount Sōkei. After Enō's death, Reitō spent the rest of his life—he died at age 95—devoted to tending Enō's stupa, which housed the kesa that Enō had received from his Master Daiman Kōnin as confirmation of his having fully awakened to the Truth. This kesa is said to be the one that Shakyamuni Buddha Transmitted to Makakashō. It is still in existence at the monastery. Ro is Enō's family name. It is used here to refer to the time when he worked as a lay laborer at Kōnin's monastery.

87

On Taking Refuge in the Treasures
of Buddha, Dharma, and Sangha

(Kie Buppōsō Hō)

Translator's Introduction: This discourse is also known as "On Taking Refuge in the Three Treasures" (*Kie Sambō*). As the postscript indicates, this discourse is an early draft which Dōgen did not finish before his death, though he apparently was planning to include it in his projected one-hundred-discourse *Shōbōgenzō*. It contains several quite long quotations, but Dōgen had not yet cited the sources of some of them in the text.

It says in the *Procedures for Cleanliness in a Zen Temple* (First fascicle, question 120), "Do you show respect for Buddha, Dharma, and Sangha?" It is quite clear that in India and China, the Buddhas and Ancestors authentically Transmitted the practice of making venerative offerings to Buddha, Dharma, and Sangha out of respect for Them. If you do not take refuge in Them, you will not revere Them, and if you do not revere Them, you will not be able to take refuge in Them. We invariably receive the spiritual merit of taking refuge in Buddha, Dharma, and Sangha whenever there is a spiritual connection between Them and us sentient beings, as well as between Master and disciple. Whether we are in some exalted celestial state, or among ordinary human beings, or in some hell, or acting like some demon or beast, if a spiritual connection takes place, we do not fail to humbly take refuge in Them. Once we have taken refuge, we promote merit in life after life, in generation after generation, in existence after existence, and in place after place as we strive to accumulate merit and achieve supreme, fully perfected enlightenment. Even if we happen to be misled by bad companions or to meet up with some devilish hindrance so that our good roots are severed for the time being, or even if we act like an icchantika,* ultimately our good roots will continue on and we will promote their spiritual merit. The meritorious virtue of taking refuge in the Three Treasures is, ultimately, not subject to extensive decay.

---

* See *Glossary.*

Taking refuge in the Three Treasures means wholeheartedly acting from pure trust—be it while a Tathagata is in the world or be it after a Tathagata has become extinct—and, with hands in gasshō* and bowed head, reciting the following aloud:

> *I humbly take refuge in the Buddha,*
> *I humbly take refuge in the Dharma,*
> *I humbly take refuge in the Sangha.*

> *I humbly take refuge in the Buddha, the most venerated*
> *among humans,*
> *I humbly take refuge in the Dharma, the most venerated*
> *among those who have forsaken their passions,*
> *I humbly take refuge in the Sangha, the most venerated*
> *among those in our assemblies.*

> *I have taken refuge in the Buddha,*
> *I have taken refuge in the Dharma,*
> *I have taken refuge in the Sangha.*

In our aspiring to the far-off wisdom that is the fruition of Buddhahood, we begin by bringing into existence just such a protective garb.[1] Thus, even though our body and our mind right now, instant by instant, are arising and vanishing, our aspiration for Buddhahood will surely long continue to thrive until we fully realize our enlightenment.

The term *kie*, 'to take refuge', is made up of two characters. The first, *ki*, means 'to keep returning to' and the second, *e*, means 'to submit ourselves devotedly to'. Thus, *kie*, 'to take refuge', more literally means 'to devote oneself to returning to'. The form of this returning is like that of a child returning again and again to its parent. 'To submit ourselves devotedly to' is like people depending on their leader. In other words, this term is synonymous with 'to be rescued by', 'to be freed by'. Because 'the Buddha' refers to our Great Master, we therefore take refuge in Him.

---

1.   That is, taking the Three Refuges acts like a suit of armor to protect us from whatever attacks us spiritually.

Because 'the Dharma' refers to good spiritual medicine, we take refuge in It. Because 'the Sangha' refers to excellent spiritual friends, we take refuge in them.

A Chinese commentary on Mahayana* Buddhism has the following dialogue:

> *Someone once asked a Master, "Why do we take refuge in* these Three Treasures?"
>
> The Master answered, "Because in the long run, by making these Three Treasures what we return to, They can help us sentient beings free ourselves from the delusion of 'life and death' and realize the Great Awakening. This is why we take refuge in Them."

These Three Refuges are ultimately of astounding spiritual merit. In India, the word 'Buddha' was pronounced like *buddhaya*, and in China, the term 'supreme, fully perfected enlightenment' was translated simply as 'awakening'. In India, the term for 'the Teaching' was pronounced as *Dharma* in Sanskrit or as *Dhamma* in Pali. In China, it was translated by the character that we read as *hō*. All meanings of *hō*—good, bad, or neutral—are called 'dharma', but the Dharma that we now take refuge in is the Dharma that is the Wheel of the Law. What we call *sōgya* is pronounced as *Sangha* in India, and is translated as 'the harmonious community' in China. The following is how we habitually speak when praising Them.[2]

---

2.   The source of the quotation that follows has not been located. It may be of Dōgen's composition.

The Three Treasures as things that physically exist
and which we preserve:

The Buddha Treasure as religious statues and pictures, along with shrines and reliquaries.

The Dharma Treasure as the Scriptural scrolls, which are made of yellow paper wound around a red rod, and which have been handed down to us.

The Sangha Treasure as those who shave their heads, dye their robes, and observe the Precepts which are the True Teaching.

The Three Treasures as the means for teaching
sentient beings:

The Buddha Treasure as the World-honored Shakyamuni Buddha.

The Dharma Treasure as His turning of the Wheel of the Law, along with the saintly Teaching that He propagated.

The Sangha Treasure as the five companions, namely, Ajnyata Kaundinya and the others.[3]

The Three Treasures as Embodiments of Truth:

The Buddha Treasure as what is provisionally called 'the five merits of the Dharma Body'.[4]

The Dharma Treasure as what is provisionally called 'the principle of the cessation of suffering through non-attachment'.

---

3.   An allusion to the five ascetics who accompanied Prince Siddhārtha while he was training as a forest hermit. They were the first of the Buddha's followers to realize the Truth and become arhats.

4.   That is, the five kinds of merit embodied in one who has realized enlightenment, namely, being free from any offences against the Precepts, being free from all delusory thoughts while remaining tranquil in heart, being possessed of wise discernment, being rid of all entanglements, and being aware of having become free of all entanglements.

The Sangha Treasure as what is provisionally called 'the merit of pursuing through one's training what is beyond conventional forms of training'.

The Three Treasures as being essentially one and the same:

The Buddha Treasure as what is provisionally called 'That which realizes the Truth as ultimate enlightenment'.

The Dharma Treasure as that which is provisionally called 'That which is immaculate and free of any taint'.

The Sangha Treasure as that which is provisionally called 'those who have realized the Truth and, in harmony with It, are neither bound nor limited by It'.[5]

This is the way that one humbly takes refuge in the Three Treasures. If people are scant of good fortune or slight in merit, they do not hear even the name of the Three Treasures, so how could they possibly take refuge in Them!

In the *Lotus Scripture*, there is the following poem:

> *All these besmirched creatures,*
> *Pass through countless eons*
> *Hearing not the name of the Triple Treasure*
> *Due to their wretched karma.* *

The *Lotus Scripture* is the karmic connection to the One Great Matter* of all Buddhas and Tathagatas. Within all the Teachings that were expressed by our Great Master, the Venerable Shakyamuni, the *Lotus Scripture* is the most sovereign and our greatest teacher. All the other Scriptures and Teachings are as the *Lotus Scripture*'s loyal subjects or as Its familial relatives. What is voiced within the *Lotus Scripture* is the

---

5.   That is, there is no tinge of fatalism in what such a one does.

Truth. All that is expressed within our other Scriptures is tinged with expedient means, which is not the fundamental intent of the Buddha. Were you to bring forth what is expressed in the other Scriptures in order to evaluate what is in the *Lotus Scripture*, you would be getting things backwards. If they were not cloaked in the meritorious powers of the *Lotus Scripture*, these other Scriptures could not exist. All these other Scriptures are waiting to return to, and be in accord with, the *Lotus Scripture*. The *Lotus Scripture* contains what is being expressed here and now. Be aware that the merits of the Three Treasures are said to be the most esteemed and most sublime.

The World-honored One once said the following:

> When ordinary people become apprehensive over something that seems foreboding, they often seek refuge in such places as mountains or parklands, as well as in some monastery, up some tree, or in some mausoleum. These refuges are not particularly of the highest quality, nor are they the most valuable. People cannot free themselves from human suffering by relying on such refuges. When people take refuge in the Buddha, as well as in the Dharma and the Sangha, then, by means of their wise discernment, they continually observe everything from within the Four Noble Truths, namely, being aware of suffering, being aware of how suffering accumulates, being aware of how suffering is transcended forever, and being aware of the Noble Eightfold Path. Taking this refuge is to take the most excellent refuge; it is the one to be most valued. Without fail, it is by means of taking refuge in this way that we can rid ourselves of suffering.

The World-honored One has stated this clearly for the sake of all human beings. Human beings, vainly acting out of fear of what is foreboding, should not seek refuge in such beings as mountain spirits or demonic spirits, or in such places as the mausoleums of non-Buddhists, for there is no escape from human suffering by relying on such places for refuge.

To put it more broadly, following the false teachings of non-Buddhists, people engage in ascetic practices which take the form of precepts for oxen, precepts for deer, precepts for rakshasas, precepts for demons, precepts for dumb beasts, precepts for deaf beings, precepts for dogs, precepts for chickens, or precepts for pheasants, and they may adorn their bodies with ashes and let their hair grow long. Or they may sacrifice a sheep, killing it after they have first chanted mantras. Or they may perform fire rituals for four months, or feast on air for seven days, or offer up hundreds of thousands of myriad blossoms to celestial beings. And they claim that, by such means, they will succeed in getting their wishes fulfilled. There is no truth in the belief that methods such as these can bring about liberation from suffering. Such methods are not praised by those of wise discernment, for people who do such practices continue to suffer in vain, devoid of any good outcome.

Because this is so, you should clearly examine whether you are vainly seeking to take refuge in some false path. Even if some method is different from the practice of the non-Buddhist precepts, if its underlying principle conforms to the principle of seeking refuge in a tree or a mausoleum, do not take such a refuge. A human body is hard to come by and the Buddhist Treasures are rarely met with. How sad it would be if you rashly spent your life as kith and kin of some demonic spirit or vainly let many lifetimes flow by while holding onto false views. By quickly taking refuge in the Three Treasures of Buddha, Dharma, and Sangha, you will not only be liberated from suffering but you will also fully realize enlightenment.

In the *Scripture on Rare Occurrences* it says, "Teaching others about the four earthly continents or the six heavenly worlds of desire so that all may realize the four stages* of arhathood does not equal the merit of one single person taking the Three Refuges." The four earthly continents are the eastern, western, southern, and northern continents.[6] Among them, those in the northern continent cannot be reached by the teaching of the Three Vehicles;* to successfully teach those in that continent how to become arhats would be rare indeed.[7] Even if such a benefit could be obtained, it would not be equal to the spiritual merit of teaching one single person how to take the Three Refuges. It is also rare for those in the six celestial worlds of desire to realize the Way. Even if we were able to help such beings attain the fourth stage of arhathood, it would not be equal to the merit of one single person taking the Three Refuges, so great and profound They are.

In the fourth of the *Āgama Scriptures* it says:

> There was once a celestial being in the Trayastrimsha Heaven who, upon seeing the five signs of his decay manifesting, knew he would be reborn as a wild boar. His bemoaning over this reached the ears of Lord Indra, who ruled over that heaven. Upon hearing the reason for his lamenting, Lord Indra called the celestial being forth and instructed him, saying, "You should take refuge in the Three Treasures." By immediately doing as he had been instructed, the being escaped being reborn as a boar.
>
> The Buddha, creating a poem for the occasion, spoke thus:

---

6.   These are the four 'continents' that surround Mount Sumeru. Mount Sumeru is considered to be the center of the universe, the pivotal point of the wheel of the six worlds of existence, as well as one's sitting place in meditation.

7.   That is, the vehicles used by shravakas, pratekyabuddhas, and bodhisattvas are not effective enough to bestir the inhabitants of the northern continent from their customarily blissful state; only a Buddha—the One of the One Vehicle—has the capacity to do that.

If beings take refuge in the Buddha,
They fall not into the three evil paths,[8]
Their passions spent, they dwell within some
human or celestial realm
And sure as sure will reach nirvana's holy shore.

Once this celestial being had taken the Three Refuges, he was reborn into a rich man's family and was also able to leave home life behind, ultimately reaching the state of one who has gone beyond being a novice.

In short, there is no scale upon which the merit of taking refuge in the Three Treasures can be weighed, for it is immeasurable and boundless.

When the World-honored One was in the world, twenty-six million hungering dragons, as a group, paid a visit to where the Buddha was staying. To a one, they were all shedding a veritable flood of tears as they addressed Him, saying, "All we desire is that You, out of Your pity, will rescue us from our suffering. O greatly compassionate World-honored One, we recall a time in a past age when we dwelt within the Buddha Dharma and had been able to leave home life behind, but we then went to great lengths to cultivate all manner of evil deeds. Because of these evil deeds, we have spent immeasurable eons in these bodies of ours, dwelling in the three evil paths. Also, because of residual retribution, we have been reborn as dragons and experience exceedingly great suffering."

The Buddha instructed the dragons, saying, "Without exception, you should forthwith take the Three Refuges and

---

8.   The three evil paths are the worlds of beasts, hungry ghosts, and those in hellish states.

wholeheartedly practice what is good. Due to these conditions, you will encounter the last Buddha in the Eon of the Wise Ones, the one named He Who Has Arrived at the Tower.[9] During the generation of that Buddha, you will be able to rid yourselves of your wrongdoings."

When the dragons heard these words, they all spent the rest of their lives in wholehearted devotion, each having taken the Three Refuges.

Aside from imparting the Three Refuges to them, the Buddha Himself had no other method or technique for helping rescue the dragons. When they left home life behind in a previous age, they had received the Three Refuges, but as retribution for their evil acts, they had become hungering dragons, and by that time there was no other means for rescuing them. This is why He had imparted the Three Refuges to them. You need to keep in mind that the merit from the Three Refuges is the most esteemed and the most sublime, mind-boggling in its profundity. The World-honored One had already clearly attested to the truth of this, and human beings should by all means accept it in faith. He did not have them recite the names of the Buddhas in the ten quarters, but simply had them take the Three Refuges. The Buddha's intention is profound, so who is there that would not sound its depths? Human beings today should quickly accept the Three Refuges rather than vainly reciting the name of every single Buddha, so that they do not foolishly remain in the dark and treat such great merit lightly.

At that time, there was a blind female dragon among those assembled.[10] Her mouth was filled with festering tumors that were

---

9.　The Eon of the Wise Ones is a reference to our present eon, so-called because there will be many who realize Buddhahood during that time.

10.　In addition to its literal meaning, a dragon woman can be understood as someone who is intellectually brilliant. Also, her being blind may be understood literally or, possibly more to the point, figuratively, as being spiritually blind.

crawling with all manner of worms, a condition that resembled excrement. It was wickedly foul, like the uncleanness within a female organ at the time of menstruation, with a fetid stench that was difficult to bear. All kinds of things were feeding off her. Pus and blood were oozing out of her, and her whole body was constantly being bitten by mosquitoes and stung by wasps, while other poisonous insects were gnawing at her. The foul condition of her body was hard to look upon.

The World-honored One, seeing the dragon woman's blindness and the depth of her suffering, asked her from His great compassionate heart, "My little sister, what conditions have caused you to have such a wretched body? What deeds in a former life have brought you to such a state?"

The dragon woman replied, "World-honored One, this body of mine is now struck with such forms of suffering that I have not a moment's respite. Even should I try to put it in words, there is no way I have of expressing it. In thinking about my past over the previous thirty-six million years, for hundreds of thousands of years I have experienced suffering like this in the form of an evil dragon up to the point that it has not ceased even for a moment, day or night. The reason for this is that in the distant past, during the ninety-first eon, I became a female monastic within the Teaching of Bibashi Buddha, but I thought about lustful things, thoughts surpassing even those of some drunken person. Further, even though I had left home life behind, I was unable to live in accord with the Dharma, so I spread out my bedding in a temple and committed impure acts in order to satisfy my greedy heart and produce great pleasure. Sometimes I would seek out what belonged to others, often taking the alms that they had been given by the faithful. For just such reasons as these, I have been continually unable to receive the body of one in the human or celestial worlds, constantly being reborn in one of the three evil paths."

The Buddha then asked her, "If that is the case, when the eon that we are now in comes to an end, where, my little sister, will you be reborn?"

The dragon woman responded, "Due to the strength of the causal conditions of my past behavior, even if I were born in some other world when this eon has exhausted itself, driven by the winds of my evil deeds, I shall still be reborn in this state." The dragon woman then made the following plea, "O World-honored One of Great Compassion, pray, rescue me! I pray, rescue me!"

At that moment, the World-honored One scooped up some water in His hand and gave her instruction, saying "We call this water 'the medicine that brings the joy of one's true wishes being fulfilled'. Now, in all sincerity, I say to you that, in the distant past, I once cast my life aside in order to rescue a dove and, to that end, I did not waver in my resolve or feel regret in my heart. If these words of yours are true, you will be completely cured of your afflictions." The World-honored Buddha then took the water into His mouth and sprayed it forth over the blind dragon woman's body, whereupon she was cured of all her sores and stench.

Now that she had been cured, she made the following plea, "I beg the Awakened One to permit me to receive the Three Refuges." Thereupon, the World-honored One gave the Three Refuges to the dragon woman.

This dragon woman had become a female monastic within the Teaching of Bibashi Buddha. Although she admitted that she had broken Precepts, once she had penetrated that Buddha's Teaching, she must have been aware of where she had become obstructed. Having now encountered Shakyamuni Buddha, she begged to receive the Three Refuges from Him. Receiving the Three Refuges from the Buddha must be said to be due to good, strong spiritual roots. The merit of meeting the Buddha must certainly have derived from the Three Refuges.[11] Although we are not blind dragons and we do not have the bodies of beasts, yet, unlike her, we did not personally encounter the Tathagata or receive the Three Refuges from the Buddha. The ability to actually encounter the Buddha is something far in the past, I am afraid to say. The World-honored One Himself bestowed upon her the Three Refuges. You should keep in mind that the merit from the Three Refuges is something that is extremely profound and immeasurable. For instance, when Shakrendra bowed to the wild fox and received the Three Refuges from it, everything depended on the depth of the merit of the Three Refuges.[12]

  Once when the Buddha was staying in a banyan grove outside the city of Kapilavastu, His lay disciple Mahānāma of the Shakya clan came to where the Buddha was and asked him, "Just what is a lay Buddhist?"

  Thereupon, the Buddha explained the matter to him, saying, "If there are good disciples, male or female, who are in possession of their faculties and have accepted the Three Refuges, they are called lay Buddhists."

  Mahānāma then asked, "World-honored One, what is meant by calling someone a ten-percent lay Buddhist?"

  The Buddha replied, "My dear disciple Mahānāma, if one accepts the Three Refuges along with one of the Ten Great Precepts, that person is called a ten-percent lay Buddhist."

Becoming a disciple of the Buddha invariably depends on the Three Refuges. Whichever Precepts we may accept, we invariably take the Three Refuges, and only

11. That is, it derived from her having taken the Three Refuges when she became a monastic within the assembly of Bibashi Buddha.

12. Dōgen will tell the story of Shakrendra and the wild fox later in this discourse. Shakrendra is another name for Indra.

then do we take Precepts. Therefore, it is in accord with the Three Refuges that one obtains the Precepts.

The following story is related in the *Dhammapada*:

> Long ago, there was a guardian deity named Shakrendra, who intuitively knew that when his present life ended, he would be reborn as a donkey. Without ceasing to bemoan his fate, he said, "The only person who can save me from the suffering of such misfortune is the World-honored Buddha."

> Thereupon, he went to where the Buddha was staying and, performing a full prostration, took refuge in the Buddha. He had not yet arisen from his prostration when his life came to an end and he arose within the womb of a donkey. The mother donkey broke free from her reins and smashed some bowls in a nearby pottery shop. The potter struck her, which ultimately caused her to abort, whereby Shakrendra reemerged in his guardian deity body.

> The Buddha said, "Just as you were dying, you were taking refuge in the Three Treasures, so the retribution for your wrongdoings had already come to an end." Upon hearing this, Shakrendra obtained the first fruits of arhathood.

In sum, the World-honored Buddha was unsurpassed in rescuing sentient beings from the sufferings and misfortunes of the world. This is why Shakrendra hastened to call on the World-honored One. While he was prostrate on the ground, his present life came to an end and he was reborn within a donkey's womb. Through the merit of his taking refuge in the Buddha, the mother donkey broke her reins and smashed dishes in the potter's shop. The potter struck her and her body was so injured that she aborted the donkey colt in her womb. Thereupon, the guardian deity returned to enter his former body. His attaining the first fruits of arhathood upon hearing what the Buddha said was due to the strength of the merit from his taking refuge in the Three Treasures.

In other words, the strength of the Three Refuges not only freed Shakrendra from the three evil paths, it also permitted him to reenter his guardian deity body. And not only did he gain the fruits and rewards from being in a celestial place, but he also became a saintly being who had realized the first stage of arhathood. Truly, the ocean of merit of the Three Treasures is immeasurable, unbounded. While the World-honored One was in the world, ordinary people and those in lofty positions enjoyed the blessings and good fortune from this. Now, in the final, degenerate five hundred years following the disappearance of the Tathagata, what can we humans do? Well, such things as statues and pictures of the Tathagata, as well as His relics, are still housed in the world. If we take refuge in these, we will also receive the merits as described above.[13]

The following is recounted in the *Scripture of Unparalleled Events*:

> The Buddha once said, "I recall a time innumerable eons ago when there was a wild fox on a mountain in the great kingdom of Vima.[14] It so happened that it was being pursued by a lion who was bent on making a meal of it. As it fled, it fell into a well and was unable to get out. After three days had passed, it realized that it was going to die there, and so composed the following poem:
>
>> *Oh, woe is me! To be thus on suffering's brink,*
>> *Losing my life, drowned deep in some hillside well.*
>> *How transient all myriad things prove to be!*
>> *Alas that I cannot leave my body for the lion's*
>> *feast.*

---

13. However, not because there is some magical power inherent in these objects, but because they are reminders to trust in Buddha, Dharma, and Sangha, and to keep to the Precepts.

14. The kingdom of Vima is a place within Jambudvipa, the legendary continent south of Mount Sumeru.

> *In homage, I take refuge in the Buddhas of the ten*
> *quarters.*
> *May They know that my heart is pure and free of all*
> *self.*

"At that moment, Shakrendra overheard someone taking refuge in the Buddha. Awestruck, his hair stood on end. Being mindful of the Buddha of old, he thought to himself, 'I, a solitary drop of dew, lack a Master to guide me as I drown myself in my addictions to sensory greeds.'

"Thereupon, along with a celestial host of eighty thousand, he flew down, desiring to explore more closely what was going on in the well. He saw the wild fox at the bottom of the well, attempting to claw its way up and out, but without success. Once more thinking only of himself, Shakrendra then said, 'Saintly person, you may well be thinking that you are lacking in some way. Though I now see the form and figure of a wild fox, clearly you are a bodhisattva* and not someone who is limited only to mundane abilities, for it was not a mundane verse that you recited, O benevolent being. I pray that you will give voice to the essentials of the Dharma for the sake of this host of celestial beings.'

"At this point, the wild fox looked up and replied, 'Even though you are a guardian deity of the Dharma, you have obviously not had instruction in It. While a Dharma Master is down below you, you have placed yourself above him. You ask for the essentials of the Dharma, but completely fail to show proper respect![15]

---

15.   In Buddhism, the traditional courtesy is to offer a meal to the Dharma Master as alms and then, after the meal, to ask the Master to give a Dharma talk whilst seated in a higher seat than those for whom the talk is intended. To ignore such a courtesy and put oneself above the Dharma Master is therefore seen as the height of disrespect. Shakrendra, so eager to hear the Teaching for His own sake, had failed to extract the wild fox from the well, much less offer him a meal, before asking for spiritual Teaching.

Because the Waters of Dharma are untainted and pure, they can save people, so how come you crave to have them by prideful means?'

"When the guardian deity heard this, he was filled with shame. The celestial beings who attended upon him were startled and laughed nervously. Then one said, 'Although our celestial lord has come down to this place, that does not greatly benefit us.'

"Thereupon, the guardian deity Shakrendra addressed the celestial beings, saying, 'I pray, do not, in this regard, hold onto your astonishment and fears. What he said is undoubtedly due to my self-deception and greed, along with my lack of virtue. By all means, we must listen to the essentials of the Dharma from this person.'

"He then lowered his celestial robe to help the fox, who grabbed hold of it and climbed out from the well. The celestial beings prepared a meal of nectar for the creature. After the wild fox had finished its meal, its vitality was restored. In the midst of calamity, it had met with such unanticipated good fortune that its heart leapt for joy, and its delight was immeasurable. The wild fox then gave extensive explanation of the essentials of the Dharma for the sake of Shakrendra and his host of celestial beings."

This story is called 'Shakrendra's bowing to an animal and taking it for his teacher'. Clearly, you need to realize that the guardian deity's taking a wild fox for his teacher is evidence of how difficult it is to hear the words Buddha, Dharma, and Sangha. Now, in accord with the help from our good deeds in past lives, we have encountered the Dharma bequeathed us by the Tathagata so that, day and night, we may hear the precious name of the Three Treasures, without regressing over time. This is surely the essence of the Dharma. Even Mara, the Lord of Bedevilment, along with his demons of desire, all escape tribulation by taking refuge in the Three Treasures. How much more can others strive to pile up merit and accumulate virtue by means of the meritorious nature of the Three Treasures! So, why, pray, would you neglect to fathom them?

To summarize, in practicing the Way as disciples of the Buddha, we first reverently bow to the Three Treasures in all ten quarters, then we call on the Three Treasures in all ten quarters to come to us as we offer incense and scatter flowers to Them, and only then do we perform our spiritual disciplines. This is an excellent example of practice from ancient times, an age-old ritual of the Buddhas and Ancestors. If there are any who have never yet done this ritual of taking refuge in the Three Treasures, you need to know that theirs is a non-Buddhist teaching and that it may well be the teaching of the Lord of Bedevilment. The Dharma of Buddha after Buddha and Ancestor after Ancestor invariably begins with the ceremony of taking refuge in the Three Treasures.

On a day during the summer retreat in the seventh year of the Kenchō era (1255), I finished making this proofed copy from my late Master's draft. It had not yet reached the stage of a clean copy, much less a middling draft. Undoubtedly, he would have made additions and deletions. Since such a process is now impossible, I am leaving the Master's draft just as it is.[16]

I made this copy on the twenty-first day of the fifth lunar month in the second year of the Kōan era (July 1, 1278), whilst staying at Shinzenkō-ji Temple in Nakahama, Echizen Province.

Giun

---

16. This first portion of the postscript is clearly by Ejō.

88

On the Absolute Certainty of Cause and Effect

(Jinshin Inga)

Translator's Introduction: In this discourse Dōgen once again takes up the kōan story of Hyakujō's fox, which he had commented on in Discourse 73: On the Great Practice *(Daishugyō).* Here, however, he presents a series of poems that various Masters had composed in relation to the subject of cause and effect, all of which Dōgen feels support non-Buddhist views. His own comments make quite clear that no one, under any circumstances, is ever free of cause and effect.

> Hyakujō Ekai was a Dharma heir of Baso. Whenever people came to hear him give a public Dharma talk, there was an old man who always came into the Dharma Hall immediately following those in the monastic assembly. He always listened to the Dharma talk and then, when the monks would leave the hall, he would leave at the same time. Then one day, he lingered behind.
>
> Thereupon, the Master asked him, "You who are standing here, who are you?"
>
> The old man replied, "To speak truly, I am a non-human being. Long ago during the eon of Kashō Buddha,[1] I dwelt upon this mountain as Abbot. Then, one day, a trainee asked me, 'Is even the one who does the Great Practice still subject to cause and effect?' I replied that such a one is no longer subject to cause and effect. After that, as a consequence, I was reduced to being reborn as a wild fox for five hundred lives. I now beseech you, O Venerable Monk, say something that will turn me around, for I long to rid myself of this wild fox's attitude of mind."
>
> Thereupon, he asked the Master, "Is even someone who does the Great Practice subject to cause and effect?"

---

1. Among the Seven Buddhas, the One whose eon directly preceded that of Shakyamuni Buddha.

The Master replied, "Such a one is not blind to causality."

Upon hearing these words, the old man had a great awakening. Prostrating himself before the Master, he said, "Since I have already shed the outer trappings of a wild fox, I have taken to dwelling on the far side of this mountain. Dare I ask the Venerable Abbot to perform for me a monk's funeral service?"

The Master had the senior monk who supervises the Meditation Hall strike the wooden gong to signal the monks to assemble so that he might tell them that, after their meal, there would be a funeral service for a deceased monk. The whole assembly was at ease with this, though they wondered about it, since there was no sick person in the temple infirmary. After the meal, the Master simply led the assembly up to the base of a rock on the other side of the mountain, where they saw him use his traveling staff to point out the corpse of a wild fox. They cremated the remains in accordance with the appropriate procedure.

At nightfall, the Master went to the Dharma Hall where he gave the monks a talk on the preceding events. His Dharma heir Ōbaku then asked him, "In the past, the man said the wrong thing to turn his disciple around and, as a consequence, was reduced to being a wild fox for five hundred lives. Suppose he had not made this mistake, what would have become of him?"

The Master said, "Come up close and I will tell you."

Thereupon, Ōbaku went on up and gave the Master a slap. The Master clapped his hands and laughed, saying, "I've always thought that the beards of foreigners were red, and here is a red-bearded foreigner."

This story occurs in the *T'ien-sheng Era Record of the Far-reaching Torch*. Even so, people doing the training who are not clear about the fundamental principle of causality fall into the error of denying cause and effect, and to no avail. Sad to say, they tend to be frivolous and casually let the authority of the words and ways of the

Ancestors go into decline. 'Not being subject to cause and effect' is surely their denial of causality, and accordingly, they fall into evil realms.[2] Clearly, 'not being blind to cause and effect' is what 'being profoundly convinced of cause and effect' means, and accordingly, those who hear this rid themselves of evil conditions. Do not doubt this: do not mistrust it. Among those of our recent generations who call themselves students of Zen practice, there are many who have denied causality. And how do we know that they have denied causality? Because they are of the opinion that there is no difference between 'not being subject to' and 'not being blind to'. Accordingly, we know that they have denied causality.

Our Nineteenth Indian Ancestor, the Venerable Kumorata, once said the following:

> For the time being, we may say that retribution for our good and bad acts has three periods, but, in general, worldly people only see a benevolent person coming to an early end while some violent person is having a long life, or see an evil one enjoying good fortune while a virtuous one is experiencing calamities, and thereby worldly people conclude that cause and effect is a dead issue and that 'wrong behavior' and 'happiness' are devoid of any significance. Such people in particular are ignorant of the fact that shadows and sounds are in accord with their source, without even a hair's breadth of discrepancy between them. And even with the passing of hundreds of thousands of myriad eons, there is no diminishing of that connection.

Clearly, we see from what this patch-robed monk says that he never denied cause and effect. Present-day trainees who have been negligent in their training with the traces left by our ancient teachers have not clarified what the kind instruction of this Ancestor of our tradition is. Those who have been negligent in this training, while at the same

---

2.   That is, the three worlds of hungry ghosts, animals, and those in hells.

time calling themselves good spiritual friends and guides for ordinary people and those in lofty positions, are malicious troops of scholars and great thieves preying on the ordinary and the lofty. Those of you who have come before me and those who will come after me, do not teach the younger generation or the veteran monks with the aim of negating the existence of cause and effect, for this is false teaching and not the Dharma of the Buddhas and Ancestors. It is due to your being negligent in your studies that you have fallen into this false view.

Patch-robed monks, among others in present-day China, are accustomed to saying, "Even though we have received a human body and have encountered the Dharma of the Buddha, we still do not know the details of one or two of our past lives. The former Hyakujō who became a wild fox was able to know five hundred of his past lives. So, it is obvious that he did not lapse into that state due to retribution for his past deeds. It must be as Meditation Master Dōan said in a poem:

> *Even if restrained by golden chains or unseen barriers,*
> *nowhere do I abide.*
> *Going amidst all manner of beings, I just roll on through*
> *cycles of birth and death.*"

This is the way that this bunch who are considered to be good spiritual friends and guides see and understand the matter. It is hard to place such a way of seeing and understanding within the house of the Buddhas and Ancestors. Among humans, and foxes, as well as those in the other worlds of existence, there are those who have the ability to get a glimpse of their past lives. Be that as it may, such an ability is not the seed of clear understanding, but is what someone experiences from having previously performed wicked deeds. The World-honored One, for the sake of the ordinary and the lofty, has spoken extensively about this fundamental principle. Not to know it is the height of negligence in one's study. How sad! Even if someone were to know a thousand of his or her past lives, or even ten thousand of them, that would not necessarily bring forth the Buddha's Dharma. There are non-Buddhists who already know of their past lives from over eighty thousand eons, but they have still not produced something we could call 'the Buddha's Dharma'. To know a mere five hundred past lives is no great ability.

In present-day Sung China, among those doing the practice of seated meditation, the folks who are the most in the dark are those who do not know that the teaching of not being subject to cause and effect is a false view. Sad to say, in a place where the genuine Dharma of the Tathagata has spread abroad and there has been a genuine Transmission from Ancestor to Ancestor, heretical gangs have formed who deny cause and effect. Those who are exploring the Matter* through training with their Master should by all means hasten to make clear the fundamental principle of cause and effect. The later Hyakujō's principle of not being blind to cause and effect means not ignoring the presence of causality. Hence, the underlying principle is clear: we feel the effects of the causes that we put into action. In sum, if you have not clarified what the Buddha's Dharma is, do not go about recklessly preaching for the sake of the worldly and the celestial.

Our Ancestral Master Nāgārjuna once said:

> If, like non-Buddhists, you argue against there being cause and effect in the world, then there could be no past or future. If you argue against there being cause and effect in the realm of enlightenment, then there could be no Triple Treasure, Four Noble Truths, or four stages* of arhathood.

Be very clear about this: no matter whether it is secular people or monastics who are arguing against the existence of cause and effect, they will be off the Path. To assert that the present is unreal is tantamount to saying, "One's physical form exists in this particular state, but one's spiritual nature has been returning to the enlightened state for ever so long, for one's spiritual nature is one's mind, and one's mind is not the same as one's body." To understand the issue in this way is to be off the Path. And there are those who say, "When someone dies, they invariably return to the ocean of spiritual nature. Even if they have not studied the Buddha's Dharma, they will naturally return to the ocean of enlightenment, at which point the wheel of birth and

---

*   See *Glossary*.

death will cease to turn. This is why there is no future life." This is the non-Buddhist doctrine of nihilism. Even if they resemble monks physically, folks who hold to such wrong views are not disciples of the Buddha at all, but simply people who are off the Path. In short, to deny cause and effect is to make the mistake of denying the existence of past and future. These people's denial of cause and effect stems from their having failed to train under a genuinely good spiritual guide. Those who train for a long time under a genuinely good spiritual guide will not hold to the false view that denies cause and effect. We need to reverently trust the compassionate instruction of our Ancestral Master Nāgārjuna and humbly place it above our head.

The monk Yōka Genkaku was an outstanding disciple of Daikan Enō. Originally, he trained in the Tendai tradition of the *Lotus Scripture*, sharing quarters with Great Master Sakei Genrō, the Eighth Chief Master of the Tendai tradition. Once while Genkaku was perusing the *Great Scripture on the Buddha's Parinirvana* a golden light suddenly filled his room, and he profoundly experienced a spiritual awakening to That which transcends birth and death. He then proceeded to pay a visit to Enō to report to our Sixth Ancestor what he had experienced. Our Sixth Ancestor then gave him the seal* that confirmed his awakening. Later, Genkaku composed "The Song That Attests to the Way", in which there are the lines:

> *Vacant-headed notions of emptiness which deny causality*
> *Bring about calamities as dire as a raging conflagration or*
> *a rampaging flood.*

Be very clear about this: denial of causality will bring about calamities. The old virtuous ones of past generations were quite clear about causality, whereas trainees in more recent times all tend to be skeptical. But even in present times, there are those who cultivate the Enlightened Heart and, for the sake of the Buddha Dharma, study the Buddha Dharma. Like the ancient worthies, they will be clear about cause and effect. To say that there are no causes and no effects is to be off the Path.

In extolling the view of cause and effect contained in Genkaku's lines, our Old Buddha Wanshi once said:

> *It's like a foot of water making a ten-foot wave:*
> *There's nothing to be done about five hundred past lives.*
> *Though people go on about 'not being subject to' or 'not*
> 　　　*being blind to',*
> *They're all still in a pit, entangled in the tendrils of*
> 　　　*discriminatory thought.*
>
> *Ha, ha, ha! What a laugh!*
> *Simply, do you get It, or not?*
> *If you're truly detached and rid of conventionalities,*
> *You'll not try to inhibit me from saying, 'Goo goo, ga ga!'"*
>
> *The gods sing and the heavenly spirits dance, as the music*
> 　　　*comes forth all by itself,*
> *And clapping hands join in with merry shouts of laughter.*

Now, the lines,

> *Though people go on about 'not being subject to' or 'not*
> 　　　*being blind to',*
> *They're all still in a pit, entangled in the tendrils of*
> 　　　*discriminatory thought,*

are tantamount to his saying that 'not being subject to' and 'not being blind to' really amount to the same thing.[3]

In short, this discussion of 'cause and effect' has not yet completely exhausted the term's fundamental principle. And why? Because even though Wanshi has shed his wild fox's attitude of mind right here and now before us, he does not say

---

3.　That is, both phrases are the product of the discriminative thinking of those who have not yet 'got It'.

that after people escape from the attitude of mind of their wild fox, they are reborn in the human world, nor does he say that they are reborn in the celestial world, nor does he say that they are reborn in any other world, but this is something we should wonder about. Once people have dropped off their wild fox's attitude of mind, those who should be reborn in a favorable world are reborn among celestial beings or among ordinary human beings, whereas those who should be reborn in an unfavorable world are reborn in one of the four unfavorable worlds.[4] Once people have dropped off their wild fox's attitude of mind, they will not be reborn in some place other than one of the six worlds* of existence. If someone says that when we die, we return to an ocean of spiritual nature or we return to a universal self, such are the views of those who are off the Path.

Meditation Master Engo Kokugon once said in a poem commenting on an ancient Ancestor's kōan* story:

When fish swim, they may muddy up the water;
When birds fly, they may shed a feather.
It is hard indeed to escape the ever-bright Mirror.[5]
The Great Void knows no bounds.

Once something has passed, it is far, far gone.
The five hundred rebirths were simply dependent on the
*   fox's Great Practice with cause and effect.*
A thunderbolt may suddenly smash a mountain and the
*   wind churn up the sea,*
But the Pure Gold, though refined a hundred times, never
*   changes Its color.*

---

4.   That is, favorable or unfavorable for hearing the Dharma.

5.   The ever-bright Mirror reflects the karmic consequences of our actions.

Even this verse leans towards denying cause and effect and, at the same time, tends to support the view of eternalism.[6]

The monk known as Meditation Master Daie Sōkō once said the following in a congratulatory poem:

> *'Not being subject to' and 'not being blind to'*
> *Are merely stones and clods of earth.*
> *Having met them along the path between the rice fields,*
> *I pulverized the silver mountain.*
> *Clapping my hands, I give a hearty "Ho, ho!" wherever I am,*
> *For here in Kōshū, this foolish Laughing Buddha is to be found.*[7]

Present-day people in Sung dynasty China consider monks like Daie to be Masters skillful in leading trainees, but Daie's opinions and understanding never reached the level of skillful means in instructing others in the Buddha Dharma. If anything, he leaned towards naturalism.[8]

Speaking more generally, there are more than thirty who have composed poems and commentaries on this story of Hyakujō's fox, and not even one of them has had the slightest doubt that 'not being subject to cause and effect' means 'doubting cause and effect'. Sad to say, these persons have not clarified what cause and effect is and have vainly wasted their lives, going astray in a state of confusion. In your

---

6. Eternalism is the belief that the self and the world are both eternal.

7. 'The silver mountain' is an allusion to a mountain that is impossible to scale. It is used in Zen Buddhism as a metaphor for the realm of enlightenment, which is beyond discriminative thought.

8. In Buddhism, naturalism is the belief that things just happen to happen, which is a denial of cause and effect.

exploring of the Buddha Dharma through your training with a Master, number one is clarifying what cause and effect is. Undoubtedly, those who deny cause and effect will, in their fierce pursuit of profits, give rise to false views and thereby become people who sever their own good spiritual roots.

To summarize, the principle of cause and effect is quite clear, and it is totally impersonal: those who fabricate evil will fall into a lower state, whereas those who practice good will rise to a higher state, and without the slightest disparity. If cause and effect had become null and void, Buddhas would never have appeared in the world and our Ancestral Master would not have come from the West. In short, it would be impossible for human beings to encounter a Buddha and hear the Dharma. The fundamental principle of cause and effect was not clear to Confucius or Lao-tzu. It has only been clarified and Transmitted by Buddha after Buddha and by Ancestor after Ancestor. Because the good fortune of those who are seeking to learn in these degenerate days of the Dharma is scant, they do not encounter a genuine Master or hear the authentic Dharma, and so they are not clear about cause and effect. If you deny causality as a result of this error, you will experience excessive misfortune, since you would be as ignorant as an ox or a horse. Even if you have not committed any evil act other than denying cause and effect, the poison of this view will immediately be terrible. Therefore, if you who are exploring the Matter through your training with a Master have put your heart that seeks awakening as the first and foremost matter, and therefore wish to repay the vast benevolence of the Buddhas and the Ancestors, you should swiftly clarify what causality really is.

On a day during the summer retreat in the seventh year of the Kenchō era (1255), I copied this from the Master's draft. It had yet to reach the state of a cleaned-up draft, much less a clean copy. Even so, I have made this copy of it.

Ejō

89

On Karmic Retribution in the Three Temporal Periods

(Sanji Gō)

Translator's Introduction: In this discourse, Dōgen discusses the good or ill recompense we receive immediately in this lifetime, in our next lifetime, or in some later future lifetime as a result of our deliberate acts. He gives the Buddhist perspective on why people who seem to be doing good deeds may experience misfortune and why people who are continually committing wrongful acts may seem to be enjoying good fortune.

When our Nineteenth Ancestor, the Venerable Kumorata, arrived at a country in Central India, there was a virtuous monk there named Shayata who raised a question with him, saying, "My parents have always had faith in the Triple Treasure, but they have continually been subject to illnesses and all their endeavors have come to naught, whereas our neighbor, who persists in behaving like Chandala the Outlaw, has always been fit and healthy and his illegal undertakings successful. How come he has had such good fortune and where have we gone wrong?"

The Venerable One responded, "Why do you entertain such doubts? The karmic* effects of good and bad actions will come to fruition in one of three temporal periods. In general, people see that the benevolent may suffer untimely or violent deaths whilst the cruel may live long, or that the wicked may be fortunate whilst the morally upright meet with misfortune. As a result of this, they say that there is no cause and effect and that 'vice' and 'good deeds' are meaningless words. Above all, they do not understand that consequences inevitably follow upon even the slightest actions, that even were hundreds of thousands of myriad eons to elapse these

---

*　See *Glossary.*

consequences would still not be wiped away, and that cause and effect are, of necessity, in accord with each other."

Once Shayata heard these words, he was immediately freed from his doubts.

The Venerable Kumorata was the nineteenth in line from the Tathagata to receive the Dharma. The Tathagata had personally mentioned his name and prophesied his future Buddhahood.[1] Not only had Kumorata clarified what the Dharma of the Venerable Shakyamuni Buddha was and received the authentic Transmission, he had also fully realized the Dharma of all Buddhas in the three temporal periods.

Having profited from his present question, the Venerable Shayata became a follower of the Venerable Kumorata and undertook the study of the authentic Dharma, ultimately becoming our Ancestral Master of the twentieth generation. Here, too, the World-honored One had prophesied much earlier that our Twentieth Ancestor would be Shayata. So, above all, you need to learn what our Ancestral Masters knew by studying their comments on the Buddha Dharma. Do not join in with the flock of that present-day worldly bunch with false opinions, who are ignorant of cause and effect, who are in the dark about karmic retribution from deliberate acts, who know nothing of the three temporal periods, and who do not know the difference between good and evil.

What we call the three temporal periods are the three time periods in which we receive the retribution from our good and evil acts. These are, first, the retribution experienced in one's present life; second, the retribution experienced in one's next life; and third, the retribution experienced in some later future life. Through your practice of the Way of the Buddhas and Ancestors you learn, first off, to clarify what the principle of karmic retribution in these three time periods is. If you do not do so, you will make many errors and fall into false views. You will not just fall into false views, you will also give rise to evil ways and undergo suffering for a long time. By

---

1.   That is, the Buddha had predicted that someone in the future would be called Kumorata, 'The Youthful One', and that he would realize Buddhahood in his lifetime.

failing to continue developing your good roots, you will lose much spiritual merit and will have long-standing obstructions on your path to enlightenment.

The karmic retribution experienced in these three temporal periods comes from both good and evil acts.

In the first temporal period, the retribution is experienced in one's present lifetime. That is to say, when we engage in karmic activities in this lifetime and then, according to the seeds we have sown, receive the fruits thereof in this lifetime, we call this 'retribution experienced in one's present lifetime'.

In other words, when there is someone who fashions his life by good or by evil actions, and then receives the consequences of those actions in this lifetime, we call that 'retribution experienced in one's present life'.

The following story is an example of creating evil and receiving the consequences therefrom in this present life.

There was once a woodcutter who had gone off into the mountains when he encountered a blizzard and completely lost his way. It was at that time when the day was coming to an end. The snow was so deep and it was so freezing cold that he knew he would certainly be dead before long. He made his way onwards and had just entered a dense, dark patch of woods when he saw a bear. There it was, right before him in the woods. Its body was a deep blue-black, and its eyes were like two glowing coals. The man was filled with terror, certain that he would lose his life, but the creature was, in truth, a bodhisattva* who had manifested in the form of a bear.

Seeing the man's dreadful fear, it then spoke in a consoling manner, counseling him, "Now you must not be afraid. Though one's parents may sometimes harbor wrong intentions towards their child, I do not harbor evil thoughts towards you." It then came forward, lifted the man onto its back, and carried him into a cave where it warmed him with its own body until it completely resuscitated him. Gathering some roots and berries, it encouraged him to eat what he would. Fearing lest the woodcutter should die, it lay down and held him in its arms. In this way it kindly tended him until six days had passed. On the seventh day, the sky cleared and the pathway became visible. The bear, having realized that the man desired to return home, again gathered sweet berries to satisfy his hunger and sustain him. It accompanied him out of the woods, and ever so politely bade him farewell. The man fell to his knees and said, "How can I ever repay you?" The bear replied, "I seek no recompense now. I only pray that, just as I protected your body these past days, you will also do the same with my life." The man respectfully agreed.

As the man was coming down the mountain shouldering his firewood, he encountered two hunters, who asked him, "What kind of creatures have you encountered on the mountain?" The woodcutter replied, "I haven't seen any creatures apart from just one bear." The hunters begged him, "Can you show us where?" The woodcutter replied, "If I can have two-thirds of your prey, I will gladly show you." The hunters agreed and they all went off together, ultimately slaying the bear. They divided the meat into three parts. As the woodcutter was just about to pick up the bear's flesh with his two hands, he lost the use of his arms, as if they were a string of pearls that had been cut or a lotus root that had been sliced off. The hunters were startled by this and, in their concern, asked him what had happened. The woodcutter, feeling deeply ashamed, gave a detailed account of what he had done. The two hunters upbraided the woodcutter, saying, "That bear had such great compassion for you! How could you possibly have carried out such a wicked act of betrayal now? It is truly a wonder that your whole body hasn't rotted away!" Thereupon the hunters, in company with the man, gave the meat in charity to a monastery.

At that time, the elderly and virtuous abbot, one who had the wondrous ability to fathom what others desired, had entered a state of deep contemplation, thereby knowing that it was the flesh of a great bodhisattva who had created benefits and joy for the sake of all sentient beings. Coming out from his meditative state, he then spoke to his assembly concerning this matter. The assembly, hearing the story, was appalled and saddened. Together, they gathered fragrant wood and cremated the bear's body. They then collected what bones remained, placed them in a stupa,[*] and made prostrations and offerings to them.

The karma from an evil act, such as the one in this story, will inevitably incur its recompense, regardless of whether its effects are received immediately or come to fruition in a future life.

Effects such as these are called 'misfortunate recompense experienced in one's present life'. To generalize, when receiving a kindness, we should intend to repay it. In doing kindnesses for others, do not seek for recompense. As in this story, one who would turn against a kindly being and thereby bring harm to such a one will inevitably receive evil karma. O my fellow beings, may you never have a heart like that of this woodcutter! Once out of the woods, he took his leave of the bear, and even though he asked how he could possibly repay the bear's kindness, when he reached the foot of the mountain and met the hunters, he greedily sought two-thirds of the meat. Being dragged by his avarice, he slew one who had shown him great kindness. May you, both laity and monks, ever have a heart that does not fail to recognize kindness. The power of evil karma to sever both your hands strikes faster than any sword could cut them off.

Long ago, King Kanishka of the nation of Gandhara had a eunuch—one born lacking normal male genitals—who supervised the affairs of the court. While momentarily departing from the city, he encountered a herd of cattle, at least five hundred in number, being led in through the city gate. He asked the herdsman, "What kind of cattle are these?" The herdsman replied, "They are bulls being taken to be castrated." Upon hearing this, the eunuch thought to himself, "Due to evil karma in a past life, I received a body lacking normal male genitals. I shall now use my wealth to rescue these bulls from just such a hardship." He ultimately paid their price and then set them all free.

Because of the power of this good karma, the eunuch's body was fully restored to that of a normal male. Filled with profound joy, he went back into the city and, standing at the palace gate, sent a messenger to ask the king's permission to enter for an audience. The king had him summoned, wondering why he had asked for an audience. Thereupon, the eunuch presented the above in great detail. Upon hearing it, the king was surprised and delighted. He generously bestowed on his servant great treasure and, in turn, promoted him to a high office, making him privy to the external affairs of state.

Good karma like this inevitably receives its fruits, either immediately or in a future life.

Clearly you need to realize that to rescue animals, even though their lives may not be treasured, earned the man good fruits. How much more so, by our honoring the kind and the virtuous, shall we garner all manner of good.[2] Effects such as these are called 'fortunate recompense experienced in one's present life'. There are many stories like these, which arise from either good or evil deeds, but there is not time enough to quote them all.

---

2.   An allusion to the four cultivated fields of merit: that derived from being kind to animals, to the needy, to one's parents, and to the saintly ones of the Three Vehicles.

> In the second temporal period, retribution is experienced
> in one's next lifetime. That is to say, when we engage in karmic
> activities in this lifetime and then, according to the seeds we have
> sown, receive the fruits thereof in our next lifetime, we call this
> 'retribution experienced in one's next lifetime'.

In other words, when there are people who have committed any of the five most
treacherous deeds, they will inevitably fall into a hellish state in their next lifetime.
'The next lifetime' means the lifetime that follows this lifetime. For other wrongdoers,
there are those who will fall into a hellish state in their next lifetime, and there are
those who would sink into a hellish state in their next lifetime were it not for some
intervening good karma. For these five most treacherous deeds, however, people
invariably fall into a hellish state along with whatever karma they carry with them
into their next lifetime. 'The next life' is also called 'one's second life'.

> The five most treacherous deeds are, first, killing one's
> father; second, killing one's mother; third, killing an arhat;[*] fourth,
> shedding the blood of a Buddha; and fifth, destroying the harmony
> within the Sangha.

With these five most treacherous deeds, those who commit just one of them will
invariably fall into a hellish state in their next lifetime. There have been those who
have committed all five of the most treacherous deeds, such as the female monastic
Utpalavarna during the time of the Kashō Buddha.[3] And there have been those who
have committed just one of them, such as King Ajatashatru who killed his father
during the lifetime of Shakyamuni Buddha. And there have been those who committed
three of these most treacherous deeds. During the time of Shakyamuni Buddha there

---

3. Utpalavarna's story is told in several discourses, with the most extensive account being
    given in Discourse 84: On the Spiritual Merits of the Kesa *(Kesa Kudoku)*.

was Ajita, who killed his father, his mother, and an arhat. This Ajita committed these acts while in home life. Later, he was permitted to leave home life behind and become a monk. The monk Devadatta committed three of the most treacherous deeds, namely, creating a schism in the Sangha, shedding the Buddha's blood, and killing an arhat. He was also called Daibadatto, which translates as Tennetsu (He of Celestial Passion).

The story of Devadatta's creating a schism in the Sangha is as follows:

> Devadatta induced five hundred monks who were either foolish or new to the training to follow him atop Mount Gaya where he promoted five false teachings, thereby splitting his followers away from the rest of the Sangha who kept true to the Buddha's Teaching. Shariputra, being weary of this, caused Devadatta to fall into a deep sleep, while Moggallana roused Devadatta's assembly and attempted to get them to return. When Devadatta awoke and saw what was happening, he gave rise to a vow that he would make the two disciples pay for their actions. Lifting up a boulder that was thirty hastas high and fifteen hastas wide, he hurled it at the Buddha.[4] A mountain spirit intercepted the stone with its hand, shattering it into shards, one of which wounded the Buddha's foot, causing it to bleed.

According to this account, Devadatta's splitting of the Sangha came first and the spilling of blood happened later. According to other accounts, it is not clear which came first, the splitting of the Sangha or the spilling of blood. Also, Devadatta beat to death with his own fists the female monk Utpalavarna, who was, by that time, an arhat. These are his three most treacherous deeds.

In his wicked attempt to split the Sangha, he tried to spread false teaching and to split himself off from the monks who kept to the Teaching of the Buddha. Attempting to spread false teaching can only occur in three of the continents, the

---

4.   A hasta is an Indian unit of measurement equivalent to roughly 18 inches.

northern continent being excluded.[5] These attempts to spread false practices began while the Tathagata was still alive and will continue to occur right up to the time when the Dharma has disappeared. False teachings such as these occurred throughout all three of these continents only while the Tathagata was still alive. After His death, they appeared only in the southern continent of Jambudvipa[*] and not in the other continents. Expounding such false teachings is the most wicked act of all.

As a result of his committing these three treacherous deeds, Devadatta fell into a hellish state of constant suffering in his next lifetime.[6] There are people who have gone to great lengths to commit all five of these treacherous acts, and there are people who have committed only one of them, and there are those who, like Devadatta, have committed three of them. All of them fall into hellish states of continual suffering. Those who have committed just one treacherous deed will spend one eon in some hellish state of continual suffering as recompense. Those who have committed all five of them may receive five types of recompense within a single eon or they may receive them one after the other.

An ancient worthy once said, "It says in the *Āgama Scriptures* and in the *Great Scripture on the Buddha's Parinirvana* alike that such a one resides for an eon in various types of fire." Furthermore, these Scriptures also state that the suffering varies according to the seriousness of their treacherous deeds. Now, Devadatta committed three treacherous acts, one after the other, and therefore will have three times the suffering which a wicked person receives from committing just one treacherous act. But Devadatta, upon reaching the end of his life, recited the word 'homage', which gave his wicked heart a bit of relief. Regretfully, he died before he could complete the phrase 'Homage to the Buddha'. Though he had fallen into the state of continual suffering, Devadatta continued to take refuge in Shakyamuni Buddha, even though He was far away, and was thus able to resume doing good deeds.

---

5.   The northern continent is excluded because it is inhabited only by blissful celestial beings, who would be impervious to what monks were up to.

6.   This state of constant suffering is known as the Avichi Hell and is the lowest hellish state among the six worlds of existence. Though the length of time someone may be in such a state is unpredictable, in Buddhism it is not a place of eternal damnation.

There were four other monks similar to Devadatta who had fallen into a hellish state of continual suffering. A monk named Kokālika was one among the thousand from the Shakya clan who left home life behind to become monks. When Devadatta and Kokālika were going out the city gate, the horse that they were riding suddenly stumbled, and the two fell off, their hats falling off as well. All those who saw this at the time said, "These two will not receive the benefits from the Buddha's Teaching." This monk Kokālika was also called Gukari. During his lifetime he slandered Shariputra and Moggallana, accusing them of committing acts that warranted expulsion from the Sangha. Although the World-honored One tried at the time to dissuade him, Kokālika did not stop, and even Lord Brahma came down to dissuade him, but again he did not stop. Due to his slandering the two venerable monks, he fell into a hellish state in his next lifetime. Even now, he is not provided with the conditions for developing good spiritual roots.

When the monk who had attained the fourth meditative state reached the end of his life, he fell into a hellish state of continual suffering for having slandered the Buddha, even though he died in the intermediate world associated with the fourth meditative state.[7] Such a condition is called 'retribution experienced in one's next life'.

We characterize the effects of the five most treacherous deeds as being without interruption, and for five reasons:

> First, because the effects that such deeds produce occur immediately. That is, no sooner has such a wicked one performed such a deed than he immediately falls into a hellish state without experiencing any intervening state.

> Second, because the suffering that this person experiences from these effects is continual. For any of these five most

---

7. The story of this monk is the subject of Discourse 91: On the Monk in the Fourth Meditative State (*Shizen Biku*). The intermediate world refers to the period after death and before rebirth.

treacherous acts, the wicked one falls into the Avichi Hell and, within the temporal space of a single immeasurable eon, experiences suffering that constantly streams on without the least moment of relief. Thus, we describe such an effect as being without interruption in accord with the suffering that it produces.

Third, because the length of time during which any being is in this hellish state is not set and is beyond our ability to calculate. Hence, we speak of the effects of these five most treacherous deeds as being incessant because one who commits any of them will fall into the Avichi Hell and, within a single span of time, will experience suffering that streams on indefinitely without the least moment of relief.

Fourth, because the span of that wicked one's life while in the Avichi Hell is equally unlimited and beyond our ability to calculate. When someone falls into the Avichi Hell due to any of these five treacherous deeds, that person remains fully awake for an immeasurable eon, knowing no diminishing of suffering. Thus, we describe this hellish state as being without interruption in accord with the effects that it produces.

Fifth, because while in the Avichi Hell, one's very existence appears to be unlimited and immeasurable, filling the hell completely. This hell is eighty-four thousand yojanas* in length and breadth. When someone enters that hell, his existence completely fills the space and then, when any other person comes to enter it, that person's existence also completely fills the space, and without the two obstructing each other.[8]

Thus, we speak of the effects of the five most treacherous deeds as being without interruption in accord with the effects these deeds produce.

---

8.   That is, for any person in the Avichi Hell, nothing other than that hellish state seems to exist.

In the third temporal period, the retribution is experienced in some future lifetime. That is to say, when we promote or entertain karmic deeds in this lifetime and then, according to the seeds we have sown, fall into a hellish state in our third or fourth lifetime, or even hundreds of thousands of eons beyond, we call this 'retribution experienced in some future lifetime'.

In other words, there are those in this lifetime who have done good deeds and those who have done evil deeds. Even if they have ceased perpetuating such deeds, they will experience their good or evil karma in their third life, or their fourth life, or even after a hundred thousand future lives. This is what we call 'the retribution experienced in some later future lifetime'. Most of a bodhisattva's merit is the retribution that he or she experiences in a future lifetime from deeds accumulated over three asamkhyeya eons.[9] Not knowing such an underlying principle, trainees entertain ever so many doubts, like the Venerable Shayata in the opening story did whilst he was still in home life. Had he not met the Venerable Kumorata, he would have had a difficult time clarifying his doubts.

When a trainee's thinking is good, his evil thoughts disappear, and when his thinking is evil, his good thoughts immediately disappear.

Long ago in the country of Shravasti there lived two men. One was always doing what was good and the other was always doing what was evil. The trainee who was always doing what was good was always practicing good deeds with his whole being, never entertaining what was harmful. The trainee who invited evil was

---

9.   An asamkhyeya eon is a period of time that is experienced as being interminably long. A bodhisattva experiences these endless-seeming stretches of time just before entering Buddhahood.

always doing bad things with his whole being, never practicing what was good.

When the one practicing good deeds approached the end of his life, a hellish intermediate world appeared before him, due to the strength of evil karma from several lifetimes earlier. Thereupon, he thought, "In my whole life I have always practiced good deeds and have never entertained evil. Surely, I should have been reborn in some celestial world. What conditions have caused this hellish intermediate world to appear before me?" Then the thought arose, "I must surely be receiving some bad karma from earlier lifetimes which has now become ripe, and therefore this hellish intermediate world has appeared." He then remembered the good karma from his practice throughout his present lifetime, and a profound joy arose in him.

Due to the thoughts of his good deeds appearing before him, the hellish intermediate world disappeared and a celestial intermediate world suddenly appeared in its place. After this, when his life had completely ended, he was reborn in a celestial world.

This person who was always doing good not only thought, "This body of mine is, no doubt, receiving retribution from wicked deeds done in several past lifetimes," but he also had a further thought, "For the good that I have practiced throughout my life, I shall surely receive recompense in the future." This was why he was so deeply filled with joy. Because these thoughts of his were true, the hellish intermediate state disappeared and a celestial intermediate state immediately appeared before his eyes, and when his life completely ended, he was reborn in a celestial world. If this person had been a wicked one, and at the end of his life a hellish intermediate world appeared before his eyes, he might well have thought, "My practice of good throughout my whole life has brought me no merit. If good and bad karma exist, how come I am seeing a hellish intermediate world?" At this moment, he would be denying cause and effect, and would be slandering the Three Treasures. Should he be like this, then when he reached the end of his life, he would fall into some hellish state. Because this person was not like this, he was reborn in a celestial world. You need to grasp this fundamental principle and be clear about it.

> When a trainee who does wicked things reaches the end of his life, he may unexpectedly see before his eyes a celestial intermediate world of existence, due to the strength of his good deeds in former past lives. He may then think, "Throughout my life I have always done wicked practices and failed to ever practice what is good. By all rights, I should be reborn in some hell. What circumstances could there possibly have been that this intermediate world has appeared before my very eyes?"

> Thus, a false view has arisen, and he denies the existence of good and evil, as well as the fruition of much earlier good seeds, because he had sown only harmful seeds in his present life. Hence, when his life came to an end, he was reborn in some hellish world.

As long as he lived, this person had consistently committed evil acts, and further, he had not practiced even one good deed. Not only that, when his life came to an end, he saw before his very eyes a celestial intermediate world, but he did not know about recompense from distant former lives. Thus, he thought, "During my whole life I committed evil acts, but I am about to be reborn in a celestial world. It is clear to me that good and evil karma have never existed." Because of the strength of his false views, he denied the existence of good and evil karma in this way, so that the celestial intermediate world that appeared fell away and a hellish intermediate world quickly appeared before him and, ending his life, he fell into some hell. It was due to this false view of his that the celestial intermediate world disappeared. So, you trainees, by all means do not hold to false views! Learn which views are false and which are true until your bodily life has exhausted itself.

First off, to deny causality, to slander Buddha, Dharma, and Sangha, and to deny both the three temporal worlds and liberation from them are all false views. You need to keep in mind that, in this lifetime, you will not have two or three bodies. Were you to vainly fall into false views and experience evil karma to no avail, how regrettable that would be! When someone, while engaged in some evil act, thinks that it is not evil simply because they hold to the erroneous belief that such an act does not produce retribution for wrongdoing, this does not mean that this person will not experience recompense for their evil deeds. According to their wrongful thinking, the recompense for good that comes may turn around and come back at them as recompense for evil.

The Imperial Chaplain Kōgetsu once asked the venerable monk Chōsa Keishin, "An ancient worthy once said, 'After we have fully understood, we see that our karmic hindrances have been empty all along. When we have not yet fully understood, then we must, by all means, pay off all our old debts.' So, how were those like the Venerable Shishibodai and our great Master Eka, the Second Chinese Ancestor, able to pay off all their old debts?"[10]

Chōsa replied, "O my virtuous one, you have not yet experienced their being empty all along."

Kōgetsu then asked, "What, pray, is this 'being empty all along?'"

Chōsa responded, "It is what karmic hindrances are."

Kōgetsu then asked, "Just what are karmic hindrances?"

Chōsa replied, "What has been empty all along."

Kōgetsu was at a loss for words. Chōsa then gave him the following poem:

---

10. Shishibodai and Taiso Eka were both executed and were, therefore, unable to complete their full natural life span.

> *What conditionally exists, from the first, is not*
>
> *That which truly exists,*
>
> *And the disappearance of the conditioned is not*
>
> *a case of there being nothing.*
>
> *The meaning of "Nirvana is the paying off of old*
>
> *debts"*
>
> *Is that our one True Nature is free from the*
>
> *discriminatory.*

Chōsa Keishin was Meditation Master Nansen Fugan's foremost disciple. He had a reputation for having explored the Matter* with his Master over a long period of time. Be that as it may, in the present story he was not able to fully grasp the fundamental principle. For instance, he did not understand what Yoka Genkaku was talking about,[11] nor had he clarified what Kumorata's compassionate instructions to Shayata were. Far and away, it was as if he had not encountered even in his dreams what had been voiced by the World-honored One. Since all that the Buddhas and Ancestors have been expressing had not been Transmitted to you, Chōsa, who could esteem and respect you?

There are three type of spiritual hindrances: karmic hindrances (which arise from our deliberate deeds), compensatory hindrances (which arise as recompense for our past deeds), and defiling hindrances (which arise from our pursuit of our passions). What we call the 'five most treacherous deeds' are an example of karmic hindrances. Although this was not at the heart of what Kōgetsu was asking, what he was saying concerning the past was based on the assumption that karma never disappears but tends to arise as karma from some distant past life. Your error, Chōsa, was that when you were asked, "What, pray, does 'being empty all along' mean?" you responded that it refers to karmic hindrances. But how could 'karmic hindrance' mean 'something that has been empty all along'? Since karmic hindrances are something created by our actions, how can something we have created be 'empty all along'?

---

11. An allusion to Genkaku's famous poem, "The Song that Attests to the Way". One translation of this is found in *Buddhist Writings on Meditation and Daily Practice,* (Shasta Abbey Press, 1994), pp. 223-241.

'Created' and 'non-created' exist only in relation to each other. If we did not create them, they would not be karmic hindrances, and if they are something that is created, they would not be something that has been empty all along. It is a non-Buddhist view that karmic hindrances are empty when their true nature has not yet been stirred up. If, as you say, karmic hindrances are 'empty all along', then human beings who indulge in creating karma would have no chance of liberating themselves. If they had no way of liberating themselves, then Buddhas could not have come forth in the world. If Buddhas had not come forth in the world, then our Ancestral Master Bodhidharma could not have come from the West. If our Ancestral Master had not come from the West, there could not have been a Nansen. If there had not been a Nansen, who would you have exchanged the Eyes of training with?

Further, when Kōgetsu asked, "Just what, pray, are karmic hindrances?" you replied, "What has been empty all along." This resembles the old 'tethering the horse' response.[12] Even so, it would appear that, due to your weak abilities, you did not fully understand the Matter and were not the equal of the shrine priest who was long in training. This must have been why you gave rise to silly words like those in this dialogue.

Afterwards, you gave him your poem, with the lines:

> The meaning of "Nirvana is the paying off of old
>   debts"
> Is that our one True Nature is free from the
>   discriminatory.

As to the one True Nature of which you spoke, just what is that 'True Nature'? Pray, which among the three natures do you consider It to be?[13] Would it be fair to say that you do not know that 'our True Nature' refers to 'nirvana being our having paid off our old debts?' When you speak of nirvana, what is this nirvana of yours? Would it

---

12.   That is, when someone asks, "Who tethered the horse?" the one asked replies, "The owner of the horse," and when then asked, "Who is the owner of the horse?" the one asked replies, "The one who tethered the horse."

13.   A reference to the nature of our deliberate acts. That is, they are good, bad, or neutral.

be the nirvana of the shravakas?* Or the nirvana of the pratyekabuddhas?* Or the nirvana of the Buddha? No matter which, yours cannot equal the meaning of 'paying off old debts'. What you are expressing is not what the Buddhas and Ancestors expressed. Further, you need to buy some straw sandals and go off hunting for a true Master. Those like the Venerable Shishibodai and our great Master Eka, the Second Chinese Ancestor, have suffered personal injury for the sake of wicked people. Why would you want to resemble those transgressors who caused such harm? This is not your final body, nor is it a body that will not have an intermediate world, so why would you not experience retribution in some future lifetime? If the time is already ripe for you to receive recompense in the future, it will not be something for you to doubt now. Obviously, you need to recognize that Chōsa had not yet clarified what the effects of karma in the three temporal worlds are.

Those who are truly serious in their training must clarify what the effects of karma in the three temporal periods are. Then they will undoubtedly be like the Venerable Kumorata. This is already the activity of those in our Ancestral tradition, so it should not be discarded or neglected. Besides that, you need to explore extensively through your training all eight kinds of karma, which includes such things as temporally unfixed karma.[14] Those who have not yet understood karmic retribution cannot have received the genuine Transmission of the Buddhas and Ancestors. Those who are not yet clear about the principle of karmic retribution in the three temporal periods should not go about recklessly calling themselves teachers and spiritual guides for ordinary people and those in lofty positions.

The World-honored One once said: "Even were hundreds
of thousands of eons to pass, the karmic consequences from what
we have created do not disappear. When dealing with causes and
conditions, we naturally receive the fruits therefrom as karmic

---

14.   The eight kinds of karma are good karma that acts within each of the three temporal periods, plus good karma that is not limited to just one of these periods, and misfortunate karma within each of these three periods, plus unlimited misfortunate karma.

recompense. By all means, you should all know that if your moral acts are completely impure, you will get completely impure results when the recompense from this matures. And if your moral acts are completely pure, you will get completely pure results when the recompense from this matures. And if your moral acts are a mix of impure and pure, you will get mixed results when the recompense from this matures. Therefore, by all means, you should avoid acts that are completely impure or a mix of impure and pure. You should make every effort to explore through your training with your Master what completely pure deeds are."

Then, having heard what the Buddha voiced, all in the great assembly rejoiced and received it in trust.

As the World-honored One has taught, when the members of the assembly have ceased to create mixed good and bad karma, even were hundreds of thousands of myriad eons to pass, they will not let our practice die out. Whenever any of them encounter causality, invariably they immediately become aware of it. Thus, when we feel remorse for our evil deeds and, in repentance, bring them to a halt, that will alter our heavy misdeeds, causing us to receive lighter consequences. If we take joy in good deeds—be they one's own or another's—we will want to increase them more and more, which is what I mean by 'not letting the practice die out'. And there is, indeed, recompense for that!

Copied on the ninth day of the third lunar month in the fifth year of the Kenchō era (March 8, 1253) whilst in the Chief Junior's quarters at Eihei-ji Temple.

Ejō

90

On 'The Four Horses'

(Shime)

Translator's introduction: This discourse is based on a widely quoted description of four kinds of trainees when they encounter the Buddhist Teaching on impermanence. The training of the four kinds is likened to the training of four types of horses.

One day a non-Buddhist came to where the Buddha was in order to pay the World-honored One a visit. He said to the Buddha, "I do not ask You whether You have words for It, nor do I ask You whether there are no words for It."

The World-honored One sat in silence for some good while.

Thereupon, the non-Buddhist humbly bowed and, in praise, said, "How fine, O World-honored One! Your great benevolence and great compassion have parted the clouds of my delusion and made it possible for me to enter the Truth." He then made a prostration and departed.

After the non-Buddhist had departed, Ananda then asked the Buddha, "What did the non-Buddhist realize that led him to say that he had entered the Truth and then, after praising You, depart?"

The World-honored One replied, "He was like a good horse who just goes forth upon seeing but the shadow of a riding crop."

Since the time when our Ancestral Master Bodhidharma came from the West up to the present, there have been many good Masters who have taken up this account and given it to those training under them. Among the trainees, there were those who took years and others who took months or even just days before they clarified the Matter* and came to trust in the Buddha's Dharma. We call this the account of the non-Buddhist

---

*   See *Glossary.*

who asked for the Buddha's explanation of the Matter. You need to realize that the World-honored One had two sorts of explanation: by spiritual silence and by spiritual explanation. Those who are able to enter the Truth via this narrative are all like a good horse who sees the shadow of the riding crop and gallops forth. Those who are able to enter the Truth via a way of explaining the Matter that goes beyond spiritual silence and spiritual explanation are also like this.

Our Ancestral Teacher Nāgārjuna once said the following, "When I explain some phrase from a Scripture for the benefit of someone, it is as if that person were a swift horse who has seen the shadow of a riding crop and takes to the appropriate path." On any occasion whatsoever, whether when listening to Teaching on that which arises and That which does not arise, or listening to Teaching on the Three Vehicles[*] and the One Vehicle, there are often those who gallop off on a false path, but just as often there are those who can see the shadow of the riding crop and thereby take to the genuine Path. If you encounter such a person in your pursuit of a Master, there will be no place where he or she does not express some Scriptural phrase for your benefit, nor will there be any time when you can say that the shadow of the riding crop is not to be seen. Those who see the shadow of the riding crop immediately upon sitting in meditation, those who see the shadow of the riding crop after three immeasurably long eons, and those who see the shadow of the riding crop after innumerable eons of eons are all capable of entering the genuine Path.

In one of the *Āgama Scriptures*, there is the following passage:

> The Buddha once told his monks that there were four kinds of horses. The first, upon seeing the shadow of the riding crop, is startled and forthwith follows the wish of its rider. The second, startled when the crop touches its hair, forthwith follows the wish of its rider. The third is startled after the crop touches its flesh. The

fourth is awakened only after the touch of the riding crop is felt in its bones.

The first horse is like the person who hears about the death of someone in a distant monastic community and forthwith feels aversion for things of the world. The next horse is like the person who hears of the death of someone within their own monastic community and then feels aversion for things of the world. The third horse is like the person who hears of the death of someone near and dear to them and then feels aversion for things of the world. The fourth horse is like the person whose own body experiences sickness and suffering, and only then feels aversion for things of the world.

This is the metaphor of the four horses in the *Āgama Scriptures*. When you are exploring through your training what the Buddha's Dharma is, this is certainly a good place to study. Those among ordinary people or those in lofty stations who emerge as spiritually good friends and guides, later, as emissaries of the Buddha, become Ancestral Masters. All of them have invariably explored this Teaching through their practice and pass it on for the benefit of their disciples. Those who do not know it are not spiritually good friends and guides for ordinary people or for those more lofty. Those human disciples who have grown good, thick roots and are intimate with the Buddha's words and ways have invariably been able to hear this Teaching. Those who are ever so far from the Buddha's words and ways have not heard it, nor do they know it. Hence, those who would be master teachers should consider presenting it without delay, and disciples should pray that they may hear of it without delay.

The meaning of 'feeling aversion for things of the world' has been given in the *Vimalakirti Scripture*, as follows:

When the Buddha gives voice to a single utterance of Dharma, sentient beings are able to free themselves from suffering in accord with their type. Some will experience fear, some will feel joy, some will give rise to aversion for things of the world, some will cut through their doubts.

The *Great Scripture on the Buddha's Parinirvana* quotes the Buddha as saying the following:

Next, my good disciples, it is like training horses. Generally speaking, there are four kinds of horses. With the first, contact is made through their hair. With the second, contact is made through their skin. With the third, contact is made through their flesh. With the fourth, contact is made through their bones. They obey the trainer's wish, depending on which part is contacted.

The situation is also like this for the Tathagata. By means of four methods, He restrains and subdues sentient beings. With the first, the Buddha explains for their benefit what 'being alive' means, whereby they accept what He says. They are like horses who follow the wish of their rider once he has made contact with their hair. With the second, the Buddha explains what 'being alive, along with aging' means, whereby they accept what He says. They are like horses who follow the wish of their rider once he has made contact with their hair and skin. With the third, the Buddha explains what 'being alive, along with aging and sickening' means, whereby they accept what He says. They are like horses who follow the wish of their rider once he has made contact with their hair, skin, and flesh. With the fourth, He explains what 'being alive, along with aging, sickening, and dying' means, whereby they accept what the Buddha says. They are like horses who follow the wish of their rider once he has made contact with their hair, skin, flesh, and bones.

O my good disciples, there is nothing assured when it comes to a rider training a horse, but with the World-honored Tathagata's restraining and subduing sentient beings, His efforts are assured and never in vain. This is why the Buddha was given the epithet of Tamer and Subduer of Those Who Are Strong in Their Determination.

This is called "The Four Horses of the *Great Scripture on the Buddha's Parinirvana*". There are no trainees who have failed to learn of it and no Buddhas who have failed to teach it. We hear it when we follow the Buddha. Of necessity, we pay heed to it whenever we encounter and offer our service to a Buddha. Once we have had the Buddha Dharma Transmitted to us, we continually give expression to It for the sake of sentient beings. When we ultimately arrive at Buddhahood, we voice It for the sake of the great assembly of bodhisattvas* and all others—worldly and celestial—who will listen, just as if it were the first time that our wish to realize the Truth had arisen. This is why the Three Treasures of Buddha, Dharma, and Sangha have continued on without interruption.

Because this is the way things are, what Buddhas teach is far from what bodhisattvas teach. You need to keep in mind that, generally speaking, there are these four methods of a trainer of horses, namely, making contact with the hair, making contact with the skin, making contact with the flesh, and making contact with the bones. It may not be apparent what the object is that makes contact with the hair, but in the opinion of virtuous bodhisattva-mahasattvas* who Transmit the Dharma, it might be a whip.[1] At the same time, among the methods for training a horse, there are those who may employ a whip and those who do not employ a whip, since the training of horses may not invariably require a whip.

Horses that stand eight feet high are called dragon horses. There are few humans who are prepared to train such horses. There are also horses called thousand-league horses, since they can run a thousand leagues in one day. When running five hundred leagues, these horses are said to sweat blood, but after five hundred leagues, they speedily run on, refreshed. Those who ride these horses are few, as are those who know how to train them. There are no such horses in China, but there are some in other lands. It seems that one does not often need to apply a whip to these horses. Even so, an old worthy once said, "In training horses, one invariably applies a whip. Without a whip, a horse is not trained, for this is the method for training a horse."

---

1.   The word *ben* translates both as 'riding crop' and 'whip'. In neither case is its use viewed as an instrument of punishment in Buddhist training. Rather, it may be considered as an instrument for getting someone's attention or pointing the way.

Now, there are the four methods of contacting the hair, the skin, the flesh, and the bones. To contact the skin while leaving the hair untouched is not possible, nor can one contact the flesh and the bones without touching the hair and the skin. This is how we know that one needs to add the whip. That this has not been explained here is due to something lacking in the old worthy's statement.[2] There are many places like this in Scriptural writings.

The World-honored Tathagata, Tamer and Subduer of Those Who Are Strong in Their Determination, was also like such a horse trainer. He subdued and restrained all sentient beings by means of these four methods, assuredly and never in vain. That is to say, there were those who accepted His words when He explained for their benefit what 'being alive' means. And there were those who accepted His words when He explained what 'being alive and aging' means. And there were those who accepted His words when He explained what 'being alive, aging, and sickening' means. And there were those who accepted His words when He explained what 'being alive, aging, sickening, and dying' means. Those who learn of the last three cannot avoid the first one. It is just as in training horses in the world: there is no contacting skin, flesh, or bones apart from contacting hair. Explaining for the sake of others what 'being alive, aging, sickening, and dying' means that it was He, the World-honored Tathagata, who taught the meaning of 'being alive, aging, sickening, and dying'. He did not do so in order to help people to cut themselves off from being alive, aging, sickening, and dying. Nor did He teach that being alive, aging, sickening, and dying is what Truth is. Nor did He teach this in order to get people to understand that being alive, aging, sickening, and dying are what Truth is. He taught this 'being alive, aging, sickening, and dying' for the sake of others in order to put before all sentient beings the Truth of supreme, fully perfected enlightenment. Thus, the success of the World-honored Tathagata's efforts to restrain and subdue sentient beings are assured and never in vain. This is why He is called the Awakened One, Tamer and Subduer of Those Who Are Strong in Their Determination.

---

2. In the original Chinese text of what the old worthy said, the word 'whip' does not occur. Dōgen's Japanese paraphrase is unclear as to whether he is referring to a whip or a riding crop.

On a day during the summer retreat in the seventh year of the Kenchō era (1255), I finished copying and proofing this from the Master's draft.

Ejō

91

On the Monk in the Fourth Meditative State

(Shizen Biku)

Translator's Introduction: In the first part of this discourse, Dōgen quotes a cautionary tale concerning a monk who misunderstood what he was experiencing in his meditation and thought that he had realized arhathood, whereas he had simply realized a state of meditative equanimity associated with the removing of delusions from within the world of form.

In the second part of this discourse, Dōgen takes up 'The Tripod Theory', a view that was popular in China at the time. It held that Chinese culture was based on the teachings of Lao-tzu, Confucius, and Shakyamuni, the respective founders of Taoism, Confucianism, and Buddhism, and that, just as a tripod needs all three of its legs in order to remain upright, so too the Chinese needed all three of these teachings in order to maintain their culture. The underlying premise for this view was that these three represented three essential ways of stating the same fundamental teaching. In refutation of this theory, Dōgen points out that Buddhism does not need Taoism or Confucianism to justify Its existence in China or anywhere else and that, in addition, the Buddha Dharma is not the same as the teachings of Confucius and Lao-tzu.

Our Fourteenth Indian Ancestral Master Nāgārjuna once said the following:

There was once a certain monk among the Buddha's disciples who, upon experiencing the fourth meditative state, became filled with conceit, fancying that he had attained the fourth stage of arhathood. Previously, upon experiencing the first meditative state, he straightaway imagined that he had attained the first stage of arhathood, that of being a stream-entrant.[1] When he experienced the second meditative state, he imagined that he had attained the second stage of arhathood, that of a once-returner.[2] When he experienced the third meditative state, he imagined that he

---

1. That is, one who has understood the Truth of the Buddha's Teachings and, as a result of following those Teachings, will be subject to no more than seven rebirths in the future.

2. That is, one who will be reborn but one more time.

had attained the third stage of arhathood, that of a non-returner.[3] When he experienced the fourth meditative state, he imagined that he had attained the fourth stage of arhathood, that of a full arhat.[4] Confident of this, he became proud of himself and did not seek to advance any farther in his training.

When his life was just about to end, he saw rising before him what appeared to be an intermediate world, one associated with the fourth meditative state.[5] Thereupon he gave rise to a mistaken notion, thinking, "There is no nirvana. The Buddha has deceived me." Because of his unrepentant mistaken view, the intermediate world of the fourth meditative state disappeared and a hellish intermediate world arose. Then, upon his death, he was reborn into a hellish world of incessant suffering.

The monks asked the Buddha, "At the end of this mistaken monk's life, where was he reborn?"

The Buddha replied, "That person was reborn in a hellish world of incessant suffering."

The monks were greatly dismayed, "Can doing meditation and keeping to the Precepts lead to that?"

The Buddha answered as before and then added, "This was all due to his being filled with conceit. When he experienced the fourth meditative state, he fancied that he had attained the fourth stage of arhathood. Facing the end of his life, he saw the appearance of the intermediate world of the fourth meditative state, and then gave rise to a mistaken view, thinking, 'There is no nirvana. Now even though I am an arhat, I am to be reborn. The Buddha has

---

3.   That is, one who will not be reborn into the world of desire again.

4.   That is, one who has cleansed his or her heart of all greed, hatred and delusion and will not be reborn into any of the six worlds of existence again.

5.   The intermediate world refers to the period between death and rebirth.

deceived me.' Because of this, he saw the appearance of a hellish intermediate world and, after his passing, he was reborn into that hellish world." The Buddha then composed the following verse:

> *Though hearing much, holding to the Precepts, and*
> *doing meditation,*
> *He had not yet acquired the method for bringing his*
> *excesses to an end.*
> *Though he had the merit from his actions,*
> *It was hard for him to have faith in this matter.*
> *It was for his slandering Buddha that he fell into a hell,*
> *Which was in no way connected with the fourth great*
> *meditative state.*

This monk is known as 'the monk in the fourth meditative state', as well as 'the monk who did not give ear to the Teaching'. We are being cautioned about mistaking the fourth meditative state for the fourth stage of arhathood, as well as being cautioned about harboring false views that slander the Buddha. All the people in His great assembly, whether ordinary people or those in lofty positions, knew about this event. From the time when the Tathagata was in the world up to this very day, both those in India and those in China, have ridiculed mistaken views in order to caution someone against being attached to what is wrong, saying, "That is like realizing the fourth meditative state and taking it to be the fourth stage of arhathood."

Let me summarize for you three ways in which this monk was mistaken.[6] In the first place, he was someone who did not give ear to the Teaching and therefore was not up to distinguishing between the fourth meditative state and the fourth stage of arhathood. And he vainly kept his distance from the Buddha as well as idly living off by himself. He was fortunate enough to live at a time when the Tathagata was in the world. Had he continually paid visits to where the Buddha was, regularly encountering Him and listening to His Teaching, he would not have made the mistakes

---

6. The first two ways are given in this paragraph and the following one. The third way is not given until later in the discourse.

that he did. Nevertheless, because he lived off by himself like a hermit and did not go to places where the Buddha was in order to hear His Teaching, he was the way he was. Even though he failed to go where the Buddha was, he could have gone to where the great arhats were and received instruction from them. To live alone to no good purpose is a mistake born of conceit.

In the second place, to attain the first meditative state and think it to be the first stage of arhathood, then to attain the second meditative state and think it to be the second stage of arhathood, then to attain the third meditative state and think it to be the third stage of arhathood, then to attain the fourth meditative state and think it to be the fourth stage of arhathood, this was his second mistake. How could he possibly have compared the way the first, second, third, and fourth meditative states appear with the way the first, second, third, and fourth stages of arhathood appear? This was due to the fault of his not giving ear to the Teaching, a fault derived from his not taking refuge in his Master and thereby remaining in the dark.

Among the disciples of Ubakikuta, there was a certain monk who, in all good faith, had left home life behind, and upon realizing the fourth meditative state, took it to be the fourth stage of arhathood. Ubakikuta, using his skillful means, had him go live in some distant place. He then made a band of thieves, along with five hundred merchants, materialize upon the monk's path. The thieves threatened to slaughter the merchants. The monk, seeing this, feared for his life, but then it suddenly occurred to him, "I am surely not an arhat. I must just be at the third stage of arhathood." [7]

After all the merchants had fled, only the daughter of a wealthy merchant remained behind. She asked the monk, "All I pray for is that, out of your great virtue, you will let me come with you." The monk replied, "The Buddha does not permit us to travel with a

7.   The fourth stage is marked by equanimity, which the monk realized that he lacked due to his feelings of fear.

woman." The young girl said, "Be that as it may, I will just follow behind you, my virtuous monk." Taking pity on her, the monk went forth, fulfilling the wishes of both by maintaining a proper distance between them.

The Venerable Ubakikuta then caused a great river to appear. The young woman said, "O great virtuous one, will you cross this with me?" The monk was downstream and the young woman was upstream when the woman fell into the water. "O great virtuous one, save me!" she cried. Then, as the monk reached out his hands to pull her from the river, thoughts of how soft she felt welled up in him, by which he knew that he was not a non-returner. Feeling intense craving for her, he picked her up and took her to a secluded place, desiring to have intercourse with her, when he saw that she was actually his Master. Giving rise to deep shame, he stood with his head hanging low.

The Venerable One then instructed him, saying, "For a long time you have fancied yourself to be an arhat, so how could you possibly want to commit such an act?" Leading the monk back to the community, He had him express his remorse to them, and explained to him the essence of the Dharma, thereby causing him to truly attain arhathood.[8]

Although this monk's mistake in the first place was having an inflated view of himself, more specifically, when he witnessed the threat of a massacre, he gave way to fear. At the time he thought, "I am not a full arhat," still he made the mistake of thinking that he must be in the third stage of arhathood. Later, when he gave rise to thoughts of how soft the woman felt, thereby allowing carnal desires to well up, he knew that he was not a non-returner. Moreover, unlike the monk in the fourth meditative state, he did not give rise to thoughts that slandered the Buddha, nor to thoughts that slandered the

---

8. This quote comes from a commentary on a text written by Master Tendai Chigi, the founder of the Tendai tradition.

Dharma, nor to thoughts that violated the Scriptures. Because this monk had the strength from having formally studied the sacred Teachings, he realized that he himself was not an arhat or even a non-returner. People today who do not give ear to the Teaching do not know what an arhat is, much less what a Buddha is, so they do not know that they themselves are not yet an arhat or a Buddha; they just recklessly go around thinking, "I am Buddha," which is an enormous mistake. Their's must be a deep-seated fault. Students of the Way must, by all means, learn first off just what a Buddha is.

A virtuous one of old once said, "Those who study the saintly Scriptures know, for the most part, what follows upon what, so, should they go beyond the proper bounds, their fault is easily recognized and corrected." How true are these words of that virtuous one of old! Though people give rise to personal opinions, if they have studiously learned even a little bit of the Buddha's Teachings, they will not be deceived by themselves or be deluded by others.

There was once a man—or so have I heard—who thought he had realized Buddhahood, but as he waited, the light of dawn did not emblazon the sky, as he had anticipated, so he thought it must be due to an obstruction by Mara. When the dawn finally came to full daylight, he did not encounter Brahma encouraging him to give voice to the Dharma. So, he knew he was not a Buddha, and thus he reckoned he was an arhat. But when others reviled him over this, his mind gave rise to negative thinking, so he knew that he was not an arhat. Thus, he imagined that he was at the third stage of arhathood. And then, when he encountered certain women, he gave rise to lascivious thoughts, thereby knowing that he was not a saintly person.

Here too was one who truly knew the forms of the Teaching and therefore was not different from the person in the previous story.

Now, those who know the Buddha Dharma recognize their mistakes all on their own. Those who are ignorant of their mistakes vainly stay in their befuddled state of mind for the whole of their lives. And it may be like this for them in life after life. Even though that disciple of Ubakikuta's had attained the fourth meditative state and took it for the fourth stage of arhathood, he was wise enough to know that he was not an arhat. Even with the monk who did not give ear to the Teaching, if upon seeing an intermediate world of the fourth meditative state at the end of his life, he had realized that he was not an arhat, he would not have committed the wrong of slandering the Buddha. And what's more, it had been a long time since he had realized the fourth meditative state, so why did he not realize upon reflection that it could not be the fourth stage of arhathood? And if he already knew that it was not the fourth stage of arhathood, why did he not correct his thinking? Instead, he idly stuck to his mistaken view, drowning in his false opinion of himself.

In the third place, as his life came to an end, he made a huge mistake. The fault was so profound that he ultimately fell into a hellish state of incessant suffering. I want to say to him, "Even if, during your whole lifetime, you were convinced that you had come to the fourth stage of arhathood, and then, at the end of your life an intermediate world of the fourth meditative state appeared, you should have acknowledged your lifelong error, realizing that you were never at the fourth stage of arhathood. How could you possibly harbor the thought, 'The Buddha has deceived me. Even though there is no nirvana, He has invented one?' This was a fault due to your not giving ear to the Teaching. This wrongful way slanders the Buddha. Accordingly, when the intermediate state of a hellish world appeared, you ended your life by falling into a hell of incessant suffering. How could anyone possibly be the equal of a Tathagata, even a saintly one of the fourth stage of arhathood?"

Shariputra had long been a saintly person at the fourth stage of arhathood. Were we to gather up all the spiritually wise discernment that exists in the three-thousand great-thousandfold world and, after excluding that of the Tathagata, treat what remained as one tenth, and then compare a sixteenth of Shariputra's wise discernment with that wise discernment that remained in the three-thousand great-thousandfold world, it would not equal one tenth of that sixteenth that Shariputra had. Even so, upon hearing the Tathagata give voice to Teaching that he had never heard before, Shariputra did not think, "What the Buddha is now saying is different from what He said earlier. Surely, He is deceiving me." Rather he says in praise of the Tathagata, "Mara the Tempter has nothing like this to offer!" The Tathagata once ferried a rich man to the Other Shore, one whom Shariputra would not ferry to the Other Shore: this is clearly the difference between Shariputra's having only realized the fourth stage of arhathood, whereas the Tathagata had realized Buddhahood.[9]

If the universe in all ten quarters were filled with folks like Shariputra and his disciples and they all together tried to fully fathom the Buddha's wise discernment, they could not succeed. And Confucius and Lao-tzu never had such meritorious virtue. Who among those who have pursued a study of the Buddha Dharma would be unable to fathom the teachings of Confucius or Lao-tzu?[10] But among those who have devoted themselves to a study of Confucius or Lao-tzu, have any ever been able to fathom what the Buddha Dharma is? Nowadays, folks in Sung China, by and large, hold to the notion that the teachings of Confucius and Lao-tzu are in agreement with the Buddha's Dharma. Theirs is a most profoundly distorted view, one we shall explore by and by.

When the monk in the fourth state of meditation took his distorted view as being true, he fancied that the Tathagata had deceived him, and turned his back on the Buddha for ever so long. The enormity of his folly was the equal of such persons as the six non-Buddhist teachers.[11]

---

9.   An allusion to a wealthy man who, at the age of one hundred, resolved to be a monk. Shariputra did not allow him to enter the assembly because of his age. The Buddha, hearing of this, did permit him to become a monk, which ultimately led him to realize Buddhahood.

10.   A thorough knowledge of the works attributed to Confucius, Lao-tzu, and, later, Chuang-tzu was considered essential for any educated Chinese male, and this continued for over twenty-five hundred years, until their writings were replaced by Mao's *Little Red Book.*

11.   They lived at the time of the Buddha and are identified in Pali Scriptures as Purana Kassapa (an amoralist who denied that good and evil exist), Makkari Gosala (a fatalist), Sanjati Belattiputta (a skeptic), Ajita Kesakambara (a materialist), Pakudha Kaccayana

A virtuous one of old once said: "Even when our Great Master was in the world, there were people with fallacious views and personal opinions. And what is worse, after His passing, there have been those who have been unable to experience meditative states for want of a Master." The Great Master referred to here is the World-honored Buddha. In truth, even those who had left home life behind and received ordination when the World-honored One was in the world found it difficult to avoid having mistaken views and personal opinions, due to their not giving ear to His Teaching. How much less can we avoid mistakes, we who live in a remote land during the last five hundred year period following the demise of the Tathagata![12] Even someone who has given rise to the fourth meditative state is like this. How much less worthy of mention are those who have not even reached the fourth meditative state and vainly drown in their craving for fame and their greed for gain, that bunch who yearn for official careers and worldly pursuits! Today in Great Sung China there are many ill-informed and silly people, who say, "The teachings of Lao-tzu and Confucius are in accord with what the Buddha Taught, so their paths are not divergent."

In Great Sung China during the Chia-tai era (1201-1205), there was a monk named Shōju who presented to the emperor a thirty-fascicle work that he had edited entitled the *Chia-tai Era Record of the Lamp Whose Light Reaches Everywhere.* In it, he said:

> Your humble subject heard the words of Kozan Chi'en who said, "My way is like a tripod, and its three teachings are like its legs. Should the tripod lack one leg, it would tip over." Your humble subject has deeply admired that man for ever so long and has explored his persuasive remarks. Thus I have come to realize that the essence of the teachings of Confucius is sincerity and the

---

(who explained the universe in terms of seven elemental factors), and Nigantha Nataputta (Founder of Jainism, who believed in the relativity of all things).

12. 'The last five hundred years' refers to the third and final five hundred year period when the Dharma will have become so degenerate as to be spiritually ineffective.

> essence of the teachings of Taoism resides in a non-judgmental heart. The essence of the Shakya's teaching resides in seeing one's True Nature. 'Sincerity,' 'non-judgmentalism,' and 'seeing one's True Nature' are different in name but the same in substance. When we reach the place that they all ultimately come down to, there is nothing to be understood except this teaching, and so forth…

People who hold such mistaken views and personal opinions are many indeed; they are not limited to Chi'en and Shōju. The error of these folks is more profound than those who have realized the fourth meditative state and think that they have experienced the fourth stage of arhathood, for they are surely slandering Buddha, slandering Dharma, and slandering Sangha. They have already denied liberation, the three temporal worlds, and cause and effect. Beyond doubt, in their jungle of entanglements and confusion, they have invited calamity and woe. They are the equals of that bunch who think that there are no Three Treasures, Four Noble Truths, or four types of monks.[13] The essence of the Buddha Dharma has never been simply seeing one's True Nature. Where have any of the Seven Buddhas* or our twenty-eight Indian Ancestors said that the Buddha Dharma is merely the seeing of one's True Nature? The *Platform Scripture* of the Sixth Ancestor contains the phrase, 'seeing one's True Nature', but this text is a fraudulent document, it is not a work associated with the Treasure House of the Dharma, nor is the phrase one of Daikan Enō's sayings, nor is it a text that the descendants of the Buddhas and Ancestors have ever relied on. Because Shōju and Chi'en did not have a clue about even a cubbyhole's worth of the Buddha's Dharma, they manufactured this false concoction of a three-footed tripod.

---

13. The four types of monks are those who are excellent in the practice, those who expound the Dharma, those who devote their lives to exploring the Dharma, and those who disgrace the Dharma.

* See *Glossary*.

A virtuous one of old once said:

> Even Lao-tzu and Chuang-tzu were still unaware of the Lesser Course's* possibility of being attached and what it is that gets attached, as well as the possibility of breaking free from attachments and what it is that gets broken free, to say nothing of actually being attached to attachments and actually breaking free from attachments within the Greater Course.* This is why their teaching is not the least bit like the Buddha Dharma. Even so, confused, worldly people who are deluded by names and forms, as well as by dubious meditative practices, have wandered off from the genuine principle. Such people would like to equate such Taoist terms as 'the meritorious function of the Tao' or 'just strolling along',[14] with the teaching of liberation in the Buddha Dharma, but how could such as this possibly be?

From ancient times, people who are confused by names and forms, as well as those who do not know what the genuine principle is, have equated Chuang-tzu and Lao-tzu with the Buddha Dharma. From ancient times, no one who has had even the slightest bit of training within the Buddha Dharma has attached importance to Chuang-tzu or Lao-tzu.

It says in the *Scripture on the Immaculate Practice That Accords with the Dharma:*[15] "Those in China call the Bodhisattva* of Moonlight by the name of Yen-hui,[16] the Bodhisattva Whose Light Is Pure by the name of Chung-ni,[17] and Kashyapa

---

14.   The latter term might find a closer equivalent today as 'just going with the flow'.

15.   This text (J. *Shōjō Hōgyō Kyō*) has long been considered one of the so-called 'spurious scriptures,' whose teaching is patently false. As a consequence, it is not included in the great collections of Buddhist Scriptures, such as the *Taishō Daizōkyō*.

16.   Yen-hui was the chief disciple in Confucius's entourage.

17.   Chung-ni was another name for Confucius.

Bodhisattva by the name of Lao-tzu." From ancient times, people have cited this teaching, saying, "Confucius and Lao-tzu were bodhisattvas and, as a consequence, what they expressed must fundamentally be the same as what the Buddha expressed." Further, they have said, "They may well have been emissaries of the Buddha, so what they expressed would naturally be what the Buddha expressed." All such assertions are wrong.

A virtuous one of old once made a comment about that text, saying, "In conformity with the catalogues of Scriptural works, all consider this so-called 'scripture' to be spurious." Relying upon this remark of his, we can say that the Buddha's Dharma is all the more divergent from the teachings of Confucius and Lao-tzu. To assert that they are already bodhisattvas does not alter this, for bodhisattvahood cannot be compared to realizing the fruition of Buddhahood. Furthermore, the meritorious action of 'concealing one's light and accommodating oneself to others'[18] is a method used only by Buddhas and bodhisattvas of the three temporal worlds. It is not something that ordinary, secular people can do. How could an ordinary, secular person who is truly keeping to his worldly occupation be free enough to accommodate himself to others? Neither Confucius nor Lao-tzu ever spoke of accommodating themselves for the sake of others. Even less did Confucius and Lao-tzu know about karmic causes from the past or their effects in the present. Their aim was simply to artfully serve their sovereign and govern their households by means of loyalty and filial piety for merely their own single generation, since they had nothing to teach future generations. They may already have been equals of the nihilists.[19] Those who felt an aversion towards Chuang-tzu and Lao-tzu and said, "They did not even know

---

18. 'Concealing one's light and accommodating oneself to others' is a technical Buddhist term. 'Concealing one's light' refers to the ability of Buddhas and bodhisattvas to 'turn down' the brilliance that may naturally shine forth due to the effects of Their spiritual attainments, which may put others into awe and thereby stimulate feelings of inadequacy in them. 'Accommodating oneself to others' refers to the ability of Buddhas and bodhisattvas to assume a presence that does not frighten people. Both abilities are used in order to help ferry beings to the Other Shore.

19. Nihilists are those who believe that there is a self which comes to an end at death.

of the Lesser Course, much less of the Greater Course!" were bright Masters of old. Anyone who says, as Chi'en and Shōju did, that the three teachings are fundamentally one and the same teaching is an ignoramus during this later, degenerate age of ours. O Chi'en and Shōju, I ask you, what brilliance do you two have that you would disregard what former virtuous ones have expressed by arbitrarily asserting that Confucius and Lao-tzu are surely the equals of the Buddha's Dharma? Your views are in no way equal to the task of discussing what is penetrable and what is impenetrable in the Buddha's Dharma. Pack up your belongings and go seek out a clear-minded Master to explore the Matter* with. O Chi'en and Shōju, the two of you are more in the dark about the Greater and Lesser Courses than that monk who mistook the fourth meditative state for the fourth stage of arhathood. How pitiful that, wherever the winds of degenerate times are blowing, there are so many devils like these two.

A virtuous one of old once said:

> According to what Confucius and the ancient Chinese emperor Chou-kung said, as well as what the legendary three emperors and five rulers of antiquity wrote, when filial piety governs a household and loyalty governs a nation, they help the nation and profit its people. Even so, this is limited to a single period of time; it does not relieve past or future suffering. Since this does not compare with the benefits from the Buddha Dharma in all three temporal periods, how could theirs possibly not be a mistaken view?

How true they are, these words of the virtuous one of old! He has arrived at a deep understanding of the Truth of the Buddha Dharma and has clarified the principle underlying the secular world. The words of the three emperors and the five rulers still do not come up to the teaching of a saintly Wheel-turning Lord* and should never be discussed alongside what a Lord Brahma or a Shakrendra give voice to.[20] The karmic recompense that these Chinese rulers would have received from their governance over their realms would have been decidedly second-rate. And not even Wheel-turning Lords, Lord Brahma, or Shakrendra himself are the equal of a monk who has left home life behind and been ordained. How much less could they be the equal of the Tathagata! Further, the writings of Confucius and Chou-kung cannot compare with the eighteen great Vedic texts, much less come up to the four Vedas themselves.[21] India's Brahmanic Scriptures are still not the equal of the Buddhist Scriptures, not even those of the followers of the Lesser Course. How sad that in a small, remote country like China there is the false doctrine of the three teachings being one and the same teaching.

Our Fourteenth Ancestor, the bodhisattva Nāgārjuna once said, "The great arhats and the pratyekabuddhas* had direct knowledge of eighty thousand great eons, whereas the great bodhisattvas and the Buddha had direct knowledge of immeasurable eons." People like Confucius and Lao-tzu never knew the past and future within their own single age, so how could they possibly have known of a couple of their past lives? How much less could they have possibly known even a single eon? How much less could they have possibly known a hundred eons or a thousand eons? How much less could they have possibly known eighty thousand great eons? And how much less could they have known an immeasurable eon? When compared with the Buddhas and bodhisattvas who have illumined and known these immeasurable eons more clearly than They knew the palms of Their hands, those like Confucius and Lao-tzu do not even warrant being called ignoramuses. Cover your ears and do not listen to such a

---

20.　Lord Brahma rules over the lowest of the four meditative heavens in the world of form. Shakrendra, Lord Indra, rules over the world of the thirty-three heavens which comprise the second of the six realms in the world of desire.

21.　The eighteen Vedic texts are the four Vedas—the Scriptures of Brahmanism—plus fourteen commentaries.

phrase as 'the three teachings are one and the same teaching', for among erroneous mouthings, it is the most erroneous.

Chuang-tzu once said, "Feeling noble and feeling base, despising suffering and craving pleasure, being right and being wrong, having and losing, are all natural states." This viewpoint was already the equal of the Naturalist perspective of non-Buddhists in India.[22] Feeling noble and feeling base, despising suffering and craving pleasure, being right and being wrong, having and losing, are all what we feel from our good or wicked acts. Because Chuang-tzu did not know about the karma that fills us up and the karma* that pulls us along,[23] or about understanding what past and future are, he was ignorant of the present, so how could he possibly be the equal of the Buddha Dharma?

There are some who assert the following:

Because the Buddha Tathagatas have broadly affirmed the ultimate reality of the universe, every tiny mote of the universe is what all Buddhas have affirmed. Thus, because both the external conditions and the internal characteristics that we receive as karmic recompense are what Tathagatas are affirming, the great earth with its mountains and rivers, the sun, moon, and stars, and the four delusions and three poisons are all being affirmed as well.[24] To see

---

22. The Indian Naturalists denied cause and effect.

23. The karma that fills us up refers to the purely individual characteristics that we may be born with, such as being born with certain abilities or propensities. The karma that pulls us along refers to the general characteristics that we share with many, such as being born as a human being.

24. The four delusions are that the physical world is permanent, that the world is a source of pleasure, that the physical world is pure, and that there exists a real, unchanging, personal self.

mountains and rivers is to see the Tathagata. The three poisons and the four delusions are nothing other than the Buddha Dharma. Seeing a dust mote is the same as seeing the whole universe. Every moment of time, without exception, is one of fully perfected enlightenment, which we call 'the great liberation'. This has been christened as 'the Way of the Ancestors, which is the Direct Transmission of and the direct pointing to the Truth'.[25]

In Great Sung China, folks like these are as prevalent as rice and flax, bamboo and reeds. The government and the general populace are filled to the brim with them. However, it is not clear just whose offspring these people are, for they have no understanding of the Way of the Ancestors of the Buddha. Even though 'the great earth with its mountains and rivers' describes what Buddhas have awakened to, that does not mean that the Great Earth with Its Mountains and Rivers is something that ordinary people might not suddenly encounter. But they have not learned or even heard of the principle that all Buddhas have come to realize. For such folks to say that seeing a dust mote is equivalent to seeing the whole universe is like their saying that being a commoner is equivalent to being a king. Further, why do they not say that seeing the whole universe is like seeing a single dust mote? If the view of these folks was equivalent to the Great Truth of the Buddhas and Ancestors, the Buddhas need not have left home life behind, our Ancestral Master Bodhidharma need not have put in an appearance, and none of us would be able to realize the Way. Even if such folks thought they had penetrated the meaning of "That which arises is the very thing that is beyond arising," it would still not be what the Truth is really saying.

---

25. This quotation borrows the vocabulary of Buddhism in order to support what is essentially a materialist perspective.

Tripitaka Master Paramārtha once said,[26] "In China, there are two fortunate things. The first is that there are no rakshasas.[27] The second is that there is no one who is a non-Buddhist." This saying is indeed something imported by a non-Buddhist Brahman from India. Even if there were no one who had deliberately followed the ways of non-Buddhists, that does not mean that there could not have been folks who gave rise to non-Buddhist views. Even though rakshasas had yet to be seen, this does not mean that there were none who were the equivalent of non-Buddhists. Because ours is a small country in a remote corner of the world, it is not the same as India or China. Though the Buddha Dharma has been studied a bit here, there is no one who has grasped what awakening is as they understood it in India.

A virtuous one of old once said:

> Nowadays, there are ever so many monks who are returning to lay life. Fearing lest they will then have to become the working dog of some lord, they enter into non-Buddhist paths. They set themselves up as teachers by stealing the principles of the Buddha Dharma and, undetected, apply them to explain Chuang-tzu and Lao-tzu. Ultimately they create total confusion, misleading innocents as to what is right and what is wrong by claiming that theirs is the view that unfolds what the Vedas taught.[28]

---

26. Paramārtha was a monastic scholar from Western India who was invited to come to South China by Emperor Wu of Liang to translate Scriptures. He arrived in 546 C.E., about a decade after Bodhidharma's death.

27. A rakshasa is a type of malevolent demon who stalks the night.

28. At the time of this quotation, the Chinese government was anti-Buddhist yet supported those who claimed to be Taoists or to have knowledge of non-Buddhist Indian philosophy.

Keep in mind that that bunch who do not know right from wrong and confuse the Buddha Dharma with the teachings of Chuang-tzu and Lao-tzu create confusion for someone who is a neophyte. They are our present-day Chi'en and Shōju. Not only is this the utmost in human idiocy, it also shows their lack of study and training, which is all too obvious, all too clear. Among the senior monks and their disciples during recent times in the Sung dynasty, not even a single one of them knew that the teachings of Confucius and Lao-tzu were not the equal of the Buddha Dharma. Although people who called themselves the offspring of the Buddhas and Ancestors were as prolific as rice and flax, bamboo and reeds, and filled the mountains and fields of the nine divisions of China, there was not a person, not even half a person, upon whom it dawned that the Buddha Dharma was foremost in insight and far beyond what was put forth by Confucius and Lao-tzu. Only that Old Buddha, my late Master Tendō, clearly understood that the Buddha Dharma was not one and the same with the sayings of Confucius and Lao-tzu, a fact that he kept affirming day and night. Though there were those who had reputations as teachers and academic lecturers on the Scriptures and commentaries, it had not dawned on any of them that the Buddha Dharma far surpasses the borderlands of Confucius and Lao-tzu. Many a modern academic lecturer over the past century has studied the customs of those who do seated meditation and follow the Way, hoping to walk off with what these practitioners had come to comprehend. Such a one, I dare say, is making a terrible mistake.

In Confucius's writings, there is 'the person with inborn knowledge,' whereas in Buddhist Scriptures, there is no one who has such inborn knowledge.[29] In the Buddha Dharma there is talk of sacred relics, whereas Confucius and Lao-tzu did not know whether there are sacred relics or not. Even if the two intended to jumble

---

29. Though neither Confucius nor Dōgen specifically identifies what this inborn knowledge is, the context of Confucius's writings implies that it refers to instinctively knowing how to behave like a sagely one, and without having to be taught. Dōgen does not seem to be as concerned with what the knowledge is about as with the notion of having any type of inborn knowledge.

their two teachings together, ultimately they would not end up with a broad, far-reaching perspective, whether it was penetrable or not.

It says in the *Analects of Confucius,* "The person who is born already knowing something is a superior being. The person who knows something through study is next. The person who learns it through great effort is next to him. The one who fails to learn it even with great effort, people will treat as the lowest." If he is saying that there is inborn knowledge, then his is the fault of denying causality. In the Buddha Dharma there is no talk that denies causality. When the monk in the fourth meditative state reached the end of his life, he immediately fell into the error of slandering Buddha. Should you think that the teachings of Confucius and Lao-tzu are on a par with the Buddha Dharma, your error in slandering Buddha during your lifetime would be profound indeed. O you scholars, you should quickly discard the notion that erroneously considers the teachings of Confucius and Lao-tzu to be in accord with the Buddha Dharma. Those who put store in that viewpoint and do not discard it ultimately end up in some evil world.[30]

O you scholars, be very clear about this: Confucius and Lao-tzu did not know the teaching on the three temporal worlds, nor did they know the principle of cause and effect, nor did they know anything about how to establish peacefulness in one continent, much less establishing it in all four continents. They still knew nothing about the six celestial worlds of desire, much less could they have known the Teaching concerning the nine divisions within the three worlds of desire, form, and beyond form. They could not have known anything about the small-thousandfold worlds or the middle-thousandfold worlds, so how could there have been a ruler who had encountered or known about three-thousand great-thousandfold worlds? Even in the singular nation of China, Confucius and Lao-tzu were petty officials who had not risen to an imperial rank. They are not to be compared with the Tathagata who was the Lord of the three-thousand great-thousandfold worlds. In the Tathagata's case, there were Lord Brahma, the imperial Shakrendra, and the Wheel-turning Lords, among others, offering Him veneration and protection day and night, and continually asking him to give voice to the Dharma. Confucius and Lao-tzu did not have merit like this. They

---

30. The evil worlds are those of the hells, the animals, and the hungry ghosts.

were merely commoners wandering about through the realms of existence. They never knew anything of the path to achieving liberation through renouncing the world, so how could they possibly have fully realized the True Nature of all things as the Tathagata did? If they had not fully realized It, how could they possibly have been the equal of the World-honored One? Confucius and Lao-tzu had no inner meritorious behavior nor any outer usefulness. They could never have reached the level that the World-honored One did. How could the Buddha have possibly given voice to the false teaching that the three are of one accord? Confucius and Lao-tzu were unable to thoroughly penetrate the borders of the world and what lies beyond those borders. They neither knew nor saw the breadth of the world, nor its magnitude. And not only that, they had not seen the most minute forms and could not have known what the shortest span of a moment is. The World-honored One saw the most minute forms and knew directly how long the shortest span of a moment is, so how could we possibly treat Confucius or Lao-tzu as one equal to Him? Those like Confucius, Lao-tzu, Chuang-tzu, and Hui-tzu were simply common men.[31] They could not have even come up to the level of a stream-entrant of the Lesser Course, so how could they possibly have been the equal of those at the second, third, or fourth stages* of arhathood?

At the same time, that you scholars, out of your ignorance, put them on the same level with the Buddhas is plainly your wandering deeper into your delusions. Not only were Confucius and Lao-tzu ignorant of the three temporal worlds and therefore did not know what the many eons are, they were unable to comprehend what a single moment of mindfulness is or to know the One All-embracing Buddha Mind. They do not even bear comparison with the celestial beings of sun and moon, nor could they compare with the Four Great Guardian Kings or the host of celestial beings. In comparison with the World-honored One, whether they be monastics or lay people, they are wandering off in delusion.

---

31.   Hui-tzu was a famous orator during the Wei dynasty.

It says in the *Biographies of Commoners:* [32]

Yin-hsi was a high-ranking government official in the Chou dynasty. He was particularly skilled in reading heavenly omens. One day, he was traveling to the east to investigate an unusual meteorological condition. Upon encountering it, as might be expected, he met up with Lao-tzu, who had composed a five thousand word text at Yin-hsi's request.[33] Yin-hsi also, for his part, compiled a nine-section work, entitled *The Barrier Gatekeeper* (C. *Kuan Ling Tzu*), modeled on the *Scripture on Lao-tzu's Converting the Barbarians* (C. *Hua Hu Ching*).[34] Later, when Lao-tzu was about to cross over the barrier to the Western Region, Yin-hsi thought he would like to accompany him. Lao-tzu said, "If what you desire within your heart is to be my follower, you must bring me the heads of seven people, including those of your father and mother. Then you will be able to come with me." Yin-hsi followed Lao-tzu's instruction, but on his return, the seven heads had all turned into those of wild boars.

---

32. The *Biographies of Commoners* (C. *Lieh Chuan*) is the major section of a classic Chinese work known as the *Records Compiled by the Historian* (C. *Shih-chi*), which is one of the Chinese dynastic histories, compiled in the first century B.C.E. by Ssu-ma Ch'ien. It was a basic text in the classical education of young boys, who were expected to memorize large portions of it, if not the whole.

33. Later known as *The Way and Its Power* (C: *Tao-te Ching*).

34. A pseudo-scriptural treatise that attempts to show through various accounts that Buddhism is an inferior, watered-down form of Taoism suited for barbarians but not for Chinese and that Lao-tzu went to India (the Western Region) where he became the Buddha and converted the 'barbarians'.

A virtuous one of old once said:

> Thus, Confucianists who are well-versed in their secular
> texts are worshipful even to carved images of their parents, but
> when Lao-tzu laid down his rules, he had Yin-hsi harm his parents.
> In the gateway to the Tathagata's Teaching, great compassion is the
> starting point of training, so how could Lao-tzu have possibly made
> such a topsy-turvy view the basis for his method of teaching?[35]

Long ago, there was that wrong-minded bunch who treated the World-honored One
as on a par with Lao-tzu, and nowadays, there are foolish fellows who treat the World-
honored One as on a par with Confucius and Lao-tzu. How can we not pity them!
Confucius and Lao-tzu cannot even measure up to the Wheel-turning Lords who
govern the secular world by means of the ten good deeds.[36] How could those legendary
three emperors and five rulers of antiquity, of whom Confucians speak, possibly come
up to the level of the Wheel-turning Lords of the Gold, Silver, Copper, and Iron
Wheels, who are equipped with thousands of the seven precious jewels* and who have
governance over the four continents or rule some three-thousandfold world?
Confucius himself cannot even be compared with those legendary ones. The Buddhas
and the Ancestors of past, present, and future have all considered the starting point of
training to lie in filial-like piety towards one's parents, one's Master and fellow
monks, and the Three Treasures, as well as in the making of alms offerings to those
who are ill, for example. Since time immemorial, They have never considered the
harming of one's parents to be the starting point of training. Therefore, Lao-tzu and
the Buddha Dharma are not one and the same. To kill one's parents will invariably
create karma that will be felt in one's next life, a life in which it is a foregone
conclusion that one will fall into a hellish world. Even though Lao-tzu may idly chatter

---

35. This quotation is from the commentary on Tendai Chigi's lectures on *Great Quietness
     and Reflection (Makashikan)*.

36. 'The ten good deeds' refers to actively abstaining from behaving contrary to the Ten Great
     Precepts.

on about emptiness, those who harm their parents will not escape the arising of retribution.

In the *Ching-te Era Record of the Transmission of the Lamp*, it says the following:

> Our Second Chinese Ancestor was wont to voice a lament, saying, "The teachings of Confucius and Lao-tzu are merely concerned with the arts of courtesy and the standards for social behavior, whereas the writings of Chuang-tzu and the *Book of Changes* have never come close to the Wondrous Principle."
>
> Then one day, he heard that Great Master Bodhidharma had taken up residence in Shaolin Monastery. "One who has reached the Other Shore is not far away. With him, I shall indeed attain the Wondrous Frontier."

People today should clearly trust that the authentic Transmission of the Buddha Dharma in China was wholly due just to the strength of our Second Chinese Ancestor. Though our First Chinese Ancestor, Bodhidharma, came from the West, had it not been for our Second Ancestor, the Buddha Dharma would not have been passed on. If our Second Ancestor had not passed on the Buddha Dharma, there would be no Buddha Dharma in Eastern lands today. In short, our Second Ancestor is not to be grouped among the masses.

It says in the *Record of the Transmission of the Lamp*, "The monk Shinkō was a broad-minded, scholarly gentleman.[37] For a long time, he resided in the Ilo district. He was well read in a wide variety of subjects and was able to discuss abstruse principles." Our Second Ancestor's being well read in a wide variety of subjects in the distant past may well be different by far from what people today read. After having awakened to the Dharma and having the kesa* Transmitted to him, he made no remarks like, "In the past, I was wrong to think that the teachings of Confucius and

---

37.   Shinkō was Great Master Eka's name when he was a young monk.

Lao-tzu were merely concerned with the arts of courtesy and the standards for social behavior." Keep in mind that our Second Ancestor had already thoroughly grasped that the teachings of Confucius and Lao-tzu were devoid of the Buddha Dharma, so why do his distant descendants go counter to their ancestral parent and insist that the teachings of Confucius and Lao-tzu are in accord with the Buddha's Dharma? You need to know that this is the spreading of false teaching. If someone were not a distant descendant of our Second Ancestor, such a one might rely upon the explanations of a Shōju or his likes. But if you would be a true offspring of our Second Ancestor, do not say that the three teachings are in accord.

When the Tathagata was in the world, there was a non-Buddhist who was called the Mighty Debater. He was of the opinion that there was no one his equal in debate, due to the enormity of his prowess, which is why he was called the Mighty Debater. Receiving the funds raised by five hundred Licchavis to pay for his services,[38] he selected five hundred difficult, debatable issues, and came to pose them to the Buddha. When he arrived at where the Buddha was residing, he asked the Buddha, "Is there one ultimate truth or, for the sake of people, are there many ultimate truths?"

The Buddha replied, "There is just one Ultimate Truth."

The Mighty Debater said, "We teachers each have our own ultimate truth, which we teach. Among non-Buddhists, each believes his own teaching is right and slanders the ways of others. Since we mutually judge what is right or wrong in what everyone else is teaching, we end up with many ultimate truths."

At that moment, Migasīsa, whom the World-honored One had already converted and who had gone beyond the stage of still

---

38.　The Licchavis were a group within the country of Vaishali who were early supporters of Shakyamuni.

being a student of Buddhism, came and stood next to the Buddha.[39] The Buddha asked the Mighty Debater, "Among the many ways that truths are expressed for the sake of others, whose is the foremost for you?" The Mighty Debater replied, "Migasīsa's is foremost."

The Buddha then said, "If his is foremost, why then did he discard his own way and become My disciple, thereby entering into My Truth?"

The Mighty Debater, fully realizing this, dropped his head in embarrassment and then, taking refuge, entered the Way. At this time, the Buddha, in order to thoroughly express the Matter, spoke the following in verse:

> *When someone thinks, "Mine is the ultimate in truth,"*
> *When someone falls in love with his own opinions,*
> *When someone assumes that he is right and all others wrong,*
> *Then none such yet knows the Ultimate Truth.*
>
> *Such people readily enter into wrangling and debate,*
> *All eager to clarify what 'nirvana' really means.*
> *In squabbling over who's right, who's wrong,*
> *Those who outwit feel elated, the outsmarted in misery sink.*
>
> *The victors fall into vanity's pit,*
> *While the bested plunge into some gloomy hell.*
> *Thus it is that those whose discernment is truly wise*
> *Fall not into either of these two ways.*

---

39. Migasīsa was a Brahman who was converted to Buddhism after he had undertaken to debate with the Buddha and ended up dumbfounded by Him. By the time of this story, he had already realized arhathood.

> *O Mighty Debater, by all means know*
> *That in the Dharma for My disciples*
> *There is no meaningless 'emptiness', no mundane 'truth'.*
> *So what is it that you so desire to seek from Me?*

> *If you desire to debase what I have voiced,*
> *Forthwith you already lack the grounds for doing that.*
> *Impossible the task to know what the whole of*
>   *knowledge is.*
> *Strive for that and you strive in vain.*

Now, this is what the World-honored One's golden words were like. O you foolish and dimwitted people in the Eastern lands, do not recklessly turn your back on what the Buddha taught, saying that there are paths equal to the Way of the Buddha, for that would be slandering both the Buddha and the Dharma. Those in India, from Migasīsa and the Mighty Debater to the Brahmacharins like Dirghanakha and Shrenika,[40] were eminent scholars, the likes of whom have never existed in Eastern lands, even from ancient times. What is more, Confucius and Lao-tzu could never come up to them. All of them abandoned their personal ways and took refuge in the Buddha's Way. If we were now to compare worldly persons like Confucius and Lao-tzu with the Buddha Dharma, even those who listened would be involving themselves in wrongdoing. And what is more, even arhats and pratyekabuddhas will all eventually become bodhisattvas, with not even one finishing up in the Lesser Courses. But when it comes to Confucius and Lao-tzu who never entered the Buddha's Way, how could we possibly say that they are the equals of Buddhas? That indeed would be an enormously

---

40. As used here, Brahmacharin refers to someone who was a Brahman priest and scholar in his younger years, and later converted to Buddhism. There is a tradition that Dirghanakha was Shariputra's father and became a Buddhist, due to his son's example. His name, actually a nickname, means He of the Long Nails, referring to his not cutting his nails because he was so deeply absorbed in his scholarly pursuits. Shrenika's pre-Buddhist teaching is discussed in Discourse 1: A Discourse on Doing One's Utmost in Practicing the Way of the Buddhas *(Bendowa).*

false view. To conclude, in that the World-honored Tathagata goes far beyond all others, He is praised and so recognized by all the Buddha Tathagatas and by all the great bodhisattvas, as well as by Lord Brahma and Lord Shakrendra. It is something that our twenty-eight Indian Ancestors and our six Chinese Ancestors all knew. In short, all who have the capacity to do the training and explore the Matter with their Master have come to know this. As people of these present degenerate days of the Dharma, do not involve yourself with the wild words of those ignoramuses of the Sung dynasty who speak of the three teachings being one, for theirs is the height of ignorance.

On a day during the summer retreat in the seventh year of the Kenchō era (1255), I finished making this copy of the Master's first draft.

Ejō

92

On the One Hundred and Eight Gates
to What the Dharma Illumines

(Ippyakuhachi Hōmyōmon)

Translator's Introduction: Except for the final paragraphs in this text, which were written by Dōgen, this work is comprised of a lengthy quotation in Chinese from the *Scriptural Collection of the Past Deeds of the Buddha (Butsu Hongyō Jikkyō).*

Gomyō Bodhisattva,* the One Who Is a Guardian of Wisdom's Light, then brought to a close His study of the family into which He was to be reborn.[1] At that time, there was a celestial palace in the Tushita Heaven named Lofty Banners. Its length and width were equal—sixty yojanas.* From time to time, the Bodhisattva would go up into this palace and give voice to the essence of the Dharma for the sake of the celestial beings residing in the Tushita Heaven. On this particular occasion, the Bodhisattva went up into this palace and, having finished His peaceful seated meditation, He gave instruction to the celestial ones of the Tushita Heaven, saying, "You who are celestial beings, by all means come gather around Me, since My present being will soon descend into a human form. I now wish to explain in their entirety the gates to what the Dharma illumines, for they are known as the gates which are the skillful means for comprehending the forms that all thoughts and things take. I leave these Teachings as My final instructions for you, that you may remember Me by Them. If you listen to what these

---

* See *Glossary.*

1. Gomyō Bodhisattva was in the Tushita Heaven, prior to His rebirth as Shakyamuni Buddha.

gates of the Dharma are, they will surely produce great joy and delight within you."

When the great assembly of celestial beings in the Tushita Heaven—including the beautiful celestial women and their entourage—heard what the Bodhisattva had just said, they came up and gathered about Him. Seeing the multitude that had gathered in the celestial palace, He desired to give expression to the Dharma for their sake.

Employing His marvelous spiritual abilities, He produced atop the original palace of Lofty Banners a celestial palace so grand and spacious that it covered the four continents.[2] So delightful was it in its ordered grandeur that few things could be likened to it. Lofty in its majesty, it was encrusted with masses of jewels. Among all the celestial palaces within the world of desire, there was none to compare with it. When the celestial beings within the world of form saw this extraordinary palace, they felt as if their own palaces resembled burial mounds.

Gomyō Bodhisattva had already performed valued deeds, planted virtuous roots, brought about much happiness, and was now endowed with much merit. He ascended to the Lion's Seat,[*] which He had so magnificently created, and sat down upon it. While seated on this Lion's Throne, Gomyō Bodhisattva adorned it with intricate patterns of jewels beyond measure. He spread over this seat all manner of celestial robes, and perfumed that seat with various types of wondrous incense which He burned in innumerable bejeweled censers. He brought forth all manner of marvelously scented flowers which he scattered over the ground. Around his lofty Dharma Seat were many treasures of great value. Hundreds of thousands of myriad light beams shone forth, magnificently illumining this palace of His. From top to bottom, the palace was

---

2.   That is, the four that lie to the north, south, east, and west of Mount Sumeru.

hung with jeweled nets, and from those nets hung many golden bells, whose tinkling sound was wondrous indeed. Countless light rays of various types shone forth from this great palace. This priceless palace was hung with thousands of myriad banners of various brilliant hues. From that great palace hung all sorts of tassels. Beautiful celestial maidens by the hundreds of thousands of millions, each carrying various varieties of the Seven Precious Jewels,* sang the praises of the Bodhisattva in songs that told of His countless past merits. The guardian lords of the earth were there by the billions, standing to His left and right, protecting this palace. The Guardian Lord Indras by the millions made prostrations before this palace, and millions of celestial Brahmas made their venerative offerings. Also, millions upon millions upon millions of bodhisattvas came to protect this palace, and the Buddhas of the ten quarters were there by untold millions, keeping watch over it. Practice and training previously done over countless eons as well as acts of freeing others from their suffering were achieving their spiritual reward. Good causes and their accompanying conditions were being fulfilled and were being promoted day and night, so that immeasurable merit was making everything magnificent. All of this is too difficult to express, too difficult to put into words.

The Bodhisattva, sitting upon that great exquisite Lion's Dharma Seat, addressed this multitude, saying, "Now, O you celestial beings, as to the hundred and eight gates to what the Dharma illumines, when bodhisattvas and monks are in a Tushita Heaven palace awaiting their next rebirth, and are about to descend through conception to be born in the human world, they must, of necessity, proclaim and voice to this celestial host these one hundred and eight gates to what the Dharma illumines, leaving them for the remaining celestial beings to memorize. O you celestial beings, with a heart of utmost sincerity, listen closely to and absorb what I am now going to voice, which is the one hundred and eight gates to what the Dharma illumines."

> *Right trust is a gate to what the Dharma illumines, for thereby we keep our persevering mind from being defeated.*
>
> *A pure heart is a gate to what the Dharma illumines, for it is not sullied by defilements.*
>
> *Joy is a gate to what the Dharma illumines, for it is evidence of a tranquil mind.*
>
> *A loving feeling of ease is a gate to what the Dharma illumines, for it purifies our mind.*
>
> *Being proper in our bodily behavior is a gate to what the Dharma illumines, for due to that, the actions of our body, speech, and mind are pure.*
>
> *Being pure in our speech is a gate to what the Dharma illumines, for it eradicates the four evil attitudes associated with beings in the hells, asuras,* ** hungry ghosts,* ** and beasts.*
>
> *Being pure in our intentions is a gate to what the Dharma illumines, for this eradicates the three poisons of greed, anger, and delusion.*
>
> *Being mindful of Buddha is a gate to what the Dharma illumines, for thereby our perception of a Buddha is clear.*
>
> *Being mindful of the Dharma is a gate to what the Dharma illumines, for thereby our seeing what is Dharma is clear.*

> *Being mindful of the Sangha is a gate to what the Dharma illumines, for it helps us to be steadfast in our pursuit of the Way.*
>
> *Being mindful of generosity is a gate to what the Dharma illumines, for due to that we do not expect rewards.*
>
> *Being mindful of the Precepts is a gate to what the Dharma illumines, for due to that we fulfill all our vows.*
>
> *Being mindful of the highest is a gate to what the Dharma illumines, for thereby we give rise to a heart that seeks the Truth far and wide.*
>
> *Being benevolent towards others is a gate to what the Dharma illumines, for thereby good roots take hold in all of life's situations.*
>
> *Being compassionate is a gate to what the Dharma illumines, for thereby we do not kill or harm any living being.*
>
> *Being morally good is a gate to what the Dharma illumines, for thereby we rid ourselves of all that is not morally good.*
>
> *Renunciation is a gate to what the Dharma illumines, for thereby we weary of the five greeds and abandon them.*[3]
>
> *Reflecting on impermanence is a gate to what the Dharma illumines, for thereby we perceive the cravings of those in the three temporal worlds of past, present, and future.*

---

3.   That is, being greedy for possessions, sexual pleasures, food and drink, fame, and sleep.

Reflecting on suffering is a gate to what the Dharma illumines, for thereby we give up all cravings.

Reflecting on there being no unchanging, permanent self is a gate to what the Dharma illumines, for thereby we refrain from fettering ourselves by thinking that such a false self is what we truly are.

Reflecting on the tranquil realm of nirvana is a gate to what the Dharma illumines, for thereby we do not disrupt the intention we hold in our heart.

Repentance is a gate to what the Dharma illumines, for thereby we experience tranquility within our hearts and minds.

Humility is a gate to what the Dharma illumines, for thereby the malevolence of others vanishes.

Sincerity is a gate to what the Dharma illumines, for, having it, we will not deceive lofty or mundane beings.

Truth is a gate to what the Dharma illumines, for, having it, we will not deceive ourselves.

Our pursuing the Dharma is a gate to what the Dharma illumines, for we are humbly submitting ourselves to the pursuit of the Dharma.

The Three Refuges in Buddha, Dharma, and Sangha are a gate to what the Dharma illumines, for they cleanse the three evil paths that those in hells, those who are asuras, and those who are beasts pursue.[4]

---

4. Traditionally, the three are beasts, those in some hell, and hungry ghosts. At the same time, asuras may resemble hungry ghosts in their constant hunger for power.

Recognizing the good intentions of others is a gate to what the Dharma illumines, for thereby we do not ignore their good roots.

Repaying our indebtedness to others is a gate to what the Dharma illumines, for thereby we do not cheat or disregard others.

Not deceiving ourselves is a gate to what the Dharma illumines, for thereby we do not go around praising ourselves.

Acting for the sake of sentient beings is a gate to what the Dharma illumines, for thereby we do not slander others.

Expressing the Dharma for the sake of others is a gate to what the Dharma illumines, for it is our acting in conformity with the Dharma.

Being aware of the limitations of time is a gate to what the Dharma illumines, for then we do not treat lightly the words spoken for our benefit.

Weeding out self-pride is a gate to what the Dharma illumines, for then we fulfill wise discernment.

Not giving rise to wicked intentions is a gate to what the Dharma illumines, for then we protect ourselves and others.

Recognizing that hindrances do not actually exist is a gate to what the Dharma illumines, for then our mind is free of doubts.

*Trusting that we may understand is a gate to what the Dharma illumines, for then we can fully comprehend the One Great Matter.**

Reflecting on what is impure is a gate to what the Dharma illumines, for then we may abandon the mind that is tainted with craving.

Ceasing from quarreling is a gate to what the Dharma illumines, for thereby we eradicate being offended and accusing others.

Not being foolish is a gate to what the Dharma illumines, for then we cease killing living beings.

Taking pleasure in the meaning of the Dharma is a gate to what the Dharma illumines, for then we are seeing what the meaning of the Dharma is.

Love of the illumination of the Dharma is a gate to what the Dharma illumines, for then we attain the illumination of the Dharma.

Seeking to hear much of the Dharma is a gate to what the Dharma illumines, for this leads to the right understanding of how all thoughts and things appear.

Right skillful means are a gate to what the Dharma illumines, for they go hand-in-hand with Right Actions.

Knowing the true name and form of all thoughts and things is a gate to what the Dharma illumines, for this clears away all manner of obstacles.

Seeing how to eliminate causes is a gate to what the Dharma illumines, for thereby we are able to free ourselves from suffering and delusion.

Freeing our mind free of 'friend' and 'enemy' is a gate to what the Dharma illumines, for when we are in the midst of those who are hostile or friendly towards us, we treat them all with impartiality.

Helping others with subtle provisional teachings is a gate to what the Dharma illumines, for we know what the suffering of others is.

Treating all elements as equal is a gate to what the Dharma illumines, for then it eradicates any need for having to harmonize everything.

Our sense organs are gates to what the Dharma illumines, for therewith we practice the Authentic Path.

Realizing that all things are beyond birth and death is a gate to what the Dharma illumines, for then we realize what 'cessation of suffering' really means.

Our body as an abode for our awareness is a gate to what the Dharma illumines, for it brings all thoughts and things to a tranquil state.

Our feelings as an abode for our awareness are gates to what the Dharma illumines, for they eradicate all entanglements with outer inducements.

Our mind as an abode for our awareness is a gate to what the Dharma illumines, for thereby we can see that our mind is like a phantom.

The Dharma as an abode for our awareness is a gate to what the Dharma illumines, for thereby our wise discernment is not blurred.

> *The four kinds of Right Effort are gates to what the*
> *Dharma illumines, for they eradicate all evil*
> *and produce all manner of good.*[5]
>
> *The four foundations of the marvelous spiritual abilities*
> *are gates to what the Dharma illumines, for they*
> *lighten both body and mind.*[6]
>
> *What lies at the root of our faith is a gate to what the*
> *Dharma illumines, for by means of it we do not*
> *blindly follow the many words of others.*
>
> *What lies at the root of our right effort is a gate to what*
> *the Dharma illumines, for by means of it we*
> *easily attain many forms of wise discernment.*
>
> *What lies at the root of our mindfulness is a gate to what*
> *the Dharma illumines, for by means of it we*
> *easily perform various positive deeds.*
>
> *What lies at the root of our concentration is a gate to*
> *what the Dharma illumines, for by means of it*
> *our heart and mind become immaculate.*
>
> *What lies at the root of our astuteness is a gate to what*
> *the Dharma illumines, for by means of it we see*
> *what all thoughts and things really are.*
>
> *The power of faith is a gate to what the Dharma*
> *illumines, for it surpasses the powers of*
> *demons.*
>
> *The power of right effort is a gate to what the Dharma*
> *illumines, for by means of it we will not regress*
> *or turn aside.*

---

5.   The four kinds of right effort are to prevent faults from arising, to abandon faults when they have arisen, to produce merit, and to increase merit that has already arisen.

6.   The four foundations are concentration of the will, concentrated effort, concentration of thought, and concentrated investigation into the principle of Reality.

The power of mindfulness is a gate to what the Dharma illumines, for by means of it we will not blindly follow others.

The power of concentration is a gate to what the Dharma illumines, for by means of it we rid ourselves of all idle thoughts.

The power of astuteness is a gate to what the Dharma illumines, for by means of it we free ourselves from the two extremes of dualistic thinking.

Mindfulness, which is a characteristic of enlightenment, is a gate to what the Dharma illumines, for it is like the wisdom inherent in all thoughts and things.

The ability to distinguish between the true and the false, which is a characteristic of enlightenment, is a gate to what the Dharma illumines, for it illumines all thoughts and things.

Right effort, which is a characteristic of enlightenment, is a gate to what the Dharma illumines, for by means of it we easily comprehend what enlightenment is.

Joyfulness, which is a characteristic of enlightenment, is a gate to what the Dharma illumines, for by means of it we attain various types of concentration.

Ridding ourselves of all evil, which is a characteristic of enlightenment, is a gate to what the Dharma illumines, for by means of it we are already managing what we do.

Concentration, which is a characteristic of enlightenment, is a gate to what the Dharma

illumines, for by means of it we recognize the
equality of all thoughts and things.

Letting go of attachments, which is a characteristic of
enlightenment, is a gate to what the Dharma
illumines, for by means of it we weary of the
world and can abandon all that arises.

Right view is a gate to what the Dharma illumines, for by
means of it we can realize the Saintly Path and
exhaust the stream of rebirths.

Right thought is a gate to what the Dharma illumines, for
by means of it we eliminate all discriminatory
judgments, as well as any lack of discernment.

Right speech is a gate to what the Dharma illumines, for
by means of it we will recognize that all names,
voicings, and words are simply like vibrations.

Right livelihood is a gate to what the Dharma illumines,
for by means of it we rid ourselves of all our evil
ways.

Right action is a gate to what the Dharma illumines, for
by means of it we arrive at the Other Shore.

Right mindfulness is a gate to what the Dharma
illumines, for by means of it we do not
intellectualize all thoughts and things.

Right concentration is a gate to what the Dharma
illumines, for by means of it we can attain the
meditative state that is beyond scattered
thoughts.

The mind that aspires to realize the Truth is a gate to
what the Dharma illumines, for it does not
dismiss the Three Treasures of Buddha,
Dharma, and Sangha.

Reliance on the Three Treasures is a gate to what the Dharma illumines, for by means of it we do not hanker after lesser courses.

Right belief is a gate to what the Dharma illumines, for by means of it we receive the Buddha's supreme Dharma.

Progressing is a gate to what the Dharma illumines, for by means of it we fully perfect the practice of developing good roots.

The practice of charity is a gate to what the Dharma illumines, for by means of it we continue in every moment to perfect a pleasant countenance, to adorn the Buddha lands, and to teach and guide sentient beings who are stingy or greedy.

The practice of moral conduct is a gate to what the Dharma illumines, for by means of it we distance ourselves from the hardships of evil paths so that we may teach and guide sentient beings who are acting contrary to the Precepts.

The practice of patience is a gate to what the Dharma illumines, for by means of it we give up all hate, arrogance, flattery, and foolishness so that we may teach and guide sentient beings who are plagued by such feelings.

The practice of zealousness is a gate to what the Dharma illumines, for by means of it we acquire all manner of morally good thoughts and things so that we may teach and guide sentient beings who are lazy or inattentive.

The practice of meditation is a gate to what the Dharma illumines, for by means of it we may perfect all manner of contemplative practices so that we may teach and guide sentient beings who are mentally scattered.

The practice of wise discernment is a gate to what the Dharma illumines, for by means of it we may eliminate the darkness of our ignorance and attachment to our opinions so that we may teach and guide sentient beings who are foolish or confused.

Provisional teachings are gates to what the Dharma illumines, for by means of them we display ourselves in accordance with the everyday dignified behavior of a monk, so that we may teach and guide others and thereby fulfill the Dharma of all Buddhas.

The four exemplary acts are gates to what the Dharma illumines, for by means of them we are accepting of all sentient beings, and when we fully realize enlightenment, we give the Dharma as alms to all sentient beings.[7]

Spiritually teaching and guiding sentient beings is a gate to what the Dharma illumines, for we neither seek self-gratification nor tire of teaching and guiding.

---

7. The four are offering alms, using kindly speech, showing benevolence, and being in sympathy with. They are also called the Four Wisdoms. Dōgen discusses these in more detail in Discourse 45: On the Four Exemplary Acts of a Bodhisattva *(Bodaisatta Shishōbō)*.

*Acceptance of the True Teaching is a gate to what the
Dharma illumines, for it eliminates the defiling
passions of all sentient beings.*

*Garnering good fortune is a gate to what the Dharma
illumines, for it profits all sentient beings.*

*Doing meditative practices is a gate to what the Dharma
illumines, for it perfects the ten abilities.*[8]

*Being tranquil is a gate to what the Dharma illumines,
for it perfects the meditative state of a Tathagata
with which we are equipped.*

*Being astute is a gate to what the Dharma illumines, for
by means of it our wise discernment is realized
and perfected.*

*Entering the realm of unimpeded eloquence is a gate to
what the Dharma illumines, for once having
received the Eye of the True Teaching, one acts
to fulfill It.*

*Entering into all manner of spiritual actions is a gate to
what the Dharma illumines, for once having
received the Eye of a Buddha, one acts to fulfill
It.*

---

8.   The ten are: ridding oneself of attachments, deepening one's devotion, effectively
teaching and guiding others, understanding what people are thinking, spiritually
satisfying people, being unceasing in exerting oneself, being accepting of all true
teachings while not abandoning the Mahayana, exuding one's Buddha Nature through
every pore of one's being, helping turn all people toward the Dharma so that one may
lead them to Its perfection, and spiritually satisfying all kinds of people with even a single
phrase.

*Fulfilling one's expressions of homage is a gate to what
the Dharma illumines, for once such a one has
heard the Dharma of any and all Buddhas, that
person can accept and maintain It.*

*Attaining unimpeded eloquence is a gate to what the
Dharma illumines, for it creates delight in all
sentient beings.*

*Being a willing follower is a gate to what the Dharma
illumines, for one is acting in obedience to the
Teaching of Buddhas.*

*Realizing the Teaching of non-arising is a gate to what
the Dharma illumines, for thereby we receive
affirmation of It.*

*Having realized the position of being beyond regression
or turning aside is a gate to what the Dharma
illumines, for it is possessed of the Dharma of
all the Buddhas of the past.*

*The wisdom that guides us from one spiritual position to
another is a gate to what the Dharma illumines,
for when the crown of our head is aspersed, we
will have fulfilled all manner of wise
discernment.*

*The position of those who have had their head aspersed
is a gate to what the Dharma illumines, for
having been born and become monks, they have
finally been able to realize supreme, fully
perfected enlightenment.*[9]

9.   The aspersing of the head marks the point when one goes from being a bodhisattva to becoming a Buddha.

At this time Gomyō Bodhisattva, having finished His instructions, addressed this whole celestial assembly, saying, "All you celestial beings, by all means keep in mind that these are the one hundred and eight gates to what the Dharma illumines, which I bequeath to you celestial beings. May you accept and keep to them, holding them always in your thoughts. I pray, do not forget them or lose sight of them."

These, therefore, are the one hundred and eight gates to what the Dharma illumines. When all bodhisattvas who are bound to be reborn one final time are about to descend from the Tushita Heaven to be born in the land of Jambudvipa,* they invariably proclaim the one hundred and eight gates to what the Dharma illumines for the sake of the celestial multitudes in the Tushita Heaven, and thereby pass on the Teaching to those celestial ones, for this is the invariable method of Buddhas.

Gomyō Bodhisattva was the name of Shakyamuni Buddha when He was in the fourth celestial heaven at the point of being reborn one more time. In the Chinese T'ien-sheng Era an imperial aide named Lee compiled the *T'ien-sheng Era Record of the Far-reaching Torch*, in which is recorded what he called 'The One Hundred and Eight Gates to What the Dharma Illumines'. Those who have explored, clarified, and understood it are few, whereas those who do not know of it are as common as rice grains, flax stalks, bamboo canes, and river reeds. I have now brought them together for the sake of you people who are beginners, as well as for you old-timers. Those of you who aspire to ascend to the Lion's Seat in order to be teachers of lofty persons and commoners should explore them in detail. Unless you have lived in the Tushita Heaven as one who is bound to only one life more, none of you is a Buddha yet, so, my practitioners, do not vainly indulge in pride. For bodhisattvas who have but one life more, there is no intermediary stage.[10]

---

10.   This is the interval between death and rebirth.

93

On Life and Death

(Shōji)

Translator's Introduction: In this text, Dōgen plays with various nuances of the word *shōji*. As 'living and dying', it refers to ever-flowing, ever-changing conditions that have no permanency, whereas 'life and death' refers to the delusion of static, unchanging conditions that are created by a judgmental mind. 'Birth and death' refers to specific moments within the flow of 'living and dying'.

"Because there is Buddha within living and dying, life and death do not exist." And in response, the following was said, "Because the Buddha did not exist within life and death, He was not infatuated with living and dying." These words are the very heart of what was said by the two Meditation Masters Kassan and Jōzan. Since they are the words of persons who had realized the Way, we can certainly profit by them, and not in vain.

Anyone who wishes to be freed from life and death should clarify this principle. Should you seek for Buddha outside of living and dying, you are like the one who pointed his cart north and drove off to the country of Etsu in the south, or like someone who faces south, hoping to see the North Star. It would be your piling up more and more causes of life and death while missing the path to liberation. Simply put, living and dying is what nirvana is, for there is nothing to despise in living and dying, nor anything to be wished for in nirvana.

At this very time, there is a distinction that frees us, right off, from life and death. It is a mistake to think that we go from being alive to being dead. Being alive is a position at one moment in time: it already has its past and it will have its future. Therefore, within the Buddha Dharma, we say that life is beyond just the act of being born. Death is also a position at one moment in time, and it too has its past and its future. Accordingly, we say that death is beyond the act of just dying.

In the time we call 'living', there is nothing except life, and in the time we call 'dying', there is nothing except death. Thus, when life comes, it is simply life, and when death comes, it is simply death. When facing up to them, do not say that you want to cling to the one or push away the other. This living and dying is precisely what the treasured life of a Buddha is. If we hate life and want to throw it away, that is just our attempt to throw away the treasured life of Buddha. And if we go no farther than this and clutch onto life and death, this too is our throwing away the treasured life of Buddha by limiting ourselves to the superficial appearance of Buddha. When there is nothing we hate and nothing we cling to, then, for the first time, we enter the Heart of Buddha.

However, do not use your mind to measure this and do not use your voice just to mouth it. When we simply let go of and forget all about 'my body' and 'my mind', relinquishing them to the Life of Buddha and letting them be put into operation from the vantage point of Buddha, then, when we rely on this—following where It leads—without forcing the body or laboring the mind, we free ourselves from life and death, and become Buddha.

And who would want to become stuck in their own mind? There is an extremely easy way to become Buddha. Simply, do not adhere to any evil whatsoever; do not become attached to life or death; have compassion for all sentient beings; respect those who are spiritually above you and have pity on those who are spiritually less advanced than you; rid yourself of the mental attitude that deplores the ten thousand things as they sprout up and the mental attitude that craves them; let your mind be free of judgmentalism and free of worry, for to do so is what we call being a Buddha. And do not seek after anything else.

94

On the Mind's Search for Truth

(Dōshin)

Translator's Introduction: Some copies of this short, undated text bear the title of "On the Buddha's Way" (*Butsudō*), but it is not a reworking of Discourse 51.

In our pursuit of the Buddha's Way, first off, we should consider our mind's search for Truth to be foremost. Those who know what the mind's search for Truth really is are rare indeed, so we need to inquire what it is from people who clearly know.

Even though people in general are said to have a mind that is searching for the Truth, there are those people who truly do not have a searching mind. And there are some people who truly have a searching mind, though it is unrecognized by others. Thus, it is difficult to know who has or does not have such a mind. For the most part, we do not listen to what foolish or wicked people say, much less do we trust them. And we should not treat our own mind as foremost, but consider only what the Buddha expressed to be foremost. Constantly, day and night, we should hold in our mind our search for Truth, desiring and praying to realize what True Wisdom is in this world of ours.

In these degenerate days of the Dharma, those who genuinely have a mind that searches for the Truth are not many. Even so, please keep impermanence in mind, and do not forget that the world is transient and human life is uncertain. And we need not consciously keep in mind the notion that, "I am thinking about the transiency of the world." Just give emphasis to the Dharma and do not take 'my body' or 'my life' too seriously. And, for the sake of the Dharma, do not be resentful towards your body or your life.

Next, you should deeply revere the Three Treasures of Buddha, Dharma, and Sangha. Be desirous of making alms offerings to the Three Treasures, even if it means changing your life or reforming your very self. Whether asleep or awake, we should respectfully keep in mind the great spiritual benefits of the Three Treasures, and, whether asleep or awake, we should respectfully call upon the Three Treasures. For instance, during the interval between abandoning this life and not yet taking up the next life, there is what we call 'the intermediate existence'. That existence lasts for seven days, during which we should keep in mind to respectfully call upon the Three Treasures, without our voice ever ceasing. When the seven days have passed, we are said to die within that intermediate world and then receive another body for seven days within that same world. However long this next existence may be, it does not surpass another seven days. At this time, one sees and hears absolutely everything perfectly, without restrictions, just as it is with our spiritual Eye. At such a time, we should diligently apply our mind and respectfully call upon the Three Treasures, mindfully and ceaselessly reciting:

> *I take refuge in the Buddha,*
> *I take refuge in the Dharma,*
> *I take refuge in the Sangha.*

When we have passed beyond the intermediate world, we draw near to a father and mother, readying ourselves bit-by-bit through Right Knowledge to entrust ourselves to a womb. Even when we are within the Treasure House of the Womb,[1] we should reverently call upon the Three Treasures. Even while we are being born, we should not neglect to reverently call upon Them. It should be our most profound wish that, through our six senses, we may reverently make alms offerings to the Three Treasures, call upon Them, and take refuge in Them.

Also, when this life of ours is coming to an end, our two eyes may suddenly become dark. At such a time, knowing that the end of our life has come, we should strive to recite the Refuges: "I take refuge in the Buddha…" and so forth. At this time, all the Buddhas in the ten quarters will have pity on us so that, due to contributing causes, even wrongdoings for which we should face being reborn in one of the three

---

1. The 'Treasure House of the Womb' is a translation of the Japanese term *Nyoraizō*, (S. *Tathāgata-garbha*), which points to the inherent Buddha Nature in all living beings and, consequently, to their potential to realize Buddhahood.

lower worlds of existence[2] are reversed, and we are instead reborn in some celestial world or reborn before the presence of the Buddha, where we may reverently pay homage to Him and hear Him give voice to the Dharma.

After darkness has come before our eyes, we should, right off, strive to recite the Three Refuges, not shirking from this even during our entering the intermediate world or our next birth. In this way, we should thoroughly expend life after life and, in age after age, reverently recite Them. We should not let up even upon arriving at the Wisdom that is the fruition of Buddhahood. This is the Path that all Buddhas and Bodhisattvas[*] pursue. We call this 'the profound awakening to the Law' and 'the Buddha's Truth inherent in every being'. Further, you must pray that you do not dilute this with opinions held by others.

Also, within your lifetime you should engage yourself in making yourself into a Buddha, and, in cultivating Buddhahood, you should offer the Buddha three sorts of alms. These three are a meditation cushion, a vessel for holding sweet water, and a light whereby to illumine one's Original Nature. These are what you should make as your alms offering.

Also, during your lifetime you should make a copy of the *Lotus Scripture*. You should reverently write It down and make a copy of It for you to retain. You should continually make It as if a crown upon your head and bow in reverence to It, worshipfully making offerings of flowers, incense, candles, food, and robes. With the crown of our head always cleansed, we should offer these alms upon the crown of our head.[3]

Also, continually put on your kesa[*] and sit in meditation. There are examples from the past of someone realizing the Truth in a third lifetime as the result of putting

---

2.   That is, the worlds of hellish beings, hungry ghosts, and beasts.

*   See *Glossary*.

3.   This is done by holding the offering with both hands and raising it <u>above</u> the crown of the head, not by literally placing it atop the head.

on a kesa.[4] It is already the garb of all Buddhas in the three temporal worlds. Its meritorious virtue is unfathomable. Doing seated meditation is not the method of those in the three worlds of desire, form, and beyond form; it is the method of the Buddhas and Ancestors.

---

4. Dōgen gives an example of this in Discourse 84: On the Spiritual Merits of the Kesa *(Kesa Kudoku)*, concerning a prostitute who once put on a kesa as a joke and, as a result, in a later life became a female monastic.

95

On 'Each Buddha on His Own, Together with All Buddhas'

(Yui Butsu Yo Butsu)

Translator's Introduction: The title of this text is a phrase that Dogen often employs. It is derived from a verse in the *Lotus Scripture:* "Each Buddha on His own, together with all Buddhas, is directly able to fully realize the real form of all thoughts and things."

The Buddha Dharma is something that ordinary people cannot recognize. For this reason, from olden times, worldly people did not awaken to the Buddha Dharma, nor did those of the two Lesser Courses[*] thoroughly explore It. Because It was realized by the Buddha all by Himself, He said that each Buddha on His own, together with all Buddhas, has been directly able to fully realize It.

When you have thoroughly awakened in spite of yourself, it will be nothing like what you thought it would be before you had awakened. In whatever way you may have imagined it would be, what you awaken to will not at all resemble what you had imagined, for actual awakening bears no resemblance to what one may imagine it to be. Thus, it is useless to try to imagine what it is like beforehand.

When you have your awakening, you will not know why it has come about as it has. Should you reflect upon this, you will see that, prior to your awakening, whatever you thought it would be like is neither here nor there when actually experiencing an awakening. And even though it will be different from all the various ways that you may have previously thought, this does not mean that those views are fundamentally wrong and have played no part in your awakening. Even your past views comprised an awakening of sorts. However, because your thinking has been topsy-turvy, you may think that such views have been useless, and you may speak of them as being so. Whenever you think that your views are useless, there is something that you need to recognize: namely, that you are afraid that an awakening will be overpowering. If your previous ideas about enlightenment could bring forth a true

---

*   See *Glossary.*

awakening, then you may feel that your realization is unreliable.[1] Since genuine enlightenment does not depend on some special capability and goes far beyond the time prior to your realization, your awakening is assisted simply by the innate power of realization. Keep in mind that delusion is something that has no physical existence, and keep in mind that enlightenment is also something that has no physical existence!

Whenever there is a person of unsurpassed enlightenment, we call such a one 'a Buddha'. When the unsurpassed enlightenment of a Buddha arises, we call this state 'unsurpassed enlightenment'. Those who do not recognize how someone looks at the time of his or her being in such a state must surely be befuddled. This so-called 'look' is that of being untainted. 'Being untainted' does not mean being deliberately devoid of any purpose or refusing to make choices, nor is it being compulsively preoccupied with trying to be aimless or glossing over everything. How could there possibly be an untainted state in which someone is devoid of any purpose and refuses to make choices! For instance, upon meeting someone, the untainted person does not bring to mind judgmental thoughts concerning just how that other person looks. And with both flowers and the moon, such a one does not think of adding anything to their present brightness and color. Such a one does not attempt to evade the feelings that a spring day is spring just as it is, or that the beauty or dreariness of an autumn day is autumn just as it is, and he or she will be aware that this is not to be taken as being separate from himself, or even as being part and parcel of himself. But such a one may reflect upon the sounds of spring and autumn as being part of himself or as being separate from himself. And there is nothing that such a one is adding to himself nor does he have any thought that even now he still has a self. This means that such a one will not see the four elements* and the five skandhas* of the present as himself, nor will he trace them back to someone else. Hence, we should not treat the images in the mind which are evoked by flowers and moon as being ourself, though we are prone to do so. If we consider that which is not ourself to be our self, well then, we do so, but when we illumine the condition where there is no color that repels us nor any that attracts us, then our everyday behavior as monks who have realized the Way conceals nothing, for this is what our original Buddha Nature is.

---

1.   Because those ideas did not produce an awakening when you first had them.

A person of olden times, Meditation Master Chōsa Keishin, once said the following:

> The whole of the great earth is our own Dharma Body, but we may not be clear about the term 'Dharma Body'.[2] If you are not clear about what the Dharma Body is, it will be impossible for you to turn yourself around even ever so slightly.[3] And still, there will be a way of extricating yourself. And what is the way whereby people extricate themselves?[4]

For those who may fail to express what this way of extricating themselves is, the very life of the Dharma Body will immediately cease to exist for them, and they will sink down into the sea of suffering for ever so long. Were the question raised like this, how would you respond so that you would keep your Dharma Body alive and not sink into the sea of suffering? At such a time you should say something to express that the whole of the great earth is your very Dharma Body. If what you offer is indeed this fundamental principle, then at the very moment when you would say, "The whole of the great earth is my very Dharma Body," you would do well not to speak. And also, at the time when you would be silent, you may get to the heart of what goes beyond words.

A monk of ancient times, who remarked that he did not say what went beyond saying, once commented, "In death there are occasions when one may be truly alive, and in life there are occasions when one may be truly dead; and there are those who are dead and are continually dead, and there are those who are alive and are

---

2.   'The Dharma Body' refers to our True Being.

3.   'Turning oneself around' translates a technical Buddhist term, which means 'relinquishing one's delusions and defiling passions, and thereby realizing enlightenment'.

4.   The last sentence can also be taken to be a declarative statement: "And the What is the Way whereby people extricate themselves."

continually alive." This is not a case where an ordinary person is trying to force things to be a certain way; it is precisely what accords with the Dharma. Thus, on the occasion when the Buddha turned the Wheel of the Dharma, He had such a glow from It, and such a voice for It, that you could recognize that He came into bodily form in order to aid all sentient beings. We call this His wise discernment that sees beyond birth and decay.

'His coming into bodily form in order to aid all sentient beings' means that His aiding all sentient beings is His manifesting what His Body is. When we focus on His giving aid, we do not call to mind His coming into bodily form, and when we see His coming into bodily form, we harbor no doubts as to His giving aid. You need to comprehend that the Buddha Dharma is being fully realized in His giving spiritual aid, and then you need to give expression to this and fully experience it. Pay attention and give expression to His act of manifesting and to His bodily form, for they are in no way different from His giving aid. All this stems from the fact that the Buddha manifested His bodily form in order to aid all sentient beings. In His fully actualizing this purpose from the dawning of His realization of the Truth to the evening of His entering parinirvana, His expressing the Truth would have been freely given, even if He had not spoken a word.

The Old Buddha, Meditation Master Chōsa, once said in verse:

> *The whole of the great earth is the Body of a True Human Being,*
> *The whole of the great earth is the gateway to liberation,*
> *The whole of the great earth is the Solitary Eye of Vairochana,*[*]
> *The whole of the great earth is our own Dharma Body.*

In other words, what we are calling real is, in essence, our True Being. You need to realize that 'the whole of the great earth' is not some provisional term, for our being is its true form. If someone were to ask you, "Why have I never known this before?" say to that one, "Give me back my words, 'The whole of the great earth is my own True Body.'" Or tell that person to say, "The whole of the great earth is the real Human Being," even though this is something he already knows.

Also, what is described as "The whole of the great earth is the gateway to liberation" means that there is nothing to get entangled with or to embrace. The phrase 'the whole of the great earth' is closely connected with the moment and with the years, with the mind and with its expressions, and so intimately are they related that there is not the slightest gap between any of them.[5] What is unbounded and extends far out beyond us is what we should call 'the whole of the great earth'. Should you seek to enter this gateway to liberation or to come out on the other side of it, this would not be possible. And why is that so? We need to reflect on whence springs the question. However much we might desire to visit a place that does not exist, that would be impossible to do.[6]

Also, when it comes to "The whole of the great earth is the Solitary Eye of Vairochana," we may speak of the One Eye of the Buddha, but do not think that It must be just like the eye of a human being. People have two eyes, so when we speak of eyes, we are just talking about human beings and we do not speak of their having two or three. What we are being taught here is spoken of as being the Eye of Buddha, or the Eye of the Dharma, or the All-seeing Celestial Eye, and so forth. You are not learning about ordinary eyes. To understand It as being an ordinary eye is hopeless. What you need to learn now is that the Eye of the Buddha is solitary and that the whole of the great earth is contained within It. There may be a thousand eyes or myriad eyes, but first of all the whole of the great earth is the One among them. There is nothing wrong in saying that it is the One among so many, and at the same time, you would not be mistaken in realizing that a Buddha has just one, solitary Eye. Eyes may be of various kinds, so it should come as no surprise to our ears when we hear that there are occasions when there are three Eyes, and occasions when there are a thousand Eyes, and occasions when there are eighty-four thousand Eyes.[7]

---

5. That is, what physically exists is inseparable from time and mind.

6. That is, enlightenment is not a place and, in that sense, is not something to be reached.

7. The Three Eyes are an awakened person's two conventional eyes plus the opened spiritual Third Eye. The Thousand Eyes are those associated with the Thousand-armed Kanzeon, who is the manifestation of the all-seeing, all-helping Compassion inherent in Buddha

Also, you need to hear that the whole of the great earth is your own Dharma Body. That which seeks to know what we truly are is the resolute heart of someone who is truly alive. Even so, those who see what their True Self is are few. Only a Buddha alone knows this Self. Others who are off the Path, such as non-Buddhists, vainly take their unreal, false self to be their True Self. The Self that Buddhas speak of is synonymous with the whole of the great earth. Thus, whether we know or do not know our True Self, in either case, there is no 'whole of the great earth' that is other than our True Self.

But let us leave to those of other times what we are talking about at this moment.

Long ago, there was a novice monk who asked the Venerable Abbot Hōju Chinshu, "When a hundred thousand myriad conditions come at me all at one time, what should I do about them?"

The Venerable One responded, "Do not try to control them."

The essence of what Chinshū is saying is "Let come what may. In any event, you cannot influence what comes." This is on-the-spot Buddha Dharma. It is not about conditions. You should not understand these words as being a rebuke, but understand them as sheer Truth. Even if you were to consider how you might control conditions, they are beyond being controlled.

An Old Buddha once said:

The whole earth with its mountains and rivers has come into being in much the same way that we human beings have. The Buddhas of the three temporal worlds of past, present, and future

---

Nature. The Eighty-four Thousand Eyes are those that a Buddha has for seeing through the eighty-four thousand forms of delusion.

have customarily done a practice that is the same as the practice that
we ordinary human beings do.

Thus, on the occasion of someone's being born, when we look at the whole earth with
its mountains and rivers, what we do not see is that person's being born has now added
another layer upon the whole earth of mountains and rivers that existed before he or
she was born. Having said this does not mean that his words may not have a deeper
meaning. So, how can it be understood? If you do not give up by saying, "I can't
understand this," then by all means, you will be able to understand, for you will be
able to ask about it. Since they are words that have already been voiced by a Buddha,
you should listen to them, and by having listened, you may also come to understand
them.

One way that you may come to understand them is to inquire from the
perspective of someone who has been born, "What is this 'being alive?'" Who of us
has clarified from beginning to end what it is? Though we do not know our end or our
beginning, even so, we have come to be alive. Well, it is like our seeing the great earth
with its mountain and rivers and treading upon it, even though we do not know its
limits. Do not be argumentative, holding to the opinion that the great earth with its
mountains and rivers is in no way like our life. You need to be clear about His having
said that the great earth with its mountains and rivers is exactly the same as our being
alive.

Further, the Buddhas of the three temporal worlds have already done the
practice, completed the Way, and fully awakened Themselves. How, then, are we to
understand this notion of the Buddhas being the same as us? Well, first off, we need
to understand what the practice of a Buddha is. The practice of a Buddha is done in
the same manner as the practice of the whole earth, and it is done together with all
sentient beings. If it were not so, all the practices of the Buddhas would not yet exist.
Therefore, from the first arising of one's intention up to the attainment of its
realization, beyond any question, both the realizing and the practice are done together
with the whole of the great earth and with every single sentient being.

Doubts may arise concerning this, but keep in mind that when we attempt to
clarify matters that appear to be all mixed up with issues that are unknowable, the

voice of such doubts is heard, so do not be skeptical about the arising of doubts being the way it is with ordinary humans. This is a teaching you need to be aware of, for you need to know that when we give rise to the intention that the Buddhas of the three temporal worlds hold to, there is invariably the underlying principle that we do not exclude our own body and mind.

However, to deliberately harbor doubts about this is already a defaming of the Buddhas of the three temporal worlds. When we tranquilly reflect upon this, the principle that our body and mind are behaving exactly like that of the Buddhas of the three temporal worlds, as well as the principle that we are giving rise to the intention to realize Buddhahood, will both be apparent. If, in reflecting, we shed light upon the before and after of this body and mind of ours, the One we will be searching for is beyond an 'I' and beyond an ordinary, mundane person. So, do not be rigid in your thinking and do not believe that you have stagnated and are therefore separated from the three temporal worlds. Such thoughts, however, do not belong to you. When the Original Mind of the Buddhas of the three temporal worlds is practicing the Way, what could possibly come from left field to turn It aside? In short, the Way should be called, 'That which goes beyond intellectual knowing and not knowing'.

One of old once said in verse:

> *Even what we cast aside is nothing other than the Body of the Dharma Lord;*[8]
> *That It permeates the three temporal worlds is beyond dispute.*
> *The mountains and rivers, along with the great earth itself,*
> *Completely reveal the Dharma Body of the Awakened Lord.*

---

8.   'To cast aside' is synonymous with Dōgen's 'to drop off body and mind'.

We people today should learn from what this person of old said. Since everything is already the Body of the Dharma Lord, there appeared a Lord of Dharma who understood that there is nothing different from the Body of the Dharma Lord. This Mind of His is like a mountain upon the earth and resembles the earth holding up mountains.

Once you have arrived at the heart of the Matter,* the time when you did not understand will not have impeded your arrival. Further, getting to the heart of the Matter has not changed the fact that, previously, you did not understand. Even so, in your getting to the heart of the Matter and in your previous non-understanding, there have been the times of spring and the sounds of autumn. The reason why you have not understood even these is because your ears have been wandering about within their voices, despite the fact that they have been giving expression to It ever so loudly. As a result, their voices have not entered your ears. Your getting to the heart of the Matter will occur when their voices have penetrated your ears and you have entered a meditative state. Do not fancy that your having arrived at the heart of the Matter is of little importance and that your non-understanding was something large. You need to realize that because you will be beyond what you conceived of as being 'you', you will not be different from the Lord of Dharma.

As to the meaning of 'the Body of the Dharma Lord', the Eye is like the Heart of It, and the Heart of It will be like the Body. Not a single hair separates the Heart from the Body, for They will be fully revealed. You will understand that within the brightness of the Light and within giving expression to the Dharma, there exists the Body of the Dharma Lord as just described.

There is a saying from olden days, "If you are not a fish, you do not know what is in the mind of a fish, and if you are not a bird, you do not know how to follow the traces of birds." People who have been able to grasp the principle of this are rare indeed. Those who fancy that this simply means that humans do not know what the mind of a fish or the mind of a bird is have misunderstood it. The following is the way to understand this. A fish together with other fish invariably know what is on each other's mind. Unlike humans, they are not ignorant of each other's intentions, so that when they are about to swim upstream through the Dragon's Gate, they all know this and they all alike make their intention as one.[9] And when they are about to swim through the nine rapids of Chekiang, again they all know this and make their intention as one, but it is only the fish that know what this intention is.

Also, when birds are flying through the sky, no beast on the ground, even in its wildest imaginings, knows what the traces of their tracks are, much less sees and follows them. Such a beast does not have even an inkling that such tracks exist. At the same time, a bird can see the various ways a swarm of hundreds of thousands of small birds have flown off, or see the traces of birds that have flown south or north. For birds, these traces are no more hidden than the tracks left on a path by a cart or than the hoofprints of horses seen on grass, since birds see the traces of birds.

This principle also applies to Buddhas. It is apparent to Them how many eons a Buddha has spent in training, and They know who is a small Buddha and who a large Buddha, even among Those who have gone uncounted. This is something that cannot possibly be known when someone is not yet a Buddha. And there may be someone who asks, "And why, pray, can I not know it?" Well, since it is with the Eye of a Buddha that someone sees the traces of a Buddha, one who is not a Buddha is not yet in possession of the Eye of a Buddha. The number of those who can see are a number that only a Buddha can count. Without realizing it, They have all been able to follow the traces of the Buddha's Path. If these traces are visible to your Eye, you are undoubtedly in the presence of Buddhas and will be able to compare Their footprints with those of others. In making that comparison, you will be able to recognize the traces of a Buddha, as well as the magnitude and depth of the traces that that Buddha has left, and, through consideration of that Buddha's traces, your own traces will become clear to you. When we learn what these traces of a Buddha are, we call them the Buddha Dharma, that is, our True Self.

---

9.   It is said that when a fish swims up through the rapids of the Dragon's Gate at Chekiang, it is transformed into a dragon. This has been used in Zen Buddhist texts as a metaphor for someone like Prince Siddhārtha becoming a Buddha, together with all other beings.

Copied at the end of the last month of spring in the eleventh year of the Kōan era (May 1, 1288), while staying in Shibi Manor, the Guestmaster's southern quarters at Eihei-ji Temple on Mount Kippō in the Yoshida district of Echizen Province.

96

On the Eight Realizations of a Great One

(Hachi Dainingaku)

Translator's introduction: According to the postscript, this text was the last that Dōgen prepared before his death. It consists mainly of passages from the *Scripture of the Buddha's Last Teachings.**

The term 'a Great One' refers not only to a Buddha, but also to virtuous monks and bodhisattvas. The term 'realization' refers not only to an intellectual understanding, but also to the act of putting the Teachings into practice, that is, making Them real.

All Buddhas are enlightened people, and because of this, we call what They discern 'the eight realizations of a Great One'. When someone discerns what this Dharma of Theirs is, It brings about nirvana, which is freedom from suffering. On the night when our Shakyamuni Buddha entered nirvana, He gave these eight realizations as part of His final Teaching.

The first is 'having few desires'. What He called 'having few desires' means not chasing far and wide among those objects of the five senses which one has not yet experienced. As the Buddha said:

> O you monks, recognize the person who has many cravings. His misery and troubles are many because he seeks for many benefits, gains, and advantages. The person of few cravings is free from seeking after things or yearning for them. Hence, he is free of such sufferings. He desires little, only esteeming what is fitting for his spiritual training and practice. By desiring little, so much more is he able to bring forth fine merits and virtues. The person of few desires is free of flattery and fawning when searching out the intentions of others. The heart of someone who behaves with

---

*   One translation of this is found in *Buddhist Writings on Meditation and Daily Practice,* (Shasta Abbey Press, 1994), pp. 247-260.

few desires is, as a consequence, even-tempered and free from gloom, anxiety, sorrow, or fear. When coming in contact with things, he finds a surplus, for he knows no insufficiency. The one who has few desires experiences nirvana, for this is the name for 'having few desires'.

The second is 'being content'. What He called 'being content' means limiting what you take to those things that you already have available to you. As the Buddha said:

> O you monks, if you wish to be free from miseries and woes, look into contentment, which is synonymous with knowing what is enough. The Teaching of contentment is none other than the location of true wealth, ease, security, and peace. The person who is contented, though he sleeps upon the bare ground, is still at ease and satisfied. Someone who is discontented, even if he were ensconced in a celestial palace would still not find this tallying with his ideas and tastes. The one who is discontented, though rich, is poor. The person who is contented, though poor, is rich. The one who is discontented always does what his five desires latch onto. He does that which causes grief to, and arouses the compassionate pity of, one who is contented. This is what I mean by 'being content'.

The third is 'enjoying the tranquility of nirvana'. What He called 'enjoying the tranquility of nirvana' means leaving behind all the noise and hubbub for the solitude of the open country. As the Buddha said:

> O you monks, if you seek to be tranquil and quiet, liberated from the insistence of the defiling passions, at ease and content, then you should part company with confusion and bustle, and dwell at your ease in some solitary place. The person who dwells in quietude continually forsakes what those in the heavens esteem so highly amongst themselves. Therefore, withdraw from those about you, as

well as from other crowds and, in a place of solitude apart from them, reflect on the source of the eradication of suffering at your leisure. If you are one who enjoys the company of others, then you will take on the woes of their company, just as with a flock of birds that gather in some huge tree, there is the lament of dead branches breaking off under their weight. When the world binds itself around us, we drown in the suffering of such company just as an old elephant, sunk down in mire, is unable to drag himself out. This is what I call 'distancing yourself from those about you'.

The fourth is 'being devoted to progress'. He called this 'being devoted to progress' because of His ceaseless devotion to performing good acts—a devotion undiluted and a progression without regressing. As the Buddha said:

O you monks, if you are diligent in your devotion to progress, training will not be difficult for you. Therefore, be diligent and devote yourselves to progress, just as a small stream, ever flowing, can bore holes in rocks. If the mind of the trainee is often inattentive and remiss, it will be just the same as making a fire by friction and blowing on it before it is hot enough to catch fire. Although your desire to train can blaze up, the fires of training are hard to arrive at. This is what I call 'being devoted to progress'.

The fifth is 'not neglecting mindfulness'. He also called it 'keeping to Right Mindfulness'. What He called 'keeping to the Dharma without losing sight of It' means keeping to Right Mindfulness. It is also called 'not forgetting to be mindful'. As the Buddha said:

O you monks, seek fine understanding, search out good assistance, and do not neglect mindfulness. If you are one who does not neglect mindfulness, the thieves of passional defilement will not be able to enter. Therefore, you monks, always keep your minds alert, for the one who loses his mindfulness loses his merits and virtues. When the strength of your mindfulness is constant and vigorous, though the five desires would break in to rob you, they will do you no harm. You will be as one who puts on armor before entering a battle and will have nothing to fear. This is what I call 'not neglecting mindfulness'.

The sixth is 'doing meditation'. What He called 'doing meditation' means abiding in the Dharma undisturbed. As the Buddha said:

> O you monks, when your mind is kept alert, then you are in meditation. Because your mind is in meditation, you are able to know the world, birth and death, as well as the characteristics of all things. Therefore, you monks should always study and practice the ways of meditation with finest diligence. When you achieve meditation, your heart is not in turmoil or your mind scattered. Just as a household that would be frugal with water arranges dikes and pond banks carefully, so a trainee does similarly. Therefore, for the sake of the water of discriminate wisdom, practice meditation well that you may prevent the loss of that water through leaks caused by the defiling passions. This is what I call 'doing meditation'.

The seventh is employing 'wise discernment'. What He called employing wise discernment means letting one's hearing, thinking, and practice naturally arise from one's realization of Truth. As the Buddha said:

> O you monks, when you have wise discernment, you will not be attached to desires. By constant self-reflection and watching what you do, you will not bring about any loss through the defiling passions. Within My Teachings, this is what can bring you to liberation. If someone denies this, not only is he not a person of the Way, he is also not an ordinary, everyday person either. Indeed, there is no name for such a one. Genuine wise discernment is the sturdy craft that ferries others across the sea of old age, disease, and death. It is also a great, bright lamp for the darkness of ignorance, a wonderful curative for all disease and suffering. It is a sharp axe for

felling the trees of defiling passions. Therefore, you monks should improve yourselves by means of this wise discernment, which you attain through hearing, thinking about, and putting into practice My Teachings. When someone has the radiance of this wisdom then, though he be blind, he will clearly see what people are. This is what 'wise discernment' is.

The eighth is 'not playing around with theories and opinions'. What He called 'not playing around with theories and opinions' means letting go of dualities and judgmentalism that one may experience. Fully realizing the True Nature of all things is what 'not playing around with theories and opinions' means. As the Buddha said:

> O you monks, if your mind plays around with all kinds of theories and opinions, it will be confused and in disorder and, though you have left home to become a monk, you have still not realized liberation. Therefore, O monks, quickly abandon your disordered mind and your playing around with your theories and notions. If you wish to enjoy the pleasure that comes from calmness and the extinction of defiling passions, thoroughly eliminate the affliction of playing around in your head. This is what I mean by 'not playing around with theories and opinions'.

These are the eight realizations of a Great One. Each and every Great One is equipped with all eight. When extended, they are immeasurable; when abbreviated, they are sixty-four.[1] They are our Great Master Shakyamuni's final voicing of the Dharma, His last instructions on the Great Course, His ultimate song in the middle of

---

1.   These two sentences that begin Dōgen's commentary are interpolations in the manuscript. 'When extended' means that there are innumerable ways in which these eight may be realized. 'The sixty-four' means that each of the eight may be coupled with each of the eight, that is, for example, one should keep to mindfulness when doing any of the eight, including keeping to mindfulness.

the night on the fifteenth of the second lunar month. After speaking the following, He did not give voice to the Dharma again, and at last, entered His parinirvana.

> O you monks, with wholehearted devotion always seek to get back on the path. Everything in all worlds, both the movable and the immovable, works to defeat and destroy all signs of uncertainty. Cease for a moment and do not ask Me to say more, for the time is nigh when I would pass and I wish for my parinirvana. These are My last Teachings and instructions.

Therefore, disciples of the Tathagata, by all means, set yourself to study these instructions of His and do not neglect to study them, for if you do not know them, you are not a disciple of the Buddha. These are the very Treasure House of the Eye of the True Teaching, which is the Wondrous Heart of Nirvana.

Even so, there are many today who do not know them, for there are few who have encountered or heard of them. That they do not know them is due to devilish disturbances. Those who have planted few good spiritual roots have also not heard or encountered them. During the long past days of the genuine Dharma and the superficial Dharma, disciples of the Buddha knew them, studied them, and explored them through their training with their Master. Nowadays only one or two among a thousand monks know the "Eight Realizations of a Great One". Sad to say, there is nothing to compare to the degeneration of the Dharma in these decadent times of ours. While the Tathagata's True Dharma is still circulating in the great-thousandfold world and His immaculate Dharma has not yet disappeared, you should hasten to learn It. Do not be slack and neglect It.

To encounter the Buddha's Dharma is difficult even in immeasurable eons. To obtain a human body is also difficult. And even if you do obtain a human body, to obtain a human body on one of the three continents is better.[2] Among these three,

---

2.   A reference to three of the four continents said to lie around Mount Sumeru. Of these three, the southern continent of Jambudvipa is considered the most favorable, since those born there can more readily experience the transiency of human life. The fourth continent

being a human on the southern continent is best, because there one can encounter Buddha, hear the Dharma, leave home life behind to become a monk, and realize the Way. Those who died prior to the Tathagata's entering His parinirvana had not heard of the eight realizations of a Great One, much less studied them. That you now have encountered and heard of them, and are studying them, is due to the strength of the good roots you planted in the past. In your studying them now, in your developing them in life after life and thereby arriving, without fail, at the supreme awakening to Truth, and in your giving expression to them for the sake of sentient beings, you may well be the equal of Shakyamuni Buddha. May there be no difference between the two of you.

Written at Eihei-ji Temple on the sixth day of the first lunar month in the fifth year of the Kenchō era (February 5, 1253).[3]

Now, on the day before the end of the summer retreat in the seventh year of the Kenchō era (August 3, 1255), I had my clerical officer Gien finish copying this text.[4] *At the same time, I have proofed his copy.*

---

is a place where beings are enjoying too much bliss to be willing to listen to the Buddha's Teaching.

3.   Dōgen is said to have died on August 28, 1253.

4.   Gien began his training under Dōgen. Upon the latter's death, he trained with Kōun Ejō, ultimately becoming one of his Dharma heirs and the Fourth Abbot of Eihei-ji.

This was our Master's last discourse, drafted when he was already ill. Among other things, I heard him say that he wanted to rework all of the Shōbōgenzō *that had previously been written in Japanese script[5] and also to include some new manuscripts, so that he would be able to compile a work consisting altogether of one hundred discourses.*

This present discourse, which was a first draft, was to be the twelfth of the new ones. After this our Master's illness worsened. As a result, he stopped working on such things as the drafts. Therefore, this draft is our late Master's final teaching for us. Unfortunately, we will never see His full draft of the hundred chapters, which is something to be greatly regretted. Those who love and miss our late Master should, by all means, make copies of this twelfth chapter, and take care to preserve it. It contains the final instructions of our Venerable Shakyamuni and is the final legacy of our late Master's Teaching.

I, Ejō, have given this final account.

---

5. As distinct from his collection of three hundred kōan stories, which were written in Chinese and are without any commentary. That collection is called Dōgen's *Chinese Shinji Shōbōgenzō*.

Glossary

Āchārya: Sanskrit for 'teacher'; in Zen monasteries, a polite form of address for a monk with at least five years of training; applied to a disciple advanced enough to teach monks and laity, but not yet deemed a Master.

Arhat: In Zen, one whose heart is cleansed of all greed, hatred, and delusion but who has not yet fully realized wise discernment or compassion.

Asura: An inhabitant of one of the six Worlds of Existence; before conversion, a heaven stormer, one who is so absorbed in attaining power that he cannot hear the Dharma, much less comprehend It; after conversion, he becomes a guardian of Buddhism.

Avalokiteshvara (C. Kuan Yin, J. Kanzeon or Kannon): The Bodhisattva who hearkens to the cries of the world; the embodiment of compassion.

Before 'father' and 'mother' were born: That is, the time before dualistic thinking arises in the mind.

Bodhisattva: When not capitalized, it refers to one who is attempting to follow the Mahāyāna (Greater Course) as the Buddha Path; when capitalized, the personification of some aspect of Buddha Nature.

A broken wooden ladle: A Zen metaphor describing someone's mind which has become free of discriminatory thinking.

A dragon elephant: Originally, a term for a particularly large elephant; used in Zen texts to describe a particularly brilliant and discerning Master.

The five treacherous deeds: Murdering one's father, murdering one's mother, murdering an arhat, spilling the blood of someone who has realized Buddhahood, and causing disharmony in the Sangha, thereby creating a schism in the order.

The four elements: Earth, water, fire, and wind.

The four stages of arhathood: (1) Stream-enterer: someone who enters into the stream of Buddhist training by abandoning false views; (2) Once-returner: someone having one more rebirth before realizing full enlightenment; (3) Non-returner: someone never returning to the realm of sensual desire; and (4) Arhat: someone who has reached a state of enlightenment and is therefore free from all defiling passions.

Gasshō: A gesture made by placing the palms of the hands together, with fingers pointing upwards, signifying the unity of body and mind. It is an expression of reverence often used during ceremonies, as well as a form of greeting when two Buddhists meet and a gesture of supplication.

Greater Course (Greater Vehicle): A translation of the term 'Mahāyāna', used to designate the Buddhist traditions that place the awakening of all sentient beings above one's personal awakening.

Hossu: A scepter-like instrument in the form of a fly-whisk carried by a celebrant during ceremonies. It represents the flowing forth of the Water of the Spirit as an expression of the celebrant's compassion.

Hungry ghost (preta): One who resides in one of the three negative modes of existence, pictured as a being who is suffering from a hunger for the Dharma and has some metaphorical deformity, such as lacking a mouth, which makes it impossible to absorb It.

Icchantika: Someone who is erroneously thought to be so amoral as to be completely devoid of Buddha Nature. In Zen, there is reference to the Great Icchantika, which is an epithet for Buddha Nature itself.

Jambudvipa: In Buddhist spiritual cosmology, the Southern Continent where people are capable of doing Buddhist training.

Kalpa: An endlessly long period of time, roughly equivalent to an eon.

Karma: What results from any volitional action, according to the universal law of cause and effect.

Kenshō: The experience of seeing into one's true nature, that is, one's Buddha Nature.

Kesa: A cloak-like robe traditionally worn by Buddhist monastics since the time of Shakyamuni Buddha. A similar type of robe is given to committed lay Buddhists.

Kōan: A statement or story used by a Zen Master as a teaching device to directly address a trainee's spiritual question; also may be used to refer to that question itself.

Lantern (stone or temple): A term often used metaphorically for a monk who stays in a monastery or temple, serving as a light to help guide a trainee.

Lesser Course: Followers of the two 'lesser' courses, namely, the shravakas and the pratyekabuddhas. They are not 'wrong' practitioners of Buddhism, but by their following a 'lesser' course it will take a longer time for their spiritual seeds to germinate and grow into the realizing of Buddhahood, since they have not yet entered the Bodhisattva Path, which involves the doing of one's practice for the sake of all sentient beings. See also the Greater Course and the Three Vehicles.

Lion Throne (Lion's Seat): The seat where a Master sits when giving a talk on some aspect of the Dharma.

Lord of Emptiness: The first of the Seven Buddhas, the one who lived during the Age of Emptiness, that is, before duality had first arisen.

Mahāsattva: An outstanding bodhisattva.

Mahāyāna: The Greater Vehicle.

Maitreya: The Buddha Yet to Come. He is said to be waiting as a Bodhisattva in the Tushita Heaven. To realize one's own Buddha Nature brings Maitreya forth.

Manjushri: The Bodhisattva who personifies Great Wisdom.

Matter (the One Great Matter): The goal of spiritual training, namely, the realization of the highest Truth.

Monjin: The act of bowing from the waist with hands in gasshō.

A pillar of the temple: A monk whose training is so strong that it supports the spiritual function of the temple or monastery in which he trains.

Pratyekabuddha: One who becomes enlightened as a result of his own efforts but does not share his understanding with others.

Samantabhadra: The Bodhisattva who is the embodiment of patient, loving activity.

Seal (Buddha seal, Buddha Mind seal, Dharma seal, and seal of certification): 'The Buddha Mind Seal' refers not only to the document written on plum blossom silk which certifies both the Master's and the disciple's Buddha Mind but also to the fact that the Minds of Master and disciple coincide and are not two separate minds. The Transmission of this seal is often referred to in Zen texts as 'the Transmission of Mind to Mind' as well as 'the special Transmission that is apart from Scriptural texts and which does not depend on words'.

The Seven Buddhas: The historical Buddha and the six Buddhas that preceded Him.

The seven treasures (the seven jewels): The seven types of jewels from which Pure Lands are fashioned.

Shashu: The way that the hands are held when doing walking meditation. There are various forms of shashu, but most involve one hand being wrapped around the fist of the other.

Shravaka: One who, upon hearing the Dharma, affirms his allegiance to It but may not yet try to put It into practice, or may try to reduce It simply to a rigid code of 'right' or 'wrong' behaviors.

The six Worlds of Existence: Those of celestial beings, humans, asuras, hungry ghosts, beasts, and those in hellish states.

Skandhas: The five skandhas comprising a living being's physical form, sensory perceptions, mental concepts and ideas, volition, and consciousness.

Skin bag: An allusion to a human as a sentient being having a physical body. Dōgen often uses the term to characterize ineffectual trainees.

Staff: The traveling staff carried by a monk when traveling to another temple. Hence the phrase 'to hang up one's traveling staff' meaning 'to have found the temple in which to permanently seek the Truth under the abbot'; metaphorically, a monk who is willing to go anywhere in order to spread the Dharma and help all sentient beings.

Stupa: Literally, a reliquary for the ashes of a Buddhist, and metaphorically, the body of a Buddha.

'Such a one' ('such a person'): Someone who has realized the Truth and automatically shows the signs of having had such a realization.

The Three Courses (the Three Vehicles): Namely, the way of training done by the shravakas, pratyekabuddhas, and bodhisattvas.

The thrice wise and ten times saintly: Those who have attained the final stage of bodhisattvahood before fully awakening and becoming a Buddha.

The tiles and stones of our walls and fences: The bits and pieces of our experiences, which we use to fashion our perception of the universe.

Tripitaka: The three divisions of Buddhist Scriptures, namely, the Buddha's Teachings (Sutras), the Precepts (Vinaya), and the commentaries on the

Sutras (Abhi-dharmas); also, the whole of the Buddhist canon.

Vairochana (the Cosmic Buddha): The Buddha who is the personification of spiritual Light and Truth, the one who represents the Pure Buddha Mind.

Vimalakīrti: A wealthy lay Buddhist renowned for his profound understanding of Mahāyāna.

A wheel-turning lord: A ruler who turns the Wheel of the Dharma in his country by governing according to Buddhist principles.

Yojana: An Indian measure of distance, understood by some scholars as equivalent to twelve or sixteen miles.

Appendix of Names

Many of Dōgen's discourses in the Shōbōgenzō are based on accounts taken from various collections of kōan stories. For the most part, these deal with notable Zen monastics who are customarily identified in the opening sentence of the story. However, since these stories have come from various sources, the name given for any of these monastics may not always be consistent. All the various names attributed to these monks would have been known to those in Dōgen's assembly but may not all be familiar to modern-day readers. To help in identifying who is who, I have taken the liberty of using the most familiar Japanese name by which these historic monks are known. For instance, Daikan Enō is referred to in the translations as Enō, whereas in some of the original texts he is referred to as Sōkei.

Also, monastic Japanese names that end in –san or –zan (Ch. –shan) may refer to the mountain on which a monastery is built, or to the monastery itself, or to the monk who was the first head of the monastery. Only context can clarify which is intended.

The numbers in parentheses by each name indicate the chapters in which a kōan story or other major reference to the person appears.

Banzan Hōshaku, C. P'an-shan Pao-chi. Zen Master. (27, 43, 82)

Barishiba, S. Pārshva. (29)

Baso Dōitsu, C. Ma-tsu Tao-i. (11, 19, 26, 29, 53, 75)

Bodhidharma, J. Bodaidaruma, C. P'u-t'i-ta-mo. (8, 19, 23, 29, 34, 41, 44, 47, 51, 69)

Bokushū Chin, C. Mu-chou Ch'en. A Dharma heir of Ōbaku.

Busshō Hōtai, C. Fo-hsing Fa-tai. Zen Master under Engo. (64)

Busshō Tokkō, C. Fa-shao Te-kuang. Zen Master under Daie Soko.

Ch'ang Cho, J. Chō Setsu. Lay disciple of Sekisō Keisho. (44)

Chimon Kōso, C. Chih-men Kuang-tso. Zen Master. (27)

Chisō, C. Chih-tsung. (51)

Chōkei Daian, C. Chang-ch'ing Ta-an. Under Hyakujō. (29, 62)

Chōkei Eryō, C. Chang-ch'ing Hui-leng. Under Seppō. (29)

Chōrei Shutaku, C. Chang-ling Shou-cho. Zen Master. (64)

Chōsa Keishin, C. Chang-sha Ching-ts'en. Zen Master. (8, 21, 35, 54, 58, 89, 95)

Daibai Hōjō, C. Ta-mei Fa-Ch'ang. Zen Master. (29)

Daie Sōkō, C. Ta-hui Tsung-kao. Under Engo. (41, 72, 88)

Daigu, J. Kōan Daigu, C. Kao-an Ta-yü. Zen Master.

Daii Dōshin, C. Ta-i Tao-hsin. Zen Master. (21, 29)

Daiji Kanchū, C. Ta-tz'u Huan-chung. Zen Master. (29)

Daikan Enō, C. Ta-chien Hui-neng. Sixth Chinese Ancestor, often known by his posthumous name of Meditation Master Sōkei. (10, 12, 15, 16, 19, 21, 28, 31, 45, 51, 60, 72, 84)

Daiman Kōnin, C. Ta-man Hung-jen. Zen Master. (21, 50)

Daini, Tripitika Master, C. Ta-erh. (18, 78)

Daitaka, S. Dhītika. (82)

Daizui Shinshō, C. Ta-sui Shen-chao. Great Master. (20)

Dōan Dōhi, C. Tung-an Tao-p'i.

Dōgo Enchi, C. Tao-wu Yüan-chih. Zen Master. (27, 32)

Dōrin, J. Chōka Dōrin, C. Niao-k'o Tao-lin. Zen Master. (9)

Echū (National Teacher), J. Nan'yō Echū, C. Nan-yang Hui-chung. (6, 18, 36, 45, 54, 67, 78)

Egaku, C. Hui-chio. Monk. (8)

Eka, J. Taiso Eka, C. Ta-tsu Hui-k'o. (29, 41, 47, 51, 60, 89)

Engo Kokugon, C. Yüan-wu K'o-ch'in. Zen Master. (22, 33, 36, 77, 88)

Enkan Saian, C. Yen-kuan Ch'i-an. National Teacher. (29)

Fuke, J. Chinshū Fuke, C. P'u-hua of Chen-chou. Zen Master. Under Ummon. (21)

Fuyō Dōkai, C. Fu-jung Tao-chieh. (29, 62)

Fuyōzan Reikun, C. Fu-jung Ling-hsün. Zen Master. (44)

Gako, C. E-hu. Disciple of Seppō. (35)

Gantō, J. Gantō Zenkatsu, C. Yen-t'ou Ch'üan-huo.

Gensha Shibi, C. Hsüan-sha Shih-pei. Under Seppō. (4, 18, 19, 22, 23, 29, 31, 48, 49, 60, 78)

Genshi, C. Yüan-tzu. (15)

Gensoku, C. Hsüan-tse. (1)

Gichū, C. I-chung. Zen Master.

Goso Hōen, C. Wu-tsu Fayen. Zen Master. (29)

Gozu Hōyū, C. Niu-t'ou Fa-jung. Zen Master. (27)

Gutei, C. Chü-chih. Zen Master. (60)

Haku Rakuten, C. Po Chü-i. Poet of the T'ang Dynasty and a lay disciple of ZenMaster Bukkō Nyoman. (9)

Hannyatara, S. Prajñātāra. Bodhidharma's Master. (20, 50)

Haryō Kōkan, C. Pa-ling Hao-chien. Zen Master. (23)

Hō'on, C. P'ang-yün. Lay disciple of Baso. (24)

Hofuku, C. Pao-fu. Disciple of Seppō. (35)

Hōgen, C. Fa-yen. (1, 59)

Hōju Chinshu, C. Chen-chou Pao-shou. Venerable Abbot. (95)

Honei Jin'yū, C. Pao-ning Jen-yung. Zen Master. (59)

Hōtatsu, C. Fa-ta. (16, 20)

Hyakujō Ekai, C. Pai-chang Huai-hai. (21, 24, 29, 33, 62, 73, 74, 76, 88)

Iitsu, C. Wei-i. Retired Abbot.

Isan Reiyū, C. Kuei-shan Ling-yu. Also known as Daii. (8, 21, 24, 29, 62)

Jimyō Soen, C. Tz'u-ming Ch'u-yüan. Zen Master.

Jinshū, C. Shen-hsiu. Chief disciple of Daiman Konin.

Jizō Keichin, C. Ti-tsang Kuei-shen. (35, 48)

Jōshū Shinsai, C. Chao-chou Chen-chi. Great Master. (18, 20, 21, 29, 34, 38, 47, 59, 62, 78, 79)

Kaie Shutan, C. Hai-hui Tuan. Zen Master. (18, 78)

Kanadaiba, S. Kāladeva. (21)

Kanchi Sōsan, C. Chien-chih Seng-ts'an. Third Chinese Ancestor.

Kashō Buddha, S. Kāshyapa Buddha. (15, 86)

Kayashata, S. Gayāshata. (19, 28)

Kazan Shujun, C. Ho-shan Shou-hsüen. Zen Master. (64)

Kegon Kyūjō, C. Hua-yen Hsü-ching. (25)

Keichō Beiko, C. Ching-chao Mi-hu. (25)

Kempō, C. Kan-feng. (58)

Kinkazan Kōtō, C. Kung-tao. Zen Master. (19)

Kisei, C. Kuei-hsing. Zen Master. (11)

Kisu Shishin, C. Kuei-tsung Chih-chen. Zen Master. (44)

Koboku Hōjō, C. Ku-mo Fa-cheng. Zen Master. (73)

Kōtō, Vinaya Master, C. Kuang-t'ung.

Kozan Chi'en, C. Ku-shan Chih-yüan.

Kumorata, S. Kumāralabdha. (88, 89)

Kyōgen Chikan, C. Hsiang-yen Chih-hsien. (8, 24, 29, 63, 65, 79)

Kyōsei Dōfu, C. Ching-ch'ing Tao-fu.

Kyōzan Ejaku, C. Yang-shan Hui-chi. Zen Master. Disciple of Isan. (18, 21, 24, 51,78)

Makakashō, S. Mahākāshyapa. First Indian Ancestor. (23, 29, 31, 52, 66, 74, 77,81, 85)

Massan Ryōnen, C. Mo-shan. Master. (10)

Mayoku Hōtetsu, C. Ma-ku Pao-ch'e. Zen Master. (3, 32)

Moggallana, S. Maudgalyayana. Disciple of the Buddha.

Musai Ryōha, C. Wu-chi Liao-p'ai.

Myōshin, C. Miao-hsin. Monk. (10)

Nāgārjuna, J. Nagyaarajuna, C. Lung-shu, Lung-sheng, or Lung-meng. AncestralMaster. (21, 82, 84, 86, 91)

Nangaku Ejō, C. Nan-yüeh Huai-jang. Under Daikan Enō. (7, 19, 22, 26, 60)

Nansen Fugan, C. Nan-ch'üan P'u-yüan. Zen Master. Disciple of Baso. (21, 34, 59,79)

Ōan Donge, C. Ying-an Tan-hua. Zen Master. (49)

Ōbaku Unshi, C. Huang-po Yün-shih. Zen Master. (21, 27, 29, 50, 73)

Ōryū Enan, C. Huang-lung Hui-nan. Zen Master.

Ōryū Shishin, C. Huang-lung Ssu-hsin.

Reiun Shigon, C. Ling-yün Chih-ch'in. Zen Master. (8)

Rinzai Gigen, C. Lin-ch'i I-hsüan. (10, 21, 24, 25, 29, 32, 50, 51, 82)

Rōya Ekaku, C. Lang-yeh Hui-chüeh. (61)

Ryūge Kodon, C. Lung-ya Chü-tun. Master.

Ryūtan Sōshin, C. Lung-t'an Ch'ung-hsin. Zen Master. (17)

Sanshō Enen, C. San-sheng Hui-jan. Zen Master. (19, 51)

Seidō Chizō, C. Hsi-t'ang Chih-tsang. Zen Master. (75)

Seigen Gyōshi, C. Ch'ing-yüan Hsing-ssu. Zen Master. (11, 15, 23, 31, 51)

Seihō, C. Ch'ing-feng. Zen Master. (1)

Seizan, C. Seizan. (75)

Sekisō Keisho, C. Shih-shuang Ch'ing-chu. Master.

Sekitō Kisen, C. Shih-t'ou Hsi-ch'ien. (11, 23, 27, 28, 51, 62)

Sempuku Jōko, C. Chien-fu Cheng-ku. Zen Master. (74)

Seppō Gison, C. Hsüeh-feng I-ts'un. (4, 19, 22, 29, 31, 35, 38, 45, 49, 60)

Setchō Chikan, C. Hsüeh-tou Chih-chien. Great Master. (52)

Setchō Jūken, C. Hsüeh-tou Chung-hsien. (64, 65, 79)

Shakkyō Ezō, C. Shih-kung Hui-tsang. Zen Master. (75)

Shayata, S. Jayanta. Great Monk. (89)

Shikan, J. Kankei Shikan, C. Kuan-hsi Chih-hsien. Zen Master. (10, 29)

Shinzan Sōmitsu, C. Shen-shan Seng-mi. Zen Master. (41)

Shishibodai, S. Simhabodhi. Great Monk.

Shōju, C. Cheng-shou. (91)

Shōkaku Jōsō, C. Chao-chüeh Ch'ang-tsung. Zen Master. (8)

Shōnawashu, S. Śānavāsa. Third Indian Ancestor.

Shūgetsu, C. Tsung-yüeh. Venerable Master.

Sōgyanandai, S. Sanghananda. Great Monk. (19, 28, 82)

Sōun, C. Sung-yün.

Sōzan Honjaku, C. Ts'ao-shan Pen-chi. (27, 30, 63)

Sozan Kōnin, C. Shu-shan Kuang-jen. Zen Master. (45)

Sunakshatra, C. Zenshō. Disciple of the Buddha who returned to lay life. (82)

Tafuku, C. Ta-fu. One of Jōshū's Dharma heirs.

Taigen Fu, C. Ta-yüan Fu. (57)

Tandō Bunjun, C. Chan-t'ang Wen-chun. Zen Master. (64, 72)

Tanka Shijun, C. Tan-hsia Tzu-ch'un. Great Monk. (64)

Tendō Nyojō, C. T'ien-t'ung Ju-ching. Zen Master. (2, 7, 20, 29, 49, 54, 57, 59, 60, 62, 66, 71, 76, 77)

Tenryū, C. T'ien-lung. Zen Master.

Tō Impō, C. Teng Yin-feng. (79)

Tōba, C. Tung-p'o. Layman in Keisei Sanshoku. (8)

Tokujō, J. Sensu Tokujō, C. Ch'uan-tzu Te-ch'ing. Under Yakusan Igen.

Tokusan Senkan, C. Te-shan Hsüan-chien. Zen Master. Disciple of Sekitō Kisen.(17, 18)

Tokusan Tokkai, C. Te-shan Te-hai. Disciple of Seppō.

Tōsu Daidō, C. T'ou-tzu Ta-t'ung. (43, 54, 63)

Tōsu Gisei, C. T'ou-tzu I-ch'ing. Great Monk. (62)

Tōzan Dōbi, C. Tung-shan Tao-wei.

Tōzan Ryōkai, C. Tung-shan Liang-chieh. (20, 24, 27, 41, 54, 61, 64)

Ubakikuta, S. Upagupta. Great Monk. (82, 91)

Ummon Bun'en, C. Yün-men Wen-yen. (35, 39, 74)

Unchō Tokufū, C. Hsüeh-ting Te-fu. Zen Master.

Ungan Donjō, C. Yün-yen T'an-sheng. (24, 32, 54, 61)

Ungo Dōyō, C. Yün-chu Tao-ying. (20, 27, 52)

Utpalavarna, J. Upparage. (82, 84)

Vasubandhu, J. Bashubanzu.

Vimalakirti, J. Yuima. (31, 70)

Wanshi Shōgaku, C. Hung-chih Cheng-chüeh. A Dharma heir of Tanka Shijun.(26)

Yafu Dōsen, C. Yeh-fu Tao-ch'uan. Zen Master.

Yakusan Igen, C. Yao-shan Wei-yen. Great Master. (11, 20, 26, 28, 70)

Yōka Genkaku, C. Yung-chia Hsüan-chüeh. (88)

Zengen Chūkō, C. Chien-yüan Chung-hsing. Great Master. (45)

About the Translator

After obtaining his doctorate in theatre criticism and the phenomenon of theatre from the University of Washington in 1972, Rev. Hubert Nearman (aka Mark J. Nearman) spent the following decade broadening his knowledge of classical Japanese and Chinese in order to devote himself to making annotated translations of the so-called 'secret tradition' writings (Japanese *hiden*) by Zeami Motokiyo, one of the principal founders of the fourteenth-century Japanese Noh theatre tradition. In 1981, he was awarded a three-year National Endowment for the Humanities grant to make similar annotated translations of treatises by Zeami's son-in-law, Komparu Zenchiku. His translations of these documents on Japanese aesthetics were published in *Monumenta Nipponica*. Also during this period he held faculty positions at the American University (in Washington, DC) and at the University of New South Wales.

In 1988 he was ordained in the Order of Buddhist Contemplatives of the Sōtō Zen tradition by Rev. Master Jiyu-Kennett and in 1992 received Dharma Transmission from her. Since then, at her request, he has devoted himself to translating major Buddhist works, including Keizan Jōkin's "Record of the Transmission of the Light" (*Denkōroku*) and his "Instructions on How to Do Pure Meditation" (*Zazen Yojin Ki*), as well as "The Scripture of Brahma's Net" (*Bommō Kyō*), the dhārani from "The Scripture on Courageously Going On" (*Shurāôgāma Sutra*), Kanshi Sōsan's "That Which is Engraved upon the Heart That Trusts to the Eternal" (*Hsin Hsin Ming*), Yōka Genkaku's "Song That Attests to the Way" (*Cheng Tao Ko*), "Bodhidharma's Discourse on Pure Meditation" (*Kuan Hsin Lun*), "The Scripture of the Buddha's Last Teachings"(*Yuikyō Gyō*), "The Scripture on Fully Perfected Enlightenment" (*Engaku Kyō*), along with the present work.

Rev. Hubert was named a Master of the Order of Buddhist Contemplatives in 2010, and died in 2016.